LATINO CITY

JUSTICE, POWER, AND POLITICS

Coeditors

Heather Ann Thompson
Rhonda Y. Williams

Editorial Advisory Board

Peniel E. Joseph
Matthew D. Lassiter
Daryl Maeda
Barbara Ransby
Vicki L. Ruiz
Marc Stein

The Justice, Power, and Politics series publishes new works in history that explore the myriad struggles for justice, battles for power, and shifts in politics that have shaped the United States over time. Through the lenses of justice, power, and politics, the series seeks to broaden scholarly debates about America's past as well as to inform public discussions about its future.

More information on the series, including a complete list of books published, is available at http://justicepowerandpolitics.com/.

LATINO CITY

IMMIGRATION AND URBAN CRISIS IN LAWRENCE, MASSACHUSETTS, 1945–2000

LLANA BARBER

THE UNIVERSITY OF NORTH CAROLINA PRESS

Chapel Hill

This book was published with the assistance of the
Authors Fund of the University of North Carolina Press.

The University of North Carolina Press has been a member
of the Green Press Initiative since 2003.

Portions of Chapters 1, 2 (including map 2), and 7 appeared previously in
different form in Llana Barber, "'If We Would . . . Leave the City, This Would Be
a Ghost Town': Urban Crisis and Latino Migration in Lawrence, Massachusetts,
1945–2000," in *Confronting Urban Legacy: Rediscovering Hartford and New
England's Forgotten Cities*, ed. Xiangming Chen and Nick Bacon (Lanham, Md.:
Lexington Books, 2013), 65–82. The Chapter 4 epigraph is from Martín Espada,
"*Toque de queda*: Curfew in Lawrence," in *Trumpets from the Island of Their
Eviction* (Tempe, Ariz.: Bilingual Press, 1987). Reprinted with permission.

Cover image: Workers in front of Lawrence Maid Footwear
Inc., 1974. Photo by Richard Graber.

LIBRARY OF CONGRESS CATALOGING-IN-PUBLICATION DATA
Names: Barber, Llana, author.
Title: Latino city : immigration and urban crisis in Lawrence,
Massachusetts, 1945–2000 / by Llana Barber.
Other titles: Justice, power, and politics.
Description: Chapel Hill : The University of North Carolina Press, [2017] |
Series: Justice, power, and politics | Includes bibliographical references and index.
Identifiers: LCCN 2016051603 | ISBN 9781469631332 (cloth) |
ISBN 9781469631349 (pbk : alk. paper) | ISBN 9781469631356 (ebook)
Subjects: LCSH: Latin Americans—Massachusetts—Lawrence—History—
20th century. | Latin Americans—Massachusetts—Lawrence—Economic
conditions—History—20th century. | Lawrence (Mass.)—Emigration and
immigration—History—20th century. | Lawrence (Mass.)—Race relations—
History—20th century. | Lawrence (Mass.)—Economic conditions—20th century. |
Race riots—Massachusetts—Lawrence—History—20th century.
Classification: LCC F74.L4 B37 2017 | DDC 305.8009744/5—dc23
LC record available at https://lccn.loc.gov/2016051603

CONTENTS

ILLUSTRATIONS

MAPS, TABLE, AND CHART

ACKNOWLEDGMENTS

I am deeply grateful. . . .

For the support I received while working on this project, including a Presidential Fellowship from the History Department at Boston College, an American Fellowship from the AAUW, and a Summer Research Grant from the State University of New York-College at Old Westbury.

To the Lawrence residents and organizers who formally shared their thoughts on the city's history with me through oral history interviews, Isabel Melendez, Jorge Santiago, Ingrid Garcia, Eric Spindler, and Armand Hyatt, and to Lawrence Housing Authority director Don O'Neill, who gave me a guided tour of the city's public housing.

To the hardworking archivists who enabled my research, Barbara Brown, Susan Grabski, and the miraculous Amita Kiley at the Lawrence History Center; Louise Sandberg in Special Collections at the Lawrence Public Library; William Maloney and the Lawrence City Clerk's office; the staff at the Andover Historical Society; Jennifer Fauxsmith and the Massachusetts Archives; the staff in Special Collections at the Massachusetts State Library; Jean Nudd and the National Archives and Records Administration Northeast Division; and Alison Pekel and the WGBH Educational Foundation Media Library and Archives. I am also grateful for the material sent electronically by Joan Keegan from the AT&T Archives and History Center. Armand Hyatt is due particular thanks for lending me his personal collection of documents regarding the Immigrant City Community Housing Corporation.

To the team at University of North Carolina Press, especially to my editor, Brandon Proia.

To my students and colleagues at Old Westbury who help keep my work oriented toward creating a just and sustainable society, Mandy Frisken, Laura Anker, Samara Smith, Sujani Reddy, Laura Chipley, and the entire American Studies Department, as well as Diana Sukhram, Amara Graf, and Jacqueline Emery. I am especially indebted to those colleagues who offered valuable feedback on portions of the manuscript, Carol Quirke, Jermaine Archer, Fernando Guerrero, Juan Pablo Galvis, and Cara Caddoo.

To the scholars who encouraged my interest in Lawrence, Marilisa Jiménez García, José Itzigsohn, Ramón Borges-Méndez, Bob Forrant, Nick Bacon, Deborah Levenson, and Cynthia Young, and particularly those who read parts or all of the manuscript, Avram Bornstein, Julio Capó, and Andrew Sandoval-Strausz.

To the dear friends who helped me keep perspective, Jason Banister, Lucy Herschel, Shauna Lavi, Gabi Moisan, Adam Freeman, Jessica Barletta, Bob and Megan English, Rachel Thompson, Brenda Laverde, Omis Wilson, Chris Kent, Christian Fernandez, and the community at Huracán Dance Studio. *Les agradezco mucho* to those friends who generously offered Spanish-language or transcription help, Paola Garcia, Nilda Hurtado, and Leora Johnson, or who read portions of the manuscript, Annie Danger and Danny Katch. I would have been simply adrift without May Lightfoot and Lindsie Bear, each of whom anchored me throughout this process.

To my mentors, Davarian Baldwin and Lynn Johnson, both of whom were tireless in offering insight and encouragement at every stage of this book, from conception to completion.

To my extended family in Providence, for their patience and support, Kim and Hok Heng, Kimnay Heng, and especially Chiv Heng, whose patience was tested more than most.

To my extended family in Lawrence, for keeping their homes open to me and for answering my ceaseless questions, Mercedes and Bill Spindler, Martiza Spindler and Julio Carrion-Leyva, Andrew Spindler, Tanya and Dylan Hawkins, and particularly to Eric Spindler, for introducing me to the city and letting me see it through his eyes.

To my sisters, Cate Barber Moran and Stephanie Barber, for whom the completion of this book was only ever a question of "when," and to my parents, Eileen and John Barber, who provided immeasurable support and love.

And finally, to my children, Cadence and Noah, who taught me that the most important work is never truly completed, so we must learn to enjoy life in the meantime.

LATINO CITY

LATINO MIGRATION AND THE RUINS OF INDUSTRIAL AMERICA

> To feel like you belong to a city and to feel intimately linked to its
> roots, it is not enough to just reside in a city. To accept a city as
> your own, you have to have lived, worked, suffered, and forged the
> history of that city.
>
> *Lawrence community organizer Isabel Melendez*

In the summer of 1984, two furious crowds faced off along a narrow, tenement-lined street in Lawrence, Massachusetts. In a race riot that would bring international attention to this small city, white and Latino rioters exploded in a rage that had been building in the city for years. TV news footage showed the two sides divided by burning trash cans, hurling rocks and insults at each other as Molotov cocktails arced through the sky, lighting up aging triple-decker apartment houses. The white rioters chanted, "Who's American? We're American," "Go back where you came from," and "U.S.A.! U.S.A.!" Both sides shouted out their anger over the course of two hot summer nights, while homes and businesses burned. Whenever the police or firefighters tried to approach, the two sides joined forces to pelt fire trucks and squad cars with rocks, sticks, or beer cans. Latino rioters made clear to the media that they were protesting both virulent bigotry from their neighbors and racialized abuse from the police. They trumpeted their fury about being excluded from city governance and the ongoing evisceration of Lawrence's economy.

Like many cities in the Northeast and Midwest, Lawrence had been an industrial giant in the early twentieth century, its colossal mills powered largely by immigrant labor from Europe. By the end of the century, however, deindustrialization, suburbanization, and urban disinvestment had devastated former manufacturing centers in the Rust Belt, and Lawrence had become one of the poorest cities in the nation, plagued by poverty, unemployment, underfunded services, and widespread frustration. This economic decline was accompanied by radical demographic changes, as white ethnics fled to the suburbs, yielding the city (although not without a fight) to a heterogeneous mix of Latin American immigrants. As the Latino population skyrocketed across the United States, Lawrence became the first Latino-majority city in New England with the 2000 census, and the city is currently nearly three-quarters Latino, mostly Dominican and Puerto Rican. The rioters in 1984 were thus not simply engaged in a unique, local conflict; they were enmeshed in much larger developments. The brutal economic collapse of industrial cities in the United States occurred at the exact historical moment of large-scale immigration from Latin America. Understanding the rioters' grievances compels us to think globally about the urban crisis in U.S. cities in the late twentieth century.

Walking through Lawrence today, it is not hard to envision the old mill city as an industrial powerhouse. Less than seven square miles, Lawrence was carved out of the surrounding towns in the 1840s to create a manufacturing center along the banks of the Merrimack River. Its economic importance quickly loomed far larger than its size. The mammoth brick mills that sprung up along the river made the city the world's leading producer of worsted wool by the early twentieth century, and tens of thousands of immigrants packed Lawrence's tenements to labor in its textile mills. In 1912, these workers in the "Immigrant City" walked out of the mills in protest against a weekly wage decrease, successfully organizing across ethnic lines in one of the most famous work stoppages in U.S. labor history, commonly known as the Bread and Roses strike.[1]

In the decades after World War II, however, Lawrence's economy suffered a stark decline. The mills closed as the textile industry moved away. Although the city managed to recruit some new manufacturing, it was never able to fill the gaping hole that the loss of textiles created in its employment stock or its tax base. The city's residents left in droves to take advantage of newly affordable suburban housing, and Lawrence steadily lost population over the next few decades. New highway construction and modern shopping centers in the suburbs encouraged the region's residents to abandon the city's downtown as well, prompting store and restaurant closings and a further diminished tax base. Insufficient tax revenue led to inadequate city services, hitting schools

View of Lawrence from the Ayer Mill clock tower in 1991. Photo by Jonas Stundzia, archived at the Lawrence History Center.

and public safety hardest and contributing to high crime and rampant arson. Abandoned properties and absentee landlords led to blight and decay in Lawrence's neighborhoods, and by the 1980s the city had essentially become an island of poverty in the midst of thriving, prosperous suburbs.

But this decline is only part of the story. At the same time that the city was undergoing disastrous disinvestment, a handful of Puerto Rican, Dominican, and Cuban immigrants began to arrive in Lawrence in the late 1950s and 1960s, to find work in its remaining factories and to make homes and communities in the very neighborhoods that white Lawrencians were leaving behind. These pioneers were followed in the 1970s by a larger wave of Puerto Ricans and Dominicans, many of whom had previously settled in New York City but then decided the big city could not provide a suitable quality of life. The Latino population in Lawrence tripled during the 1980s and continued to grow in the 1990s, with many Dominicans and Puerto Ricans migrating directly from the islands to join family in Lawrence. This remarkable Latino immigration reversed the city's population decline. Latinos reinvested in Lawrence's economy and institutions and revitalized its streets, parks, and other public spaces. In this most basic sense, Latinos saved a dying city.

Yet many white residents saw the relationship between the city's decline and Latino immigration differently. They believed, mistakenly, that Lawrence was in a state of crisis because Latinos had *brought* poverty, blight, and other "urban problems" to the small city. This effort to pin the effects of economic restructuring on a racialized scapegoat manifested in intense anti-Latino prejudice, discrimination, and even violence, as was evident in the 1984 riots. White Lawrencians broadly rejected Latinos' right to the city, including their right to live and work in Lawrence, to walk its streets unharassed, to maintain and celebrate their language and cultures, to participate in city governance, and to access quality public services such as schools and, when needed, welfare. The transition of the city to a Latino majority was not a simple demographic change; it required decades of Latino organizing and struggle to claim a right to the city in the face of white hostility. White residents and city officials often dismissed Latinos' demands by fixating on their presumed foreignness. These rights were for "Americans," they argued, and so Latinos had no valid claim on the public spaces and resources of the city.

This book braids together these aspects of Lawrence's history: urban economic decline based in suburbanization and deindustrialization, Latino migration from a largely U.S.-dominated Caribbean, and white resistance to Latino settlement in a highly racialized metropolitan landscape. While Lawrence is a small city, its population never reaching above 100,000, this is not just a parochial study of a faded, obscure mill town; the forces that transformed Lawrence impacted cities across the nation. Throughout the United States, particularly in the Northeast and Midwest, white flight, racialized disinvestment, and deindustrialization provoked an urban crisis from the mid-1960s through the early 1990s. Immigration from Latin America skyrocketed during this same era, partially the fruit of the long history of U.S. military and economic intervention in the region. Latinos came to be the largest "minority" in the nation, and immigration brought about profound changes in many U.S. cities. As in Lawrence, these shifts often involved decades of protest and organizing in order for Latinos to assert their right to the city. Finally, the white backlash against poor urban communities of color was certainly not unique to Lawrence either, as the nation moved away from the liberalism of the New Deal and Great Society eras during the 1970s toward a conservatism that rejected shared responsibility for "urban problems." These major historical developments were inextricably interwoven and dramatically visible in Lawrence. In stark and vivid detail, this small city's history allows us to see the connections between several of the most important transformations of the late twentieth century.

Immigration history has long been focused on mobility: of people certainly, but also of ideas, cultures, resources, and capital. Indeed, immigration and migration studies are by definition studies of movement. Yet there is also substantial (and growing) attention in immigration studies to the limits of mobility, particularly to the role of national borders, immigration policy, and regimes of detention and deportation in restricting the movement of people.[2] This emphasis on borders and constrained mobility dovetails well with the concerns of urban studies, particularly as the field has been influenced by the discipline of geography. Urban historians have long been attentive to the concrete realities of place and have emphasized the importance of internal borders: state and municipal boundaries, for example, and their attendant political economies, residential segregation along the lines of race and class, and incarceration.

Although urban historians and immigration scholars have often shared a focus on U.S. cities, their approaches have been quite different. Immigration scholars have documented skyrocketing immigration in the latter half of the twentieth century, particularly from Latin America. Their emphasis has frequently been on the transnational networks of people, capital, and communication that migrants have formed, and the cultural and economic impact of immigration on U.S. cities. Scholars of Puerto Rican and Dominican migration have been particularly important in documenting the role of U.S. imperialism in spurring migration and the complicated positioning of Latinos in the racial hierarchy of the United States.[3]

This attention to race and empire is essential because a full consideration of transnational migration must take into account not only what encouraged Latino settlement but also what limited or channeled it. Pushed to migrate by conditions shaped by U.S. intervention, Dominicans and Puerto Ricans entered not only a racialized U.S. *social* arena but also a racialized U.S. *spatial* arena, a metropolitan geography that had already been profoundly shaped by the U.S. racial order. As such, migrants confronted a racially and economically segregated landscape and an ongoing urban/suburban competition over resources that preceded their arrival. Being racialized as nonwhite in a historical moment when white privilege was becoming spatialized in segregated suburban development had a profound impact on both the Puerto Rican and Dominican diasporas. Understanding why Latinos concentrated in Lawrence also entails understanding the obstacles to their settlement in the city's surrounding suburbs—suburbs with none of Lawrence's danger and decay, and where many of the jobs Latinos came to fill were actually located. Understanding why Latinos dispersed from New York City to Lawrence (and other secondary cities) requires looking at the historical development of urban crisis and gentrification in New York. Such an emphasis on structural factors is not meant to obscure migrants' own agency. Without understanding the factors that constrained Latino residential and employment choices, however, we cannot truly understand the *stakes* of Latino migration and activism; finding a place in the United States to build a home and community was often a struggle.

Urban studies scholarship offers important analytical tools to understand these processes of segregation and disinvestment, to understand the spatialization of privilege and hardship. Urban historians have demonstrated that racialized political conflicts over metropolitan social, spatial, and economic organization are central to understanding U.S. history in the twentieth century. They have linked urban crisis and white flight to the massive government and private investment in suburbanization after World War II and to the myriad forms of discrimination that kept African American communities, particularly in the Northeast and Midwest, overwhelmingly restricted to central cities in the postwar decades, as urban economies crumbled in the wake of the flight of industry and retail to the suburbs. Indeed, urban historians have persuasively argued that this racialized metropolitan political economy played a major role in the nation's turn to conservatism in the late 1970s and the dismantling of the welfare state.

Taken together, existing scholarship has emphasized four constituent elements of urban crisis from the mid-1960s through the early 1990s: concentrated racialized poverty and joblessness in urban neighborhoods; a host of related fiscal and social problems, including crime, blight, arson, and inadequate public services; protest against these circumstances, both organized and spontaneous (especially rioting); and a national media preoccupation with the seemingly intractable dangers and dilemmas of the "inner city." Some of these elements had existed in earlier eras, of course, but beginning in the 1960s these circumstances combined with population loss, deindustrialization, and a declining tax base in many of the nation's major industrial centers, leading to widespread perceptions that this not only was a crisis *in* U.S. cities; rather, this was a crisis *of* U.S. cities. This perception was not entirely accurate, as many cities in the South and West actually experienced growth and prosperity in the postwar era. Yet even these Sunbelt cities generally saw white flight and racialized disinvestment on a neighborhood scale, often leading to similar patterns of ghettoization, stigma, and protest for communities of color. Indeed, the 1965 Watts uprising in Los Angeles, far outside the Rust Belt, is a major part of what brought the urban crisis to national attention.[4]

To date, Latinos have been woefully underrepresented in this scholarship. There has been some excellent work documenting Latino experiences in postwar U.S. cities, and the history of Puerto Rican and Chicano urban activism in the 1960s and 1970s is particularly well developed; but there remains so much more to be excavated.[5] As in Lawrence, Latino immigration absolutely transformed U.S. cities in the late twentieth century, revitalizing their economies, radically shifting their demographics, and in many instances reversing their population decline. By 2000, Latinos were a majority in major cities like Miami and San Antonio and a near-majority in Los Angeles at 47 percent. More than 2 million Latinos lived in New York City alone, constituting a full quarter of the population.[6] Latino urbanism is not a new phenomenon, however. Both Puerto Rican and Mexican American communities were mainly concentrated in cities in 1960, as the crisis era dawned, and Latinos remained a predominantly urban population through at least the 1990s—that is, through the entire urban crisis era. Indeed by 1990, Latinos resided in central cities at a rate nearly equal to that of African Americans (52 and 57 percent, respectively), while only a quarter of non-Hispanic whites lived in central cities.[7] Given the disproportionate concentration of Latinos in U.S. cities during the era of urban crisis, their relative absence from the historiography is shocking.

As Lawrence's history powerfully illustrates, poor and working-class immigrants in the postwar era often confronted the racialized political economy of urban crisis, occupying a complicated position in the late twentieth century's deeply segregated landscape of spatialized inequality. While many scholars have emphasized the role of immigration in reversing urban economic decline in the late twentieth century, far less attention has been paid to the *experience* of immigrants with urban crisis—how dreams of security or prosperity evaporated in the harsh light of segregation, concentrated poverty, and disinvestment.[8] As Eric Tang has written of Cambodian refugees resettled in the Bronx hyperghetto, "Refuge [was] never found." Instead, what these immigrants encountered in the Bronx and other crisis cities was "an urban reality characterized by racialized geographic enclosure, displacement from formal labor markets, unrelenting poverty, and the criminalization of daily life."[9] Across the country in the crisis era, Latinos and other immigrants poured into cities and urban neighborhoods that whites (and capital) were abandoning. There is no way to completely grasp the history of immigration or U.S. cities in this era without a fuller understanding of this process.

Detroit has been the paradigmatic crisis city in urban studies scholarship.[10] Its postwar history has been well documented by Thomas Sugrue and others: deindustrialization, suburbanization, severe segregation, job discrimination, poverty, blight, fiscal emergency, white bigotry, and Black protest, including rioting.[11] It would be a mistake to assume that the experiences of Puerto Ricans and Dominicans in Lawrence could be cleanly deduced from this classic urban crisis narrative; Lawrence is not simply the Latino Detroit. Yet there are countless echoes of Detroit's history throughout this book, and of Black experiences with urban crisis more generally. Segregated into a city suffering from economic decline and compelled to reckon with the impact of concentrated poverty and racialized disinvestment, Latinos in Lawrence encountered forms of structural racism similar to those faced by African Americans in the crisis era. This occurred not necessarily because Dominicans and Puerto Ricans in Lawrence were racialized as Black (although many were indeed partially of African descent), but because they were racialized as nonwhite and specifically "urban" in an era when cities had been shaped to contain Black poverty and protest. Of course, the mixed-race heritage of most Puerto Ricans and Dominicans contributed to their being marked as nonwhite, but the prejudices they faced in Lawrence were distinctly anti-Latino, often emphasizing presumed foreignness, the use of Spanish, and Third World poverty. These anti-Latino prejudices, however, also incorporated ideas about the "inner city" that relied on and recycled anti–African American stereotypes, invoking assumptions that urban communities of color were lazy, pushy, welfare dependent, immoral, dangerous, criminal, etc. Thus, independent of any individual Puerto Rican's or Dominican's skin color, the experiences of urban Latinos in the crisis era were inextricably tied to the structures and discourses of anti-Black racism.[12]

While the causes of urban crisis have been amply documented, scholars are just beginning to understand where Latinos fit in this history, and there are still many unanswered questions. Have Latinos experienced, as "people of color," the same forms of segregation, discrimination, disinvestment, and pernicious racist harassment as African Americans? Have they had access to racial privileges vis-à-vis African Americans?[13] It should surprise no one that the answers to these questions vary immensely. Class, national origin, immigration status, skin color and physiognomy, and geographic location have all played major roles in shaping Latinos' experiences of race and racism in the United States, and those roles have also changed over time. There can be no single narrative of "the Latino experience" of racism in the United States. Similarly, there can be no overarching history of Latino urbanism.

Cubans in Miami, Chicanos or recent Mexican immigrants in Los Angeles, Salvadorans in Washington, D.C.—no one book could possibly capture the range of their very different experiences. It is this very diversity, however, that makes excavating the past of Latinos so essential, as these histories compel us to rethink basic assumptions about culture and identity, urban economics, spatial inequality, political coalitions, social citizenship, and most obviously, the complicated process of racemaking in the United States.[14]

LATINO CITY

Even within the small city of Lawrence, the history of Latino experiences is multifaceted. This single city contains the stories of Dominicans, Puerto Ricans, and a range of other nationalities; of immigrants, citizens, and colonial subjects; of the poor, the working class, and professionals; of the hopeful and of the disenchanted. It is a history of community building, of transnational economic and kinship networks, of hardworking families persevering in the face of deindustrialization and decline, of Latinos forging and celebrating an ethnic identity in the multicultural United States. But it is also a history of persistent, outspoken, and even insurgent Latino activism, of fierce claims on public space and battles for self-representation, and of disappointment, failure, and disillusion. As Henri Lefebvre has argued, cities are not only the sites of protest and contestation but their stakes as well.[15] Dominicans, Puerto Ricans, and white ethnics struggled not just *within* the city but *for* the city, for access to and control over its land and resources, and for the right to transform the city and shape its future.

Chapter 1 locates the roots of Lawrence's economic decline in suburban development from World War II until 1980. It focuses on white flight from the city and the divergent housing markets that developed between Lawrence and its suburbs. In addition, it traces the decline of Lawrence's economy and tax base in the postwar decades, arguing that suburban competition for industry and retail played a major role in eviscerating Lawrence's economy. Chapter 2 analyzes Latino settlement in Lawrence during the 1960s and 1970s, as the city's declining manufacturing sector recruited Latino workers. I emphasize the push factors driving migrants from Puerto Rico and the Dominican Republic, as well as from New York City, where the crisis provoked by racialized disinvestment and deindustrialization was already well advanced. The postwar metropolitan political economy ensured that suburban housing, particularly in Massachusetts, was largely off limits to working-class Latinos, so this dispersal from New York was marked by a re-concentration within small cities like Lawrence. A second wave of deindustrialization in the late 1970s was especially destabilizing for Latinos concentrated in the city's manufacturing sector.

The next three chapters explore Latino activism and white resistance in Lawrence. Many white residents correlated the economic decline of the city with the contemporaneous Latino immigration and so scapegoated the city's newcomers for Lawrence's decline. Resisting Latino settlement in the city became a way to hold on to an idealized past or to hopes for a future renaissance. Chapter 3 examines attempts by whites to discourage Latino immigration into the city. Faced with this white hostility, Latino efforts to settle and build community in Lawrence were a form of quotidian activism, aimed at claiming an equal right to the city's homes, jobs, and public spaces. Latino activism and community formation are viewed through the life and work of Puerto Rican organizer Isabel Melendez. Chapter 4 offers a narrative account of the riots of 1984 and an analysis of how white and Latino Lawrencians viewed the rioting in the context of the city's larger transformations. The riots were the most spectacular and devastating example of the racialized clash in the city, as whites and Latinos attempted to stake their claims with knives, rocks, guns, and Molotov cocktails. Chapter 5 addresses the impact of the riots, including the major media spotlight trained on the city. Latinos successfully used the riots as leverage to press for changes in the city, finding allies in state and federal antidiscrimination agencies. This chapter also includes a discussion of the successful voting rights lawsuit brought by the Department of Justice against the city in the late 1990s that greatly increased Latino political power in Lawrence.

The final two chapters focus on the late 1980s and 1990s. Chapter 6 recounts the decimation of Lawrence's public services, with an emphasis on public safety and education. Major metropolitan centers experienced a "tale of two cities" phenomenon in this era (substantial reinvestment in some neighborhoods along with deepening crisis in others); in smaller postindustrial cities, however, economic decline often continued to define the city as a whole. I situate Lawrence's crisis in the larger battles over public spending in the late twentieth century, especially state-level education and welfare reform legislation. These reform efforts illustrate a distinctly suburban political agenda that came to reject the liberal welfare state when many voters saw it as privileging poor, urban communities of color. Finally, Chapter 7 traces Lawrence's transition to a Latino-majority city with the 2000 census, including the tremendous increase in immigration during the 1980s that led Lawrence to become home to the largest concentration of Dominicans in the United States outside New York City. The city's Latino population came to define Lawrence's public culture in this period, and the long push for Latino political power in the city was ultimately successful in many ways. This chapter discusses the transnational activities that brought new vitality to Lawrence's economy and its public spaces, yet larger structural forces continued to create obstacles to Latinos finding in Lawrence the better life they pursued. I conclude with some thoughts on Lawrence in the twenty-first century.

As a small, globalized city, Lawrence is not unique.[16] Throughout the nation, immigrants have completely reconfigured the demographics, economies, and public cultures of many small cities, and this is particularly evident in New England. Chelsea and Holyoke in Massachusetts resemble Lawrence in many ways.[17] Lowell, Massachusetts, has one of the highest concentrations of Cambodians in the country, and even Lewiston, Maine, has developed a sizable population of Somali refugees.[18] Some might argue that these small cities, often located in the shadow of major metropolitan centers like Boston, are actually best considered global suburbs. Suburban studies scholars have done formidable work excavating the history of suburban diversity and challenging the model of white, middle-class homogeneity; not all suburbs were "lily white" bastions of homeownership and picket-fenced prosperity.[19] Suburbs have become increasingly diverse since the 1980s, and sizable immigrant communities have formed outside large cities.[20] The Latinization of the United States has occurred across urban, suburban, and rural settings, and municipalities of various sizes with pronounced Latino majorities exist throughout the Southwest and in southern Florida. Lawrence has much in common with small, dense, "inner-ring" suburbs in metropolitan New York and Los Angeles, places such as Union City, New Jersey, or Maywood, California, which are both economically struggling and thoroughly Latino (85 and 97 percent, respectively).[21]

I argue, nonetheless, that it is important to disaggregate small or second-tier postindustrial cities from suburbs, particularly in the Northeast and Midwest, or else risk losing sight of the distinct historical trajectory of former industrial centers. By new census definitions adopted after the 2000 count, Lawrence is no longer officially a principal city in its metropolitan area, but this new suburban designation obscures more than it reveals. For a municipality of Lawrence's size to be considered a city by the new criteria, it would need to have a substantial daily influx of commuters. So Lawrence's economic marginality has rendered it a suburb, while Waltham and Framingham (suburbanesque municipalities along Route 128 that boomed

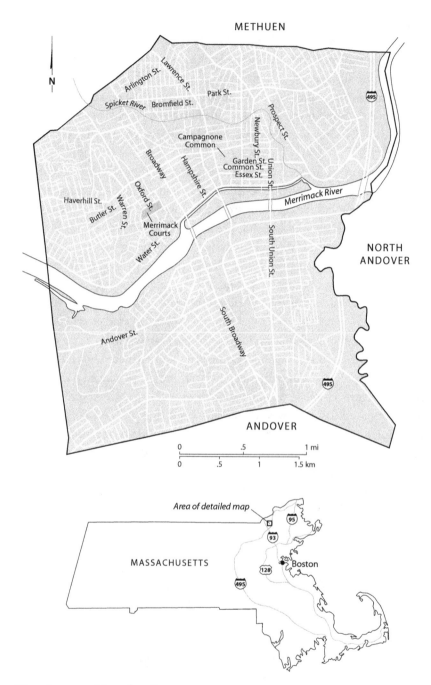

METHUEN

N

Arlington St.

Lawrence St.

Park St.

Spicket River   Bromfield St.

Prospect St.

Campagnone
Common

Newbury St.

Garden St.   Union St.
Common St.
Essex St.

Broadway

Hampshire St.

Haverhill St.

Butler St.

Warren St.

Oxford St.

Merrimack
Courts

Merrimack River

Water St.

South Union St.

NORTH
ANDOVER

South Broadway

Andover St.

ANDOVER

0		.5		1 mi
0	.5	1		1.5 km

Area of detailed map

95

93

MASSACHUSETTS

128

495

Boston

Map 1. Lawrence, Massachusetts

in the postwar era) are now principal cities.[22] This is problematic, of course, because if employment patterns are considered in the very definition of city/suburb, then the historic migration of jobs from city to suburb is eclipsed, and the impact of suburbanization on urban economies becomes invisible.

Indeed, in many ways, disinvestment has been most extreme and persistent in the nation's small or second-tier postindustrial cities. While major metropolitan centers saw an economic recovery beginning in the 1980s—a patchwork reinvestment and repopulation by the rich and professional class—many smaller cities have not experienced this turnaround. These cities, often with a population that is majority African American or Latino, remain economically marginal and in a state of continued fiscal crisis. Flint, Michigan, for example, recently made headlines for the public health crisis precipitated by its postindustrial economic decline. Flint is a Black-majority city with fewer than 100,000 residents, more than 40 percent of whom live in poverty. Once an auto manufacturing hub, deindustrialization had left the city in a state of economic crisis. While under the fiscal control of a state-appointed emergency manager, Flint officials switched the source of the city's drinking water from Lake Huron to the Flint River in 2014 in order to save the city money. The corrosive water from the Flint River released highly poisonous lead from the water pipes into the tap water, resulting in elevated lead levels in the blood of children in the city.[23] When examined through the lens of major metropolitan centers like New York or Boston, some U.S. cities seem to have fully transitioned to a new era of prosperity and growth, but when seen through the lens of small postindustrial cities like Lawrence or Flint, some urban centers clearly still experience many of the problems of the era of urban crisis.

Undoubtedly, the stark line between city and suburb has blurred in the past twenty years. In 2016, as I write, not only changing census definitions but also urban gentrification and the growing diversity of the suburbs have undermined the crisis-era model of an impoverished city, populated largely by people of color and surrounded by a ring of prosperous and almost exclusively white suburbs. Yet complicated does not mean integrated. Patterns of intrametropolitan segregation and inequality persist, even if they do not lie cleanly along urban/suburban lines. Poor and working-class municipalities still neighbor wealthy, well-served municipalities, and race still plays a significant role in determining in which municipality one will reside. Even in the most conventional of suburbs, poor and working-class Latinos often remain segregated, laboring in towns where they cannot afford (and are rarely welcome) to live.[24]

Ultimately, I refer to Lawrence as a city because of its history of urban crisis. In the second half of the twentieth century, Lawrence underwent transformations that were widely typical of northeastern and midwestern cities in this era: deindustrialization, economic decline, population loss, social upheaval, and dependency. Immigration had such a pronounced impact in Lawrence precisely because of these urban transformations. Meanwhile, Lawrence's suburbs experienced equally typical patterns of growth, exclusion, and autonomy. Adopting the idea of Lawrence as a suburb would render invisible its position in these larger historical developments. Further, analyzing Lawrence as a suburb, or jettisoning the urban/suburban binary, would risk obscuring the important cultural role played by narratives of "urban" danger and decay in the city's history.[25] The national preoccupation with urban crisis from the 1960s through the early 1990s generated a tremendous stigma attached to the inner city, a deep narrative association between cities and crime, blight, dysfunction, welfare, and a racialized population of undeserving and pathological poor. This stigma played a major role in shaping Lawrence's political economy and the experience of its residents. While scholars of the twenty-first century can perhaps afford to reject the city/suburb binary, for historians to do so risks obscuring the immense cultural resonance of these terms and blinds us to the impact that being branded with the term "urban" could provoke during the crisis era.

EMPIRE, CRISIS, AND RAGE

The history of Latinos in Lawrence, Massachusetts, is one of grassroots urban revitalization: a postindustrial city given new life by immigration. It is also, however, a history of marginalization, suffering, disappointment, and anger, of Latinos fighting for their right to the city in the face of racism and urban economic collapse. And like many histories of Latinos in the United States, it is fundamentally an account of the imperial migrations set in motion by U.S. intervention in Latin America. Although this book strives to situate Lawrence in its global and regional context, my main focus is on events within the city's borders, as this is, above all else, an attempt to document Latino experiences of urban crisis. The decision not to make this a truly transnational study, with an equal emphasis on sending and receiving societies, is partly an academic one; there is already ample scholarship on U.S. imperialism in Latin America, especially in the Caribbean, and the ties between U.S. intervention and Latino migration have already been thoroughly documented. The Latino experience of urban crisis, however, is nearly absent from the historiography.

The history of how Latinos were forced to reckon with segregation and racialized disinvestment in U.S. cities is an essential coda to the history of imperial migration and an equally essential corrective to the mythology of immigrant opportunities and a bootstrap American Dream. If Dominicans and Puerto Ricans came to Lawrence for "a better life," as so many migration stories attest, two questions remain: Why wasn't that better life available in their home countries? And did they find the better life for which they had migrated?

It is impossible to answer the first question—Why wasn't that better life available at home?—without running up against the history of U.S. intervention in Latin America. Throughout the twentieth century, and particularly during the Cold War era, U.S. priorities shaped the development of Latin American nations in many ways, often foreclosing opportunities for a better life at home. The United States repeatedly either thwarted or circumscribed Latin American efforts to create democratic, sovereign governments that were genuinely responsive to people's needs or that prioritized social development and national autonomy. Whether through the constraining terms of aid and investment, covert support for military coups, or direct military occupation, the United States shaped conditions in Latin America. Of course, local actors played major roles in this history as well, but the influence of the United States is undeniable, especially in Puerto Rico and the Dominican Republic. As such, Latinos in Lawrence were not foreign immigrants, coming from abroad, but imperial migrants, coming from within the sphere of U.S. intervention, their migration set into motion at least partially by U.S. policy and practices.[26]

And the answer to that second question—Did they find a better life in Lawrence?—is complicated, because many did not. Lawrence was a city in crisis, wracked by deindustrialization, unemployment, and underfunded services, a bleak New England landscape of condemned mills and crime. There was no American Dream for these new immigrants to Lawrence; this was an urban nightmare. This nightmare was shared by many poor and working-class Latinos who settled in U.S. cities in the crisis era. While there are certainly numerous examples of immigrant success stories, they should not overshadow the reality that many Latinos encountered a type of urban dystopia: a profoundly racialized, segregated landscape of disinvestment, joblessness, homelessness, underfunded and neglected public school systems, arson, blight, absentee landlords, inadequate housing, drug and gang violence, racial discrimination, and even racial violence. Over and over again, in interviews and in literature, many Latinos expressed that what they found in U.S. cities was not only thwarted opportunities but decay, frustration, and disappointment.[27]

Interweaving the history of urban crisis and imperial migration is necessary not only to make sense of individual Latino experiences but also to expose the transnational history of U.S. racism and empire more broadly. To illustrate this, I would like to juxtapose two quick stories (both of which I discuss in more detail later in the book). These stories could be told separately, but I argue that they belong together, part of a single history that crosses national borders.

The first: In 1965, more than 20,000 U.S. troops landed in the Dominican Republic, preventing a popular uprising from reinstating the democratically elected leader, Juan Bosch, because U.S. officials feared he was not sufficiently anticommunist. Instead, the United States oversaw the rise to power of Joaquín Balaguer, a former aide to the infamous dictator Rafael Trujillo. Balaguer, with pronounced U.S. support and stark disregard for the human or civil rights of his opponents, ruled the Dominican Republic for twenty-four of the next thirty years, putting in place economic policies that still impact the island today and significantly underfunding the nation's health and education sectors.

The second: In 1991, three-quarters of the public school students in Lawrence, Massachusetts, were Latino, mostly Dominican and Puerto Rican, and the city's fiscal crisis had left the school system dangerously underfunded. Latino students endured pest-infested and leaking school buildings, science classes with no labs, classrooms with too few desks where students were forced to sit on the floors or stand along the edges, no fields for high school athletes, and outdated textbooks that administrators had to beg as hand-me-downs from their suburban neighbors. Seventy percent of the bilingual classes were out of compliance with mandated teacher/student ratios. How does this image of young people of color experiencing the failure of urban education read differently when told alongside the story of a U.S.-supported autocratic ruler in the Dominican Republic refusing to invest in education?

In the same way, the Lawrence riots of 1984 take on a different resonance in the context of the history of U.S. imperial rule in Puerto Rico. In 1898, U.S. troops landed on the island, ostensibly as part of their war against Spain. When defeated, Spain yielded Puerto Rico to the United States, along with the Philippines and Guam. As Puerto Ricans came to realize that they would be ruled over as a colony rather than incorporated as a territory, many escalated their calls for independence. To silence these calls, the U.S. Congress passed the Jones Act in 1917, making Puerto Ricans U.S. citizens. Under U.S. rule,

16   *Introduction*

the island was transformed into a sugar economy, with poorly paid, seasonal labor leading to widespread hardship, particularly in the 1930s. The economic dislocations produced by colonial modernization schemes in the postwar era drove hundreds of thousands of Puerto Ricans to the mainland United States to look for work, and today more than half of all Puerto Ricans live in diaspora.

How does the story of an urban race riot read differently in the context of U.S. colonial rule in Puerto Rico? Does the story of white rioters screaming "Who's American? We're American" at Latinos in Lawrence take on a different resonance when we remember that most of those Latinos were Puerto Rican, made "American" unilaterally more than half a century before, essentially through conquest? Powerful on their own, these stories belong together because they are connected by migration. Latinos arrived in Lawrence displaced from home countries that had been ravaged by U.S. rule or intervention, a process Juan González has termed the "harvest of empire."[28] Told as a single narrative, these stories illuminate a broad history of U.S. empire, racism, and spatialized inequality, as well as a wide range of Latino strategies to survive and contest those forces.

There has been an impressive acceleration of Latino activism since 2006, and the growing political strength of this tremendously diverse group is incontrovertible. Yet calls for Latino inclusion in the United States, as Arlene Dávila and Gina Pérez have both emphasized, have often relied on the image of hardworking immigrants with a strong commitment to their families and a remarkable pro-U.S. patriotism, a discourse that portrays Latinos as more true to "American values" than U.S. Americans are.[29] The double standard here is obvious: Why should Latinos have to be "more American than Americans" to justify their claims on social membership? And who is left out of this narrative? Where is there space in this discourse for the jobless, the disaffected, the incarcerated, or the welfare reliant? This narrative of Latinos as well-behaved, family-oriented, hardworking, and patriotic doesn't have room for the radically critical, for revolutionaries like the Young Lords or the Brown Berets, or for the young Puerto Rican men hurling Molotov cocktails in Lawrence in 1984. After the Lawrence riots, a Latino scholar and activist argued, "Riots among Hispanics are highly unusual. . . . Things have got to be extremely serious when rioting breaks out among Hispanics."[30] While attempting to highlight the rioters' valid grievances, comments like these also domesticated the riots, rendering them an isolated unruly incident from an otherwise obedient social group. But of course, all people have the potential to riot under certain conditions; in fact, urban Latino communities rioted more than forty times in the late 1960s and early 1970s alone, and Latinos were major participants in the Los Angeles and Washington Heights uprisings of 1992.[31] The narrative of the hardworking, family-values immigrant is based on a very real, but inevitably partial, truth about Latino communities. As long as Latino claims on space and resources rely on this narrative, the insurgence of the alienated and the outraged can seem to undermine rather than reinforce Latino demands for change.

It is here that recalling the interwoven histories of imperial migration and urban crisis becomes imperative. The white residents and city officials who rejected the efforts of Latino Lawrencians to claim their right to the city invoked discourses of foreignness, of Latinos as outsiders and latecomers attempting to gain illegitimate access to that which did not belong to them. The history of U.S. intervention in displacing Latinos to the United States is a powerful counternarrative, an implicit invocation of the common protest slogan "We didn't cross the border; the border crossed us," correcting the myth of U.S. American innocence and entitlement. The history of suburbanization, racialized disinvestment, and urban decline is a further corrective to the idea of the United States as a land of immigrant opportunities in terms of jobs, wealth, education, and political freedom. The truth is that these opportunities were divided unequally across the U.S. landscape, and race played a central role in determining access to them. As one Latino Lawrencian explained frankly after the riots, "I do not see those opportunities here for everybody." For this speaker, disillusion was transformed into anger, into a fierce commitment to demand the opportunities that migration had promised but not provided: "What it [may] come to is that we will have to fight for these things . . . and believe me, if it comes to that, we will fight."[32] Told together, these histories help to anchor a protest narrative that does not rhetorically rely on well-behaved Latinos and to recognize Latino activism that is oppositional and radical, aimed at transformation, not just inclusion. By tracing the global and local obstacles to a better life that poor and working-class Latinos faced in the late twentieth century, historians can contribute to creating a discursive space for the type of anger expressed during the 1984 riots, anger that might otherwise be read as ingratitude in a more normative discourse of immigration-as-opportunity.

In essence, the larger questions guiding my work are these: How do we write an anticolonial Latino history that holds the United States accountable to those affected by its imperialist interventions? How do we write histories of Latinos in the United States that take as their premise the idea that migration is a human right? And how do we apply that premise not only to challenge the exclusions at, and militarization of, national borders but to challenge racial and economic segregation, mass incarceration, and the displacement provoked by gentrification—to challenge all the spatial constraints on Latino social mobility, all the obstacles to that better life that drew so many Puerto Ricans and Dominicans to Lawrence?

And how do we recognize the limits of migration in a globalized world? Whether on the islands or in Lawrence, Latinos essentially found the same neoliberal economic order: a system that rendered quality education, health care, housing, and public safety privileges only for those who could pay. They found ostensibly autonomous governments crippled by deficits and debt, desperate to attract private investment, too blinded by revenue needs to attend to the survival needs of their people, too dependent to truly be self-governed. And they encountered the devastating mobility of capital, which was constantly migrating elsewhere in search of lower wages and less regulation, creating racialized spaces with such widespread un- and under-employment that laboring became a privilege.[33] Telling the history of imperial migration and urban crisis together begs the question of where, exactly, that better life was to be found.

A NOTE ON TERMS, SOURCES, AND TONE

This book will at times seem to play fast and loose with the terms "immigration" and "migration," as neither is precisely adequate. "Immigration" is generally reserved for migrations that cross formal national borders, and this is inaccurate for Puerto Ricans. Although I argue that both Dominicans and Puerto Ricans (and many other Latinos) ought to be understood as imperial "migrants," I do not intend to collapse distinctions between Puerto Ricans and other groups by this choice of terms or to obscure the substantial advantages conferred by U.S. citizenship in this era. In addition, I rely on the term "immigration" in a very broad sense to refer to migration *into* an area, even when referring to Puerto Ricans. I use the term "Latino" when discussing groups of mixed national origins or when the national origin of the source or subject is unknown. Although I highlight intentional efforts to engage in pan-ethnic Latino organizing in Lawrence, these efforts certainly did not erase individuals' pride in or identification with their (or their parents'/grandparents') home countries. Yet all too often, the sources I've relied on refer only to Latinos or Hispanics, rendering a more nuanced or comparative analysis difficult. One of the biggest challenges in writing about such a small city is that very little of its history has been archived; even many official government documents are missing. As a result, there are many questions I could not answer simply because I was unable to find suitable sources. I leave it to future scholars to discover more creative archives that will yield a fuller picture of Lawrence's past.

Finally, Lawrence has endured countless slights and insults over the past several decades, as have many of its Latino residents. Writing about such a city, it is tempting to focus only on the positive, to help reclaim for the city and its residents some of the respect due to them. I have been cautioned by concerned Lawrencians that writing about the riots or the arson or the poverty in Lawrence will only reinforce the city's bad reputation. I share that concern, but ultimately I believe that clarifying the structural roots of Lawrence's troubles is fundamental to portraying the city and its residents positively. If showing a city in a positive light means telling only happy stories of privilege, success, and well-being, then this book fails in that regard. Instead, this book tells stories of individuals and communities overcoming obstacles, fighting for their rights, and insisting on fairness and justice. These are the stories that have inspired me for the past decade, that have given me goosebumps and awoken my outrage, but they cannot be told without also focusing on unfairness, injustice, and seemingly insurmountable barriers. So I hope Lawrencians will forgive yet another account of the city's struggles; to me, these fierce stories of tenacity, passion, and commitment in the face of hardship are positive indeed.

ONE

THE URBAN/
SUBURBAN DIVIDE

Nowhere was the transition more dramatic, the extremes of
prosperity and adversity so marked, as in Lawrence.

"City That Wouldn't Die," Boston Globe, *1960*

In 1965, the cover of the town of Andover's annual report featured a simple, striking illustration of a Pilgrim wearing an astronaut's space helmet.
There could not have been a better image to capture the postwar identity
of Lawrence's suburban neighbor. The small New England town of Andover
prided itself on its three-and-a-half-century history and its democratic traditions, with major decisions still made via a town hall meeting open to all
voters. In the postwar decades of suburban growth, Andover had carefully
controlled development, maintaining ample open space, a pastoral aesthetic,
and property values sufficiently high to ensure a well-heeled, patrician population. It was an old town with a long history of wealth and prestige. Yet
the astronaut's helmet placed Andover solidly in the space age, reflecting an
equally important aspect of the town's character: its growing importance as
a high-technology manufacturing site, especially for the defense industry.
In the postwar decades, Andover was still home to tasteful houses on gently
rolling hills, but it was also increasingly home to well-insulated industrial
parks where companies like Raytheon manufactured the latest in military
and other technology. This controlled, successful growth created a spiral of
prosperity, as the swelling tax base expanded the town's capacity to provide
services to its residents (particularly quality public schools), thereby further
increasing the town's desirability and, by extension, its property values.

Lawrence, however, was encountering a completely opposite spiral, one that was intimately bound up with the growing prosperity of Andover and its other neighbors. In the postwar decades, Lawrence experienced a massive exodus of its residents to the suburbs, the collapse of its economic backbone (the textile industry), and the evisceration of its retail sector and downtown business district. Its tax base gutted, the city struggled desperately to provide basic services to its residents and to recruit private industry to the city to generate jobs. Lawrence was essentially competing with its suburban neighbors to house, and thus tax, the region's middle class and its industry, offices, shops, and restaurants. And Lawrence was losing.

In the decades before World War II, Lawrence was in many ways the heart of its small metropolitan region. People from the suburbs flowed into the city to work, to shop, to see movies, and to visit with family. By the 1980s, this had reversed. The suburbs were flourishing and the city was in a state of profound crisis. Suburban residents drove in a wide arc around Lawrence to avoid traveling through it; some even talked about demolishing the city and starting over.[1] Although there were still a few suburbanites who worked in the city (often as teachers or social service workers), it was more common for people from Lawrence, or at least the lucky ones with jobs and access to transportation, to travel out to the suburbs to work or to shop.

This transition was extreme in Greater Lawrence (i.e., Lawrence and its surrounding suburbs), but it was most certainly not unique to the old mill city. Throughout the country, suburbs boomed in the postwar decades, while the flight of industry, retail, and white residents devastated cities. Of the twenty-five largest cities in the country in 1950, eighteen lost population over the next few decades, and the media began to fret over the death of American cities.[2] Urban decline was particularly evident in the "Rust Belt" of the Northeast and Midwest, as older, densely settled cities were hit hard by the flight of industry and population to the suburbs or to the sprawling "Sunbelt" cities in the rapidly developing South and West.[3]

While cities atrophied in the postwar decades, the nation's suburban population actually doubled between 1950 and 1970. By 1970, the United States had more people living in suburbs than in cities.[4] Suburbanization was not simply a shift in residential population; it was a radical transformation in political economy. As the suburbs grew, they quickly ceased to be bedroom communities for urban professionals and often became the economic engines for their metropolitan regions. By the end of the 1980s, a majority of jobs in metropolitan areas were located in suburbs.[5] This transformation completely undermined the relationship that had previously existed between cities and suburbs, a relationship enshrined in the very term "*suburban*." As Kenneth Jackson, the groundbreaking historian of suburbanization, explained in 1985, while the term "suburban" "once implied a relationship with the city, the term today is more likely to represent a distinction from the city."[6] By the 1980s, the suburbs were no longer viewed as subordinate to cities, but as their antithesis.

This chapter will explore the causes of suburban growth, both nationally and in the Greater Lawrence region, and its consequences for cities like Lawrence that lost their central economic role as a result of suburban competition. As Latinos began to arrive in Lawrence in large numbers in the 1970s and 1980s, they were viciously and violently scapegoated for the city's decline, but the reality was that Lawrence's economic crisis was already well under way as a result of these broader shifts in urban/suburban political economy. Suburbanization, deindustrialization, and disinvestment ravaged cities across the country in the postwar era (again, especially in the Northeast and Midwest), and this small industrial city was certainly hit hard. The real growth of Lawrence's Latino population, however, occurred decades after the city's economic transformations had gotten under way. The policies and practices that enriched the suburbs and impoverished the city in the postwar era formed the economic landscape that greeted Puerto Rican and Dominican newcomers to Lawrence, and thus profoundly shaped their experiences.

SUBURBAN NATION

The decades after World War II were an era of unprecedented prosperity in the United States. Individual aspirations, private investments, media discourses, and government commitments coincided to make homeownership an achievable dream in this era of growing affluence. The proportion of American families owning their own home exploded. In 1940, only 44 percent of American households owned their own home; by 1960, that proportion had jumped to 62 percent and continued to climb slowly for the rest of the century.[7] Although each home purchase has an individual story of a homebuyer's hard work, hope, and investment in the future, this national transformation was also the result of a much larger shift in the country's political economy, particularly the intervention of the federal government into the realm of home financing.

The mortgage industry, and the housing industry more broadly, looked very different before the 1930s. Until then, mortgages were generally short term (5 to 10 years) with variable interest rates and often required that the buyer pay half the purchase price up front. This financing structure kept owning one's home out of reach for most working families. Then as unemployment skyrocketed and home values plummeted during the Great Depression, even those families who had been able to purchase homes began to default on their mortgages, and the nation faced a rash of foreclosures. The federal government responded by creating the Home Owners' Loan Corporation (HOLC) in 1933 to refinance mortgages to help stave off foreclosures. Although the HOLC only made loans until 1936, it set a crucial precedent, pioneering the long-term, fixed-rate, self-amortizing mortgage.

In 1934 the Federal Housing Administration (FHA) was created and began to guarantee the mortgages provided by approved lenders; this meant that lenders would be protected by the federal government against financial loss if the homeowner defaulted on the mortgage. Although these "guarantees" did not protect the homeowners themselves from foreclosure, they did eliminate much of the risk for lenders, making them more willing to lend. In 1944, the GI Bill created the Veterans' Administration mortgage insurance program, providing low-interest loans to veterans, and in 1948, the FHA made purchasing a home even easier, allowing thirty-year instead of twenty-year loans. In 1956, the required down payment was reduced from 20 percent to only 5 percent for new construction. All of these changes dramatically increased the financing available to potential homebuyers.[8]

In sum, the federal government began in the 1930s and 1940s to massively invest in the expansion of the mortgage industry, making lending less risky for banks and making homes easier to afford for potential buyers, in what was essentially an unacknowledged form of "welfare." Yet the true impact of these new lending policies was not felt during the Depression, as so few people had the funds to purchase homes and as construction lagged in the crippled economy. During the war that followed, the nation's industries were focused on the war effort, not on home construction. Not until after the war did this new approach to mortgages have its most pronounced impact: when industries returned to domestic production, when returning veterans faced a housing shortage, when federal decentralization policies encouraged suburban growth with new highways, when the baby boom suddenly ramped up the number of new families, and when realtors, developers, and the media inspired the nation with a suburban dream of leafy streets, white-picket fences, and children playing happily in the yard. As new home construction boomed in the suburbs, the federal mortgage policies that brought homeownership within reach of working families found their market, and the suburbs exploded.[9]

Not everyone in the United States was able to leverage this postwar government largesse into suburban homeownership, however. As the federal government was expanding access to the suburbs in many ways, it was also developing policies that restricted residential mobility to the suburbs for people of color, and it condoned private policies that had the same effect. These influential HOLC and FHA practices discouraged lending in neighborhoods considered to be a risky investment. Neighborhoods could be "redlined" (a term that referred to risk-assessment maps that marked off neighborhoods according to their presumed safety as investments) based on the age or quality of their housing stock or their proximity to industry or other undesirable neighborhood qualities. Yet federal policies also explicitly discouraged lending in neighborhoods with "undesirable" racial demographics—neighborhoods of color or integrating neighborhoods—assuming that such neighborhoods were inherently risky investments. As the FHA explained in a prewar underwriting manual, "If a neighborhood is to retain stability, it is necessary that its properties shall continue to be occupied by the same social and racial classes."[10] Although the federal government removed such explicitly racialized obstacles to mortgage access in the late 1940s, this type of discrimination in federal lending existed well into the 1950s and was broadly adopted by private lenders as well until the passage of the Fair Housing Act in 1968. People of color's access to home financing was thus severely limited in the postwar decades.[11]

Other practices limited the suburbanization of people of color in the postwar decades as well. Developers often designated new suburban developments to be for white people only, using restrictive covenants or deed restrictions to prohibit the sale or leasing of homes to people of color. The U.S. Supreme Court ruled racial restrictive covenants unenforceable in 1948; but they were still widely used, and there was little federal intervention to press developers to open new suburban housing to people of color.[12] Realtor "steering" (only showing prospective homebuyers homes in certain neighborhoods based on race) and racist violence and harassment also discouraged the suburbanization of people of color, particularly African Americans, in the postwar era.[13] These factors combined to ensure that the vast majority of people rushing to the booming suburbs in the decades after World War II were white, and that suburbanization constituted a form of white flight from postwar U.S. cities.

In addition to these racial limits on suburban expansion, most suburbs worked to enforce some degree of class uniformity in this era as well. Suburbs regulated growth by enacting zoning requirements designed to prevent neighborhoods from becoming overdeveloped, run down, or mixed with undesirable elements, like waste disposal sites. Suburban municipalities strove to balance their desire for growth (necessary to expand the tax base) with their desire to preserve open space and an exclusively residential character, and to maximize lot sizes in order to drive up property values. The emphasis on single-family zoning and the upward spiral relationship between a municipality's exclusivity, desirability, tax base, and quality of its public services, especially education, continued to render many suburbs virtually off limits for people from urban communities of color even as explicit racial barriers fell in the post–Civil Rights era. Suburban home-ownership was affordable for average working-class U.S. Americans in the 1950s in a way that it rarely was by the 1980s, especially in the crowded Northeast, and zoning restrictions often limited the availability of rental housing to cities.

This economic exclusivity was an intentional part of suburban planning. As Robert Engler noted in his 1971 study of nearby metropolitan Boston, "Restrictive zoning practices . . . succeeded in reducing the availability of residential land and raised its price such that any housing that can be built in the suburbs excludes all but the middle class." Engler noted people who had moved out to the suburbs from the city were especially adamant that their municipalities should exclude low-income and particularly subsidized housing, so that more urban residents could not follow them out. He quoted one resident of Newton who explained, "It took me twenty years to make it out of Dorchester and I'm not going to pay for these people to move in and ruin it."[14] The postwar era was one of unparalleled social and spatial mobility as the suburbs mushroomed, yet access to that mobility was seriously circumscribed by race and class.

SUBURBANIZATION IN GREATER LAWRENCE

Lawrence is completely surrounded by three suburbs: Andover, North Andover, and Methuen. Observers sometimes also included Salem, New Hampshire, directly over the New Hampshire border from Methuen, in their discussions of "Greater Lawrence" as well. Lying just north of Methuen, Salem would come to be the closest major retail center in tax-free New Hampshire and a heavy retail competitor with Lawrence in the postwar decades.[15] The four suburbs had somewhat different characteristics: Andover and North Andover, lying to the south of Lawrence (in other words, on the Boston side), were much more prosperous than Methuen and Salem, lying to the north. Yet all four suburbs experienced dramatic growth and increasing prosperity in the decades after World War II.

In 1940, 66 percent of the population of Greater Lawrence lived in Lawrence proper (on only 5 percent of the region's land), but this shifted after the war.[16] Between 1950 and 1960, Andover, Methuen, and North Andover all saw major population gains, while just over the New Hampshire border, Salem saw its population almost double. As Lawrence's suburbs grew in this decade, however, the city itself lost 10,000 residents, or 12 percent of its population, and between 1960 and 1970, Lawrence's population declined another 6 percent. By 1980, Lawrence's total population decline had slowed (although it still managed to reach a new low of 63,175), but this apparent stability was entirely due to Latino immigration. If we consider only the white residents of the city, Lawrence lost another 20 percent of its population in a single decade during the 1970s. Significantly, the bulk of those leaving the city in the postwar era were young adults, as new families opted to buy homes in the suburbs, leaving behind an aging population in the city.[17]

For many white families across the nation, flight to the suburbs was a way of maintaining segregated communities, schools, and public spaces in the face of postwar racial integration in U.S. cities.[18] Lawrence, however, was 99 percent white in the immediate postwar decades and had never developed a sizable African American community, so the paradigm of white residents leaving the city as people of color moved into their neighborhoods simply does not apply to Lawrence in this era. Yet even without a racial motivation, Lawrence whites still fled the city. In fact, between the 1940 and 1980 census, Lawrence lost nearly 40 percent of its white residents, before substantial Latino migration to the city. In this sense, Lawrence's population decline emphasizes the "pull" factors of white flight: the myriad privileges and opportunities that enticed white urban residents out into the suburbs.

The draw of Lawrence's suburbs in these early decades was not that they offered an escape from the racial tension of the city (although white flight from Lawrence would rapidly accelerate as the Latino population in the city grew after 1980); rather, the pull of the suburbs related to changes in the metropolitan political economy that allowed the suburbs to develop at Lawrence's expense and enabled the suburbs to restrict economic diversity through exclusionary zoning practices.[19] These changes in metropolitan political economy were national changes that were racialized in their *origins* (an effort to create and preserve prosperous, independent, "lily-white" suburbs), and they would come to be tremendously racialized in their *impact* on the Greater Lawrence region as Latinos settled in the city. These transformations were not, however, specifically racialized in their early application in Greater Lawrence, as there was no sizable urban community of color from which to flee—or to exclude. Despite the white racial homogeneity of the region in these first decades of suburbanization, early white flight from Lawrence did indeed conform to national patterns in that it created prosperous, independent, politically powerful, and overwhelmingly white suburbs, as well as the economically segregated geography that would funnel future Latino migrants into the central city.

In 1950, at the beginning of this suburban growth, median home values and household incomes were similar in Lawrence and its suburbs. This is important because it meant that suburban homeownership was in reach for even average-earning Lawrence residents. Within a few decades, this would no longer be the case; unequal urban/suburban development would create a massive divergence in property values and housing costs between Lawrence and its suburbs. In 1950, the median value of a single-family home in the city of Lawrence was $8,989 ($88,248 adjusted to 2015 dollars, to give a sense of change over time), quite near the median home value for the Greater Lawrence area as a whole, $9,210 ($90,418 adjusted).[20] This cost was just over three times the median household income of Lawrence residents, in other words, generally affordable to average, hardworking Lawrencians. Considering that much of the federal support for homeownership was geared toward new construction, it was most likely easier for Lawrencians in 1950 to buy a home in the booming suburbs than in the city. In the immediate postwar era, however, when the economics of homeownership were so egalitarian, the racial politics of homeownership were their most exclusionary. By the time an enforcement mechanism (however inefficient) was in place in the 1970s to discourage housing discrimination, a solid gap had already grown between urban income and suburban housing prices.

By 1980, the difference between urban wages and suburban housing prices had become pronounced. In Andover, the median home value had grown to $80,684 ($231,672 adjusted), nearly six times the median household income in Lawrence. By 2000, at $344,895 ($473,878 adjusted), the median home value in Andover was nearly twelve times the median household income in Lawrence. The average, hardworking Lawrencian could not possibly dream of purchasing an average home in Andover, no matter how diligently she or he saved. Even in a less prosperous suburb such as Methuen, the process was similar. By 1980, the median home value had only grown to $50,004 ($143,579 adjusted), just three and a half times the median household income in Lawrence, steep but not impossible for an average Lawrence worker. By 2000, however, the median home value in Methuen had exploded to $159,000 ($218,462 adjusted), or five and a half times the median household income

The Urban/Suburban Divide

in Lawrence. Average household incomes in Lawrence declined slightly over these decades, but the true responsibility for this huge gap lay in the incredible growth of suburban housing prices. As historian Robert Self noted in his study of Oakland, California, and suburban Alameda County, at the same time that explicitly racial barriers to suburban living were being eradicated in the 1960s, "property value differentials hardened across space."[21]

While many urban workers had been priced out of buying homes in Lawrence's suburbs by 1980, the quantity of affordable rental housing in the suburbs had also been dramatically limited through exclusive zoning and staunch public opposition. The suburbs strongly opposed the construction of multifamily rental and subsidized housing. By 1980, between 87 and 94 percent of homes in Andover, Methuen, and North Andover were only in single-family dwellings.[22] This reflected a conscious suburban zoning strategy to protect property values, limit the burden on municipal services, and promote a pastoral aesthetic in what had generally been farmland before World War II.

In 1936, for example, the Town of Andover approved zoning bylaws "in order to promote the health, safety, convenience, morals, and general welfare of the inhabitants" and "to improve and beautify the town." The bylaws divided the town into distinct uses: residential, educational, business, industrial, and agricultural. Each district had its own set of standards and building requirements. The bylaws specified that new buildings or alterations in the residential district must be single-family detached houses, except where two-family houses were already typical of the neighborhood (very rare). Any new residential properties were required to have lot frontages of at least 75 feet and total land areas of not less than 10,000 square feet. Even before World War II, Andover residents were planning ahead to shape the type of development that could occur within their town's borders.[23]

As demand for housing in Andover grew in the postwar era, Andover voters responded with even more restrictive zoning in 1948 and 1955. Rather than a single residential district, voters approved, by a huge margin, the creation of three separate residential districts, each with much larger lot size requirements than those required by the 1936 bylaws. Zone C, for example, required at least 200-foot frontages and a minimum lot size of one acre. In response to the rapid development of housing in Andover, the town consciously raised the bar on land parcels for new homes. As land costs made up a major part of property values, such zoning restrictions helped to ensure high-value development. At the same time, they also served to exclude the creation of affordable housing within the town's boundaries. Although Andover residents approved very small parcels of land as "Multiple Residence Districts" (initially to create a public housing project for the town's veterans immediately after the war, before public housing became stigmatized), the overwhelming majority of land in Andover was zoned only for single-family houses on large lots.[24]

Andover residents consciously legislated and organized to maintain the pastoral nature of their town. The Andover Village Improvement Society (AVIS) had been formed in 1894, but its activities had been largely limited to town beautification until the 1950s. With the postwar boom in suburban development, Harold Rafton transformed the organization into a conservation group. Rafton argued that AVIS must work quickly to set aside open space before the town's growth made it impossible and all the land was "gobbled up by thoughtless building," and AVIS began to acquire acreage through purchase and donation. The town formalized these efforts by creating the Andover Conservation Commission in 1957 and the Conservation Fund in 1966.[25] Andover had the resources and political will to effectively channel suburban growth.

To counter the exclusionary zoning widespread in Massachusetts's postwar suburbs, the state legislature passed the Affordable Housing Act, also known as the Comprehensive Permit Act (Chapter 40B), in 1969. This landmark law became popularly known as the Anti-Snob Zoning Act, as its goal was to override restrictive zoning laws in order to permit the development of affordable housing throughout all Massachusetts communities, even the suburbs. Chapter 40B empowered developers to bypass municipal zoning requirements, as long as 20 to 25 percent of their units were set aside for affordable housing and provided that developers agreed to limit their own profits from the development. Communities in which 10 percent of existing housing units were already affordable for low-income residents were exempt, but few suburban enclaves met this target. In most Massachusetts suburbs, like Andover, the bulk of the land available for development was zoned for single-family houses on large lots. Multifamily rental housing—the only type of housing in the Massachusetts market with a reasonable chance of being affordable for low-income residents—was considered anathema to neighborhood property values. By enabling developers to override local zoning laws, Chapter 40B basically gave them the right to force suburban communities to accept dense, multifamily developments. Suburban municipalities did not submit to this presumed violation of their autonomy without a fight, frequently rejecting proposed developments until they were forced by the courts or the Massachusetts Housing Appeals Committee to permit them.[26]

North Andover was an early test case for anti-snob development. In 1973, the Archdiocese of Boston proposed a 144-unit townhouse development for families of low and moderate income on church-owned land next to the Holy Sepulchre cemetery. The archdiocese emphasized the community's moral responsibility to provide affordable housing, but the town rejected the proposal. North Andover residents argued that the development would turn the town into a "slurb"—a suburban slum. The *Boston Globe* noted that this fear of being a "slurb" was sparked by North Andover's position next door to Lawrence. "The town [of North Andover], characterized by expensive single-family homes, borders the city of Lawrence which is rowed with triple-deckers and skylined with mammoth mill buildings that now house mostly minimum-wage shops." North Andover residents saw themselves as holding the line against creeping urbanization. Many, the article noted, were former Lawrencians themselves; having moved out of Lawrence to the suburbs, they could not then let the city follow them into North Andover. They viewed opposing multifamily developments as necessary to protect their upward mobility and their investment in suburbia.[27]

The state's Housing Appeals Committee and courts saw the issue differently, however, and required the town to permit the development in 1977. The Planning Office for Urban Affairs, Inc., a nonprofit established by the archdiocese to develop affordable and mixed-income housing, completed Wood Ridge Homes in 1979, a cooperative development with 230 units, a portion of which were (and remain) subsidized.[28]

This was a major win for the dispersal of affordable housing into the suburbs, but such wins were not common. In general, suburban affordable housing development in the state remained painstakingly slow, and the subsidized suburban units that were built were most often for the elderly, not for low-income families.[29] By 1976, Lawrence's nearest suburbs had a total population greater than the city itself. Yet combined they contained only 694 total units of subsidized housing, more than three-quarters of which were reserved for the elderly. Fewer than 150 units were available for low-income families in Lawrence's suburbs. The city, meanwhile, had 2,203 units of subsidized housing, three-quarters of which were available to families.[30]

By 1980, subsidized and even private multifamily rental housing was extremely concentrated in the central city through exclusionary zoning, constraining renters' choices considerably. Median home prices in most suburbs were beyond the means of the average Lawrence worker and were particularly out of range for most Latino workers in the city, whose wages were significantly lower than the Lawrence median. The overwhelming majority of

Latinos who settled in the Greater Lawrence region thus had little opportunity to find a home outside the city. As Puerto Ricans and Dominicans were drawn to the region, these housing policies concentrated Latino settlement into the deteriorating city, determining not only their living conditions but the educational opportunities available to their children. The suburbs were flourishing, but the privileges of suburban homeownership were, by design, not for everyone.

URBAN RENEWAL AND DISPLACEMENT IN LAWRENCE

While the suburbs pulled people, especially young adults, from the city in the postwar decades, there were a number of factors that effectively pushed residents out of Lawrence in these decades as well, further encouraging suburban settlement. Urban renewal projects were government-sponsored plans to demolish and rebuild "blighted" areas of U.S. cities in the postwar decades. City governments used the power of eminent domain to appropriate large swaths of property in poor and working-class neighborhoods. This property was then generally razed, and the cleared land was given at low cost to private developers to rebuild with newer, more modern housing or commercialized leisure sites. The Federal Housing Act of 1949 provided federal money to fund this broad remaking of U.S. cities. The roots of subsequent neoliberal urbanism were evident in this structure for urban renewal, as government funds and concessions were marshaled to attract private capital to the city to counter disinvestment.[31]

Poor and working-class residents undoubtedly bore the brunt of urban renewal, or "slum clearance," in most U.S. cities, suffering from eviction from their homes and businesses, demolition of their neighborhoods, and displacement from their communities. African American and Latino neighborhoods were especially vulnerable to demolition, leading critics of urban renewal to label it "Negro removal" or "spic removal,"[32] but many working-class white ethnic neighborhoods were also targeted.[33] Displaced residents of color were often resettled into the cities' newly built public housing projects, while white residents displaced by urban renewal often had more options, including moving to the suburbs.[34] Lawrence, with its older, tenement neighborhoods and its hunger to generate economic activity, was eager for federal redevelopment funds. Yet, as in many cities, the process of urban renewal in Lawrence created tremendous upheaval, uncertainty, and ultimately displacement, all of which served as one more incentive for Lawrencians with sufficient means to relocate to the suburbs.[35]

The Urban/Suburban Divide

The Lawrence Redevelopment Authority (LRA) was created as a renewal agency via the 1949 Housing Act. The LRA received federal funds to acquire "blighted" properties. Generally, the federal government paid two-thirds of the cost of acquiring a site, with the final third the responsibility of the city, but in Lawrence's case, state funds often made up much of the balance. The first step to acquiring federal funds was to designate a renewal area. In November 1959, the LRA voted to initiate the General Neighborhood Renewal Area (GNRA) of 200 acres (a substantial portion of land, given that the entire city of Lawrence is less than seven square miles). The city would carry out five distinct neighborhood renewal projects within this GNRA over the next two decades. When the renewal plan was announced in 1959, however, Lawrence residents had no concrete information on which neighborhoods within the GNRA would be demolished or what the timeline for renewal would be, and instead rumors swirled throughout the city.[36]

Although city officials maintained high hopes for urban renewal, neighborhoods throughout the GNRA, as they were constituted in 1959, were essentially doomed. Even those that were not in the end selected for renewal experienced paralyzing uncertainty, disinvestment, and decay. As Nicolas Pernice explained in his history of the city's renewal, inclusion in the GNRA "stopped neighborhood growth and development right in its tracks."[37] Pernice described this as a "self-fulfilling 'blight' scenario" in which functioning, if modest, working-class neighborhoods were declared "blighted" in order to gain access to federal redevelopment funds; this declaration then set off a chain of disinvestment and disrepair leading to *actual* blight.[38] Herbert Gans's scholarship on urban renewal in Boston's West End drew similar conclusions: A working-class white ethnic neighborhood was targeted for renewal based on the city's allegation of blight, but pronounced decline and disinvestment in the neighborhood actually occurred afterward, in the six years between when the plan was announced and when neighborhood demolition began.[39] In the postwar context of widespread slum clearance, labeling a neighborhood as blighted could very quickly make it so.[40]

The city acquired the renewal property using eminent domain, the legal right of the government to acquire private property for public use. The LRA reserved the right to take even well-maintained properties if they were in otherwise "blighted" neighborhoods, so property owners were reluctant to invest in homes that they might lose shortly thereafter. Generally it is the responsibility of the government to compensate the property owner, but in the case of urban renewal, property owners often had very little leverage to negotiate a fair price, further discouraging upkeep.[41] As a result, residents in the renewal area either left their neighborhoods when they became slated for demolition or watched them deteriorate before they were taken by the city and torn down to make way for new construction. It was a devastating triad for the city's residents: deterioration followed by demolition and displacement. This uncertainty and disinvestment expanded throughout the city in the 1960s and 1970s as other neighborhoods feared they might also become subject to renewal. Stable working-class ethnic neighborhoods were eroded or demolished by the renewal process throughout much of the city in the postwar decades.[42]

The Plains urban renewal project comprised the rectangle of land bounded by Lawrence Street, Haverhill Street, Hampshire Street, and the Spicket River, and it characterizes well the impact of urban renewal on Lawrence's working-class white ethnic communities. The fifteen-block tenement neighborhood was home to long-standing Italian, Syrian, Armenian, and other immigrant communities. Although the neighborhood was vibrant with businesses and social clubs, one consulting report declared frankly, "The neighborhood has no prestige in terms of social standing."[43] In addition, local banks generally refused mortgage financing in the neighborhood, viewing it as an investment risk.[44] This redlining contributed to the vulnerability of the Plains and inhibited grassroots renewal in the neighborhood.[45]

Tenement neighborhoods in Lawrence were extremely congested, but that did not necessarily mean local residents were aching to get out. As one resident of the Plains neighborhood recalled, people living in the tenements found ways to adjust to the overcrowding, and the congestion could even facilitate strong social connections within the neighborhood. "Those tenement houses were squeezed together so closely, that when you went up to the roof to dry your mint . . . we could actually jump from one roof to the other. We in the tenement world, the asphalt world, we didn't have many spots to plant, so what we'd do is utilize the rooftops, and we'd grow tomatoes and we'd grow cucumbers. . . . This is what the community gardens looked like." This close living may actually have facilitated social bonds, even across ethnic lines. As one resident recalled, "The Plains was really a mixture of Lebanese, Italian, Irish, Polish. It was really, really a melting pot."[46]

This "melting pot" was broken up by dispersal of the residents to the suburbs once urban renewal got under way. As one Plains resident recalled, "Most of the Jewish people moved to Andover and the Italian people moved to Methuen; the Irish moved to North Andover."[47] Another resident also recalled the scattering of the ethnic groups who had previously shared the neighborhoods, either to the suburbs or to the sections of Lawrence with

The Urban/Suburban Divide

more single-family houses, Prospect and Tower Hills or South Lawrence. "I think those with Italian background moved to Prospect Hill (Lawrence) or to the valley, in Methuen. . . . The Lebanese moved—you name it—some to Methuen, some to Salem, NH."[48] Although many residents wanted to continue to live close to their friends and families in the neighborhood, they were reluctant to move within the city for fear that their new neighborhood would also eventually be slated for renewal. Moving to the suburbs was a much safer investment. The suburbs provided a powerful pull for Lawrence residents, yet it is important to recognize the impact of urban renewal in pushing residents from Lawrence as well, in addition to contributing to deterioration and disinvestment in the city.

Desperate residents organized to challenge the renewal projects. One Plains resident recalled, "We got a community organization and we had stickers put out saying 'Save Your Home.' We tried to petition the city council and the Mayor to do spot cleaning up. Spot removal of houses that were below standards of human habitation," rather than demolition of entire neighborhoods, was preferred by many in the community. But he remembered the city government being uninterested in such a solution: "Of course they didn't want anything to do with it, the city council and Mayor Buckley, because it was obvious that there were two developers who were ready to build their apartments."[49] Not only was urban renewal a way to garner federal redevelopment funds; it also aimed to attract private development in an era of disinvestment. The city government and the LRA hoped to anchor and expand the city's tax base, particularly through reinforcing the importance of the downtown shopping sector and recruiting higher-income residents to the city.

In the end, however, the city was not able to create high-end housing in the Plains to recruit and retain middle-class residents and boost the downtown's retail sector. Instead, the neighborhood saw the construction of more than 1,000 units of housing and assisted living for the elderly. While ensuring adequate housing for the elderly is an important function of city government, it was not the goal of the city's urban renewal plan, and it did not significantly increase tax revenue for the city. In addition, the Plains neighborhood lost over 90 percent of its businesses after renewal, which certainly could not have helped the city's tax base.[50]

Most importantly for understanding the divergence between Lawrence and its suburbs, urban renewal created what Pernice calls a "sifting" process among long-term Lawrence residents. As residents were displaced, those with the means left for the suburbs (or the few suburbanesque neighborhoods within the city), and those without the means stayed behind, often moving to subsidized family housing or into the new developments for the elderly. In the Plains renewal project, a total of 742 families were uprooted, as well as 155 individuals and 126 businesses. By 1969, the owner-occupancy rate in the neighborhood had been slashed nearly in half to 11 percent.[51]

As I discuss in later chapters, longtime Lawrence residents often blamed Latinos for blight and deterioration in their neighborhoods, yet the city's decline was rooted in the broader policies and practices of the postwar era, such as urban renewal, that preceded the city's demographic shift. Even before Latinos began to arrive in the city in large numbers, the threat of property being seized by the city and demolished in waves of urban renewal provided a serious disincentive for owners to maintain their properties. In addition, those displaced were either forced to scramble for other substandard housing in neighborhoods that might become the city's next targets, or if they had sufficient resources, they were encouraged to move to the suburbs to be safely outside the renewal zone. Although some Latinos were directly impacted by this process during the North Common renewal of the 1970s, the bulk of the deterioration, demolition, and displacement actually occurred during the 1950s and 1960s, when the residents of those neighborhoods were overwhelmingly working-class white ethnics. These immigrant and second-generation families from the city's industrial heyday watched their neighborhoods crumble and their communities shatter. Many responded by leaving for the suburbs, but those who stayed in the city were left with the very real impression that the city of their youth had deteriorated beyond recognition.

THE BIGGEST MONEY BATTLE THIS AREA HAS KNOWN

Urban renewal radically transformed residential neighborhoods, but city governments that undertook renewal projects in the postwar era generally had twin goals: both the creation of improved housing *and* the creation of higher-end sites of consumption. Urban renewal projects aimed at commercialized leisure had a number of different motives: to build tax revenue by increasing consumer spending and economic activity within the city, to help attract/maintain middle-income residents to the cities, to anchor further private investment in urban neighborhoods, and to provide jobs for lower-income city residents. This is especially evident in the construction of Lincoln Center in New York City in the 1950s and 1960s, in which a large tenement neighborhood on the city's west side (home to many Puerto Ricans) was razed to create a high-culture hub housing the Metropolitan Opera and other elite performers. The creation of Lincoln Center was intended to spur a wave of private investment in luxury condominiums and high-end shops and restaurants in the surrounding area. Improved housing was often just one small part of a larger municipal strategy to reinvigorate urban neighborhoods.[52]

These types of urban renewal projects were efforts to counter white flight, to attract middle-class and wealthy consumers back into the city, ideally as residents but at least as consumers. This twin emphasis in urban renewal on housing and consumption was evident in Lawrence as well and coalesced into a city priority to attract "first-class" tenants (both residential and commercial) through the use of state and federal urban renewal funds. One of Lawrence's five major urban renewal ventures was the Broadway Essex project, focused on the city's main downtown shopping district. Lawrence's downtown allegedly suffered not only from deterioration and blight but also from heavy traffic, lack of parking (newly essential in the postwar era), and incompatible land uses. In the Broadway Essex urban renewal project, there was widespread renovation but not complete demolition. In addition to revitalizing the downtown shopping district, the plan added a 320-car parking garage. City leaders initiated urban renewal to help make their commercial district competitive with mushrooming suburban shopping plazas and malls. In Lawrence, as in other cities throughout the country, urban renewal was a response to commercial disinvestment in the postwar decades, as suburbs became the new major sites for retail consumption and commercialized leisure.[53]

Although unemployment skyrocketed in the late 1940s and early 1950s as the textile industry left the city, Lawrence's downtown retail and entertainment sector was still vital into the 1960s. Indeed, when longtime white residents or former residents of Lawrence talk about a renaissance in the city, about bringing Lawrence back to its former glory and prominence, they are not usually romanticizing Lawrence's industrial past (a time when most residents lived in slum tenements and had little in the way of free time or available capital for commercialized leisure); rather, they are generally referring to the World War II and early postwar years when Essex Street thrived and drew residents of the entire region to its shops and theaters. More than the loss of industry—although related to it—the loss of Lawrence's retail sector damaged both the city's tax base and its morale. Already in 1974, an article on a well-known Lawrence restaurant described the heyday of the late 1940s with nostalgia: "But those were different days—days when laughter came more easily and Lawrence was alive with lights and fancy clubs and 'every night there was a party.'"[54] By the 1970s, the loss of the city's retail sector and the no-longer-bustling streets of Lawrence's downtown symbolized the end of an era to many of the city's residents.[55]

The decline of the city's retail sector began in the mid-1950s as Methuen and Salem gradually became the consumer hubs of the region.[56] The looming danger of suburban retail competition was not lost on Lawrence's leadership, who commissioned urban planners in 1957 to study how they could regain their competitiveness. The report focused on the city's "Central Business District," mainly along Essex Street. Sales in the district had declined in spite of it being "the center" of the Greater Lawrence area, according to the report. Many businesses had closed, one prominent block had one-third of its retail floor space vacant, and "some new stores have come into the C.B.D. to service primarily the lower-income group." This decline in Lawrence's retail sector, the report pointed out, was not due to decreased buying power in the region, as Greater Lawrence's "effective buying income" had actually been increasing. Rather, the decline was due to white residential flight and the loss of workers coming into the city since the textile mills had shut down.[57] As in other deindustrializing communities, the closing of Lawrence's textile mills had a ripple effect throughout the city's economy, impacting its stores, restaurants, and theaters.[58]

The report continued, however, to point out what city elites were probably most reluctant to hear: "The people of the Greater Lawrence Area are doing business outside [downtown]."[59] Suburban shopping centers were springing up around Lawrence, and traveling to them was becoming easier thanks to the rapidly expanding highway system. Shopping centers in the suburbs were new and well designed; they were conveniently located and included huge parking lots. Retail establishments came to thickly line Route 28 in Salem, New Hampshire, in the following years. The town's growing importance as a consumer site was aided by Massachusetts's decision to introduce a sales tax in 1966, which made the quick drive over the New Hampshire border (to one of the few states left in the country without a sales tax) quite appealing.[60] The *Journal of Greater Lawrence* called the commercial sector along Route 28 in Salem "a sizzling strip of neon and a motorist's nightmare," but it was clearly a shopper's dream.[61]

The final blow to Lawrence's retail sector was dealt in the early 1970s with the construction of the Methuen Mall. In November 1973, journalist Andrew Coburn wrote, "Excuse the messy metaphor, but one hell of a heavyweight is flexing its muscles for the biggest money battle this area has known. . . . the Methuen Mall versus every other shopping scene (particularly plazas) from here to Newburyport." The Methuen Mall would be the biggest of its kind in the region, posing an immediate threat even to suburban shopping plazas. At the time, the mall was only partially open, with less than half of its projected seventy-five stores up and running, but Coburn reported that it "already [was] doing damage in downtown Lawrence." Coburn called the suburban mall "one huge consumer circus with something for everybody," noting that it had "huge stores like Sears and Howland's, with all the latest gimmicks, advertising money, and promotional fanfare to draw crowds from far and wide." Sears had just left its longtime location on Essex Street in downtown Lawrence, and so its relocation to the Methuen Mall must have caused some Lawrencians particular chagrin. Whatever hope Lawrence elites may have had for returning downtown to its prior prominence suddenly became unrealistic, as the Methuen Mall laid Essex Street down for the count.[62]

Lawrence elites, however, clung tightly to the idea of a reinvigorated downtown. A 1978 redevelopment proposal for Essex Street focused on the "Sears Block," where the former Sears building remained vacant, leaving a large, unsightly gap in Lawrence's downtown. The proposal acknowledged the "vast" suburban competition that Lawrence faced by the end of the 1970s, with seven suburban shopping centers in southern New Hampshire, along with the Methuen Mall, the North Andover Mall, and several other nearby suburban shopping centers. The flight of professionals from Lawrence's downtown area to "suburban office parks" had also affected Lawrence's retail sector, the authors noted, as fewer people came through downtown each day. The authors warned that the suburbs were "increasingly self-sufficient," noting that "they have attracted industries of their own, built numerous shopping centers and office parks and continued to build new housing." This suburban "self-sufficiency" was harming Lawrence economically, the proposal argued, and stigmatizing Lawrence as deteriorating and decayed. Already there was a "strong prejudice against Lawrence" that kept suburban residents out of the city.[63]

Suburban competition and Lawrence's bad reputation, however, did not hinder the authors' optimism that the city's downtown could have a renaissance. The key, the proposal argued, was to gear development toward high-end consumers. Renovation of the Sears Block should focus on creating "an image of superiority" in order to attract high-end businesses. The proposal explicitly warned against accessible, or affordable, development, arguing that "low price is not the way to attract 'first-class' commercial tenants."[64] This vision of Lawrence redevelopment marked a persistent strategy among city elites over the next decades. City officials and business leaders believed that a renaissance in the city was only possible by attracting "first-class" commercial or residential tenants, by investing city, state, and federal money in high-end development. Such a renaissance was premised on the exclusion and marginalization of the city's low-income residents or businesses designed to serve them. Subsequent chapters will detail the struggle of community groups to counter this elite strategy with a plan for Lawrence redevelopment premised on improving the lives and building the assets of the city's low-income residents. For now, it is sufficient to note that this neoliberal strategy of investing public money to attract private investment failed repeatedly in Lawrence; the city became increasingly poor and working class, and its downtown remained a hollow shell of its past glory. Ultimately Lawrence would not see a renaissance on Essex Street or a resurgence of commercial activity citywide until the expansion of Latino-owned and Latino-oriented businesses in the 1990s.

INDUSTRY

While the growth of racially and economically homogenous suburbs raised property values and tax bases in suburban Massachusetts, and suburban shopping centers drew the region's consumers out of the city, suburban industry also experienced rapid growth. In the middle of the twentieth century, New England's manufacturing economy was radically transformed. Particularly in Massachusetts, the textile mills that had clothed the nation and provided the backbone of the region's economy had been struggling for decades, and the industry essentially shut down soon after World War II, as some manufacturers headed South or overseas and others folded completely in the face of competition from southern industries and synthetic fabrics.

As textile production was in decline, however, electronics and other high-tech manufacturing was ascending in New England, aided by government support for education and for defense development. Along Route 128, in the suburbs of Boston, a high-tech industrial corridor began to develop, changing the industrial base of the state from textiles to electronics. In Lawrence, this shift was seismic. As the city had been at the center of the textile industry, it would also demonstrate the most significant drawback to New England's industrial transition: Whereas textile manufacturing had been largely an urban mill town phenomenon, electronics development and manufacturing would come to be largely a suburban process. This transformation left former mill towns grasping for a new economic base.[65] As the *Boston Globe* reported, "New England adjusted gradually to the changed economic world, but nowhere was the transition more dramatic, the extremes of prosperity and adversity so marked, as in Lawrence."[66]

As with suburban residential and retail growth, this shift in economic activity to the suburbs was not limited to Greater Lawrence. Across the country, companies located or relocated their production, research, and office spaces in the suburbs in the postwar decades. Federally supported highways made access to the city from the suburbs much easier in the postwar era, of course, but this was only part of the impetus behind relocation. Cold War concerns about a nuclear attack encouraged decentralization of production; suburbs recruited industry through utility development and tax breaks; and suburban facilities could be expansive and pastoral with ample space for parking, a necessity in the postwar era. In addition, postwar suburbanization for many companies was a way to avoid the rapidly desegregating cities and maintain a racially homogenous labor force. As white flight shrunk the available white urban labor force and as civil rights activism pressed companies to broaden their hiring, shifting to the suburbs became a way to bypass the pressure to integrate. In her detailed study of this relocation, Louise Mozingo contrasted corporate perceptions of city and suburb in the postwar era: "The center city was noisy, diverse, crowded, unpredictable, inflexible, expensive, old, and messy—a dubious state of affairs for postwar capitalists bent on expansion." In contrast, "the suburbs were predictable, spacious, segregated, specialized, quiet, new, and easily traversed—a much more promising state of affairs." Corporate suburbanization was so pervasive that, by the end of the century, the suburbs (not urban downtowns) contained most of the office space in the United States.[67]

Lawrence, with its extreme racial homogeneity in the postwar decades, would not necessarily have provoked this racialized corporate flight, but once again Greater Lawrence was swept up in a national trend that was highly racialized in its origins. And as with housing, the suburbanization of industry, research, and office spaces would also be highly racialized in its impact, as it concentrated economic activity, jobs, and tax dollars in Lawrence's suburbs, denying the city's soon-to-burgeon Latino population equal access as the decades progressed.

Greater Lawrence's suburban growth was not only part of this national trend; it was also tied to the spectacular growth of suburbs in the Boston metropolitan area. Lawrence and its suburbs have generally been considered to lie just outside Metro Boston, but the economic development of Andover and North Andover clearly benefited from proximity to the high-tech industrial corridor along Route 128 in Boston's western suburbs. In the decades after World War II, federal defense spending and the nearby presence of world-class educational institutions contributed greatly to the growth of high-technology industries in Boston's suburbs. Defense research led to innovations in consumer goods as well, most obviously in computing, but also in other spheres. For example, in its efforts to develop microwave radar technology, Raytheon discovered microwave cooking.[68]

As the state initiated construction on Route 128 in 1948, electronics firms opened along the new highway, in suburban towns like Waltham and Lexington. Most of the investment capital initially came from Boston investors, but once new ventures were up and running, federal defense dollars maintained a thriving high-technology research and production economy in the suburbs along Route 128. Sixty-eight new plants were constructed along the highway between March 1954 and June 1956. Just seven years later, there were 400 new plants. While the number of jobs in Boston was declining in the immediate postwar era, the suburbs along Route 128 saw a 22 percent increase in available jobs.[69]

Local suburban municipalities were essential in the growth of high-tech research and production plants along Route 128, providing exceptions or changes to their zoning requirements to accommodate these new research and production facilities. Boston's higher-education infrastructure was also key, as many research sites, in particular, were partnerships with local universities or university affiliates; by 1979, 300 computer or computer-related companies had opened within just a few miles of MIT. Jack Tager, a historian of Route 128's development, concluded that federal dollars were essential to this suburban development: "Defense spending reversed Massachusetts' economic decline and moved the state toward a material well-being unknown since the nineteenth century." This remarkable economic growth culminated in the "Massachusetts Miracle" of the 1980s, in which the suburban high-tech sector expanded greatly, giving Massachusetts one of the lowest unemployment rates and highest per capita incomes in the nation.[70] Lawrence's deindustrialization took place in the context of the state's industrial expansion, a "miracle" that bypassed the crisis city.

DEINDUSTRIALIZATION IN LAWRENCE

As the former woolen-worsteds capital of the world, Lawrence had already struggled through a hard time in the 1920s when manufacturers had bolted from the city on account of its perceived labor militancy after industrywide strikes in 1912 and 1919.[71] The Great Depression exacerbated these troubles, but like most of the country, Lawrence enjoyed an economic recovery during World War II and for a couple of years after the war ended. Beginning in 1947, however, the textile mills began to close for good, and tens of thousands of workers were laid off.[72] Textile manufacturing had long operated cyclically, with times of high demand and lots of work and times of low demand and lots of layoffs, so at first, few in the city were worried. Unemployment benefits and a union-negotiated "stagger system" for layoffs kept income coming in to families, as did the fact that Lawrence had long been a city with multiple workers in each household. For many low-paid textile laborers, unemployment benefits, with added allowances for children, were actually comparable to what they earned in the mills.[73]

By 1949, the city was making headlines for its monstrous unemployment, with *Business Week* ranking Lawrence the country's number one unemployment problem.[74] In 1952, Francis W. White, head of America's largest manufacturer of woolen and worsted fabrics, American Woolen Company, addressed the Lawrence Chamber of Commerce's annual dinner. At the time, American Woolen owned twenty-four mills, twenty-two of which were in New England, and the company was one of Lawrence's major employers and major taxpayers. American Woolen had paid over $200,000 in taxes to the city of Lawrence the year before and had paid over $21 million in wages and benefits to 20,000 textile workers in Greater Lawrence.[75]

In his speech, White noted that the company had just finished an exceptionally profitable year thanks to government defense contracts, but he was not there to congratulate workers on a job well done. On the contrary, the bulk of his address focused on the company's recent purchase of a mill site down South and notification to the textile unions that northern workers' contracts would not be renewed. American Woolen was considering closing all of its New England operations and moving its manufacturing entirely to the South. He argued that the South offered higher productivity, a lower wage scale, fewer union restrictions, and lower state and local tax payments. American Woolen had paid Massachusetts and its communities nearly $2.3 million in taxes in 1951. In the South, the total tax bill for the same operations would have been just $861,467, approximately a third of the taxes due in Massachusetts. White warned that unless New England was prepared to compete in these respects, American Woolen's movement to the South would be inevitable.[76]

American Woolen's textile production in Lawrence ground to a halt soon after the speech. Throughout the late 1940s and early 1950s, the city's mammoth textile mills shut down, including the Ayer, Monomac, and Wood Mills. The Pacific Mill closed in the winter of 1957, marking the end of the textile era in the city.[77] By 1953, Lawrence had lost a total of 18,000 textile jobs (from a city whose entire population never exceeded 100,000) and had a 20 percent unemployment rate.[78] Members of the city's political and business elite were not waiting passively for the city's industrial boom to return, however. They had initiated a concerted booster campaign to draw new industry to Lawrence, with a clear goal of maintaining the city's emphasis on manufacturing but diversifying the products manufactured. In 1951, former World War II colonel John J. Buckley, still in his thirties, was elected mayor on a "diversify industry" platform. He quickly pulled together a team of the city's business leaders into the Greater Lawrence Citizens Committee for Industrial Development and outfitted them with city funds to begin the work of drawing new industry to Lawrence. Buckley would remain mayor for twenty-one of the next thirty-four years and would still be mayor when the riots struck the city in 1984. He presided over some of the most dramatic changes to affect any city in the nation, and his influence is notable in the elite vision for the city that emphasized drawing in "first-class" industry and residents, a vision that pervaded official redevelopment throughout the late twentieth century.[79]

Buckley and his boosters did successfully recruit some new diversified industry into the city and managed to maintain some of the nontextile manufacturing that was already there.[80] These industries would play a major role in drawing Latino migrants to the city in the 1960s and 1970s, as I discuss in Chapter 2. Shoe manufacturers, particularly, were prominent in post-textile Lawrence and would become major employers of Lawrence's Latino population. When the New England shoe industry went into crisis in the late 1970s, however, the city experienced a new wave of deindustrialization and unemployment. Although Lawrence maintains some small amount of manufacturing to this day, its status as an industrial city came to an end with a second round of deindustrialization in the late 1970s and early 1980s, and it was this later deindustrialization and joblessness that would help provoke the 1984 riots.[81]

SUBURBAN INDUSTRY IN GREATER LAWRENCE

While Lawrence underwent industrial decline in the postwar era, its suburbs experienced industrial expansion. In the decades after World War II, the largest and most profitable manufacturers in the Greater Lawrence area were either located in or relocated to its suburbs. In an effort to remain competitive, the city built a suburban-style industrial park in South Lawrence in the 1960s, but by 1977 it was still not fully occupied.[82] Suburban industries provided jobs for many Lawrencians but contributed nothing to Lawrence's tax base or its municipal services.

The two most notable suburban manufacturers in this era were Raytheon in Andover and Western Electric in North Andover (which would become AT&T and then Lucent Technologies). Western Electric demonstrates cleanly the arc of urban/suburban competition for industry in the postwar era. During World War II, Western Electric produced communications equipment for both consumer and defense uses. In the postwar era, the company expanded into Lawrence, beginning to manufacture and warehouse in the former Monomac Spinning Mill in 1951. As a company brochure described, "Lanolin stains on the shop's wood floor from the wool used as raw material lingered as a reminder of the textile industry's heyday in Lawrence." City elites were proud that they had managed to recruit Western Electric, a bright symbol that Lawrence could diversify its industrial base and be a part of the new high-tech manufacturing sector that was on the cusp of blossoming in the state.[83]

Just two years later, in 1953, however, Western Electric broke ground on a larger, more modern plant in North Andover. By 1960, the plant in North Andover covered more than 150 acres, compared with the Lawrence plant's 6 acres, and had space for 1,500 cars to park. By 1978, after years of rumors and decades of gradually transferring its operations and its workers to North Andover, Western Electric closed the Lawrence plant. Meanwhile, the North Andover plant was thriving, having expanded seven times in the intervening years. Although Western Electric continued to provide employment for a substantial number of city residents for almost two more decades after its Lawrence plant closed, it was no longer directly contributing to the city's tax base, the upkeep of its old mill buildings, or its reputation.[84]

North Andover was not the only pastoral suburb eroding Lawrence's status as the region's industrial powerhouse. In the same year (1955) that Andover expanded the lot sizes and frontages required of its residential districts, it also voted to create an industrial committee "to endeavor to encourage desirable industrial development in Andover with a view to balancing the community and providing a broader tax base." The industrial committee proposed two articles, approved the next year, designed to rezone two large parcels of land for industrial use. These measures contained an array of building and land use restrictions to "insure desirable industry," including stipulations that "no plot shall be less than five acres" and no plant could occupy more than one-quarter of the total owned land.[85] In order to expand its tax base, Andover voted to recruit industry, but it was intent on using its zoning powers to make sure that industry did not spoil the town's pastoral landscape (and thus property values).

The town's Development and Industrial Commission engaged in a booster campaign to recruit industry to Andover, "sending promotional materials to key executives in major corporations throughout the country." In 1960, however, the commission complained that the town provided inadequate infrastructure for industrial development, arguing that the lack of utilities was the greatest deterrent to attracting more industry. The commission pushed the town to provide expanded water capacity, and Andover responded by greatly increasing municipal services (water, sewer, and transportation) for the industrial zones, with impressive results over the next few decades. The combined impact of these municipal efforts (zoning changes, the industrial commission's boosterism, and investment in expanded services) was the pronounced, but still tasteful and unobtrusive, growth of industry in the small but venerable old New England town, beginning in the late 1960s.

In 1968, Andover sought to diversify its tax base even further by creating new industrial zones as well as zoning for an "Office Park District."[86] To residents potentially resistant to the industrialization of their town, boosters responded with an appeal to their pocketbooks: "On the one hand, each of us can dig more deeply into our own pockets and pay our increasing property tax bills. On the other hand, we can take steps to broaden our tax base in terms of property use and development principally by attracting and retaining desirable industries and, in so doing, spread the tax base."[87] A tax base overly reliant on residential properties, boosters argued, necessarily meant high tax rates and a high tax burden for residents. Recruiting and supporting industrial growth could ensure quality municipal services without adding to residents' tax burden. Voters were persuaded, and Andover's commitment to industrial and office space expanded.

The most important industrial giant in Andover was Raytheon Company. Raytheon had played a prominent role in developing radar technology during World War II and, in the postwar era, became a leader in the development of missile technology, including defensive missiles that could intercept attacks.[88] In 1956, Raytheon opened a production facility in the Shawsheen Mill in Andover (a remnant of rural Andover's involvement in textile production). By 1968, the company's assessed tax value was $5 million and it had become the town's largest single taxpayer. It hoped to expand its operations and build new office and production facilities on a much larger lot in a more rural section of town, but this would require a zoning change from town voters. Raytheon's proposal would require the rezoning of 155 acres of land, the installation of water and sewer lines, as well as drainage, and the construction of two roadways. The estimated value of the completed plant, however, was $22 million, and boosters noted that would mean a minimum tax contribution to the town of $600,000, "or the equivalent of almost $4.00 on the Town's tax rate at the present level of assessed property valuations." Boosters translated this directly into public services: "This amount of income is enough to meet the bond payments of three existing elementary schools and two senior or junior high schools or most of the present annual salaries of our policemen *and* firefighters."[89] To Andover's industry boosters, the connection was clear between supporting industrial expansion and improving municipal services and/or decreasing residential tax rates. To ensure that residents' quality of life was not affected, the deal included the requirement that between ten and fifteen of the acres purchased by Raytheon would not be zoned industrial but would be maintained as a buffer between industry and residents. In addition, the company would donate two or three acres to Andover as a park. A special town meeting drew a remarkable 2,770 registered voters, and the required zoning change was approved unanimously. Raytheon completed construction on its new facility in 1970.[90]

Raytheon's valuation and tax contribution to the town increased dramatically after the construction of its new facility and for decades afterward. Its Andover facilities were valued at approximately $5.5 million in 1970, $17.5 million in 1980, and $107.3 million in 1990, and it consistently paid more than $1 million a year in property taxes to the small town from 1980 forward. Federal defense dollars were central to Raytheon's prosperity, of course. A 1982 report from the Massachusetts Division of Employment Security noted that Massachusetts was one of the top recipients of U.S. military contracts through the 1970s. In 1978, 80 percent of those military contracts went to "missile and space systems, aircraft, engines, and electronic and communications equipment." In that same year, Raytheon was awarded $110.3 million in military contracts, a full 10 percent of all contracts in the state.[91]

As a "prestige community," as described by the chair of the Board of Selectmen in 1985, Andover's tax base relied mainly on residential property taxes. Yet these active attempts to broaden the town's tax revenue were incredibly successful, increasing industry's share of the tax base considerably, even as residential property values increased. In 1968, industry was only 6 percent of Andover's tax base. By 1970, that figure had doubled to 12 percent, and by 1972, it was 15 percent. This broadened tax base reduced the tax rate for residential property, further increasing Andover's desirability as a residential community.[92] In 1980, the Development and Industrial Commission reported that most of the land in the new industrial park, Andover Technical Center, had gone to "large, high technology firms of international reputation."

The commission celebrated that Andover had achieved "a greatly expanded and high quality industrial tax base, achieved at little capital or service cost to the town, with little disruption or inconvenience to the community," and argued that this development was "testimony to the recognition of Andover as 'the jewel in the crown of Massachusetts development.'"[93]

By 1990, the top ten taxpayers in the town made up nearly 20 percent of Andover's entire tax levy. At the top of the list, of course, was Raytheon, valued at $107.3 million, contributing over $1.6 million in taxes to the town, nearly 4 percent of the town's levy. A number of other industrial giants were in the top ten: Digital Equipment Corporation, Gillette Company, and Hewlett Packard, as well as real estate and insurance companies and the elite private school Phillips Academy.[94]

Andover officials congratulated themselves and the town's residents for achieving this remarkably lucrative industrialization. In 1980—a year in which the town's tax base expanded by a full 19 percent—the town manager reflected on the past several years of sustained industrial growth. He emphasized how *intentional* this industrial growth had been: "Andover's ability to accommodate and provide for major industrial development of extraordinary quality is the result of and credit to the years of prior planning and cooperative effort of many people over many years and capital investment in a water supply and distribution system, sewer system and road network." Andover's prosperity and the superior municipal services that its ballooning tax base could provide were not just a fortuitous outcome of the town's inherent desirability, but a conscious strategy to broaden and expand the town's tax base through recruiting and investing in industrial growth. Later, the town's Finance Committee would acknowledge that, although Andover provided the direction for this development, much of the funds actually came from elsewhere. Particularly, "state grants have paid significant portions of the costs of major school building, water, and sewer projects,"[95] and of course federal dollars supported necessary highway construction as well as defense spending for major Andover industries. It was not simply cleverness on the part of Andover's boosters that led to the town's remarkable prosperity; the national shift toward the suburbanization of industry and office space played a major role, as did the infusion of taxpayer dollars, including Cold War military spending.

Andover's successful industrial expansion made it emblematic of postwar suburban industry in many ways. Its manufacturing was high tech and substantially reliant on defense dollars; its plants were tasteful and unobtrusive; and rather than undermining property values (as urban industry often

The Urban/Suburban Divide

did), Andover's industry supported residential prosperity by contributing to improved municipal services and reducing property tax rates, thereby enhancing the town's desirability and property values. In the early twentieth century, Lawrence had been an industrial powerhouse; but by the early twenty-first century, pastoral Andover rivaled only Boston for the largest number of manufacturing jobs in the state, and Raytheon was the largest single industrial employer in Massachusetts.[96] As the Andover boosters anticipated, it is simply impossible to overstate the impact of suburban industrial development on tax revenue, tax rates, public services, and thus property values. While economics is never a zero-sum game, Lawrence was clearly competing with its suburban neighbors for industrial development in the postwar era; it was a high-stakes game that the city could not hope to win.

ALMOST SINFUL: THE URBAN CONCENTRATION
OF INDUSTRIAL LABOR

In light of the urban/suburban competition for industry, discussions of "Greater Lawrence" were not without tension. By the 1970s, it became obvious that Lawrence was invested in suburban development far more than the suburbs were invested in Lawrence's development. Increasingly, the new industries looking to locate in Greater Lawrence were drawn to its suburbs. As a result, any hope of reducing unemployment for Lawrence residents seemed dependent on *facilitating* industrial growth in the suburbs, not challenging it. When Hewlett-Packard wanted to locate in Andover in the early 1970s, for example, it required Lawrence's approval to link into the city's sewer lines. The Lawrence Development and Industrial Commission (LDIC) claimed that this approval could be taken as a given and cited it as an example of the spirit of cooperation the LDIC was trying to foster with the commissions of Andover, North Andover, and Methuen.

Yet the LDIC hoped for something in return: more affordable housing in the suburbs. The LDIC's goal was to "stem the tide" of growing poverty in Lawrence through dispersing the region's poor and working families. It noted in its newsletter that "cooperation ... is never a one way street.... Lawrence, for many years, has taken on the problems of the Greater Lawrence Area. It is time that the surrounding towns start sharing some of these burdens."[97] All four development commissions had recently signed a "declaration of intent" to work toward regional cooperation, and Lawrence elites wanted suburban officials to recognize poverty as a shared, metropolitan problem. The LDIC argued that Lawrence could have had "plush" housing like the suburbs, but instead it bore a disproportionate responsibility to house the region's poor and working families. The LDIC believed that the suburbs ought to share responsibility for housing the region's low-income residents because these were the very people who labored in suburban industry and retail. "It seems almost sinful for the outlying communities to want prosperity through business and industry and not expect to provide housing for the people working in their stores and factories." As Massachusetts Secretary of Communities and Development Thomas I. Atkins explained of the suburb's eagerness to hire but not house urban workers, "They can't have their cake and eat it too."[98]

By asking the suburbs to develop housing that would be accessible to urban workers in suburban industries, the LDIC highlighted the fact that suburban prosperity was based on the labor and consumption of urban workers, while suburban zoning and housing development made that prosperity inaccessible to those same workers. "Almost sinful" it may have been, but ultimately these efforts to shame the suburbs into expanding affordable housing were largely unsuccessful, and the region's poor and working families remained concentrated within the city limits.[99]

CONCLUSION

The postwar decades were marked by white residential flight from the city to its suburbs. Yet the expansion of economic activity in Lawrence's suburbs makes clear that they were certainly not bedroom communities; on the contrary, Lawrence's suburbs became economically central in the metropolitan region. Methuen and Salem became major sites of retail consumption, while Andover and North Andover became home to much of the region's industry and office space. The booster emphasis on metropolitan integration and cooperation could not hide Lawrence's growing irrelevance in the metropolitan economy. In a telling move, even the local paper, the *Lawrence Eagle-Tribune*, left its Essex Street location for North Andover in 1968, and in 1987 it removed the word "Lawrence" from its name.[100] By 1980, the suburbs had effectively won the battle for Greater Lawrence's middle-class residents, its major industry, and its retail sector. The crisis city was, in many ways, economically irrelevant.

While the suburbs were experiencing an upward spiral of property values and commercial/industrial development, Lawrence was experiencing extreme disinvestment and decline. Lawrence's economy sharply diverged from that of its suburbs in the postwar era. This is evident in the

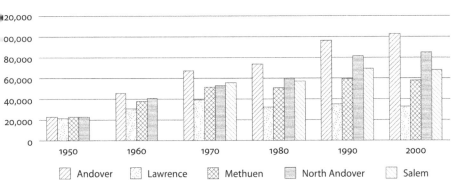

120,000					
00,000					
80,000					
60,000					
40,000					
20,000					
0					
	1950	1960	1970	1980	1990	2000

▨ Andover   ▢ Lawrence   ▩ Methuen   ▦ North Andover   ▢ Salem

Median Household Income for Lawrence and Its Suburbs, 1950–2000. Data from the *United States Census*, adjusted for inflation (2005 dollars). Note that in 1950, disaggregated data for the suburbs is unavailable, so the number for the entire metropolitan region is used. Actual median incomes in the suburbs may already have reflected the slight edge held by Andover that is evident by the 1960 figures.

median household incomes for Lawrence and its suburbs from 1950 to 2000 (see chart). Lawrence was poorer than its suburbs in 1950, 1960, and 1970, but not outrageously so. Andover was clearly wealthier than both Lawrence and the other suburbs in those decades, but not in an extreme way. By 1980, however, a clear divergence is visible between the incomes of Lawrence residents (increasingly comprising the elderly, those without the resources to move to the suburbs, and a small but growing Latino population) and the incomes of suburban residents, with the median household income in Andover more than twice that in Lawrence.

The divergence in tax bases is quite similar. In 1945, Lawrence's budget was more than six times that of Andover's. By 2000, Lawrence's budget was only 70 percent greater than Andover's (in spite of the city having more than twice the suburb's population), and more than two-thirds of Lawrence's budget came from state aid. In 1945, Lawrence collected more than six times as much as Andover in real estate taxes. By 1980, this had reversed, due to the massive increase in Andover's real estate valuation. By 2000, small, suburban Andover actually had more than twice the tax revenue from real estate than the city. In 1992, Lawrence's equalized tax valuation per capita was $29,091, while in Andover it was over $100,000.[101]

Although Lawrence has historically been considered to lie outside the Boston metropolitan area, it is certainly in the shadow of the much larger and more prosperous city. Lawrence's extreme decline is undoubtedly related to its small size and status as a second-tier city in the region. While major metropolitan centers like Boston, New York, and Chicago also experienced population loss, job loss from deindustrialization, fiscal crises, and profoundly racialized disinvestment in the postwar era, they never completely lost their economic backbone in the way that smaller industrial cities did. They maintained middle-class and even wealthy neighborhoods, prestigious hospitals and universities, and a functioning FIRE (finance, insurance, and real estate) sector to anchor their economies. Persistent efforts at urban renewal transformed into massive reinvestment in the 1980s, and gentrification has since reversed the tide of economic decline in America's largest cities. Urban economic crisis was both more thorough and more persistent in smaller postindustrial cities like Lawrence, as I discuss in Chapter 6. As one journalist explained, Lawrence had "all the problems of a Boston, but none of the glory."[102]

Far from reinvestment and economic recovery, Lawrence experienced the worst of its economic crisis in the 1980s and early 1990s, while the suburbs flourished. The goal of careful suburban growth had been to increase property values and swell the tax base to provide higher-quality municipal services (and thus increase property values even further in an upward spiral of prosperity). So it is not surprising, then, that the intrametropolitan divergence that was already obvious in 1980 became only more extreme over the next two decades. By 2000, median household incomes in Andover were more than triple those in Lawrence, and even Lawrence's poorest neighbor, Methuen, had nearly twice the median household income of city residents.[103] The divergence of urban and suburban development both concentrated the region's poor within the city and fundamentally stripped the city of sufficient resources to address "urban problems." As Latinos began to arrive in Lawrence from New York City, Puerto Rico, the Dominican Republic, and elsewhere in Latin America, this growing divide between declining city and prospering suburbs would profoundly shape their experience.

TWO

WHY LAWRENCE?

It's not like New York City. It's quiet. It's nice people. You can walk
in the night. You don't have to be worried about somebody hitting
you or something, killing you, like in New York City.

Dominican teenager explaining her preference for Lawrence

In 1992, the director of Lawrence's Minority Business Council, Jose Zaiter,
told his family's migration story to the local paper, explaining that it was
typical of how many Latinos ended up in Lawrence. His family had moved
from the Dominican Republic to New York City in 1965. A year later, his uncle
left New York for Lawrence and got a job in the city's garment industry. While
living in Lawrence, his uncle returned for frequent visits to New York, tout-
ing Lawrence to his relatives as a safe city where jobs were plentiful. In the
context of Lawrence's infamous reputation as dangerous in the early 1990s
(when Zaiter was telling his story to the paper), he described the fact that
safety motivated his family's immigration to Lawrence as "ironic." But crime,
drugs, and arson were already tearing through low-income neighborhoods in
New York City during the 1960s and 1970s, while Lawrence had yet to experience the full brunt of disinvestment. The presence of jobs in Lawrence must
have seemed no less ironic to Zaiter, as the city had a nearly 25 percent Latino
unemployment rate in 1990.[1] Decades earlier, however, when his family had
first come to the city in the 1960s, not only were there "many jobs available,"
but companies even used to pay $50 bonuses to people who recruited new
workers. After Zaiter and his family moved to Lawrence, his mother kept
in touch with friends in New York, encouraging them to make the move as

well, stressing that in a city with such an "immigrant flavor" from previous generations of European immigrants, it was easy to "blend in."[2]

Zaiter's story demonstrates many of the ironies or apparent contradictions of Latino settlement in Lawrence. The idea of a tiny, seven-square-mile city on the border of New Hampshire, more than a thousand miles from the nearest Latin American country, becoming home to one of the highest proportions of Latinos in the nation seems preposterous. Lawrence is certainly not a major urban center with obvious name recognition, nor is it the home of a long-standing Latino community, like New York City. Further, as I will discuss in the next few chapters, the city administration and many white residents worked hard to make it unappealing as a Latino settlement site, through both official policy and quotidian harassment. Finally, when one considers the severe economic crisis facing the city, the pull of Lawrence seems puzzling indeed! Why would tens of thousands of Latinos settle in a small, obscure city with a resistant white population and a troubled economy? Why would they choose a deteriorating, often bigoted New England city over New York, with its established Latino neighborhoods, businesses, and communities and its reputation for racial tolerance? Why would so many Latinos move *into* Lawrence just as so many white families and businesses were moving *out*? As community development scholar Ramón Borges-Méndez aptly phrased it, "Who in their right mind, looking for a job and looking for better economic opportunity ... would move to Lawrence?"[3]

First, as Zaiter's story illustrates, Latino migration was shaped by family and social networks that channeled migration and aided in settlement. Lawrence was suggested as a settlement site by family and friends who were already established there. Countless Latinos migrated to Lawrence to rejoin family or because the presence of kin made Lawrence an easier place to settle. As Jessica Andors described, kinship networks were "overlaid like so many ligaments and tendons on the bare bones of economy necessity."[4] Suggestions from kin generally emphasized the ways in which Lawrence could provide what other places could not: the economic opportunities and quality of life that eluded potential migrants in their home countries or the safety and quiet that eluded them in New York City. Understanding the "pull" into Lawrence therefore also entails understanding the "push" out of Puerto Rico and the Dominican Republic and the "push" out of New York City, historically the main settlement site for both Puerto Ricans and Dominicans in the mainland United States. The migration narratives of Latinos in Lawrence overwhelmingly focused on the "better life" they hoped to find, but clearly there were broader social, political, and economic forces channeling those hopes into this small, troubled city. This chapter will explore those forces.

U.S. intervention played a key role in spurring Latino migration, as scholars have amply documented. Particularly for Dominicans and Puerto Ricans, the long history of U.S. imperialism shaped the countries they left behind, foreclosing dreams of a better life at home. Like colonial and post-colonial migrants around the world in the era of globalization, Dominicans and Puerto Ricans were pushed from the periphery to the metropole, to the heart of the American empire. And yet, in reality, Lawrence was hardly the metropole, hardly the center of anything; rather, this move from the Caribbean to the crisis city was essentially a move from one type of margin to another: from (semi)colony to ghetto. Latino settlement in crisis cities seriously complicates the idea of immigration as opportunity. Full access to the benefits of living in the United States could be restricted based on race, class, and/or immigration status, as well as by a racialized geography that privileged the suburbs over cities in the era of urban crisis.

For poor and working-class Puerto Ricans and Dominicans, postwar shifts in metropolitan political economy (suburban growth/exclusion and urban decline/disinvestment) were absolutely essential in shaping both their settlement patterns and their experiences. First, white flight, deindustrialization, displacement, and racialized disinvestment in New York City persuaded many Latinos that New York was not a suitable place to make a life for themselves and their families in the urban crisis era. Second, the exclusive political economy of suburbanization constrained the settlement options of poor and working-class people of color in the Northeast, making the question of where to settle really a question of in which *city* to settle.[5] As Latinos dispersed from New York, these factors served to concentrate and segregate them within Lawrence's municipal boundaries.

Latino immigration to Lawrence began with a trickle of Puerto Rican, Dominican, and Cuban settlers in the late 1950s and early 1960s and grew so dramatically that today Lawrence is nearly three-quarters Latino. The history of this profound demographic transformation is best understood when broken into two phases. The first phase, what I call the labor phase, took place in the 1960s and 1970s. In this era, Latino migrants to Lawrence were mostly Puerto Rican, although there were many Cubans and Dominicans as well. Rather than arriving directly from their home countries, many Latino newcomers during this era were secondary migrants from New York City. During this labor phase, Latinos were recruited into the city's nondurable goods manufacturing sector and found homes in Lawrence's public and multifamily rental housing, already partially emptied out and worn down from white flight and urban renewal. Yet the city's remaining manufacturing sector began to collapse in the late 1970s, leading to high rates of unemployment and deepening Lawrence's fiscal crisis. By the 1980s, migrating to Lawrence for a job was a gamble. In this later era, what I call the Latino City phase, migrants (increasingly Dominicans) settled in Lawrence for somewhat different reasons, as I discuss in the final chapter. For now, I will focus mainly on the labor phase of Latino settlement and the impact of the city's deindustrialization.[6]

Ultimately, although deindustrialization, white flight, and economic decline devastated Lawrence and created hardships for many of its residents, in some ways disinvestment actually created opportunities for Latino settlement by opening up the city's jobs and housing and by allowing Latinos to develop a community infrastructure unimpeded by waves of urban renewal or gentrification. In his study of Latino community development in Lawrence, Lowell, and Holyoke (other small industrial cities in Massachusetts), Borges-Méndez concluded that disinvestment was a major part of what enabled Latinos in Lawrence to develop a strong network of community organizations and Latino-owned businesses, because their growth was never seriously undermined by displacement. As he noted, however, this effectively blank slate for community development came "at the price of widespread neighborhood deterioration, growing segregation, and rising poverty."[7] Latinos settled in a city that was being rapidly abandoned through suburbanization and deindustrialization, but they were then, of course, forced to reckon with the consequences of that abandonment.

EMPIRE AND IMMIGRATION

Popular narratives of immigration point to divergent living standards between the United States and Latin America to explain the growing presence of Latinos in the United States. This conventional view assumes that everyone would prefer to live in a rich, modern, powerful nation rather than in a poor, underdeveloped nation if given the opportunity. This line of thinking, however, homogenizes both the United States and Latin America, obscuring the pronounced poverty that exists in parts of the United States and the considerable wealth that exists in parts of Latin America. Perhaps more importantly, this common narrative obscures the long history that accounts for the disparities between the United States and much of Latin America, particularly the Spanish-speaking Caribbean. There is nothing natural or foreordained about the global geography of inequality.

In order to grasp why Dominicans and Puerto Ricans would leave their home countries to settle in Lawrence, it is important to understand the history of these islands, especially their economic development. It is a history in which the United States has played a notably active role. The home countries that Dominicans and Puerto Ricans left for Lawrence had been shaped by U.S. political, military, and economic power throughout the twentieth century. It is this history that has led Juan González to refer to Latino immigration as the "harvest of empire"; Latinos who arrived in the United States were displaced, in many senses, from their home countries as the result of more than a century of U.S. imperialism and/or intervention.[8] The United States did not just "pull" migrants by providing economic opportunities and dreams of a better life; the U.S. also helped "push" migrants out of their home countries by foreclosing economic opportunities and eroding dreams of a better life at home.

This reality complicates the myth of the United States as a benign refuge for the world's "huddled masses." As a Puerto Rican woman in Lawrence argued, "Poorer Puerto Ricans don't come here because they love the United States. They come with a colonial mentality, to suffer and endure so they and their families can survive."[9] It shouldn't be shocking to find such a critical mindset among Puerto Ricans, given the long history of colonial rule on the island, but Dominican migration was also spurred by a surprisingly similar process of U.S. intervention and exploitation. As a Dominican in Lawrence summed it up, "*Sabes por qué tantos dominicanos han venido aquí? Es porque los Estados Unidos han cogido toda la riqueza de nuestro país* [You know why so many Dominicans have come here? It's because the United States has taken all the wealth of our country]."[10] These comments place Latino immigration to Lawrence within a transnational history of U.S. imperialism and economic globalization, a context that is worth fleshing out in detail, even if it may already be familiar to scholars of Latina/o studies.

PUERTO RICO

Most colonies in Spanish America won their independence in the early and mid-1800s, but Spain retained control of Cuba and Puerto Rico in the Caribbean, as well as the Philippines in the Pacific. In 1898, nationalists in Cuba and the Philippines were on the verge of winning their independence from Spain after a protracted struggle. Their timing, however, was unfortunate, as it coincided with the U.S. desire to expand overseas. Although European nations had taken colonies across the globe by 1898, creating vast empires in Asia and Africa, the growing industrial power of the United States had limited itself to continental expansion, claiming the northern half of Mexico in 1848, Alaska in 1867, and the overwhelming majority of Native American land across the continent by 1890. This continental expansion constituted colonialism in many respects, of course, in that violence was used to take over territories in which other peoples lived and were sovereign, and those peoples were then forced to surrender their sovereignty and conform to U.S. laws that rarely protected their property or their human rights.[11]

By 1898, however, the United States already stretched "from sea to shining sea," and many business and government leaders in the U.S. worried that without further expansion, without new markets and new resources, their growing industrial economy would collapse. Expansionists pressed Congress to enter the war against Spain in order to ensure good economic relations with the new nations after the war, especially with nearby Cuba, where U.S. businesses already had sizable investments in sugar production. The entrance of the United States into the war helped speed its conclusion, but not before the U.S. landed troops in Cuba, Puerto Rico, and the Philippines. In the treaty to end the war between Spain and the United States, Spain surrendered its rights to Cuba and Puerto Rico and sold the Philippines to the United States for $20 million. Expansionists quickly pushed for, and won, annexation of Puerto Rico and the Philippines to the United States, and the removal of U.S. troops from Cuba was conditioned upon Cuban acceptance of the Platt Amendment, authorizing future U.S. intervention and giving the United States a perpetual lease for a military base in Guantánamo Bay.[12]

Using tortured logic, Congress and the Supreme Court established a legal framework within which a democratic nation, otherwise committed to the ideal that government derives its authority from the consent of the governed, could hold a colony whose people were subject to the United States but unable to participate in its government. In the Foraker Act of 1900 and the Supreme Court's Insular Cases, the U.S. government defined Puerto Rico as an unincorporated territory (distinct from the status of incorporated territory that preceded statehood) and ruled that the Constitution thus did not necessarily apply there. As Senator Joseph Foraker explained, "Puerto Rico belongs to the United States, but it is not the United States, nor a part of the United States."[13] The United States established a civilian government for Puerto Rico in which top posts were appointed by the U.S. Congress (and consistently held by U.S. Americans) and any laws created by the Puerto Rican government were subject to being vetoed or changed by the U.S. Congress. Puerto Rico was given no voting member in Congress. This obviously colonial status, in which Puerto Rico was to be ruled by but was not a part of the United States, was inflammatory. The representatives of Puerto Rico who had been elected under Spanish colonial authority beseeched Congress not to hold Puerto Ricans as "subjects of an arbitrary and imperialistic power."[14]

U.S. colonialism in Puerto Rico rapidly transformed the island's economy. U.S.-imposed currency changes led many independent farmers to lose their land, and large (often U.S.-owned) sugar plantations came to dominate the island's economy. As one historian described it, "Puerto Rico had been turned into little more than a plantation."[15] In addition, new U.S.-imposed tariffs and shipping requirements made Puerto Rico dependent on the United States both as a market for the island's sugar exports and for all of its imports and shipping. These colonial economic regulations even left Puerto Rico dependent on imported food from the United States, leading to higher food prices on the island than in New York City by the 1930s.[16]

As it became clear to Puerto Ricans that the island would not be formally or equally incorporated into the United States, an independence movement grew. To silence these calls for independence, the U.S. government in 1917 passed the Jones Act, unilaterally giving Puerto Ricans U.S. citizenship. The elected members of Puerto Rico's House of Delegates unanimously voiced their objection to the act, but it was implemented over their objection. As one U.S. politician explained to applause from Congress, independence was a nonstarter: "Porto Rico will never go out from under the shadow of the Stars and Stripes."[17]

The already struggling Puerto Rican economy declined even more precipitously in the 1930s, leading to massive underemployment, unemployment, and hunger and provoking widespread protest on the island. Nationalist agitation grew, as did government repression of nationalist activism. Many independence leaders, such as Pedro Albizu Campos, argued that Puerto Rico would never be prosperous until it could determine its own economic policy; political independence was a precondition of economic independence. Other leaders, however, like Luis Muñoz Marín, came to believe not only that economic development could be accomplished within the context of U.S. rule but that U.S. aid would be essential to that development.[18]

Muñoz and his Partido Popular Democrático cooperated with the United States to help subdue nationalist agitation on the island and downplay Puerto Rico's colonial status on the world stage, in exchange for a limited form of self-government and U.S. support for the island's economic development.[19] In 1948, Puerto Ricans were permitted to elect their own governor, and in 1952, Congress approved granting Puerto Rico "commonwealth" status (known as *Estado Libre Asociado*, or free associated state, in Spanish). Under the commonwealth system, which exists to this day, Puerto Rico became theoretically self-governing but ultimately subject to federal laws. Island residents cannot vote in federal elections and have no voting representative in Congress, but they are still subject to any U.S. military draft. They pay some forms of federal taxes and can receive some federal benefits, although often at lower rates than stateside residents.[20]

The United States invested heavily in Puerto Rico's economic development after World War II. Not only did the United States want to avoid the risk of protests and upheavals near its key Caribbean military bases, but it was also eager to showcase the island as a model for capitalist development throughout Latin America during the Cold War. In line with these development goals, in 1947 Puerto Rican leaders initiated Operation Bootstrap (Manos a la Obra in Spanish; the closest translation would be something like "Let's get to work"). The goal of Operation Bootstrap was to industrialize and modernize the island's economy. In 1950, the Puerto Rican legislature created the Administración de Fomento Económico (Economic Development Administration, commonly referred to as just Fomento) to organize the process of "selling Puerto Rico as an industrial location," mainly by offering tax exemptions to U.S. manufacturers.[21] In addition, Fomento undertook a widespread media campaign in Puerto Rico, trumpeting the values of modern living and progress. This campaign drew Puerto Ricans en masse out of the sugar fields toward higher-waged industrial jobs and modern living in the island's cities.[22]

Yet this "industrialization by invitation" did not produce nearly enough manufacturing jobs on the island for all those who wanted to "flee the cane," and those jobs that were generated evaporated over the next few decades as the tax exemptions expired and the Puerto Rican minimum wage was raised.[23] In an era of newly accessible air travel, and with their U.S. citizenship, many Puerto Ricans chose to pursue the modern living celebrated by Fomento in the mainland United States instead. Indeed, the migration of Puerto Ricans from island to mainland was a key part of the island's economic development strategy; reducing the sheer number of poor people on the island seemed easier than raising their incomes.[24] In the decades after World War II, hundreds of thousands of Puerto Ricans migrated to the United States, overwhelmingly concentrating in New York City. This migration was supported by the Puerto Rican government's Migration Division, formed to aid in migrant settlement and assimilation as well as to maintain a good public image of Puerto Ricans on the mainland.[25] This huge resettlement of Puerto Ricans in New York City is not properly understood as immigration, and not solely because of their U.S. citizenship; Puerto Ricans were imperial migrants, their move stateside precipitated by economic deprivations and dislocations for which U.S. colonial rule was largely responsible.

Operation Bootstrap made Puerto Rico a prominent competitor for the textile production that had previously been centered in Lawrence. One of the first major U.S. textile companies to move production overseas was Textron, which bought out the Lawrence mammoth American Woolen Company in 1955. Textron began relocating production to Puerto Rico in 1947 in response to Operation Bootstrap incentives. Not only did Puerto Rico offer a lower wage scale and nonunion workers, but the Puerto Rican government agreed to build Textron a $4 million factory in Ponce, ensuring that the move overseas involved very little capital outlay. As Puerto Rico was a U.S. possession, there was no duty shipping cotton into Puerto Rico or shipping the finished textiles back stateside. Companies operating in Puerto Rico were exempt from federal taxes until the funds were brought back stateside, according to the internal revenue code, and as an added incentive, Puerto Rico gave recruited companies a ten-year tax exemption.[26]

This neoliberal strategy (using public funds and tax breaks to recruit private industry and investment as a means of providing jobs and stimulating the economy) was effective in drawing New England industries overseas: to Puerto Rico and Colombia and, later, to the Dominican Republic and other nations throughout the Caribbean and beyond. Capital mobility, however, ensured that industry rarely remained after the tax exemptions expired or if lower wages or looser environmental or safety regulations could be found elsewhere, provoking a global "race to the bottom."[27] Interestingly for the study of Lawrence, while some manufacturers, like Textron, effectively chose to move production from New England to Puerto Rico, other manufacturers attempted to recruit Puerto Ricans and other Latinos to work in Lawrence industries in the hope that such a strategy would allow these industries to remain competitive, as I discuss more below.

Labor-intensive industries recruited through Operation Bootstrap left the island for cheaper wages in the 1970s, exacerbating Puerto Rico's struggles with poverty and unemployment. The Puerto Rican government encouraged the development of capital-intensive industries in the 1970s, including high-tech and pharmaceuticals, but this was not sufficient to solve the problem of unemployment on the island. Lest joblessness lead to desperation and unrest, the U.S. government extended Nutrition Assistance benefits (commonly known as "food stamps" in English or *cupones* in Spanish) to the island in the 1970s, and by 1980, approximately 60 percent of Puerto Rican families relied on food stamps.[28] While the provision of these benefits helped stave off hunger, it did nothing to remedy the larger colonial economy that had impeded Puerto Rican self-sufficiency.

Migration stateside slowed in the 1970s but resumed in the 1980s. Precise numbers are hard to obtain because Puerto Ricans were, of course, not counted by immigration officials, and many traveled back and forth between the island and the mainland several times. By the 2010 census, however, there were more Puerto Ricans living stateside than on the island (4.6 million stateside versus 3.7 million in Puerto Rico). Puerto Ricans initially concentrated in New York City, with 88 percent of stateside Puerto Ricans living in New York in 1940, but then gradually dispersed. By 1970, only 59 percent of stateside Puerto Ricans lived in New York City, and in 2000, less than a quarter did. Latino settlement in Lawrence and other industrial cities in the Northeast and Midwest was an important part of this diaspora.[29]

There has been consistent debate over the past half-century about how to end Puerto Rico's semicolonial status and improve its economic situation. Nationalist movements on the island have historically met with fierce repression, and with more than half of Puerto Ricans now living on the mainland, the idea of Puerto Rican independence seems increasingly remote.[30] By the turn of the twenty-first century, most economic indicators highlighted Puerto Rico's ambiguous status: The island was poorer than any state in the United States and profoundly reliant on U.S. aid and investment. Yet it was also wealthier than most nations in Latin America and certainly wealthier than any of its neighbors in the Spanish Caribbean, largely because of its ties to the United States. In a relative sense, Puerto Rico is an island of prosperity, as illustrated by the many Dominicans who have risked their lives in small boats (*yolas*) to immigrate to Puerto Rico without authorization.[31]

The reality of Puerto Rican relative prosperity and economic reliance on the United States discourages calls for independence, yet critics have pointed out that true sovereignty has been elusive for all nations in the Caribbean. As Ramón Grosfoguel has noted, "Caribbean nation-states live under the regime of 'global coloniality' imposed by the International Monetary Fund (IMF) and the World Bank (WB)." In contrast, "Puerto Rico benefits from massive annual metropolitan transfers that never reach the shores of Caribbean nation-states." He notes that an oft-heard sentiment in Puerto Rico is "*Para ser independientes como la República Dominicana o Haití, mejor ser colonia* [If independence means being like the Dominican Republic or Haiti, it's better to be a colony]."[32] Being attached to the United States, even in a permanently subordinate position, has its privileges as well as its costs, given the larger context of global capitalism.

Of course, this regime of "global coloniality" in the Dominican Republic did not begin with the IMF; U.S. intervention there goes back more than a century. Although many U.S. leaders harbored annexation hopes for the island in the nineteenth century, U.S. power in the Dominican Republic ultimately came in the form of economic control via debt servicing and military intervention. The decades after Dominicans gained their final independence from Spain in 1865 were marked by an often bloody competition between regional leaders, or *caudillos*, to consolidate power over the country.[33] To strengthen their position, Dominican leaders often borrowed freely from foreign creditors while in power and printed money as needed in order to maintain dictatorial control of the country. As a result, the value of the Dominican peso plummeted in the late 1800s and the nation's debt skyrocketed. Loans to the Dominican government not only were often profitable in themselves but could also ensure generous economic concessions from indebted politicians, and U.S. businesses quickly recognized the opportunity. By the end of the 1800s, the San Domingo Improvement Company, a privately owned U.S. firm, controlled the Dominican Republic's foreign debt and held a monopoly on the transportation of passengers and freight into and out of the country. The company was granted authority over the country's customs receipts (the main source of government revenue), ostensibly to ensure debt repayment. Increasing U.S. investments in this era transformed the Dominican economy and infrastructure, as U.S. sugar companies bought up wide tracts of land and imported workers from the West Indies to work them, and as U.S. companies received lucrative government contracts to build railroads and modern utilities.[34]

After the death of dictator Ulises Heureaux in 1899, Dominicans learned that he had left the nation $34 million in debt, most of it to foreign creditors.[35] As the nation struggled to repay its enormous debt, the United States feared that European governments would engage in military action to force repayment to their banks. In response, President Theodore Roosevelt successfully convinced the Dominican government to place U.S. officials in charge of Dominican customs revenue and debt repayment in 1905, justifying this action with his Roosevelt Corollary to the Monroe Doctrine (which essentially argued that U.S. military and diplomatic power could be put at the service of the private sector in order to guarantee repayment of loans made to foreign banks).[36] In the context of political upheaval on the island, the United States continued to consolidate its control over Dominican finances. As World War I expanded in Europe,

President Woodrow Wilson demanded that the United States be allowed to appoint U.S. Americans to important posts in the Dominican government and to replace the Dominican army with a U.S.-trained national guard. Dominicans said no, and Wilson froze their customs revenues. Dominican government employees rallied, working without pay in order to protect what remained of their sovereignty. But in May 1916, partially fearing that Dominicans would ally themselves with Germans in the war, Wilson sent in the U.S. Marines to take over the island and push through the resisted reforms. Under military occupation, the Dominican legislature was dissolved and martial law was imposed. Through press censorship and the incarceration and repression of dissenters, the United States quashed opposition to the occupation.[37]

Even before the occupation, the Dominican government had been persuaded to implement a number of reforms beneficial to U.S. sugar companies, including making sugar produced for export tax exempt and dividing communally held lands so they could more easily be purchased by U.S. companies. The eight-year U.S. military occupation (1916–24) transformed the Dominican economy even further, opening up huge tracts of land to U.S. sugar companies and making the country dependent on U.S. imports. The Customs Tariffs Act of 1919 (enacted during the occupation) allowed 245 U.S. articles to enter the country duty-free and 700 more to enter with reduced tariffs. Not only did this eliminate a crucial source of government revenue, but it subjected local producers to competition with the flood of imports, including food imported from the United States.[38] Although the Dominican Republic was never formally a U.S. colony, these policies imposed by the United States shaped the Dominican economy so that it bore a striking resemblance to the export-oriented, U.S.-dependent sugar economy of its colonized neighbor, Puerto Rico.

The U.S. Marines also created a new national police force, which became the national army after the Marines left. Rafael Leónidas Trujillo rose up through the ranks of this new U.S.-constituted army and was elected president in 1930 with the help of a violent terror campaign by his soldiers. Trujillo remained a brutal, notorious dictator for the next thirty-one years, but the United States generally supported him, largely because his iron-handed rule maintained stability. Trujillo combined economic development and modernization with major graft and corruption, accumulating an immense personal fortune through government contracts. Widespread assassinations and torture of dissenters (as well as their families) combined with comprehensive control over the media and personal control over huge sectors of the Dominican economy all helped ensure Trujillo's position.[39]

Yet, after the Cuban Revolution in 1959, the United States came to fear that Trujillo might provoke a similar uprising, and the CIA supported his assassination in 1961. After his death, populist reformer Juan Bosch won the country's first democratic election. Once Bosch was in office, however, his efforts at land reform and his unwillingness to repress the country's communist movement led to conflict with sugar planters, business and military leaders, and the U.S. government. In 1963, a military coup forced Bosch into exile, but he remained popular and protests against the ruling powers in the country increased. Two years later, when a small group of army officers tried to restore Bosch to power, much of the country rose up to support their democratically elected leader. When the popular uprising seemed on the verge of success, President Lyndon Johnson sent in 26,000 U.S. troops to squash it, as the United States believed there were communists dominating the Constitutionalist supporters of Bosch. This second U.S. occupation brought to power former Trujillo aide Joaquín Balaguer, who commenced a repressive campaign against his opposition; government-supported death squads kidnapped and murdered as many as 5,000 of Balaguer's political opponents in the first twelve years of his rule.[40]

There was very little Dominican migration to the United States during Trujillo's reign, as he made it extremely difficult for Dominicans to acquire passports to leave the country. Yet, after his death, the government faced immense popular pressure to restore to Dominicans their right to travel, after which petitions for tourist, student, and immigration visas to the United States accelerated rapidly. The U.S. State Department facilitated the acquisition of visas, particularly for activists and opponents of the regime, in the hope that island politics would stabilize if Constitutionalists left the country. With Balaguer in power, emigration became an important strategy for pro-democracy activists in order to avoid government persecution. Rendered political exiles by U.S. intervention, these imperial migrants shaped the early wave of Dominican settlement in New York City in the 1960s.[41] Yet even in this politically tumultuous era, many Dominicans immigrated to the United States not to flee government repression but simply to find a better life than what they believed they could find at home. Although the Dominican Republic had experienced substantial economic growth, development, and modernization under Trujillo, this prosperity did not exist equally across the Dominican population, and unemployment and poverty remained high.

With the support of the United States, Balaguer restructured the Dominican economy, opening it to foreign investment and relying largely on U.S. aid. His goal was to industrialize the island using an import substitution model, in which products could be manufactured locally rather than imported, but this policy was only partially successful. During Balaguer's first two terms, from 1966 to 1974, the country did indeed experience considerable economic growth, thanks largely to foreign aid and foreign investment (mostly from the United States), as well as the high price for sugar. As had been true under the Trujillo regime, however, the benefits of this growth were not evenly distributed, and high rates of unemployment and poverty persisted. Balaguer's economic policies neglected social spending in particular, and health and educational services suffered dramatically. Improved health care and educational opportunities would thus come to be essential elements of that "better life" Dominican immigrants were searching for in the United States. In addition, the country's reliance on imports actually increased in this era, creating a trade deficit that Balaguer's government addressed by taking on debt.[42]

Balaguer's emphasis on industrialization and foreign investment wreaked havoc on the island's agricultural sector. His policies encouraged the consolidation of land into large cattle and sugar latifundios (either requiring very little labor or using imported labor from Haiti, respectively), making it increasingly difficult for small farmers to maintain their land. By 1981, less than 2 percent of landowners held more than 55 percent of the country's arable land. With the decline of small farms, the domestic production of food also declined, and the Dominican Republic became further reliant on imported food. These transformations in the agricultural economy significantly cut rural Dominicans' employment options. In 1960, there were 1.1 million people employed in the agricultural sector, nearly one-third of the entire population. By 1991, only 458,000 Dominicans had work in the agricultural sector. Many people responded to the evisceration of small farming and agricultural employment by moving to cities, especially Santo Domingo. But as in Puerto Rico, there were far more migrants leaving the country's rural areas than there were available jobs in the cities, and many migrants found themselves concentrated in urban slums, without running water, sewage systems, paved streets, schools, or health care facilities.[43] Other Dominicans (like many of those who settled in Lawrence) left the agricultural Cibao region to find economic opportunities in New York City, as the policies of a U.S.-supported authoritarian ruler created economic deprivation and dislocation at home.[44]

In some senses, democracy was largely restored when Balaguer yielded power in the election of 1978, but his economic policies had already helped set in motion the brutal economic collapse that hit the Dominican Republic in the 1980s. The global oil shocks of the 1970s led to radically increased prices for imports, while the price of sugar plummeted on the world market.

In 1975, sugar sold for 76 cents a pound, but by 1985, it had dropped to just 4 cents a pound, less than what it cost to produce it. The decimation of the country's sugar sector was exacerbated in 1982 when President Ronald Reagan yielded to pressure from U.S. sugar growers and restricted sugar importation with new quotas, cutting access to the major market for Dominican sugar.[45] This decline in export revenue coupled with the steep increase in import costs exacerbated the nation's trade deficit, but it is important to keep in mind that the deficit was already long standing by the 1980s and had long been financed by borrowing from international institutions. In 1970, foreign debt was already $290.6 million, but it ballooned in the 1980s, reaching an astounding $3.84 billion by 1988.[46]

In 1982, the Dominican Republic entered a state of extreme fiscal crisis and became unable to continue to pay its debt. The IMF intervened to stave off economic collapse, but it imposed a structural adjustment (or "austerity") program on the country, requiring the government to raise taxes, freeze wages, and reduce government spending. A follow-up agreement with the IMF in 1984 required the government to reduce subsidies and price controls, devalue its currency, and reduce import restrictions. These policies had a disastrous impact on the standard of living in the Dominican Republic and provoked extreme inflation.[47] Although the IMF is not commensurate with the United States, the U.S. has had an outsized influence on the organization since its inception during World War II, and the neoliberal ideals of the IMF have long paralleled the U.S. emphasis on "free trade."[48] The structural adjustment program imposed on the Dominican Republic was not unique, but it was a common response to the debt crises precipitated throughout the Third World when decades of trade imbalances and debt ran up against the inflation and rising costs of imports provoked by the oil crisis of the late 1970s.[49]

Given the Dominican reliance on imported food, the rise in the cost of imports and the extreme inflation provoked by IMF policies seriously undermined the ability of many Dominicans to feed themselves and their families, leading to some of the worst structural adjustment–related food riots in the world in 1984, as Dominicans protested IMF-imposed austerity by taking to the streets. In that year, 41 percent of Dominican children under five were malnourished, and the infant mortality rate nearly doubled between 1980 and 1985.[50] While the nation's middle class was not necessarily forced to struggle with hunger, inflation in the 1980s still severely undermined their economic opportunities. Dominican economist Bernardo Vega has called the 1980s the country's "lost decade."[51] Even for the nation's urban, educated professionals, emigration increasingly came to seem like the only path to economic security and an improved quality of life.

Although the Dominican Republic had long ceased to be any nation's formal colony, its economy was fragile and ultimately reliant on decisions made beyond its borders, particularly in the United States. Efforts to restructure the Dominican economy after the crisis concentrated on attracting foreign investment, either in tourism, in nontraditional export agribusiness, or in tax-free light manufacturing in Free Trade Zones. By 1991, there were 285 firms operating in 26 such zones in the country, assembling products largely for export to the United States. Foreign companies, often U.S. multinational corporations, were attracted to the Dominican Republic because of its low wages, high unemployment rates, and the tax incentives offered by its government.[52] This incentivized industrialization made the Dominican Republic one of the major competitors for the remains of U.S. nondurable goods manufacturing, further undermining the industrial core of cities like Lawrence. Manufacturing and tourism have provided jobs for many workers, notably women, in the Dominican Republic in the past few decades, but the jobs provided are often unstable, lack suitable worker protections, and are poorly paid. So long as U.S. and other foreign companies are locating production in the Dominican Republic specifically *because* of the low wages they can pay there and the taxes they can avoid, foreign investment is unlikely to be a long-term solution for Dominican development or any improved economic circumstances for its residents.[53]

It was in the "lost decade" of the 1980s that Dominican migration to the United States, and to Lawrence, expanded at truly unprecedented levels. The 2000 census indicated that the overwhelming majority (75 percent) of the nearly 700,000 foreign-born Dominicans in the country had immigrated after 1980. Dominicans overwhelmingly concentrated in New York City in the late twentieth century, although they have begun to disperse somewhat in the past few decades. Nearly three-quarters of Dominicans in the United States lived in New York City in 1980, but just over half did by 2000. Still, a huge majority remained in the Northeast, 82 percent as of the 2000 census. Lawrence today has the second-highest population of Dominicans in the country, after New York City, of course.[54]

The huge increase in Dominican migration during the 1980s is clearly related in part to the country's economic crisis, although it is important to keep in mind that widespread poverty and unemployment existed even during the economic growth of the late 1960s and early 1970s, and that the dislocations provoked by changes to the agricultural sector preceded the economic crisis. Yet this rapid expansion of Dominican migration is also related to chain migration. The major way in which Dominicans obtained access to highly prized immigration visas was through family members who were already citizens or legal permanent residents in the United States. Indeed, the current configuration of U.S. immigration law makes it a reality that, without a close family member in the United States, the chances of getting an immigration visa are exceedingly slim, as the quota of available visas is generally taken up with those who have a family-preference priority. Even those with a close family member in the United States often have to wait many years to obtain a visa.[55]

It is important to add here that immigrating illegally requires either considerable resources or the willingness to take extreme risks. Any Dominican seeking a student or tourist visa to visit the United States temporarily must be well enough established in the Dominican Republic (with cash, property, a good job, etc.) to convince the U.S. authorities that she or he has no plans to stay once her or his visa has expired.[56] The other illegal immigration option is to attempt to secretly cross into Puerto Rico by *yola*, a dangerous and often unsuccessful journey. Given the extreme risks and challenges of unauthorized immigration, most Dominican migrants come to the United States legally, and the emphasis on family unification in U.S. immigration law encourages the expansion of immigration as the number of Dominicans already in the country increases.[57]

Pushed out of their home country partly by the effects of U.S. (and IMF) policies, Dominicans are, like Puerto Ricans, best understood as imperial migrants, attempting to move from the periphery of the U.S. empire to its center to pursue the opportunities foreclosed at home. This parallel, however, should not blind us to the very real difference that U.S. citizenship makes; Dominican access to the United States is severely restricted by policies and practices that limit immigration, divide families, condemn those without visas to a precarious existence, and render even legal permanent residents subject to deportation. Puerto Rico and the Dominican Republic have had very different histories of U.S. imperialism, and those histories shape the experiences of migrants to this day.

Many other nations in Latin America experienced similar constellations of military and economic intervention, particularly during the Cold War and in the post–Cold War era of economic globalization, and so this "harvest of empire" intellectual framework is applicable for many other Latino nationalities as well.[58] Certainly not all of the blame for poverty or political instability in Latin America can be laid on the U.S. government, the IMF, or U.S. corporations, but nor would it be accurate to say that nations in Latin

America were truly sovereign in the twentieth century, able to direct their own economic or political development without interference from U.S. officials or investors. At the same time that U.S. imperialism cut off avenues to improve conditions at home, it also drew Latin American nations closer to the United States in many ways, forging links along which migrants would then travel.

HAY TRABAJO, PERO NO HAY VIDA:
WHY CHOOSE LAWRENCE OVER NEW YORK?

The bulk of Latino settlement in Lawrence during the labor phase was made up of secondary migrants, primarily from New York City. Although some direct migration from the islands occurred in the 1960s, accounts from long-term city residents and community organizers agree that as the population grew in the 1970s, a major portion of both Dominican and Puerto Rican migrants to Lawrence came from New York.[59] As prominent community worker Isabel Melendez described the 1970s, "Lawrence filled-up with New York."[60]

New York City has historically been the major settlement site for both Puerto Ricans and Dominicans in the mainland United States. In the early postwar era, it was not hard for Puerto Ricans to find jobs in the big city's manufacturing sector, especially in the garment industry.[61] But like cities throughout the Northeast and Midwest, New York began to experience a period of decline in these decades, as a result of suburbanization, deindustrialization, and disinvestment.[62] This history parallels that of Lawrence in many ways, although on an earlier timeline and on a much larger scale. Between 1940 and 1970, New York lost approximately 2 million white residents as the suburbs surrounding the city boomed, largely restricted to white families through an array of discriminatory developer, realtor, and bank practices.[63] Massive urban renewal and highway construction campaigns displaced entire communities in these decades, accelerating white suburbanization and the frequent relocation of poor and working-class families of color. Public housing construction centered in low-income neighborhoods of color, further concentrating poverty and stigmatizing those neighborhoods. The struggle to find new housing, often in unwelcoming neighborhoods, left Puerto Rican families paying more in monthly rent ($49) than white families ($37) and African American families ($43) by the mid-1950s. In addition, frequently being displaced to new neighborhoods often compelled Puerto Rican youth to engage in violent battles for turf, as Italian American and Irish American young people attempted to resist the entrance of these newcomers into their neighborhoods by force.[64]

Deindustrialization and the suburbanization of offices and the retail sector eviscerated New York City's job base in the 1970s. The city lost 100,000 jobs *per year* between 1970 and 1975, with the bulk of those losses in manufacturing, and the city's unemployment rate rose from 5 percent to 12 percent.[65] Puerto Rican workers were hit particularly hard by the loss of manufacturing jobs. In 1977, the median income for Puerto Rican families was just $10,499, below that of African American families ($13,999) and half that of white families ($20,998). Impoverished mothers turned to welfare: in 1969, 328,000 New Yorkers relied on welfare; by 1972, 1.25 million did, and 40 percent of the city's welfare recipients were Puerto Rican.[66]

Displacement and disinvestment devastated low-income communities, and crime began to rise dramatically in the 1960s. Although this was true of cities across the country, circumstances in New York were especially dire. Robberies increased 825 percent between 1960 and 1968, and the homicide rate doubled. Residents of poor neighborhoods were far more likely to be the victims of crime than those who lived in wealthier neighborhoods.[67] This perilous rise in crime was partially tied to a dangerous increase in heroin use and addiction in the late 1960s and 1970s, as well as the larger geography of abandonment in the city. As Eric Schneider explained, "Heroin was a city-killing drug, and in the early 1970s the American city appeared to be on its way to the morgue."[68] As joblessness expanded in the 1970s, crime, drugs, and arson exacerbated the overwhelming sense of decay and despair in New York City.

This sense of crisis was solidified with the city's fiscal breakdown in 1975. The provision of municipal services in the huge city was expensive, and white flight and deindustrialization had undermined New York's tax base. The city addressed this deficit through borrowing. By 1973, however, the city's debt was so profound that banks began to question the soundness of these loans. In April 1975, the private financial sector refused to support new municipal bonds, and the city was on the cusp of bankruptcy. In the compromise to restart lending and avoid an economic catastrophe in the city, oversight of the city's finances was given to two newly created state agencies, both dominated by bankers and businesspeople.[69] As historian Robert Snyder explained, "Bankers, Republicans, and fiscal conservatives seized on the opportunity to discipline New York [and] restructure its political economy."[70] As in the Dominican Republic in the 1980s, deficit and debt were the mechanisms by which control over economic policies was surrendered to elite financiers beyond the reach of democratic processes.

These postcrisis policies entailed severe cutbacks to municipal services (in essence an austerity program parallel to the structural adjustment measures imposed in the Dominican Republic by the IMF). As a result of these cutbacks, 60,000 municipal employees were laid off, and the city lost a quarter of its teachers. Class sizes in New York City public schools were increased, while counseling and other programs were decreased. Two thousand full-time faculty at City University of New York were dismissed. The 130-year-old policy of tuition-free higher education at the university was ended, and enrollment dropped by 63,000. Fewer trains ran, and trash piled up in the streets. Cutbacks in municipal services were particularly devastating for poor neighborhoods, especially police, firefighting, and public transportation services. The justification for these cutbacks was articulated most clearly by the head of the city's Housing Development Administration, Roger Starr, in his support for "planned shrinkage": Cutting back services in struggling neighborhoods would encourage those residents to leave and move elsewhere. Although Starr ultimately lost his job for his incendiary comments, the cutbacks remained in place.[71]

The combined impact of disinvestment and cuts in municipal services was most powerfully illustrated as poor and working-class neighborhoods went up in flames. Already by late 1960s, low-income neighborhoods of color often suffered paradoxically from both overcrowding and abandonment, as many landlords no longer found profit in paying the maintenance and tax costs for their buildings. In this environment of racialized disinvestment, arson began to spread. As Deborah Wallace and Rodrick Wallace explained, "Fires became virulently epidemic in 1968."[72] This epidemic was exacerbated by the city's decision to scale back fire services over the next few years, with the cuts in services concentrated in the neighborhoods that needed them most. But in the years after the fiscal crisis and its austerity cuts, the arson epidemic reached extreme proportions and drew national attention. During the 1977 World Series, cameras panned the streets surrounding Yankee Stadium as Howard Cosell interrupted his play-by-play to announce, "Ladies and gentlemen, the Bronx is burning."[73]

As historian Joanne Reitano summed up New York City in the crisis era, "A startling conglomeration of ills confirmed New York's image as the worst of all possible worlds. Rampant arson, ravaging disease, surging welfare rolls, high unemployment, untrammeled drug use, brazen crime, filthy streets, sprawling graffiti, crumbling schools, huge rats, extensive homelessness, fiscal bankruptcy, police corruption, and political scandals horrified the nation. Gotham epitomized the problems everyone else hoped to avoid. It symbolized the urban crisis."[74]

Clearly, the 1970s were a particularly bleak moment in New York City's history. Overwhelmingly concentrated in New York, Puerto Ricans and Dominicans were forced to reckon with this crisis. After the massive white flight of the immediate postwar decades, New York lost another 1.3 million white residents between 1970 and 1980.[75] Many of those who could leave the city did so in this era, but opportunities to move somewhere safer were not available to everyone; the constraints imposed by race were formidable. Latino migration narratives demonstrate that many Latinos chose to settle in Lawrence in the 1960s and 1970s because they believed it provided an escape from New York. They explained that urban crisis had made New York an inhospitable, unsafe environment to live in and raise their families.

Although Latinos have often been described as labor migrants, moving in search of a job, this is only partially true in Lawrence.[76] Like millions of families who left cities wracked by poverty, crime, and inadequate public services in the postwar era, Latinos left New York City searching for a better *life*, not just a better *livelihood*. In the context of the constrained choices available to most Latinos in the Northeast by exclusive suburbanization (i.e., not where to settle, but in which city), life in Lawrence seemed preferable to life in New York. As the Dominicans interviewed by Patricia Pessar often repeated, in New York, "*Hay trabajo, pero no hay vida*"; there were jobs in New York, but it wasn't the place to make a life.[77]

The Latinos who eventually settled in Lawrence were not just searching for a job; they were searching for a better life, broadly defined. This idea is evident throughout their migration narratives, phrased in myriad ways: "a better life," "better opportunities," "a better way of living," and so forth.[78] As one Puerto Rican in Lawrence explained, this better life generally required a job in order to maintain it, but the job itself was not the goal: "We've all come because we want better work, health, schooling. We'll do any work to get them."[79] A better life (in this example, not just a job but a good job, plus improved access to health and education services) was what spurred migration, and the impulse behind much of the early immigration to Lawrence was ultimately a desire for safety and a better quality of life.

Although Lawrence would come to be known, at least regionally, for its economic problems and its crime and poverty, many of the Latinos who chose to move there during the labor phase were looking for the closest thing they could get to small-town life in the United States. Constrained by the exclusionary practices of suburbanization, Latinos looked for a small city where they could build community, raise children, and start businesses in safety and escape the perceived danger and anonymity of life in New York. One Dominican woman explained that migrants were searching for "*la tranquilidad. . . . Tú sabes que Lawrence es pequeño y está fuera de las grandes urbes* [peace and quiet. You know that Lawrence is small and outside of the large urban centers]."[80]

Many Lawrence Latinos had lived in small towns in their home countries: Juana Díaz in Puerto Rico or Tenares in the Dominican Republic, for example. The relative *tranquilidad* of Lawrence resembled the life many had lived before migration: "*Se parece más a nuestros barrios, a nuestro pueblo* [It more closely resembles our neighborhoods, our towns]." Latino settlers in Lawrence believed that this small-town life provided a safer environment in which to raise children: "*Los muchachos pueden jugar en las calles, pueden estar fuera de su casa hasta tarde, sobre todo en el verano; eso no puede suceder en otras ciudades* [The children can play in the streets, they can be outside until late, above all in the summer; this wouldn't be possible in other cities]."[81] One Latina explained that she came to Lawrence from New York City in 1981 not because she had been told about jobs in the area but because she had been told that "it would be more peaceful for my children."[82] A young Dominican man explained to the *Eagle-Tribune* why his mother chose Lawrence, and the paper reported that she "first went to New York for a year and then she found Lawrence. To her . . . the city was like a church—quiet and peaceful. It was a much safer place to send her children to school."[83] A report on Dominican immigration to the city recounted, "We heard again and again that 'it is quieter here.' 'Lawrence is more peaceful than New York.'"[84] The desire for safety and tranquility drew Latinos from New York City to Lawrence.

Among both Puerto Ricans and Dominicans, family and commercial links between Lawrence and New York City remained quite strong even after migration directly from the islands accelerated in the 1980s and 1990s. In fact, many Latinos continued to move from New York in this later era, or to compare Lawrence with New York. Crime rates in New York City worsened after the emergence of crack cocaine in the late 1980s. The citywide murder rate in the early 1960s was 7.6 per 100,000 (at the time an unprecedented high), but it rose to 25.4 by the late 1980s. The violence of the drug trade terrified city residents, especially those who lived in neighborhoods where drug sales were concentrated, such as Washington Heights.[85] In 1990, a poll found that 73 percent of New York City residents considered the city dangerous, and 59 percent would rather live somewhere else.[86] It should not be surprising that Dominicans and Puerto Ricans would be among those wanting to leave.

A young Dominican woman came to Lawrence with her father in the late 1980s as a teenager but moved to New York City to live with her mother when she became pregnant. She returned to Lawrence a few years later, however. As she explained, "I moved to Lawrence because New York is, I don't consider a nice place for a child to be raised in. You know, I was thinking about my kids to be raised in a nice city, not gangs, stuff like that, bad things." She explained what she liked best about Lawrence: "It's not like New York City. It's quiet. It's nice people. You can walk in the night. You don't have to be worried about somebody hitting you or something, killing you, like in New York City."[87] New York's urban crisis, particularly its crime, was cited again and again as a reason to leave for Lawrence.

Another Dominican woman who came to the United States in 1963 never lived in New York City but was affected by its urban crisis nonetheless. She landed in a New Jersey airport, and her husband's cousin picked them up to drive them up to Boston. On the way, they drove through Harlem. What she saw there provided a strong contrast to what she expected to find in the United States: "I envisioned [the United States] like a land with the streets paved with gold, beautiful, streets immaculately clean. . . . And when we came in, we came through Harlem . . . and when I saw the mess, I couldn't believe it. I talked to my husband and I told him, 'This is the United States of America?' I couldn't believe it. I really couldn't. So in that way, I was disappointed."[88] The racialized disinvestment in U.S. cities in the latter half of the twentieth century shocked immigrants who expected that a wealthy nation should be free of such poverty and degradation. The urban crisis in New York City spurred Latino dispersal, as Dominicans and Puerto Ricans continued to search for an elusive American Dream.

IMMIGRATION AND DEINDUSTRIALIZATION

It may seem paradoxical, but in some ways the process of urban decline actually opened the city's job market and housing to Latinos. Lawrence's nondurable goods manufacturers welcomed and even recruited Latinos to Lawrence in the 1960s and 1970s as a means of remaining competitive with southern and overseas manufacturers. This initial migration formed the basis of a Latino community in the city that was then fed through kinship networks, even after the employment incentive to settle in Lawrence receded. White flight made rental housing available in the city, although it was not necessarily "cheap" relative to Latino wages. At the same time, as discussed above, Lawrence's abandonment was so long standing that the Latino community was allowed to grow relatively undisturbed by gentrification or large-scale urban renewal. The absence of gentrification in the city enabled long-term community and small-business development, virtually uninterrupted by the displacement suffered by many Latino communities in larger cities.

In the 1960s and 1970s, the availability of jobs in Lawrence's nondurable goods sector was a central factor in encouraging Latinos to move to Lawrence (the nondurable goods sector mainly includes textile, garment, and shoe manufacturing). As the local paper described, "Often, enough to make a family head for Lawrence, was the help-wanted section of the *Eagle-Tribune* received from a friend."[89] Although Lawrence manufacturers welcomed Latino workers, the work was often poorly paid, unstable, and even dangerous. In this era, increased global competition was undermining the primacy of U.S. manufacturing. As the manufacture of nondurable goods was transferred overseas in search of cheaper labor costs (often to the very countries migrants were leaving to come to the United States), Lawrence's remaining manufacturers were eager to hire Latinos, eager to exploit the same workforce their competitors were exploiting "offshore," but without the need to relocate.

Latino Lawrencians described manufacturing jobs as easy to come by until the late 1970s, with local bosses paying recruiting fees to workers who brought in family or friends as new employees. Although no record of *why* Lawrence manufacturers decided to recruit Latino workers exists, a study of similar firms in Boston in 1973 noted that they recruited Puerto Ricans because employers considered them less "intractable" than local African American workers.[90] While Lawrence never had a substantial African American population, the perception of Latinos as a docile labor force may still have been operative. Lawrence employers may have also recruited Latinos out of a belief that they would accept lower wages than native-born white workers. A 1980 Greater Lawrence booster pamphlet pointed out to prospective businesses that the real wages of factory production workers had actually *declined* since 1967.[91] Certainly, the upward mobility of the white working class in this era must have also played a role. As the Immigrant City lost its white ethnics to the suburbs, manufacturers scrambled to replace them with a new wave of migrants.

Although most Latinos in Lawrence in this era were Puerto Rican, employers also seem to have been aware of the particular vulnerability of undocumented Latino workers. Julia Silverio, a Dominican who worked in the personnel office of a shoe factory in the early 1970s (and who later became a prominent politician in the city), noted that, during slack times, "the employers used to call the INS department. Dominicans, many of whom were undocumented and scared to be deported, used to abandon their jobs. After a while, ads looking for workers would be posted and Dominicans and others would be rehired as new workers. . . . Workers were always new and, when they were not needed, they were simply let go in this manner." In this context, the preference for Latinos seems to have been due partly to the belief that they would be less likely to protest the periodic layoffs inherent in an industry in decline. It is no surprise that the shoe factory that Silverio worked in closed a few years later.[92]

Jobs in Lawrence's factories played an undeniable role in facilitating early Latino settlement in Lawrence. These jobs, however, were often poorly paid, unstable, difficult, and dangerous, and they contributed to the profound disappointment that many Latinos felt at the huge gap between the lives they had hoped to create for themselves in the United States and the lives they actually lived in Lawrence. This disappointment became even more pronounced when Lawrence's remaining manufacturing sector basically collapsed in the late 1970s and 1980s, leading to widespread unemployment and poverty but also undermining the city's tax base and thus eroding its social services, particularly education and public safety. This transition from bad work to no work is most evident in Lawrence's shoe industry, a sector that specifically employed large numbers of women.

Many early Latina settlers in Lawrence worked at the local shoe factories, such as Lawrence Maid or Jo-Gal Shoes. Father John J. Lamond, who directed a church-based center aimed at helping Latinos settle in the city, recollected hearing about job openings at a local shoe factory. He recounted that he brought a young Latina who was looking for work over to the factory one morning, and the manager hired her on the spot, asking, "Did she bring her lunch?"[93] An Argentinian woman recalled a similar story. She explained that she went to Jo-Gal Shoes, a shoe factory at the corner of Essex and Union Streets, with her daughter. She could not understand English at the time, but the owner told her daughter that if she wanted to work, she could start the very same day. "I said 'yes' and that same day I filled out the necessary paperwork. I told him I was an illegal [alien] and he said not to worry, things would work out." She worked adding shoelaces and rubber to the shoes and was eventually promoted to forelady.[94]

The Lawrence Maid shoe factory was one of the most important employers of early Latina settlers in Lawrence. With only one exception, every Latina interviewed by the Lawrence History Center who arrived in the city before 1980 and mentioned a job in her interview recalled working for Lawrence Maid. While this may be a sampling bias, and while men certainly worked there too, the centrality of Lawrence Maid, and the shoe industry more generally, for Latina workers cannot be underestimated. In 1974, the short-lived progressive Lawrence newspaper, *Today in Greater Lawrence*, did an exposé on Lawrence Maid titled, "New Immigrants in Old Sweatshops," offering a detailed window into work conditions at the factory. *Today* invoked Lawrence's history as an industrial center but noted the changing times: "The

Workers in front of Lawrence Maid Footwear Inc. in 1974. Photo by Richard Graber, reproduced with permission from Jennifer Graber. Print provided by Linda and Jurg Siegenthaler.

textile industry has retreated south, leaving the old mill buildings as shadows of what they once were—unless you happen to be there at 3:30 when the new mill workers are spilling out, and the place comes to life as if the turbines were still running. . . . The faces are Spanish now, high-boned and sleek-haired." In spite of that awkward description (high-boned?), Puerto Ricans did account for more than 40 percent of Lawrence Maid's workforce in the early 1970s.[95]

Yet conditions at Lawrence Maid did not reflect a golden opportunity. "Not one of nine workers interviewed batted an eyelash about saying there are accidents of various sorts, and varying degrees of severity, all the time, '*todo el tiempo*.'" One worker explained: "The same guy got hurt four times in one day. . . . I see the old man in the bathroom crying. A strong man. An American. Maybe 40. *Muy viejo y muy joven*, very old and very young. . . . Each time the machine took a little [of the man's finger]." The hourly rate on the floor was $2.15, just pennies above the federal minimum wage and *less* than what many manufacturing jobs paid in Puerto Rico.[96] Many workers did piecework. One Italian woman explained that you could make a "good dollar" on piecework "if you're fast . . . if you don't mind conditions. . . . It's a dog eat dog rat-race. It's kill, it's really kill. If your machine doesn't run, you suffer. It hasn't changed." Workers also complained of the patronizing behavior of the bosses: "They talk hard to us . . . like, 'you, you got to do this.' They don't say please." "They treat us like kids—'*como hijos*,' like sons." These were clearly not the circumstances migrants were dreaming of, yet the author argued that many Latinos were resigned: "It's still harder to make a buck in Puerto Rico, they say. 'There are more opportunities here.' Now that I've been here so long, I'd have to begin again." One Latino worker explained, "You get used to it . . . [except that you feel] old and tired, *viejo y cansado*."[97]

The availability of low-wage jobs drew Latinos to other small industrial cities in these early decades as well. Dalia Díaz's story of why her family left Miami and ended up in Chelsea is illustrative (she later settled in Lawrence and Methuen). Díaz and her family landed in Miami after a harrowing boat journey fleeing Cuba in the early 1960s. The Cuban Refugee Center gave them $100 a month; but they were paying $87 for rent, so they were desperate for work. Díaz's mother and stepfather went to work in the tomato plantations in Homestead, outside Miami, but as she described, "people were greatly exploited at that time in 1963." They worked long days at less than minimum wage, but "they couldn't complain, they couldn't go anywhere because Miami wasn't what it is today. There were no industries, factories, banks. It was just plantations and people had to leave Miami." She explained, "The Cuban Refugee Center was going crazy at the time, trying to get rid of us, sending us anywhere—a one-way ticket anywhere in the country." The refugee center was encouraging dispersal from Miami, but her parents were slow to take up the offer. She remembered that her stepfather went to Boston and wrote to his family a week later "saying that he was making a dollar sixty an hour in a factory in Chelsea, and that in two weeks after he finished the training process he would be making—watch this—two dollars and two cents an hour. We thought we were going to get rich!"[98]

For Díaz and her family, the economic opportunity provided by low-wage factory work in Chelsea, another small industrial city outside Boston, was a compelling alternative to sub-minimum-wage agricultural work in Florida's tomato plantations. Further, the sheer number of different employment alternatives in Massachusetts allowed Díaz and her family to resist exploitation by changing jobs until they found a good fit, something they did not feel able to do in still-developing Miami. In addition, as their time in the United States lengthened and their English-language skills improved, they were able to leverage those skills into better, and better-paid, work. Díaz remembered that at sixteen she went to work shelling shrimp in Boston, in an area "that was all fishing piers and dingy little houses and warehouses and the boats used to come in that area and unload the fish. I went to work there shelling shrimp. That was my first job.... Sixteen. Ice water up to my knees." From there, Díaz moved to a factory in Cambridge, "stitching because I had learned how to sew in Cuba. All girls in Cuba had to learn to sew and to do embroidery." Contrary to the frequent depiction of Lawrence Latinos as unskilled laborers, Díaz is one of many Lawrence Latinos who came to the United States with skills learned at home. Within months, she had learned enough English to get a job at American Built, a shoe factory in Chelsea, where her father already worked packing rubber soles and heals. She remembered changing jobs frequently, although she would have rather been in school. "That was my dream, to get an education, and I didn't."[99]

Although many Latinas in Lawrence's nondurable goods sector worked for low wages, it was not for lack of skills.[100] Like Díaz, many Latinas who ended up in the factories used skills they had learned before migrating. Daniel Rivera came to Lawrence from the Bronx as a child in 1975. Rivera (who would be elected mayor of Lawrence in 2013) explained, "My mom was a seamstress in the Dominican Republic and she learned her trade under the dictator Trujillo, and when she came to the United States, she worked primarily in the garment district in New York, and heard there was seamstress work here in Lawrence to be had." His mother worked at Grieco Brothers, in Lawrence, and at a suede company in Haverhill.[101]

It would be only a partial truth to say that these miserable conditions and low wages were what caused Latino migration to Lawrence and other industrial cities in Massachusetts; rather, jobs like those at Lawrence Maid were what Latino migrants *endured* in order to achieve other aims. Low-wage jobs were viewed as a stepping-stone to better jobs, improved economic opportunity, and most importantly, better health and education services—a better life for workers and their families. Latinos took the miserable jobs that were available as a way to stay in the United States and eventually gain access to the better life they believed staying could provide. Many were never able to find work commensurate with their education or training, however. As one Dominican man explained, "*[En mis] diez meses residiendo aquí he tenido que trabajar en seis lugares; ninguno de estos tienen nada que ver con la formación académica que yo tengo de Santo Domingo . . . [pero] estos trabajos nos han permitido seguir sobreviviendo aquí* [(In my) ten months residing here I have had to work in six places; none of these had anything to do with the academic background that I have from the Dominican Republic . . . (but) these jobs have permitted us to keep surviving here]."[102] The low quality, low wages, and instability of the jobs Latinos found in Lawrence were far from the American Dream; rather, Latinos were drawn into an industry that was rapidly globalizing, engaged in an international "race to the bottom."

Even these less-than-ideal jobs in the city's declining manufacturing sector were to prove short lived, as Lawrence Maid was already going through layoffs in 1974, affecting both the day-to-day operations of the factory as well as hopes of workers to unionize. *Today* noted, "Dust from machines, [one worker says], is thick enough to choke on. When Lawrence Maid laid off 500 last November, four of the five janitors for the five story structure got the axe." The worker elaborated, "And we have to eat on dirty machines because there's no workers lunch room. *El polvo es el postre* [The dust is the dessert]."[103] By 1978, Lawrence Maid was down to just 750 employees, from 2,200 a decade earlier.[104] Between 1964 and 1974, eighty-seven Massachusetts shoe factories closed, and the number of leather-shoe workers was cut nearly in half. As the vice president of a New Hampshire shoe company summed it up, "We're exporting our labor-intensive industry abroad."[105]

By the early 1980s, much of Lawrence's remaining nondurable goods manufacturing had shut down, provoking the massive unemployment protested in the 1984 riots.[106] As the State Office of Affirmative Action noted, "Many Hispanics migrate to Massachusetts to pursue employment opportunities. Yet many cannot find work and those who are employed are stuck in low-paying jobs in the secondary sector of the economy with little opportunity for mobility. . . . This threatens to make Hispanics a permanent underclass in the Commonwealth."[107] Indeed, the 1980s were a time of widespread national discussion of whether disinvestment and segregation were creating a potentially permanent "underclass" among urban African Americans and Latinos, concentrated in cities from which economic opportunities had fled, entire communities with little hope of steady employment and thus little hope of gaining the resources for spatial or social mobility. Lawrence's history illustrates well the challenges of migrating *to* a city only to watch the jobs migrate *away*.[108]

Given that many Latino Lawrencians came from New York during the labor phase, or at least had kin in New York, it is worth comparing the economic opportunities available to Latinos in Lawrence with those in New York City. A look at the census data for the two places confirms that jobs were plentiful in Lawrence in the 1960s and 1970s and even that Lawrence might have offered a better economic opportunity in those early years, as Lawrence Latinos had somewhat higher median incomes than New York City Latinos. Latinos in Lawrence were concentrated in the manufacturing sector, however, so the city's second wave of deindustrialization in the late 1970s and early 1980s was economically devastating. In 1970, 83 percent of Lawrence's employed Latinos worked in manufacturing, compared with only 34 percent in New York City, as the diversification of New York's economy was already well under way. The fact that manufacturing was the absolute basis of most Latino Lawrencians' income in 1970 boded ill, as shutdowns and layoffs continued. The effects of deindustrialization were evident by the 1980 census. In real terms, Latino households in Lawrence experienced a 25 percent decline in income, adjusted for inflation, over the 1970s. By 1990, there was a pronounced gap between median Latino household incomes in New York and Lawrence. The median income for Latinos in Lawrence was less than $15,000, compared with more than $20,000 in New York, and Lawrence's Latino unemployment rate was nearly 25 percent (compared with just 13 percent in New York).[109] Lawrence's Latinos were clearly suffering from the small city's deepening economic crisis by the 1980s.

The decline of Lawrence's manufacturing sector in the late 1970s and 1980s hit the city's Latino labor force incredibly hard, and it was especially brutal for Latina women, who had been even more concentrated than Latino men in the city's nondurable goods manufacturing. In 1970, more than 60 percent of Latinas were in the labor force in Lawrence, compared with only 35 percent in New York, and they were overwhelmingly concentrated in manufacturing (81 percent of employed Lawrence Latinas were operatives, compared with just 36 percent in New York). In the next two decades, Latinas in Lawrence experienced an explosion of joblessness as the city deindustrialized. From an unemployment rate of only 3 percent in 1970 (half the male unemployment rate), Latina unemployment rose to a merciless 25.4 percent by 1990, and labor force participation declined to just 51 percent.[110] By the end of the 1980s, the very jobs that had brought Latinas to the city had evaporated. In sum, while Lawrence may have offered a relative advantage over New York in the 1970s and 1980s in terms of its small size and relative safety, Lawrence offered no real economic advantage as the mill city's deindustrialization progressed. Whether in New York or Lawrence, urban crisis rendered a "better life" elusive for poor and working-class Latinos.

SUBURBANIZATION AND SEGREGATION

In her study of Dominicans in Lawrence, Jessica Andors offered the story of "Alma" to demonstrate the main themes in Dominican immigration to Lawrence.[111] Alma's parents, of "humble background," left the Dominican Republic in the early 1960s after the death of Trujillo and settled in New York. Friends and family followed them to the city, in what scholars refer to as "chain migration" and Alma described as "the domino effect" (in an interesting appropriation of Cold War military language). In the late 1960s, one person from her circle of kin followed rumors of work to Lawrence, and the chain migration/domino effect began all over again—this time from New York City to Lawrence. Like Zaiter's family, Alma remembered that local manufacturers were paying referral fees to make use of migrant kinship networks to recruit new workers in this early era. Both male and female members of Alma's circle of friends and family found nondurable goods manufacturing jobs, sewing coats and shoes. In the late 1970s, when Lawrence underwent its second deindustrialization, many in Alma's circle went to work for suburban electronics manufacturers—Raytheon, Lucent, and Western Electric—what Alma described as "the elite of immigrant working class" jobs.[112] The story of Alma's family demonstrates the role of employment opportunities in encouraging early Latino settlement in Lawrence. Yet it also demonstrates the transition to suburban manufacturing that occurred in the late 1970s (each of the firms named above was located in Andover or North Andover), a transition that left many Latinos unemployed at the same time that it eviscerated the city's tax base, as discussed in Chapter 1.

Lawrence's share of jobs in the region declined considerably in the postwar decades, as the suburbs successfully competed for the region's industry and retail establishments. The proportion of jobs that were located in the suburbs markedly increased in the 1980s, while deindustrialization tore through Lawrence. Less than 39 percent of Latinos in Lawrence's labor force actually had a job *within the city itself* in 1990.[113] Many Latinos were unemployed, but many more commuted to the suburbs to work. In the 1990s, Andors interviewed representatives of three local temporary employment agencies, noting that the majority of the workers they staffed were Latino, and concluded that many Lawrence Latinos were "serving the temporary and seasonal labor force needs of manufacturers in North Andover, Haverhill, Wilmington, and other neighboring towns and cities."[114] Many Latinos who had jobs in the 1990s worked as "permatemps," laboring regularly in suburban industries through a temporary contracting agency without ever being hired on directly.[115] Given the importance of suburban jobs for Lawrence Latinos, it is important to acknowledge why poor and working-class Latinos were so residentially concentrated within the city itself.

A common speculation has been that Latinos concentrated in Lawrence (and other urban centers) because cities had cheap rent. Certainly, housing in Lawrence was more affordable for working-class and poor Latinos than in the surrounding suburbs, but more affordable does not mean "cheap," as Latinos often paid sizable portions of their income toward housing. The existence of relatively affordable housing in Lawrence is better understood as a *lack* of affordable housing in other areas.[116] As discussed in Chapter 1, mid-twentieth-century suburbanization was premised on single-family homeownership and the allure of quiet, tree-lined streets. With their increased tax base and political power, most suburbs throughout the nation success- fully fought against the creation of multifamily, rental housing, and they particularly fought the creation of public or subsidized housing in their neigh- borhoods, arguing that it would lower property values. This is certainly true of the suburbs around Lawrence. Poor and working-class Latinos looking to settle in northeastern Massachusetts would have had few options for apart- ments to rent outside cities like Boston, Lawrence, or Springfield. Many of the very qualities that migrants were searching for—tranquility, safety, small communities, and even access to jobs—would have been more easily found in the suburbs around Lawrence, not in the crisis-wracked city itself, but exclusive suburbanization served to limit Latinos' residential options.

Historians are still uncovering the mechanisms responsible for Latino residential segregation in the second half of the twentieth century. Which of the factors that kept many suburbs "lily white" in the postwar era impacted Latinos? Certainly, the upward spiral of property values in suburban Greater Lawrence excluded the city's largely poor and working-class Latino popu- lation, but to what extent was racial discrimination an independent factor? Were the restrictive covenants, discriminatory mortgage lending, realtor steering, and racial violence that excluded most African Americans from sub- urban homeownership in the postwar era applied in the same way against Latinos? If so, were they applied against all Latinos or only certain national groups or only those with dark skin? Were they common in all parts of the country or only in certain regions? The remarkable racial, national-origin, and geographic diversity of Latinos makes questions such as these difficult to answer, as does the reality that substantial Latino settlement in many cities occurred in the post–Civil Rights era, when explicit discrimination was illegal. Of course, this does not mean that such discrimination did not occur; it just means that it left fewer archival traces.

There is ample evidence in oral history interviews, however, that in addition to the economic exclusiveness of suburbanization, Latinos in the Northeast experienced some degree of explicitly racial/ethnic housing discrimination that contributed to their residential segregation.[117] While I have found no records of any formal testing for housing discrimination in Greater Lawrence, there was an investigation in nearby suburban Framingham in 1988. This investigation marked the first time that the Massachusetts Commission against Discrimination (MCAD) specifically tested for housing discrimination against Latinos, and it is suggestive of the experiences Latinos likely had in nearby Lawrence's suburbs as well. MCAD investigated six different real estate agencies and one property management company using "matched" testers (i.e., individuals who were essentially equivalent in all major respects except race). Testers posed as homeseekers and inquired about available rental units. While the report concluded that discrimination against African American renters was "subtle," investigators found that discrimination against Latino renters was "overt." "Hispanics had a more difficult time in arranging for appointments and they were more likely to be told that [no units were] available." Overall, real estate agents offered white testers an average of 3.55 units; African American testers, 2.64 units; and Latino testers, only 1.55 units. MCAD found that Latinos experienced much more discriminatory treatment from real estate agents in this rental market than did African Americans.[118]

Popular perceptions of Latinos sometimes place them on a racial continuum between white and Black, and scholars have argued that Latinos' fluid and complicated racialization has often subjected them to racism, but rarely to the same degree as African Americans. Indeed, scholars of Philadelphia have noted that Latino neighborhoods created a quite literal buffer between Black and white neighborhoods.[119] The extreme discrimination against Latinos evident in this test, and the racist harassment, disenfranchisement, and disinvestment that Latinos suffered in Lawrence documented throughout this book, should caution us against applying that model to all Latino nationalities, in all parts of the country, in all eras. Not only were Puerto Ricans, nationally, far more segregated from non-Hispanic whites than other Latinos (even when controlling for socioeconomic indicators), but Latinos were far more segregated in Massachusetts's small cities than could be predicted from national trends.[120] As Barry Bluestone and Mary Huff Stevenson documented, "At the national level, black segregation from whites is typically higher than Hispanic or Asian segregation, but this pattern is frequently broken within Greater Boston." In Bluestone and Stevenson's study of Greater Boston in the early 1990s (within which they included Lawrence and its suburbs), Latinos were actually *more* segregated from whites than African Americans in half of the communities studied, particularly the state's small cities.[121] Of course, the goal is not to rank oppression but to explore how racial constructions vary over time and in different places. Clearly, Latinos in Massachusetts in the late twentieth century, mainly working-class Puerto Ricans and Dominicans, experienced virulent prejudice, and it seems undeniable that this prejudice contributed to their residential segregation and urban concentration.

Of course, the desire to live near kin certainly played a role in concentrating Latinos within Lawrence as well, and as the Latino community evolved in the 1980s and 1990s, the institutions and services that were developed added to Lawrence's gravitational pull. To some extent, as I will discuss further in Chapter 7, the concentration of Latinos in Lawrence reflected migrants' desire to live in a distinctly Latino community, to maintain their language and culture. I argue, however, that this preference worked *alongside* an array of structural factors to overdetermine the concentration of Latinos within the city limits. As is clear in map 2, Latinos did not choose just to settle *near* Lawrence (and thus maintain access to kin and to the cultural hub the city provided); they overwhelmingly, almost exclusively, settled *within* the city boundaries. Moving to Lawrence was a choice, but a choice constrained by the racial and economic geography of the postindustrial Northeast.

For European immigrants in the early twentieth century, the upward social mobility of the second and third generations was paralleled (and enabled) by a spatial mobility into the suburbs after World War II. But the postwar metropolitan political economy that encouraged the consolidation of these predominantly white, wealthy, and politically powerful suburbs by the 1970s narrowed the choices of later Latino immigrants. The decline of the traditional manufacturing sector in central cities across the Northeast and Midwest and the national transition to a two-tiered service economy undermined the possibility for migrants to achieve a living wage or experience upward mobility from the low-wage manufacturing and service jobs they found in the cities. In addition, as also discussed in Chapter 1, the cost of suburban housing

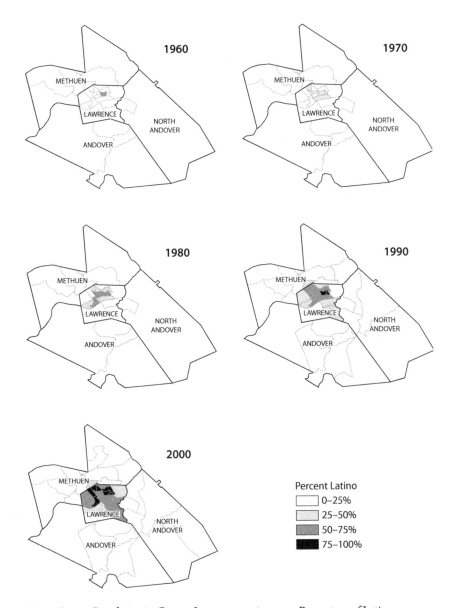

Map 2. Latino Population in Greater Lawrence, 1960–2000. Percentage of Latino residents in Greater Lawrence census tracts between 1960 and 2000. With the exception of southwest Lawrence, every part of the city had experienced substantial Latino settlement by 2000 (defined as census tracts that were at least 25 percent Latino), while with the exception of a small section of south-central Methuen, no area in the suburbs had experienced substantial Latino settlement by 2000. Map based on an original map drawn by Nicholas Bacon.

relative to working-class wages skyrocketed in Greater Lawrence from 1950 to 2000. Therefore, even independent of discrimination, these employment and housing trends reinforced the persistence of Latino segregation and urban concentration into the 1980s and 1990s, even for U.S.-born generations. The impact of these combined processes is evident in the extreme segregation between Latinos in Lawrence and their white suburban neighbors, as can be seen in map 2. By 2000, only one suburban census tract had developed a sizable Latino presence (a section of working-class Methuen, filled with Lawrence-style triple-decker houses), while Lawrence had been demographically transformed.

CONCLUSION

For many Latinos in Lawrence, migration was a survival strategy after U.S. imperial penetration of Puerto Rico and the Dominican Republic sharply curtailed economic opportunities on the islands. Once migrants were stateside, however, a number of factors combined to influence their settlement sites. Racism and urban crisis shaped Latino experiences, and secondary migration to cities like Lawrence was an attempt to resolve this dilemma, a way to pursue the economic opportunities presented by life in the United States without risking or enduring the perceived danger and decay of major urban centers in the crisis era. Migrants moved to Lawrence because they craved the peace and tranquility they could not find in New York City. While the prospect of life in a small New England city seemed to offer an escape, in reality the metropolitan political economy significantly limited the access of Latinos to the amenities they sought, such as good schools and safe neighborhoods. Increasingly, such amenities were found almost exclusively in the suburbs, especially in the Northeast, suburbs that were out of reach to poor and working-class Latinos. In the end, the cities that were intended to serve as an escape from urban crisis were really only a small step up from places like New York at the height of its crisis. They were smaller and quieter, yes, but on the same track of increasing joblessness and poverty, substandard housing, and perhaps most importantly, deeply inadequate educational and public safety services.

The remarkable Latino immigration to Lawrence occurred at the same time as white emigration from the city. Just as thousands of white Lawrencians were deciding that Lawrence was unlivable, thousands of Latinos were deciding to call Lawrence home. The simultaneous immigration and emigration that Lawrence experienced in the second half of the twentieth century highlights

Why Lawrence?

the impact of race on determining the range of choices available. Whites and Latinos encountered very different situations in Lawrence, and the decision whether to live there was made in the context of a field of radically different and profoundly racialized options. Most whites came to see Lawrence as worse than their other options (suburban homeownership), while many Latinos came to see Lawrence as substantially better than their other options (poverty or economic stagnation in the Caribbean or New York City's urban crisis). Understanding "Why Lawrence?" is only possible in this broader context of constraints.

THREE

STRUGGLING FOR THE CITY

Lawrence today is not the Lawrence of yesteryear. They ruin it; the people who come now ruin it all.

Elderly white Lawrencian in the 1980s

Si yo hubiese sido cobarde, no existiera nada, no existiera nada de lo que ves, te lo digo yo, no existiera nada [If I had been a coward, none of this would exist, none of what you see, I tell you, none of it would exist].

Lawrence community organizer Isabel Melendez

Latino settlement in Lawrence was no simple matter. As the city's economy spiraled downward, and as neighborhoods deteriorated from waves of demolition and white flight, many Lawrencians looked for a scapegoat. The growing number of Latinos in Lawrence in the 1970s correlated with the city's decline, and some white residents became convinced that Latinos were actually the cause of this decline—that these newcomers had *brought* poverty and blight to the small New England city, carrying the "urban problems" of crisis-era New York with them into Lawrence. Thus, rather than welcoming the newcomers as a source of reinvigoration for the struggling city, many white Lawrencians worked instead to discourage Latino settlement, hoping that by reversing the tide of Puerto Rican and Dominican migration they could restore the city to its imagined prime.

For Latinos attempting to make a home for themselves in Lawrence in the 1970s and 1980s, this white hostility created a serious obstacle. Not only did these imperial migrants have to struggle with all of the structural factors impoverishing the city, devastating its services, and limiting opportunities for work and social mobility, but they often had to face bitter prejudice, harassment, and discrimination as well. Settling in Lawrence required more than finding a landlord willing to rent to Latino tenants, although that itself could be an endeavor; it required repeated acts of courage to claim a space in the city's streets and public spaces. These conflicts reached their apex in the 1984 riots, but they began before the riots and were not settled by them. Latinos in Lawrence had to actively assert their right to the city.

As Robin Kelley and others have persuasively demonstrated, formal politics are often only the most visible manifestation of a more diffuse contest for control over space and resources, much of which takes place *outside* officially recognized political arenas.[1] In this sense, streets, parks, schools, businesses, restaurants, and even homes became political spaces in Lawrence, the sites of struggles for an often racialized claim to the city. Latinos in the crisis city forged a persistent and dispersed culture of opposition to racism, manifested in an array of quotidian acts of confrontation, cooperation, and self-expression. The movement toward political empowerment often blurred with celebrations of identity and community formation across ethnic lines. Marginalized and excluded from official sites of political power, Latino Lawrencians carved out alternative spaces from which to advocate for themselves.

Latino efforts to claim the city in this era included the creation of community-based social service organizations, rapid-response condemnation of any expressions of prejudice from the media or city officials, collective and individual protests against Latino exclusion from housing and the city's public spaces, and pan-ethnic organizing to celebrate a diverse but united Latino community in Lawrence. All of these forms of activism had essentially the same goal as the more quotidian contestations over public space: to assert the right of Latinos to build lives in the city and to challenge the efforts of whites to deny them that right. Settling in Lawrence required Latinos to defend themselves against the steady pressure to leave the city; they built lives in Lawrence in spite of the chilly welcome they received, and they collectively challenged white visions of the city that did not include a Latino presence.

The first section of this chapter will outline the broader story of white resistance to Latino settlement in the 1970s and 1980s. While this section will focus sustained attention on white bigotry and prejudice in the city, it is not meant to eclipse the reality that some white people in Lawrence accepted their Latino neighbors with equanimity or even friendship. Nor, of course, is it meant to elide the myriad structural means by which residents of Lawrence's suburbs were able to shield themselves from residential integration. White families in Andover never had to test their own willingness to live next to working-class Latinos or to become a "minority" in their own town. Those were issues with which Andover residents were never compelled to grapple, as the political economy of suburbanization sheltered them from the city's changing demographics.

Given the caveats above, why focus so much attention on white bigotry in Lawrence at all? I believe that the history of white opposition to Latino settlement in the city is necessary because it shows us the stakes of Latino activism. Only by understanding the often fierce and bitter resistance that many white Lawrencians mounted can we truly appreciate the courage and commitment of those Latino residents who insisted that Lawrence was their home. As the quote from Isabel Melendez at the beginning of this chapter illustrates, if early Latino settlers in Lawrence had been "cowards," the city's history would look quite different. Melendez was speaking of her forty years of community organizing and activism with the Greater Lawrence Community Action Council (GLCAC), but she could have been speaking for any of the countless activists and community organizers in the city, any of the families who had been the first Latinos on their block, any of the teenagers who dared to speak Spanish in public in the face of harassment from adults, or any of the young men who tossed a Molotov cocktail into the crowd of furious white faces shouting "Spic!" during the riots. The second half of the chapter will focus on this Latino activism, broadly conceived, because if the early generation of Latinos who settled in the city had been cowards, Lawrence's profound transformations would have been impossible; truly "none of this would exist."[2]

WHITE FIGHT

For a variety of reasons detailed in other chapters, Lawrence's economic decline occurred at the same time as Latino settlement in the city. Yet to many white residents, the correlation between decline and immigration needed no explanation, as they believed it was self-evident that Latinos had *caused* Lawrence's deterioration. As indicated in the quote at the beginning of the chapter, many white Lawrencians believed simply that "the people who come now ruin it all."[3] Although most white people in Lawrence were themselves immigrants or the children of immigrants from an earlier generation—"white ethnics" in the era's terms—they evinced little faith that this new immigration could benefit the city.[4] On the contrary, many believed that a renaissance in Lawrence, a return to "the Lawrence of yesteryear," could only be possible if the tide of Latino immigration was stemmed or, ideally, reversed. As a result of this belief, many white Lawrencians rejected the very presence of their Latino neighbors, greeting them with vocal expressions of prejudice and frequent harassment.

For Latinos, inadequate housing, unstable employment, and substandard health and educational services were frustrating, as was their exclusion from city government. Yet one of the most trying obstacles to feeling at home in the city was the day-to-day experience of this white prejudice and harassment. Although urban disinvestment, or "white flight," created challenges for Latinos in the city, "white *fight*" was also a significant obstacle to settlement in Lawrence, and Latinos had to struggle individually and collectively to hold fast to their right to remain in the city.[5]

The postwar white flight of Lawrencians to the suburbs accelerated in the 1970s and 1980s as Lawrence's Latino population grew and as the city's economy continued to decline. Simply put, most white people with the means to leave did so in this era. There were many whites, however, who could not or would not leave the city. Some lived in South Lawrence, where the bulk of the city's single-family housing stock was concentrated and where the effects of urban crisis had not hit as hard (beyond the school system, which could be circumvented with private schools). Some whites were invested in Lawrence as homeowners, business owners, or politicians and insisted that Lawrence was on the verge of an imminent renaissance. Others, particularly in North Lawrence, simply did not have the resources to leave; many were elderly, early twentieth-century immigrants whose second-generation, upwardly mobile children had moved out to the suburbs without them. Many were poor: low-income working families, single mothers, or other families or individuals with fixed incomes, often from Social Security or welfare.

It was those without the means to easily leave the city who most often shared neighborhoods with newly arriving Puerto Ricans and Dominicans, as discrimination concentrated most Latinos into the poorest parts of the city. Unlike suburban residents, those whites who remained in Lawrence were unable to distance themselves from these demographic changes through zoning restrictions or ostensibly neutral market practices. Working-class white Lawrencians who shared urban space with Latinos had fewer options: They could either befriend, or at least tolerate, the new arrivals (as some did), or they could try to show Latinos that they were unwelcome in order to discourage them from staying. As one resident explained after the riots, "Token liberalism isn't a luxury people in [the housing projects] can afford. They either really believe in brotherhood, or they hate."[6]

This section will focus on these more direct forms of resistance to Latino settlement in the city, "white fight" rather than "white flight," but not because I consider these quotidian acts of white hostility to be more racist; on the contrary, the structural forces described in other chapters created far more effective obstacles to Latino residential and social mobility. These stories of white resistance, however, give a sense of the day-to-day contestations that occurred in Lawrence between white and Latino residents. Daily incidents of bigotry, prejudice, and harassment worked in concert with larger structural exclusion and marginalization to limit the opportunities of Latinos and to give many the impression that they were not welcome in the city. It is hard to overstate the virulent bigotry that Latinos faced in the city in this era. As a local journalist summed it up, "For this is the town where Hispanics have been called 'Spics' on the police log, where racial war is played out regularly on the graffitied walls of public restrooms, and where a former school com-mitteeman once stated publicly that Americans introduced Hispanics to shoes."[7] Official expressions of bigotry combined with insults in public spaces like bathroom walls to create an atmosphere of aggression and unwelcome.

Much of the hostility focused on the right of Latinos to even be in Lawrence, a mindset that misrecognized these imperial migrants as for-eigners, presumably with no right to the city. As one Puerto Rican woman explained, "Hispanics are INVADERS, they think. You can see it on people's faces. It really hurts me. After all, Americans were invaders, too. How can they forget how hard it is?"[8] Given the Immigrant City's long history of new arrivals struggling to overcome exploitation, marginalization, and nativist prejudice, this Puerto Rican resident expected a warmer welcome, a longer memory from the city's white ethnics regarding the hardship of migration and reset-tlement. A forty-year-old white Lawrencian expressed his animosity toward the city's Latinos and his desire that the government could remove them from Lawrence: "I wish to hell they'd send them all back, to be honest with you."[9] Puerto Ricans were particularly outraged by these sentiments, given their U.S. citizenship; as one Puerto Rican pointed out, "It's our country, after all."[10]

Often white animosity centered on language, on many Latinos' need or desire to communicate in Spanish. As one white woman argued about Puerto Ricans, "I think they should try to speak more English. They can, but they pretend they can't. If they figure out they're an American citizen, they should talk our language. Then we could communicate."[11] The argument that all Puerto Ricans could speak English but were pretending they couldn't demonstrates an extreme paranoia, and the phrase "if they figure out they're an American citizen" reflects not only the belief that English is and ought

Struggling for the City

to be the official language of the United States but also the strange idea that Puerto Ricans might be unaware of their somehow secret citizenship, rather than intensely aware of the long colonial subjection of the island by the United States, including the U.S. history of imposing policies designed to force Puerto Ricans to adopt English.[12] Finally, the idea that if Puerto Ricans spoke their hidden English, "then we could communicate," completely rules out white Lawrencians learning Spanish as a means of cross-cultural communication.

Some white residents felt so certain of their right to deny Latinos their language that they resorted to physical remonstrations. One Latino teenage male recalled, "I was at Burger King, one time, and I was speaking Spanish. An old lady behind me in the line says, 'I hate Spanish!' and just then the counter guy hands me my burger and she snatches it away and throws it on the floor." This racialized encounter during the commonplace activity of purchasing fast food demonstrates that virtually all sites were ripe for contestation, ripe for a struggle to determine whether Latinos had the right to truly be at home in Lawrence. Latinos were certainly not passive recipients of this animosity; they firmly asserted their right to defend themselves, although in this case the teenager demonstrated restraint. Another Latino teenager present at the interview replied to the story, "I hope you hit her!" and the young man who had lost his hamburger answered that he had not, "How could I? She was 60 years old." He continued, though, with a warning reminder that he would not, as a rule, stand for such behavior, adding, "Now if she'd a been 20 . . . ."[13]

It seems that young Latinos, like the teenager above, were especially vulnerable to such expressions of white animosity. A collaborative high school report, "Growing Up Hispanic in Lawrence," noted that young Latinos were more likely than adults to feel that "the white people are always looking down on you." Young Latinos explained that they walked through the city expecting the "disapproving (or downright angry) stares that greet them as soon as they open their mouths, whether to speak Spanish or accented English." The authors of the report asked if the young Latinos "ever [got] used to that kind of thing." They all replied at the same time, "No, no, no, we never do."[14] Perhaps teenagers conjured particular fears of crime and disorder in white minds, or perhaps their youth signaled to some whites that they could express their contempt without the potential ramifications of confronting full-grown adults.

In addition to outright hostility, many whites, including those in the media, expressed negative stereotypes about Latinos. In the months before the riots, one interviewer summed up these stereotypes bluntly: "Hispanics are stereotyped as dirty, violent, welfare recipients who are bringing Lawrence down."[15] As brutal as this depiction might seem, it succinctly summarized the common complaints of whites against Latinos in the city. Carlos Ruiz had lived in the city since the 1960s. By the early 1980s he served as the president of the Alliance of Latins for Political Action and Progress, and he worked as the equal opportunity specialist for Western Electric (a major employer of Latinos located in North Andover). He explained that Latinos were often accused of being dirty and that whites even charged that Latinos brought cockroaches to the city, to which he replied confounded, "How can they say that? Do they think we imported them? Cockroaches have been around for millions of years."[16] Latinos were often relegated to the worst housing in the city, housing that was often neglected by its landlords (including the Lawrence Housing Authority) and in disrepair. Clearly, this did not stop white Lawrencians from blaming the victims of this neglect. The stereotype of Latinos as dirty was clearly painful for settlers in Lawrence. As one Dominican woman explained, "When you hear 'They're all filth,' you get hurt."[17]

The stereotype that Latinos were violent was also prevalent and contributed to the view of Lawrence as fraught with particularly "urban" (i.e., nonwhite) dangers. A few months before the riots, an *Eagle-Tribune* reporter interviewed fifty white and Latino Lawrencians about race relations in the city. She concluded, "None of the Anglos interviewed for this story had experienced violence at the hands of a Spanish-speaking person in Lawrence, but most said they were afraid to walk the streets because of Hispanics." She quoted a middle-aged white resident who elaborated on this fear of Lawrence's presumably violent Latinos: "I fear for my mother and father. My father's been robbed before with a knife and they just robbed the battery out of his car after he just got one. He lives in a heavily Hispanic neighborhood." When he was asked if the attackers were Hispanic, however, he replied, "Tell you the truth, I don't remember."[18]

The stereotype of Latinos as violent must have been especially painful to those Latinos who had faced racist violence at the hands of white Lawrencians. The interviewer quoted a Puerto Rican woman: "My other daughter, a deaf mute, was raped by five white boys in back of a garage on Andover Street three years ago. It was 10:30 at night. Three of them watched outside. . . . The police came. When she was found, she was walking the streets, all muddy." The interviewer elaborated, "That 'other daughter' is now 23, a fine-boned woman of delicate beauty who lives on Tower Hill with her husband and newborn son. Communicating in sign through her 10-year-old sister-in-law, the young woman confirms her mother's story and suggests that her attackers may have had a racial motive." The interviewer was quick to point out, however, that such a brutal experience of racialized, sexualized subjugation did not harden the young woman's heart into prejudice, as the man she eventually married was white.[19]

The final aspect of the stereotypes summed up by the interviewer above was that all Latinos were on welfare, presumably without deserving such aid. Some expressions of this stereotype focused on rumors of a sign directing Latinos to Lawrence. Given the city's economic troubles by the early 1980s, white Lawrencians could not imagine a reason for Latino settlement in the city other than to get welfare. As the *Eagle-Tribune* explained, "There is supposed to be this sign somewhere. San Juan, Santo Domingo, southern Florida—no one can place it exactly. But on it, so the rumor goes, are large letters exhorting in Spanish, 'Come to Lawrence for welfare.' You can find hundreds of 'white' Lawrence residents who have heard—or told—the story of the sign. And none who has actually seen it."[20]

In spite of the paranoia evident in the fears of the sign, the belief that all Latino Lawrencians were on welfare was prevalent among whites in the city and would be a huge factor in racialized Lawrence politics after the riots. The condemnation of welfare use was often offered in conjunction with a celebration of earlier European immigrants' work ethic. One white man justified his use of racial slurs based on the ethnic labeling he had endured and his belief that Latinos were lazy: "I call 'em 'Spics,' like when I was a kid they called me 'Guinea' and 'Wop.' . . . My grandparents are from Italy. They worked from the day they got here to the day they died, seven days a week. . . . The Hispanics don't do that, absolutely not." A retired white woman argued, "The immigrants coming over now—the government has made it too easy for them. If they can't get a job, they're taken care of with food stamps and welfare. The first immigrants, if they didn't have a job, had to scrub floors or whatever to support their families."[21]

At least the woman quoted above gave Latinos the benefit of the doubt— that they were on welfare because they "can't get a job." Others decried Latinos for a presumed *refusal* to work. A white man explained: "I know everybody's got their beautiful car. If you go shopping and buy food, I never saw the Puerto Rican pay with money. He's got the food stamps. That means most everybody's on welfare. . . . Most of them don't want to work." That this man was speaking in stereotypes is evident from his use of the singular "the Puerto Rican," although he deduced from his narrow experience that "most" Puerto Ricans were on welfare. Like the woman who suspected that Puerto Ricans were hiding their English skills, this man implied that poor

Puerto Ricans actually had a hidden source of funds, as "everybody's got their beautiful car."[22]

The dishonesty and lack of a work ethic that some white Lawrencians attributed to Latinos, particularly Puerto Ricans, was reminiscent of the "culture of poverty" discourse that blamed African Americans and Puerto Ricans for their own hardships, based on allegedly cultural traits that supposedly prevented them from being able to lift themselves out of poverty. Although today common stereotypes of Latinos emphasize their *labor*, either by celebrating hardworking immigrants or by condemning "illegals" who "take our jobs," stereotypes about poor and working-class Puerto Ricans (and later Dominicans) in U.S. cities during the urban crisis era were quite different, instead emphasizing Latino joblessness, welfare reliance, and poverty. From the 1960s through the early 1990s, these Latinos were often lumped together with African Americans in media discourses on "inner-city" deviance, blamed for crime, gang violence, drug sales, and welfare fraud. While this shared stigma was partially related to the fact that many Caribbean immigrants were of African descent to some degree, and thus were often considered Black in a U.S. racial context, the same stereotypes were often attached to inner-city Chicano communities in this period as well. During the crisis era, urban Latinos faced stigmas similar to those of African Americans not simply because of shared Blackness (although that certainly played a role) but also because, like African Americans, they had largely been segregated in neighborhoods from which jobs and capital had fled.[23]

This attention to Latino morality—or the purported lack thereof—in white expressions of prejudice was nearly ubiquitous. Some of the very strategies Latinos employed to overcome Lawrence's hostile environment were used against them as signs of their presumed lack of values. As a young Dominican woman explained, "We tend to put more people in a household than Anglos do. We have many relatives and many friends who, when they're in need, we provide them with a place to stay." Opening their homes to kin in need was not only an act of extreme generosity but also a community survival strategy in the face of a housing crisis in the city that was especially acute for Latinos. Many white Lawrencians, however, did not see it this way. As a white man explained, "I really don't think they have any morals as far as having two or three families, mother and father situations, under one roof. I would almost maybe refer to it as a Kentucky or a mountain situation, but those people seem to have more on the ball than the Puerto Rican people do—I've heard of kissing cousins, but these people carry it too far."[24] This condemnation of extended family sharing a home is one more example of how Latino

Lawrencians were blamed for the very obstacles they had to overcome in the city.[25]

In the larger context of white hostility, ostensibly neutral issues could become sources of bitterly racialized tension. One Dominican Lawrencian who lived in the Lower Tower Hill neighborhood where the 1984 riots would take place recalled the tension leading up to the explosion. She described frequent arguments in the neighborhood, as white and Latino residents yelled and cursed at each other about seemingly superficial things that had become racialized only in the context of the larger changes in the city, such as "'why are you parking here?' or things like that. Or 'pick up your garbage.'" White and Latino Lawrencians even fought over whose music would fill the neighborhood's air: "Something that really was big [was] the music, it was everywhere and it was just opposite each other."[26] In 1984, one presumably white resident summed up how racial tension was reflected in cultural terms in his assertion that Lawrence needed "more Van Halen and less Michael Jackson," essentially more white rock and less Black pop.[27] That this cultural battle involved Michael Jackson, rather than a more typically "Latino" artist, should not be surprising, as many of the city's Puerto Ricans and Dominicans had come to Lawrence from New York City and would likely have been steeped in the vibrant fusions of Black/Puerto Rican culture that emerged from New York in this era, evident in mambo, boogaloo, hip-hop, and free-style. Indeed, for many Latino youth in Lawrence in the 1980s, breakdancing was another popular way to claim the streets.[28]

Even where hostility was absent, true compassion and empathy were not necessarily forthcoming. "Growing Up Hispanic in Lawrence" explained that "several Hispanics told us that 'Americans' were superficially friendly, but too busy with their material concerns ever to be close 'in the way we're used to. . . . So few Anglos understand our culture—or care about it.'" This lack of will-ingness to learn about Latino cultures was evident in the tendency for many white Lawrencians to lump all Latinos together as "the Puertoricans," which the report argued was particularly galling to Dominicans.[29]

Of course, many Latinos were simply shocked at how radically divorced these stereotypes were from reality. Isabel Melendez recalled hearing the frequent complaints that Puerto Ricans were dirty and refused to care for their homes, which led to the city's blight. She described the accusations that Puerto Ricans "were very dirty, that they were garbage eaters." She flat-out rejected any possibility that the inadequate living conditions Latinos endured in Lawrence were related in some way to Puerto Rican cultural traits. She described cleaning rituals on the island: "If you've seen Puerto

Rico . . . I remember, even if they didn't have a broom, I remember cutting out *las ramas de los árboles para hacer escobas y barrer, y los sábados . . .* with the hose, *tirando agua a las casas, limpiando* [the branches from the trees to make brooms and sweep, and Saturdays . . . with the hose, spraying water at the house, cleaning]." Melendez countered these accusations of Puerto Ricans' putatively cultural disregard for cleanliness with an account of how hard Puerto Ricans on the island worked, in spite of poverty, to maintain clean homes.[30]

Occasionally even city officials publicly expressed these stereotypes or exposed their prejudices. Biased remarks from the "city fathers" took place in the context of the near-complete exclusion of Latinos from city government and municipal jobs such as firefighters and police officers. The publicly expressed bigotry of city officials spurred the Latino community into action with incredible force because it exposed the bias that was often hidden in the post–Civil Rights era; it demonstrated that the very people who were supposed to be working to ensure equal protection of all city residents were not committed to that equality. When a member of the school committee, for example, heckled a group of Latino parents, making fun of their accents and insisting they came to the United States poor and homeless, Latinos responded in force.[31] As International Institute director Kathy Rodger explained, "I saw the Hispanic community come together just once, for one reason—when they were out to get Callahan (Edward J. Callahan, Lawrence school committeeman, known for negative remarks about the Hispanic community). They were just about kissing each other. It would kill him to know that he was the one to unify the Hispanics." Although such depictions of divisions among the Latino community were often overblown, it is not surprising that official proclamations of racism from city leaders would have a galvanizing and unifying effect.[32]

In the face of white hostility, young Latinos sometimes felt compelled to defend themselves with violence. Shortly after the release of the movie *The Warriors* (1979), a fictional account of street gangs in New York City, the *Eagle-Tribune* ran a profile of white and Latino youth gangs in the city. Reporters concluded from their interviews that there was no such "gang warfare" in Lawrence but that white and Latino youth did join gangs in the city for "security and friendship." As the Dominican leader of the Getaway Brothers, a mostly Puerto Rican gang, explained, "When the cars pass by and the Americans say 'Hey Spics' I always step in front. If they wanna be friends with us, we say 'Hey, that's all right.'" But then he added, "I fight if I have to fight." Of course, white people calling "Hey Spics" out their car

Struggling for the City

Lawrence teenager standing in front of "Latin Place, No Honkeys" graffiti on the wall of the Essex Street projects, 1979. Photo by Rose Lewis. Reprinted with permission from the *Eagle-Tribune.*

windows were probably not interested in interracial friendship, and the article euphemistically acknowledged that gang fighting in the city reflected "racial tensions." The Latino youth interviewed explained that these tensions "were provoked by 'Americans' who drove by and threw eggs and called them 'Spics.'" Reflecting the broader pan-ethnic Latino alliances in the city, the profile noted that "it is almost an unwritten law in Lawrence that Hispanic gangs do not fight among themselves." As a Puerto Rican ex–gang member explained, "We're Spanish. We ain't gonna have fighting between our own people."[33] Gang membership in this era was at least partially about finding security and claiming space in a racialized landscape. A photograph of one of the Getaway Brothers included graffiti on the brick wall of the Essex Street housing projects that captured these competing claims on public space well; it read, "LATIN PLACE, NO HONKEYS."[34]

DENIED SERVICE IN LAWRENCE

Civil Rights activists in the postwar era had worked hard to desegregate public accommodations, to ensure that no one could be denied service at a store or restaurant on account of race.[35] The goal of completely unfettered access to white-owned businesses remained elusive, however, and not only in the U.S. South. In Lawrence, Latinos protested for equal service in local business establishments. One resident, Eric Spindler, recalled a story told to him by his uncle, who had migrated from the Dominican Republic as a child. As a teenager in the 1970s, his uncle, Louis, had gone to a corner store in Prospect Hill, an overwhelmingly white neighborhood at the time, with his younger sister, Miriam. Spindler recounted, "They go to a store to get some ice cream, and Miriam comes out and she's crying and Louis says, 'What's up?' and Miriam says, 'They won't serve me, he says he won't serve spics,' and Louis comes in and says, 'I just told her the same thing I'm gonna tell you: I don't serve spics,' and something happens where Louis hits him." Whatever assumptions the storeowner might have made regarding his power to exclude and insult the two young Dominicans, Louis's response demonstrated his unwillingness to be a passive victim of such exclusion and harassment, although he was indeed arrested for hitting the storeowner. Spindler felt that this story, "fighting to get ice cream in Lawrence, Massachusetts," summed up well the struggles of many Latinos in the city: White Lawrencians were not held accountable for their discrimination, and Latinos had to literally fight for basic rights.[36]

Although other such incidents of Latinos being refused service in restaurants and shops likely went unreported, one Lawrence merchant garnered media attention for denying service to Puerto Ricans when he posted a sign in the window of his sandwich shop. In August 1971, the cover of the *Eagle-Tribune* carried a photo of the sign reading, "This store closed to all Purto Rican [sic] in this building and all their bum friends." Store manager Joseph Green elaborated to the newspaper, arguing that he was not trying to exclude all Puerto Ricans: "If they can talk English and we know what they want, they can come in." He was not unaware of the risks involved in refusing service to such a large group, noting that he could lose his license, but he was convinced that he would have the support of the local government: "A lot of people will back me up at City Hall." He explained his feelings against Puerto Ricans: "I'm not against their rights, there's just too many of them on welfare." He complained of noise late at night, banging on the doors after the store was closed, and Puerto Ricans who, he believed, drove cars without a license and who sold "dope."[37]

Although the sign was taken down shortly after its photo ran in the paper, it sparked a dramatic protest. The *Eagle-Tribune* reported that over a hundred "Spanish-Americans" had gathered in front of the store in protest that night before moving the demonstration to the city's Common. The next day's paper showed a photo of jubilant Latino youth, two of whom held up peace signs and one with a raised fist, above the caption "Spanish-speaking Lawrencians demonstrate against discrimination." The protest continued the next day, until Green came out and apologized for his comments, saying that he would sell the shop.[38] While Lawrence today draws Latino consumers from throughout the region, this transition was not inevitable; rather, it was the result of Latino Lawrencians insisting (individually and collectively) on their right to the city, on their entitlement to equal access to Lawrence's public spaces and services.

Struggling for the City

In the minds of many Latinos, the structural problems they faced as a result of Lawrence's economic decline merged with the prejudice they encountered to form their overall perception of the city as a difficult place to live. A 1970 *Eagle-Tribune* profile of a young Puerto Rican girl, Juanita, and her family sums up many of the challenges that Latinos faced in the city in the early decades of Latino settlement. These challenges included prejudice and harassment, of course, but it is clear from the family's explanations that it was the combined impact of hostility and economic marginalization that was responsible for the family's disappointment.

According to the profile, "Juanita was five years old and playing with a rubber ball on a Newbury Street sidewalk the first time she heard the word 'spic.'" Her family had migrated from Puerto Rico to Lawrence only a few months earlier, but already they were having second thoughts. The prejudice their children suffered combined with other troubles the family was having "caused Juanita's father and mother, who consider themselves typical of the Puerto Rican parents in the city, to wonder how wise a move it had been to leave Puerto Rico." This was during the labor phase of Latino migration to the city, and the article was careful to be clear that Juanita's parents had jobs; but the types of jobs available for Latinos in Lawrence did not necessarily give them access to the "better life" that had spurred migration. "They have found jobs, but now, with cutbacks in the textile and shoe industries, wages are down and security has gone out the window." The *Eagle-Tribune* discussed their issues with housing as well: "They have rented apartments (despite landlords who know ways to avoid renting to Puerto Ricans), but the apartments have never been much more than shelters and rents are currently soaring." As argued in the last chapter, "cheap rent," often cited as the reason for Latino settlement in Lawrence, is an inadequate explanation, given persistent lack of affordable housing (relative to wages) available in the city.[39]

The prejudice faced by their children and the low wages and job insecurity in the declining manufacturing sector of the city, as well as the difficulty finding landlords who would rent to Puerto Ricans and the inadequacy of the apartments and the high rents, all combined to make Juanita's parents question if they were better off in Puerto Rico. Juanita's father had learned his English as a draftee in the U.S. army, and at the time of the interview he was making an average of $80 a week in a shoe factory, where his hours were often cut to four per day. This U.S. veteran explained, "There is a lot that makes us believe we haven't found a home in Lawrence. . . . Too many people show us no respect. . . . They act like we are all bums and thieves and selling narcotics and that we all live like pigs and the only reason we come to America is to get welfare money." This imperial migrant was experiencing the brunt of the manufacturing industry's decline, and he was deeply disenchanted by the disrespect Latinos faced in the city as a result of the stereotype that Puerto Ricans were dirty, violent criminals who abused welfare. His wife elaborated: "Puerto Rican people, even our children aren't trusted here. . . . It makes you sad when they don't give your children a chance."[40]

For Juanita's family, economic disappointments merged with their experiences of white prejudice to make them question their decision to come to Lawrence. They had not "found a home" in Lawrence or the "better life" that drove Puerto Rican migration. The day-to-day hostility from white Lawrencians was not encountered in isolation but in conjunction with the structural inequalities that made settling in Lawrence difficult. The hopes that had brought this Puerto Rican family to the city were dashed by the reality of racism and urban crisis.

THE LIFE AND ACTIVISM OF ISABEL MELENDEZ

Latinos organized in countless ways in Lawrence: demonstrating against discrimination; registering Latino voters; advocating for bilingual education and affordable housing; creating social clubs, cultural celebrations, and store-front churches to serve the community's social and spiritual needs; forging a Latino-oriented service sector to provide a safety net for the community's survival—the list could go on for pages. Although a comprehensive account of these organizations, programs, and campaigns would be impressive, it would also be simply exhausting to read. Instead, I would like to tell the story of Latino organizing in Lawrence in this early era through the life story of Isabel Melendez, undoubtedly the city's most prominent Latina/o activist during this time. My focus in this section on a single individual should not be taken as support for a "great leader" model of social movements, in which successful social change is attributed to one person's wisdom and charisma.[41] On the contrary, the fight for Latino empowerment in Lawrence was truly grassroots, as the wealth of examples throughout this book should illustrate. In fact, Melendez's strength ultimately lay in her ability to draw people together at key moments via networks that she spent her entire lifetime feeding and nourishing through community service. Yet in virtually every major action and campaign for Latino equality in Lawrence that I uncovered, I found Isabel Melendez somewhere near the center of it. As such, her fascinating life story and her decades of activism provide an inspiring and effective lens through which to view the history of Latino activism in the city.

Isabel Melendez moved to Lawrence from Juana Díaz, Puerto Rico, in 1959, when she was twenty-two years old. Like Juanita, profiled above, her migration story was initially one of extreme disappointment, an American Dream cut short by the gritty urban reality of life in Lawrence. The hardship she suffered in Lawrence decidedly shaped her later activism, so it is worth exploring in depth. Melendez had gone to university in Puerto Rico and had been working as a teacher before coming to the United States. She described her disappointment as she realized that her education back in the U.S. territory would not be applicable stateside: "When I first came, I started looking for a job. . . . I went to the employment office, I remember. I says, in my broken English—back then, remember, there was no bilingual, there was nothing bilingual, ok?—and I says, I'm *maestra, yo soy maestra*. I teach in Puerto Rico." The employment office responded by sending her over to nearby Merrimack College. Melendez was thrilled, because she assumed they were sending her there to study, to prepare to be a teacher in the United States. But that was not the case. "When I went there, I brought my transcript. When they read it . . . the first words that they said, and this stays in my mind, 'That's no good!' . . . That broke my heart!"[42] Like many Latino arrivals in Lawrence, Melendez found that her existing professional qualifications were not recognized, and the career she had practiced in Puerto Rico (and for which she had been educated) was not available to her.

Melendez's dream of continuing her work as a teacher came to a quick end. Before this major disappointment, she had had high hopes for living in the United States. Her education in Puerto Rico had persuaded her that opportunities on the mainland abounded. "Reading the American history, I always thought that in the United States you get everything, everything." Her disillusionment exacerbated her homesickness as she resigned herself to looking for a job in the city's manufacturing sector: "Every day, I was crying, I want to go back to Puerto Rico." Like many Lawrence Latinas, Melendez got a job working for Lawrence Maid, with a starting pay of $1.00 an hour. She remembered that she only lasted there one week before she got ill. The smell of the shoe factory overwhelmed her, and communication issues made work very difficult. The limited English she had learned in Puerto Rico was not useful, and it was hard to spend all day without talking to anyone. "Today I says to people, if you go to the Lawrence Maid, where I worked, maybe my tears they're still on the floor because I used to cry all day."[43]

After staying with her cousin for two months, she and her husband found their own apartment on Union Street. She remembered that it was not difficult to find an apartment in those days, but the quality of apartments in the fading mill town left much to be desired. Melendez's first apartment had no bathtub, just two big sinks for dishes and clothes. She had to go out and buy a big plastic tub to bathe in. She recalled her shock at the miserable living conditions in Lawrence: "I come from a poor family . . . but we have a bathtub!" She remembered asking herself in disbelief, "Nobody here takes a bath?" This absence of a bathtub was not rare, however; as late as 1970 the census reported that 6 percent of housing units in Lawrence lacked full plumbing facilities, and Latinos were disproportionately likely to live in the city's worst housing.[44] Although her life in the city eventually improved, she remembers the move to Lawrence as a terrible disappointment and disruption in her life. "Believe me, I suffered when I came, I did suffer. . . . I was expecting so many things . . . that didn't happen to me."[45]

Melendez's efforts to make a home for herself involved reconstituting the sense of community that she had left behind in coming to Lawrence. She and her husband formed the first Latino social club in the city (for former residents of Juana Díaz, Puerto Rico), opening the Club de Juanadinos Ausentes on Garden Street in 1964. Together they ran the social club for fourteen years, eventually moving to Common Street after a fire in the first location.[46] The club provided a place for community gatherings and celebrations. Melendez made the space freely available for people to celebrate major family events, like baptisms, or holidays, like Mother's Day. Over the next few decades, Latinos formed countless social clubs in the city, such as the Dominican club Los Trinitarios. These social clubs filled important roles as centers for celebration, community formation, and political organizing.

Melendez was also involved in establishing, in 1964, an adult baseball league for the city's early Latino residents. Participants kicked off the league with a parade through the city streets, and Isabel Melendez described the furious reaction the parade encountered: "When I opened the first one, [the league for] adults, that was crazy! . . . Because we did a parade in the city. Oh my god! And the people . . . decían: Mira ese parece uno del zoológico. Oh my god! We receive many insults [the people were saying: Look at that; it looks like a zoo]."[47] Latino community building took place in the face of cruel dehumanization and bitter resistance to their public presence in the city.

In 1970, Melendez opened a clothing store, Casa Melendez, on Newbury Street in Lawrence. To obtain merchandise for her store, she would regularly travel down to Orchard Street in New York City, leaving Lawrence at four o'clock in the morning and returning near midnight with her car full of things to sell at the store. As a business venture, the store was a disaster; Melendez never made a profit and soon shut the store down. But her calling was to community service, not retail, and the very things that made Casa Melendez ineffective as a business made it profoundly important for the community, as Melendez turned it into a hub for settlement aid. After having faced such hardship adjusting to life in Lawrence, Melendez committed herself to easing the transition for subsequent arrivals. As she later stated, "I dedicated my life to the newcomers."[48] People regularly came to Casa Melendez for help finding an apartment or a job, and she would close the store for hours at a time to bring them to suitable contacts around the city. New migrants from Puerto Rico and the Dominican Republic often arrived without adequate winter clothes, and Melendez freely gave away coats and sweaters from the store to those in need. "It became the store for the community and the place where people would go and ask . . . where is a job, where is an apartment? I used to close the store and tak[e] people out looking for jobs, and that's how I learn services and the agencies." Melendez eventually formalized her role as community aide and advocate through four decades of work at GLCAC, but her earlier community service via Casa Melendez illustrates the tremendous informal support networks that made Latino settlement in Lawrence possible.[49]

It is impossible to overestimate the importance of the formal and informal settlement aid provided for (and usually by) Latinos in Lawrence. Arriving in a strange city where you don't speak the language and where the institutions and habits of the people are largely foreign; finding a home, a job, and adequate clothes for the New England winter; enrolling your children in school; obtaining food that you know how to cook; navigating the bureaucracy of leases, bank accounts, medical insurance, and perhaps immigration law—these are all formidable tasks! And what if there is an emergency? What if a child falls severely ill and needs to be hospitalized? What if a breadwinner has an accident at work that leaves him or her disabled? What if your home is broken into or burns down, or you are evicted? These would be major upheavals even for locally born, English-speaking citizens with ample resources; imagine how much more devastating they would be for recently arrived migrants, particularly those who may have exhausted their resources just to arrive in Lawrence.

Even the most independent and entrepreneurial migrant cannot settle in a new place without guidance, information, and support. Most often this support is provided informally through kinship networks. Family and friends who have already settled in the new place provide information and resources for their newly arrived kin, including a place to stay, help finding a job, warm clothes, perhaps interpreting services, and most certainly ample information and advice. This was absolutely true in Lawrence. Kinship networks were especially important for Dominicans because of family-preference visa requirements, but even Puerto Ricans needed the support that friends and family provided as they navigated the challenges of settling in the city. Catholic priest John J. Lamond created a Spanish center in his church in 1965 that offered English classes and children's programs and also helped with court interpretation. He remembered, however, that the Spanish center rarely had to help Latinos find apartments in this era, because "most of the time they would do it through friends of their own." Informal settlement aid functioned well in the 1960s, as "the people who had been here for quite some time kind of took care of the newcomers."[50]

There will inevitably be times, however, when this informal settlement aid is insufficient, and two conditions can potentially render more formal settlement services indispensable: (1) During times of rapid, heavy immigration, the sheer number of new arrivals can strain informal support networks, and (2) in communities where even established kin themselves are mostly working class or poor, informal networks may simply not have sufficient resources to support newer arrivals, particularly in times of crisis. Both of these conditions existed in Lawrence, especially during the 1970s and 1980s: Immigration to the city was heavy, and kin often lacked the resources to comfortably provide support to new arrivals, as most work was poorly paid and unstable. In response, Latino community leaders such as Melendez worked both to formalize newcomer settlement aid and to provide a safety net for all the city's Latinos, whether immigrant or not. This led to the creation of a new bilingual and bicultural social service infrastructure in the city, as well as pressure on the city and state to better tailor their services to the city's growing Latino population.

The long history of earlier waves of immigration to Lawrence seems to have played a role in ensuring an existing infrastructure for settlement aid. In addition to Casa Melendez and the Spanish center started by Father Lamond, Lawrence's International Institute offered support for new immigrants to the city as well. The International Institute was a network of immigrant social service organizations established in the early twentieth century in fifty-five industrial cities. Started by the YWCA in New York City in 1910, the International Institute movement celebrated cultural pluralism and ethnic diversity during an era when many immigration-related services stressed assimilation and "Americanization."[51] The Lawrence branch was founded in 1913 and is still functioning today; its service to the city's immigrant population bridged the city's industrial (largely European) and postindustrial (largely Latino) immigration eras.[52]

The most prominent organization for Latino settlement aid and advocacy, however, was GLCAC. GLCAC was one of countless local organizations across the country formed out of President Lyndon Johnson's War on Poverty program in the 1960s, through which the federal government provided funds for local, community-based organizations to provide services for poor communities. The program was unique in that it advocated the "maximum feasible participation" of the poor in designing and implementing services, and as a result many of these organizations became important sites of empowerment and advocacy in poor communities.[53] GLCAC was formed in 1965 in Lawrence, although the small Latino population in the city at the time was not its main focus. GLCAC did, however, create a Spanish coordinator position, a Latino or Latina staff member who was responsible for coordinating services for the Latino community.

Isabel Melendez gained the position of Spanish coordinator at GLCAC in 1973 after applying and being rejected each year since 1967. (Before her, only men had been hired for the position, because, as she explained it, "back then, remember, they didn't believe in women.") She recalled that she was particularly eager to get the job because she had been unofficially providing settlement and other services for the Latino community for years, and spending time on those activities had, as mentioned above, been ruining her retail business.[54] As Spanish coordinator for GLCAC, she did not have to take time away from her work to give to the community; helping the Latino community in Lawrence *became* her job, and she worked at GLCAC until her retirement in 2010. Under her stewardship, the Spanish program at GLCAC "became the emergency room for the Latino community."[55]

Puerto Ricans like Melendez may have appreciated the advocacy and services that GLCAC provided, but as citizens they did not need assistance specifically related to immigration. Many other arrivals to the city certainly did, however, and as the "emergency room" for Latinos in Lawrence, the Spanish program ended up providing a range of immigration-related services. Melendez recalled that at first she had neither the skills nor the knowledge to provide such services, but the overwhelming need of Dominicans in her community for help with their own cases, and for help reuniting with their families still on the island, pressed her to learn very quickly.[56] GLCAC provided this immigration support as a form of community service, and Melendez emphasized that "*la primera gente que llegó aquí, nunca pagaba dinero, nunca, en ningún momento pagó un centavo* [the first people who arrived here never paid money, never, not once did they pay a cent]."[57]

The work of GLCAC in providing immigration aid is significant because it highlights the role played by Puerto Ricans in creating a social service infrastructure that could facilitate further Latino settlement in the city, including non–Puerto Ricans, as would become increasingly evident after the 1984 riots. As U.S. citizens, Puerto Ricans, of course, had no immediate concern with the vagaries and heartbreak of U.S. immigration policy; nor was providing immigration support crucial to building a strong, stable Puerto Rican community in the city. Melendez highlighted that, as a Puerto Rican, she had never had personal experience with immigration: "*¿Qué sabía yo de inmigración si venía de Puerto Rico* [What did I know about immigration, if I came from Puerto Rico]?" Yet she devoted herself to learning the system, and GLCAC quickly became able to help immigrants and their families with all phases of the process: "*Y yo aprendí, aprendí a hacer las cosas, yo le hacía todos los trabajos de inmigración, desde la petición hasta el final* [I learned how to do things, and I did all the work of immigration, from the petition to the end]." Melendez recalled making frequent phone calls and even trips to Boston to support petitioners. She traveled to the Dominican Republic five times to learn more about the immigration process and to build connections there, even meeting with President Antonio Guzmán.[58] As citizens (and often as an earlier wave of Latino settlers, given that large-scale Puerto Rican migration to the United States began a full generation before large-scale Dominican migration), Puerto Ricans were in a relatively privileged position to build a community service infrastructure and indeed to mediate between the U.S. government and Latino communities.

In the 1960s and 1970s, lack of adequate interpreting services in the city caused many Latino Lawrencians great difficulty, particularly when interacting with the government, schools, and doctors. Community activists consistently reiterated the need for Spanish-speaking police officers, and court interpretation was inadequate or absent. In 1970, weak legal services even resulted in a defendant relying on his own accuser to translate for him! It is no surprise that the man was convicted.[59] In that same year, a U.S. court finally ruled that the criminally accused have a right to a court-provided interpreter (in the case of *United States ex rel. Negron v. State of New York*).[60] Engaging with children's teachers and principals often required interpreters as well, or else children were left to mediate between schools and their parents. In 1970, Oscar Rodriguez, president of the Puerto Rican Civic Association, alleged that approximately 300 of the city's school-aged Latino children did not attend school. He argued that the reason for this was that Spanish-speaking parents did not know how to register their children and the city had done nothing to reach out to them or to make the process accessible.[61]

Several years later, organizers undertook a petition campaign to get the Lawrence public schools to provide bilingual education. Melendez remembered that she and Father Hervio Caravallo from the Holy Rosary Church went door to door gathering signatures. She recalled, "I was very involved getting *padres* and people, *tú sabes, buscando a la gente, yo revoluciono a la gente, ¿tú sabes? Yo busco a la gente, sé buscar a la gente y traer la gente y buscando el apoyo y necesitamos esto y vieron la necesidad ¿tú entiendes? Eso me pasó con el programa bilingüe* [I was very involved getting parents and people, you know, finding people, stirring people up, you know? I find people, I know how to find people and bring people together, and find support, and make clear 'we need this' and they would see the necessity. That's what happened with the bilingual program]."[62] Ultimately, these parents that Melendez helped to stir up formed the Bilingual Parents Advisory Council, an organization that would play a major role in the city, not only in demanding students' access to bilingual education but also in advocating for Latino equality more broadly.

Communicating with schools, police, and courts was clearly imperative. Yet what many Latinos were most concerned about was their inability to communicate clearly with their doctors and nurses. In a survey taken in the late 1960s, Latino families strongly emphasized the dangerous lack of Spanish-speaking doctors as a major problem in their neighborhoods.[63] The lack of a bilingual social service infrastructure obstructed Latinos' access to health care. GLCAC made access to adequate health care a central priority and helped found the Greater Lawrence Family Health Center in 1980. The creation of the health center was a response to the changing metropolitan political economy and racial demographics of these years. By the 1970s, many of Lawrence's primary-care doctors had left for the suburbs, leaving many city residents without access to suitable primary care, a situation exacerbated by widespread poverty and language barriers. Emergency rooms became overburdened with residents who lacked access to primary care, and the hospitals began to work with GLCAC to create the health center. The Greater Lawrence Family Health Center now runs six primary-care clinics and serves over 56,000 patients.[64]

Lawrence today is thoroughly bilingual; signs, information, voting materials, and letters home from school are consistently written in both Spanish and English. Bilingual employees are the norm in virtually all of the city's businesses and offices. But this bilingualism evolved gradually in the city, and Latinos had to specifically organize to have interpreting services, bilingual signage, and bilingual/bicultural services. Melendez recalled an especially memorable incident in the 1960s when a Puerto Rican farmworker had an accident that left him hospitalized. Witnessing his desperate desire to communicate with the medical staff motivated her to organize for better interpreting services in the city. "I remember one time I was in the emergency room, back then there was no interpreters, ok? And this guy had an accident and he was yelling. I was outside and I could hear him, '*Busquen en mi cartera, busquen en mi cartera que allí está el teléfono de mi hija* [Look in my wallet, look in my wallet. My daughter's telephone number is there].' Nobody, nobody. I remember the situation, oh my god! . . . I fought for that, to bring interpreters to the emergency room."[65] Today Massachusetts law requires emergency rooms to have trained interpreters available for patients at all times.[66] Each bilingual sign and service in the city, however, is a reminder of the persistent organizing and activism required to make such bilingualism the norm in Lawrence.

The most visible way that Latinos claimed public space in Lawrence in this era, however, was the creation of a pan-ethnic Latino cultural celebration in the city, Semana Hispana, or Hispanic Week. Organizers, including Melendez, began the festival in 1979 as a way to bring different Latino groups together to celebrate what they had in common and to explore what made each unique. The festival was, from the beginning, also about empowering the Latino community politically; it was a way to claim space in the center of the city and clearly announce their public presence. In addition, it was also intended as a way to register Latino voters who, in the words of one organizer, "were intimidated to go to city hall to register to vote."[67] Organizers carved out an alternative space to empower Latinos politically. Over the years, the annual festival grew into the largest event in the city, drawing tens of thousands of people from throughout the Northeast into the heart of Lawrence.[68]

Melendez remembered the desire to create a pan-ethnic Latino celebration as at the root of the creation of Semana Hispana. She recalled, "*Cuando yo llegaba aquí, yo iba a Boston por el* Puerto Rican festival [When I arrived here, I went to Boston for the Puerto Rican festival]. *Pero*, one year I was with two girls: a Guatemalan and a Cuban. . . . Those people that were on the stage [were] saying '*Viva Puerto Rico*.' I'm Puerto Rican and I didn't want to raise my hand either, because I have a girl on my side who is not Puerto Rican and they're going to feel bad [if I'm] raising my hand and they could not."[69] Residing and organizing in a city that was home to immigrants from throughout Latin America and accompanied to this celebration of Puerto Rican people and culture by two non–Puerto Rican Latinas, Melendez was conscious of wanting to establish an event that could celebrate the diversity of Latin American cultures.

This pan-ethnic focus was partly about shared friendships and commonalities but also partly a response to the racism Latinos encountered in the city. Even if many Latino Lawrencians would have preferred to maintain an identity based on their home country, the daily prejudice they experienced reminded them of their shared position in the city's racial hierarchy. To many white Lawrencians, Latinos were all "Spics" at worst, all "Spanish" at best. Many community organizers thus chose to embrace a pan-ethnic Hispanic or Latino identity as a way of building a coalition to organize against bigotry and exclusion in the city. Although there was certainly a good deal of tension between different nationalities, many political organizations in this era, such as the Alliance of Latins for Political Action and Progress, consciously adopted a pan-ethnic Latino framework.[70]

Semana Hispana, in particular, emphasized shared *latinidad* as a means to build community and claim a space for Latinos in the city. Many organizers were eager to showcase the commonalities among Latinos, as their political marginalization was often attributed to lack of unity. This emphasis was reflected in the festival's slogan, "*Juntos en Armonía*," or "Together in Harmony." Community leaders argued that Latinos of all nationalities had an intrinsic affinity, based on a common language and many shared values and similar traditions. Yet the challenge was to express and celebrate a pan-ethnic identity that didn't collapse differences between groups, that allowed Latino Lawrencians to embrace a Latino identity *through* their national identities, not *in place of* them.[71]

Semana Hispana was an effort to showcase the diversity of Latin American cultures, for Latinos from different countries both to share their traditions with each other and to educate white Lawrencians. Melendez explained: "When you go to Guatemala, even though we talk in, you know, Spanish, *pero cuando tú ves la cultura y la artesanía de ellos es muy diferente a la de Puerto Rico. Cuando tú vas a la República Dominicana . . . ya tú ves otra cosa, cuando vas a Argentina, Ecuador, entonces tú entiendes . . . el plan que tuvimos era traerlos todos* [but when you see the culture and the artisanship in Guatemala, it is very different than that of Puerto Rico. When you go to the Dominican Republic, you see something else; when you go to Argentina, Ecuador, you understand. . . . The plan was to bring it all]." For the first Semana Hispana, Melendez recalled Puerto Ricans constructing a *bohío*, a type of straw hut adapted from the indigenous Taíno. She explained: "*Había mucha cultura que tú veías ahí y en el escenario era cultura, era el mejor baile que había en la República Dominicana, aquí era lo mejor de Argentina, algo típico que era de allá* [There was so much culture that you would see there and on the stage was culture, was the best dancing they had in the Dominican Republic, there was the best of Argentina, something traditional from there]." Semana Hispana was a means of showcasing the best (at least according to festival organizers) of Latin American cultures and traditions, and thereby celebrating the talents and contributions of Latinos. In the process, the festival helped to envision a pan-ethnic Latino identity that respected national differences.[72]

Yet this seemingly innocuous cultural celebration had to fight for its very existence. At first, the city government attempted to deny the organizers a permit to use the Common to hold the festival. Julia Silverio (who became a well-known Lawrence politician and business owner) recalled, "You see, these were the times when there was a lot of racism and antagonism against us in the city. We had to fight the city to be able to get a permit to use the park. Some authorities claimed that we were going to use the park to get drunk and other bad things." In the years that followed, Semana Hispana frequently struggled with the city for the continued right to hold the festival in the Common and to shape the event the way they envisioned it. One of the most substantial controversies in the years leading up to the riots was over whether or not the festival could serve as a voter registration site as well. Officials' reluctance to allow organizers to use the city's public space to celebrate Latino cultures and controversy over including voter registration as part of the festivities demonstrate the clear political element inherent in this collective celebration.[73]

LAWRENCE CANNOT AFFORD TO BE A CITY
OF THE POOR AND THE ELDERLY

None of the above accounts of white resistance is meant to obscure the fact that some white Lawrencians accepted their new Latino neighbors with neutrality or occasionally even enthusiasm. Evidence of cross-racial friend-ships, work relationships, and even marriages abounded, even during the thick of the riot era. Although such positive interactions were nowhere near as prominent as examples of tension or bigotry, this is perhaps because they were deemed less newsworthy than negative interactions. If so, we should not repeat the media's mistake in obscuring the very real presence of neighborli-ness, solidarity, friendship, and kinship between some whites and Latinos in the city. Further, Latino community organizers were not without white allies. Particularly in religious and social service organizations, Latinos teamed up with sympathetic whites to struggle against discrimination and for equal access to the city's spaces and resources, especially housing. Nunzio DiMarca, for example, was an Italian American, fluent in Spanish, who was a consistent part of Latino organizing in the city. He worked with Latino activists during the riots, and he even became the head of Semana Hispana organizing for a time in the mid-1990s.

One of the most prominent examples of interracial organizing was the creation of the city's first community development corporation: Immigrant City Community Housing Corporation (ICCHC). ICCHC was a successful interracial effort to keep affordable housing in the city, as a handful of white professionals in Lawrence aligned themselves with Latino organizers and residents displaced by urban renewal to advocate for affordable housing in a North Common neighborhood. Although ICCHC was an interracial effort, its battle against city leaders reflected two competing visions for Lawrence that were profoundly racialized. Many Lawrence elites, including the city government, had long been engaged in a steadfast booster campaign to draw and keep industry and middle-class residents in the city. The urban renewal efforts described in Chapter 1 were part of that push for a renaissance in Lawrence that would bring middle-class residents back to the city. Latino Lawrencians, however, were generally working-class or poor, and they pointed out that the renaissance envisioned by city leaders did not include a place or role for lower-income Latino residents. On the contrary, many Latinos understood that this imagined renaissance was premised on their displacement.

As part of the urban renewal effort described in Chapter 1, nine blocks north of the Common were razed in 1978, and the predominantly Latino residents of the demolished neighborhood were promised priority access to housing in the new development. As the *Eagle-Tribune* described the demolition, "A giant has plucked out all the houses and buildings in the heart of the city," and nearly 300 households and 45 stores had been displaced. Representative Kevin Blanchette discussed the importance of the nine-block section that had been decimated by what he termed "urban removal," calling the neighborhood "the last frontier for development in the city."[74] When bids were requested for the new development in the early 1980s, however, the mayor, the city council, and the Lawrence Redevelopment Authority (LRA) made clear that they wanted the development to be specifically designed for middle-income residents, as part of the long-standing plans to draw middle-class residents into the city.

Lawrence business elites were major advocates for the elimination of low-income housing from the proposed development. Under the leadership of Andover's Nicholas Rizzo, these elites formed Lawrence Strategy, an organization to advocate for middle-income housing on the North Common site. Lawrence Strategy argued that middle-income tenants in the North Common were key to Lawrence's retail sector, and they lobbied for "upward mobility" for the site.[75] As Rizzo explained, "A family of four making $22,000 is going to spend money on Essex Street. But a family of four making $15,000—well, it's just not there."[76] Mayor John Buckley concurred: "Lawrence is faced with the loss of our greatest resource—our young people and middle-income residents who have been moving out of the city. . . . Lawrence cannot afford to be a city of the poor and the elderly."[77]

This view of city elites—that Lawrence would be best served by attracting middle-income residents and by purging itself of poor residents—contrasted sharply with a letter from the leaders of twelve Latino churches in Lawrence, who urged Mayor Buckley to "support inclusion of low income housing units." The Latino religious leaders explained that "many of our members are working people who earn $13,000–$15,000 [a year] who could not obtain a unit if none were available in that income level." They informed the mayor of the housing crisis Latinos faced in the city: "Housing is a very severe problem for our church families and others in the community, who though their incomes are low, would make very good residents of that neighborhood and would bring stability to the North Common, which has been deteriorating for a long time."[78]

The Latino clergy who authored this letter detailed a vision of the city very different from that put forward by Lawrence Strategy, as well as a different idea of how Latinos could contribute to the city. The clergy were clear that the neighborhood decline had been long standing. Stability in the neighborhood, they argued, required residents who would be committed to staying in Lawrence, unlike middle-income people who had been abandoning the city for decades. While Lawrence Strategy advocated "the highest, financially feasible income level for this area" in order to make a "top-flight development,"[79] Latino clergy and ICCHC wanted homes for the Latino residents of the city who were experiencing a crisis of housing availability, affordability, and quality. They pushed city leaders to focus on improving the lives of the people already living in Lawrence, not on trying to recruit mythical "first-class" tenants to save the city.

ICCHC had formed in the early 1980s as a coalition of displaced North Common residents; Latino community organizers, including Isabel

Melendez; and white supporters of affordable housing and community-based development, such as lawyer Armand Hyatt. As they described themselves, "Immigrant City Community Housing Corporation (ICCHC) is a non-profit corporation whose membership is composed, in significant part, of Hispanic residents of Lawrence. . . . Its purpose is to help alleviate the shortage of low and moderate income family housing in Lawrence through development of cooperative housing for the various immigrant groups, specifically including minorities, who live and work in the City of Lawrence community."[80]

ICCHC submitted a bid to build co-op apartments on the North Common site. Their bid was denied in late 1983 by an LRA aligned with the conservative city leadership, who were committed to a project that did not include low-income or cooperative units. ICCHC drew up a lawsuit alleging that the city's insistence on a development without low-income housing was illegal, as it did not conform to the city's urban renewal plan. The primary funding for the project so far had come from community development block grants totaling $6 million over the past eight years. The conditions of these grants required the adequate relocation of residents from what was formerly a lower-income and minority neighborhood, as well as "priority access" to the new development for "Hispanic and other minorities of the City who have suffered from a lack of housing opportunities."[81] ICCHC's lawsuit was designed as a class-action suit and argued that the civil rights of several displaced Latino residents had been violated, both by the refusal to prioritize low-income housing and by the lack of Latinos involved in the process stemming from the city's abysmal minority hiring record.[82] As a result of the threatened legal challenge from ICCHC, the chosen developer withdrew its bid in February 1984. Rather than choose between the two remaining proposals, however, the LRA decided to re-solicit bids and maintained its commitment to exclusively middle-income or "moderate-income" housing.

Although it would seem that state and federal funding the city was receiving for the project would require the inclusion of at least some affordable units, in early August 1984, the state advised that the project could go ahead without an affordability component and build only middle-income housing. The local paper trumpeted the decision with the headline, "Mayor, Council Score Victory as Low Income Homes Banned."[83] Days later, the Lower Tower Hill neighborhood across the city erupted in the 1984 riots. Some speculated that the blatant message of unwelcome sent by city elites to Latinos displaced from the North Common may have contributed to the tension that erupted in the riots. Whether or not the North Common controversy played a direct role, the competing visions of the city evident in the conflict over the North Common site (one plan that included Latinos and another that excluded them) were mirrored in the riots. Indeed, the riots were interpreted by many as a militant call for improved affordable housing in the city. In their wake, with a new city council in place, a compelling legal challenge drawn up, and strong community support, ICCHC eventually won the new bid and constructed 140 cooperatively owned units on the North Common site in 1989.[84]

The fight to include affordable housing on the North Common site was part of a larger Latino effort to claim a right to the city, to be at home in its public and private spaces, as well as a right to assert a vision for Lawrence's future that included Latinos. The elite vision for the city had often been premised on drawing in "first-class" people and businesses and, by extension, on the displacement of poor and working-class Latinos. In the daily incidents of harassment and violence discussed above, white residents were attempting to do on a street level what city officials had long been trying to do with urban renewal and middle-income housing: deny Latinos a place in Lawrence.

CONCLUSION—I CAME HERE TO STAY

This chapter includes such detailed information on the hostility that Latinos faced in Lawrence not just to document the fact that Latinos had to fight against white racism in order to settle in Lawrence but also to trace the strategies, narratives, and impact of white resistance to Latino settlement. The bigotry on the part of some city officials is important to note, for example, lest we fall into the trap of believing that Lawrence's white working class was the sole source of the animosity directed against Latinos. All classes of white people in and around Lawrence (not necessarily all white people, but all *classes* of white people) resisted Latino immigration. While city elites may not have thrown rocks or shouted "Spic," many resisted Latino settlement in other ways: by trying to reduce low-income housing in the city, denying Latinos the use of the Common, or refusing to hire Latino employees or provide Spanish-language services. Suburban whites, meanwhile, were sheltered from Lawrence's conflicts by restrictive zoning practices that kept multifamily and public housing contained in the city, as well as by a metropolitan political economy that protected suburban schools from regional desegregation. These were more legal and classier (pun intended) forms of resisting Latino settlement, but their impact was in many ways more powerful than the day-to-day hostility of working-class whites. The bias of their white neighbors certainly made many Latinos feel hurt and outraged, but ultimately it was the institutionalized and customary practices of whites *in power* that truly created a struggle for survival.

Again, understanding the full scope of white resistance to Latino settlement is also crucial to understanding the stakes of Latino activism. Although Isabel Melendez has been in Lawrence since 1959, she rarely speaks in interviews about the bigotry of her white neighbors, not even the prejudice she saw or experienced during the early decades of Latino settlement. Melendez has long worked in interracial coalitions and even dipped briefly into a formal bid for mayor in 2001, so it is not surprising that her public recollections focus on achievements gained through organizing and coalition building, rather than on bitter reminiscences of slights and prejudice. Yet she has occasionally offered glimpses of the bigotry and harassment she personally endured as a Latina activist in the city. "How many times I was told 'go back to Puerto Rico,' 'learn English' 'why don't you stay in Puerto Rico?'" Her point in recalling these insults, however, was not to complain about the bigotry of her white neighbors but, rather, to highlight her commitment to the city. She explained that she always answered these types of insults in the same way: "'because I came here to stay.' I always said that, 'I came here to stay; I'm not leaving. I came here to stay.'"[85] It is in that spirit that I draw attention to white resistance to Latino settlement in Lawrence. "I'm not leaving" is a much bolder statement when said in response to violent or hateful demands to "go home."

Latino organizing during the 1960s, 1970s, and early 1980s played an important role in providing a safety net for the city's poor and working-class Latinos. But there is more to making a place a home or a community beyond ensuring that everyone's basic needs are met. Building community in Lawrence also meant providing ways to reinforce and expand connections between friends and family and to maintain connections with home-country kin and cultures. To this end, Latinos in Lawrence established social clubs, storefront churches, restaurants, and other small businesses to create and strengthen communities in the city. Organizing to provide for one another what the city denied them, and to provide it in a way that respected or even celebrated Latino culture, was an implicit assertion of Latinos' right to the city. The most basic aspects of Latino community formation—opening small businesses to serve the community, helping new arrivals find work or fill out immigration papers, forming social clubs—were all ways of collectively laying down roots in Lawrence and making the city a home. Not all of these ventures had a pan-ethnic Latino focus, but taken together, these endeavors contributed markedly to the Latinization of Lawrence's public life.

The work of providing services and organizing cultural celebrations often blended seamlessly into community organizing and formal politics, crossing all boundaries of public and private and playing an indispensable role in empowering Latinos in Lawrence. Melendez, for example, spent her professional life in community service, but she also used her extensive network as formidable political leverage, fiercely and relentlessly pressing City Hall to be responsive and accountable to the city's growing Latino population. Melendez became one of the most powerful figures in Lawrence politics throughout the 1980s and 1990s, culminating with her becoming the first Latino person, of any gender, to win the Democratic mayoral primary in 2001 (although she was defeated by Republican Michael Sullivan in the general election by fewer than a thousand votes).[86]

Latino political empowerment in Lawrence emerged from decades of individual and collective assertions that Latinos had a right to make a home in the city. These day-to-day contestations and formal organizing efforts remind us that Latinos were not passive victims of white racism in Lawrence. Aside from the obvious fact that, from a crude perspective, Latinos "won" the battle for Lawrence, as the city transitioned to a Latino majority by 2000 and the public culture of the city today is overwhelmingly Latino, quotidian battles over the right to public space, over the right to live and work and walk the streets in Lawrence unmolested, were all a form of Latino activism. Yelling back or throwing punches when called a "Spic" or even hanging out on your front stoop and talking loudly in Spanish were ways of insisting that Latinos had a right to the city. Both carrying the Dominican flag through Lawrence's streets during Semana Hispana and organizing for affordable housing were ways of laying claim to Lawrence. The struggle for Latino empowerment in Lawrence was evident not only when Latinos registered voters or ran for office but also when they resisted white attempts to make them disappear, "go home," or immediately assimilate. This deeply racialized effort to claim the city would explode in the riots of 1984.

FOUR

THE RIOTS OF 1984

The mobs are gone: white adolescents
who chanted USA and flung stones
at the scattering of astonished immigrants,
ruddy faces slowing the car to shout spick
and wave beer cans.

Martín Espada,
*from "*Toque de queda*: Curfew in Lawrence"*

For two nights in August 1984, hundreds of white and Latino Lawrencians faced
off along Oxford Street in Lawrence's Lower Tower Hill neighborhood. Banging on metal garbage cans and yelling racial slurs and insults, the two crowds
hurled rocks and Molotov cocktails at each other as neighbors shouted down
from triple-decker balconies or cowered in fear inside their apartments. Whenever police or firefighters appeared to disperse the crowd or put out the blazes
in the firebombed buildings, the two sides joined together to throw rocks and
beer cans at the advancing squad cars and fire trucks, temporarily putting aside
their animosity to struggle against a common target. Both white and Latino
Lawrencians rioted, claiming the streets and raging at the injustices in their city.

The riots are a spectacular example of how city residents claimed and
contested public space in this era as they negotiated a rapid and major shift
in Lawrence's racial demography, as well as the brutal effects of their city's
impoverishment. The shouted slurs and burning buildings were a dramatic
commentary on urban disinvestment and a fierce assertion of divergent white
and Latino visions for the city. As Chapter 3 demonstrated, many white

Lawrencians blamed Latinos for their city's decline. For some whites, the desire to restore Lawrence to an imagined earlier state of safety, prosperity, and neighborliness inspired them to violently reject Latino settlement in the city using rocks, Molotov cocktails, and shouted demands for Latinos to "go back where [they] came from."[1] While Latino Lawrencians had been formally organizing for decades to render the city a safe place to settle, the riots were an insurgent, street-level refusal to be scared out of their homes and neighborhood, a furious and unmistakable insistence on their right to the city.

Even before the glass was swept from the streets and the burned-out buildings were bulldozed, a debate raged over what to call those two nights of disturbances. The media that converged in Lawrence marked the riots immediately as an "urban problem," tied to the economic decay and racial tension that were considered specifically endemic to inner cities by the 1980s. As one reporter summed up, "They don't riot in the suburbs."[2] Indeed, there was near-universal agreement that the two nights of fighting indicated a larger crisis in the city, but a heated debate took place over what, exactly, that crisis was.

For urban historians, riots are rich opportunities to examine the political, economic, and social systems of a city, made visible precisely by their failure. Riots are like a fever—a sure sign of illness in the city's systems—and thus they present an opportunity both to diagnose the illness and to theorize what's necessary for healthy city systems. In addition, riots are one of the few occasions in which journalists, academics, and government officials converge to actively seek out and record the opinions of ordinary people on the state of their city. As a result, riots create a unique archive that allows historians unparalleled access to the views, thoughts, and frustrations of regular city residents, beyond oft-quoted politicians and media-savvy activists. Riot-provoked interviews with city residents give a priceless glimpse at how Lawrencians understood their own city's crisis. More broadly, they offer insight into how working-class white ethnics and Latinos thought about race, government, the economy, and urban/suburban divides in the 1980s.

Interpretations of the Lawrence riots drew on narratives of urban crisis that had been circulating nationally since the "ghetto revolts" and "urban uprisings" of the 1960s. In these uprisings, Black communities had rioted to protest segregation, discrimination, urban poverty, and police abuse. Beginning in Harlem in 1964 and Watts in 1965, the rioting quickly spread to other cities throughout the nation. In 1967, there were 164 race-related riots in the United States, most prominently in Newark and Detroit (the most lethal riot of the decade, in which forty-three people were killed). After Dr. Martin Luther King Jr. was assassinated in 1968, there were another 200 riots in cities across the country and 500 more incidents in 1969. These urban uprisings continued throughout early 1970s. Activists and community leaders helped render these upheavals articulate by highlighting the valid grievances that had fed rioters' rage. The federal government then lent weight to these interpretations via a national commission charged with analyzing the roots of the violence. The National Advisory Commission on Civil Disorders (aka the Kerner Commission) report, released in 1968, validated the rioters' complaints, ultimately concluding that systemic racism was largely responsible for the rioting and that, even in the aftermath of civil rights legislation, the United States was "moving toward two societies, one black, one white—separate and unequal."[3]

While the rash of rioting had slowed by the late 1970s, a major upheaval in Miami in 1980 brought these issues back into the national spotlight. By 1984, then, there was already an established framework through which to make sense of the conflict in Lawrence.[4] Yet there were many ways in which the Lawrence riots challenged the common explanatory narrative forged in the urban uprisings of the 1960s era. First, it was the middle of the 1980s. Was the nation still trapped in the same state of extreme racial polarization as it had been twenty years earlier, and were urban communities of color still as impoverished and alienated? The Lawrence riots demonstrated that, although much had changed in the post–Civil Rights era, the urban crisis had clearly not been resolved. This would be played out on an even larger stage with the rioting in Crown Heights, Brooklyn, in 1991 and Los Angeles in 1992.[5] Second, these rioters were Latino, not African American. While Latino communities had actually rioted more than forty times between 1964 and 1971, racial divisions nationally were still generally viewed through a Black/white lens, and a stereotype of Latino political docility had somehow managed to persist in spite of these uprisings and the revolutionary Puerto Rican and Chicano activism of the 1960s and 1970s.[6] As a prominent Cuban scholar and activist in Massachusetts noted after the Lawrence riots, "Riots among Hispanics are highly unusual. . . . Things have got to be extremely serious when rioting breaks out among Hispanics."[7] While attempting to justify the rioting of Latino Lawrencians, this comment implicitly contrasted them with African Americans, who were presumed to be more militant. The reality was that circumstances were indeed "extremely serious" for many Latino communities, and like urban African Americans, Latinos who were concentrated in segregated and impoverished neighborhoods protested in a wide range of ways, including rioting. This, too, would be evident on a larger national stage with the Latino participation in the Los Angeles riots of 1992 and the Dominican riots in Washington Heights that same year.[8]

A third way in which the Lawrence riots diverged from the paradigm of ghetto revolts was that white Lawrencians took to the streets as well. White rioting was not unprecedented, of course. Whites had been the main perpetrators of earlier eras of race riots, using violence as a tool to maintain white supremacy in the face of real or perceived threats to the racial order, for example, in the New York "Draft Riots" of 1863 or the East St. Louis riot of 1917.[9] And white racial violence had certainly not disappeared in the latter half of the twentieth century, as brutal white terrorism against Black activists in the South during the Civil Rights movement illustrates, as do the multiple incidences in New York City during the 1980s in which young Black men were killed by white mobs or vigilantes.[10] In Boston, just ten years before the Lawrence riots, white residents had responded to a federal order to desegregate local public schools with what historian Jack Tager has described as an "outpouring of staggering violence, almost daily and continuous for three years" beginning in 1974.[11] The countless examples of white rioting and racist violence, however, had not been incorporated into the standard narrative of postwar race riots, which were viewed almost exclusively as Black protest.

Finally, the distinctly nativist tenor of the Lawrence riots complicated the paradigm even further. White nativist violence was certainly already evident in this era, especially in the murder of Vincent Chin in 1982. But the Lawrence riots also foreshadowed a distinctly anti-Latino nativism that would grow in the 1990s and 2000s. This rise in nativist violence was most prominently illustrated when a mob of teenagers beat and killed Ecuadorian immigrant Marcelo Lucero in Patchogue, Long Island, in 2008. Anti-Latino hate crimes presumed the foreignness of Latinos and viewed their presence in the United States as inherently illegitimate. In a disturbing echo of white shouts that Latino Lawrencians should "go back where [they] came from," a man who attacked a Latino in Colorado in 2008 explained, "I hit him because he shouldn't even be here."[12] The Lawrence riots have much to show us not only about the changes and challenges in the city itself but also about the persistence of urban crisis and racial divisions after the 1960s, the racialization of urban Latinos and the range of Latino protest strategies, and the trajectory of white racial and nativist violence in the post–Civil Rights era.

WEDNESDAY, AUGUST 8, 1984

Many industrial cities in New England are filled with tightly packed, three-story apartment houses (commonly referred to as triple-deckers) built to hold an earlier generation of immigrant laborers. Oxford Street in Lower Tower Hill in

The Riots of 1984

Lower Tower Hill neighborhood after two nights of rioting, 1984. Photo reprinted with permission from the *Baltimore Sun*. All rights reserved.

Lawrence was crowded with these triple-deckers and other apartment houses, many with porches, balconies, and small yards.[13] Beginning in the early 1970s, the demographics of Lower Tower Hill had begun to shift. Previously, the neighborhood had been dominated by ethnically French Canadian white residents, but by 1980, half the residents were Latino, mostly but not exclusively Puerto Rican. Latinos accounted for three-quarters of the 5,000 people living in two low-rise public housing projects in the neighborhood, and there were also numbers of Latinos spread throughout the triple-decker tenements.[14]

It is hard to pinpoint exactly how the long-standing racial tension in Lower Tower Hill suddenly escalated on that hot Wednesday night. A confrontation during the day, apparently retaliation for an even earlier offense, snowballed into massive, open street violence when night fell. As one reads the conflicting accounts of what catalyzed the riots, however, it seems clear that the anger and frustration on both sides was so immense and the quotidian struggles over turf, respect, and safety were so persistent that the slightest incident could have provoked the riots. As many observers noted afterward, the riots emerged out of a personal conflict, but they were not *about* that conflict; they were *about* the much larger issues of economic decline, scapegoating, and marginalization (or viewed differently, they were *about* fighting for the right to live, work, and participate in a vibrant, safe Lawrence).

On Wednesday, August 8, a group of angry young Latinos went to the home of three whites, John Ball, Gary Gill, and Rick Brady, to confront them over a broken window. According to Anna Ocasio, a Puerto Rican woman, Ball and his friends had thrown a rock through her apartment window the night before, shattering the glass next to her five-month-old baby. Ball (known to friends as "The Hawk") was sitting outside his house on the corner of Oxford and Haverhill Streets with the others when Ocasio's avengers showed up, and a fight quickly ensued. As the *Eagle-Tribune* described it, "Insults and obscenities flew back and forth. Someone grabbed a bat and started clubbing a dog belonging to the owner of the house. The riot began."[15]

Accounts of this confrontation varied widely, of course. Some witnesses argued that the young Latino who allegedly clubbed the dog was actually just a boy, and that he really only kicked the dog through a fence. In addition, these witnesses noted that dozens of people saw the boy get "slapped around" by the group of white men as a result.[16] On the other hand, Ball's friend Rick Brady recounted that about "40 Puerto Ricans" suddenly attacked the white men with bats. Brady said he and his friends threw rocks at the Puerto Ricans because "we figured by throwing rocks at them, they would back off." This story is suspect, of course, because it would be difficult to throw rocks at someone close enough to be clubbing you with a bat, but it is clear that the group of Puerto Ricans did not "back off." They remained in the fight, barricading the street with burning trash cans while white residents massed at the corner of Oxford and Haverhill Streets.[17]

Over the course of the next several hours, between 200 and 300 people gathered on opposite ends of the street, evenly divided between white and Latino, each shouting at the other side, and many throwing rocks at each other, at the surrounding houses, or at any cars that braved the intersections. Police and firefighters were met with substantial resistance whenever they attempted to restore order, as the mob redirected its anger at this common target.[18] There were ten police on duty that night, and the outnumbered officers and unprotected firefighters decided to go back to their respective stations and wait for reinforcements. As police captain Frank Foley explained, "If I had sent ten men up there, they'd get their a—s kicked in."[19] As a result of this retreat, the melee continued without police interference for hours. At 11:00 P.M. rioters broke into Pettoruto's liquor store. The *Eagle-Tribune* reported that at first the two groups fought over the liquor, but then they cooperated to divide it up and share it, after which "a lull followed with a lot of public drinking."[20]

This odd reprieve could not have been long lived, because by 12:15 A.M., the liquor store was on fire. Firefighters attempted to reach the burning building, steering their trucks around the flaming barrels in the road, only to be turned back by the crowd. Although it seems the rioters could put aside their rage at each other long enough to divvy up the looted liquor, this same tolerance did not extend to the police or the firefighters. As the *Eagle-Tribune* described, firefighters "had to duck the rocks and beer cans aimed at them by people in the street and others hanging out of tenement windows." The newspaper interviewed firefighter Raymond Pelletier, who "paced in circles around the Lawrence Fire Station." He admitted, "I've never been scared of anything in my life. . . . A guy's house can be on fire and I'll go right in. I've never been afraid . . . until tonight."[21]

Many neighborhood residents did not join the crowd in the street during the riots, but a number of them still watched, shouted, and even threw things from their porches and balconies. As a result, the line between riot participant and bystander was quite blurry. As the *Eagle-Tribune* reported, "Home-owners and tenants stood on the porches and screamed down at the rioters, who responded with rocks, slingshots and warning shots from pistols and sawed-off shotguns."[22] One Dominican resident recalled that she didn't participate, only watched, but still felt somewhat involved because of the racialized nature of the conflict: "Of course whoever you are, you know, you had your sides."[23]

There were many other neighborhood residents, however, who were simply terrified by the riots, and the *Eagle-Tribune* gave these "innocent bystanders" a good deal of attention. The paper focused on families trapped in their homes, cowering in fear, desperate for some type of police protection that was not forthcoming. The paper reported on residents' terrified phone calls to the local and surrounding police stations, saying, "We're trapped" or "I'm laying on the floor and I'm scared." Some residents called the *Eagle-Tribune* directly. One tearful woman pleaded with the paper, "We're innocent victims being held prisoners in our own house. I'm afraid something terrible is going to happen, please get us help. . . . This has been going on for three hours, but no one is coming to help us." An hour later she called back crying that the police had not arrived: "These things [fire bombs] are coming in the windows. Someone is going to be hurt. It is women and innocent children. I have four families in here, we're huddled."[24] For many residents of the neighborhood, abandoned by the police, the riots were simply a nightmare.

When police reinforcements finally did arrive, including forty officers from the regional tactical unit and thirty state troopers, they joined the ten

Lawrence officers. The *Eagle-Tribune* described them as a "fearsome paramilitary force," as the eighty heavily armed officers in all-black riot gear marched along the darkened streets. By the time the police force had gathered together and traversed the five blocks to Oxford Street, however, the rioting had mostly run its course. The firefighters were already beginning to battle the blaze at Pettoruto's, and the fighting in the street had ended. There was nothing between the police and the fire besides "overturned barrels, piles of trash and broken glass." Despite the dramatic, theatrical march to the scene, the police had missed much of the action. Officers encountered just a small, milling crowd that reluctantly dispersed, overturning trash cans and breaking windows at the Haffner's gas station as they went. Even with tear gas, the crowd moved away slowly while "taunting the police," according to the press.[25]

As the first night of rioting wound to a close, no one had been killed, and no one had been critically injured. Judging from the last names of those arrested (an inaccurate method, of course), five Latinos were apprehended for riot-related activity, mostly disorderly conduct. One white man was arrested for driving under the influence and possession of marijuana. All of those arrested were in their late teens or early twenties. Gary Gill, one of the three white men involved in the catalyzing fight, was taken into protective custody.

THURSDAY, AUGUST 9, 1984

The next day, glass lay scattered through the intersection of Haverhill and Oxford, although the streets were far from deserted. The *Eagle-Tribune* described the scene as "almost carnival-like as neighbors leaned off their porches and through windows, anxious to talk to anyone." The paper continued, "Women wheeled toddlers in strollers over broken glass and garbage. A pregnant girl in a cotton smock giggled with friends outside a house that had been pelted with rocks the night before."[26] The overwhelming presence of children helped create an almost relaxed, festive atmosphere. Some young people dragged cardboard out into the middle of the glass-strewn intersection to breakdance.[27] In most of the TV coverage, kids grouped together behind the reporters to stay in the camera's frame, leaning on the handlebars of their bikes or jumping up and down.[28] One boy rode his bicycle in circles around the people and reporters filming on the closed street, exclaiming to his friends, "It's just like a movie."[29]

The media were an overwhelming presence in the neighborhood the next day. The *Eagle-Tribune* listed the following: "The riots led both Boston daily

Teenagers and children parody the press attention during the riots with a fake camera and microphone, 1984. Photo by Cheryl Senter, archived at the Lawrence History Center. Reprinted with permission from the *Eagle-Tribune*.

newspapers, Boston radio and TV news reports and United Press International's national wire report. The second night of rioting made page three of *USA Today*. Both days led NBC's Today Show. Covering from the scene were Boston television stations 4, 5, 6, and 56 and channels 9 and 50 from New Hampshire. Shortwave radio buffs reported hearing the news over a Russian station. Calls were received from a national Hispanic network in California and a Montreal newspaper." The television stations, in particular, drew attention with their massive equipment, including a ninety-foot crane, two fifty-foot antennas, and spotlights when night fell. Jose Colon, age nine, and Eddie Santiago, twelve, mockingly impersonated a TV news team. They toured the riot neighborhood with a fake camera made out of a disposable diaper box and a flashlight and a fake rubber microphone, in a brilliant parody of the media's sudden fascination with their small city.[30]

Ten local church leaders, both white and Latino, including the Reverend Daniel Rodriguez from the Hispanic Baptist Church, organized a bilingual religious ceremony for early Thursday evening, in order to calm the residents through Bible readings and songs. The ecumenical service took place outdoors in front of an abandoned firehouse on Oxford Street.[31] As Canon Rudolph Devik of Grace Episcopal Church explained, "We're telling them that Lawrence is made up of people who can live together with unity, with love." The ceremony took place near the building that had been burned out the night before.[32]

The church leaders and residents prayed for peace; but just moments after the religious ceremony ended, the crowd broke up into two groups, and the conflict began again. According to the *Boston Herald*, "Hundreds of Hispanic men formed in one section of Oxford Street and hundreds of whites banded together at the other. The Hispanics began beating on garbage cans and both they and the whites shouted racial slurs at one another." A line of Lawrence police moved in between the two groups, and shortly thereafter Molotov cocktails began to fly.[33] The *Eagle-Tribune* stated, "The music from the bilingual service at Engine 4 faded as the crowd swelled. The first man was led out of the crowd in handcuffs. There were cheers. There was chanting, raised arms and clenched fists. A group of white men shouted, 'U.S.A., U.S.A., U.S.A.,' and 'Who's American? We are.'"[34] The *New York Times* added that white rioters were also shouting, "Go home. We were here first," but there is no record of what exactly the Latino rioters were shouting.[35]

TV news coverage showed two groups massed at opposite ends of a narrow street, with what looked like less than a hundred feet of empty space between them. In the dark of the summer night, the cameras followed the arc of a firebomb that was thrown from one side at the other, crashing just shy of its presumed target and exploding in flames on the street.[36] One Dominican woman who lived just outside the riot area recalled that she could see the fires from her apartment as cars and buildings were set alight.[37] As in the first night of rioting, much of the anger and violence was directed by both groups at the police. In fact, the cover of the *Boston Herald* implied that the riots were more a battle between police and rioters than between whites and Latinos. The article, "New Riot Hits Lawrence: SWAT Team in Action against Wild Mob," was accompanied by a graphic picture of a cop holding a bloody, racially indeterminate man in a headlock.[38]

The police made clear to the media that racial violence in Lower Tower Hill was nothing new. Two weeks before the riots, police had found a pipe bomb loaded with gunpowder. A few weeks before, when the police went to the neighborhood to break up a fight, they found several Molotov cocktails and a homemade bomb fashioned out of a car battery. Another police officer said, "There hasn't been a secure night on Oxford Street. This has been festering for two months. We found an arsenal of rocks and bottles. There have been five or six fires there recently and there was a major fire this past weekend. They're burning each other out. Shooting and stabbing each other." The anti-police sentiment in the neighborhood wasn't new either; the president of the police union said that a street department worker who went to the neighborhood to turn off a fire hydrant the week before had had gasoline thrown in his face.[39]

The disturbances continued until the early morning. At 10:30 that night, the head of the Northeast Middlesex County Tactical Police Force "arrived to find Lawrence police pinned down—lying on the ground to avoid gunshots, rocks, bottles and Molotov cocktails." An early contingent of forty Lawrence police officers and the regional SWAT team had been no match for the hundreds of rioters who claimed the streets. By 12:30, however, the reinforced police force organized to clear the streets of Latino rioters. Between 200 and 300 officers, including local police from the surrounding towns and state police from six barracks, marched in cadence down the streets, pushing the Latino rioters in front of them, herding them to the Merrimack Courts (Essex Street) projects, where virtually every newspaper account assumed all the Latino rioters lived. The *Eagle-Tribune* said, "As police marched toward them, rioters scattered and ran towards their Merrimack Court homes. 'Let's go, move it! You've got homes, let's get back to them,' police yelled."[40]

Latinos lived throughout the neighborhood, however, and it is highly unlikely that all the Latinos at the riot site lived in the Essex Street projects. One can only imagine the scurry of nonresidents to find someone who would let them into their home or the panic of residents who were not involved in the rioting as the police charged into Merrimack Courts, clearing the sidewalks and streets. Elsie Rodriguez had simply been standing in front of one of the buildings in the projects when she was clubbed by a police officer before she could run into her home. She explained, "I feel like I was abused even though I wasn't involved." Another project tenant, Joseph Miner, said police "marched in here like the Gestapo throwing tear gas for nothing."[41]

As the police herded Latinos into the Essex Street projects, the hundreds of white rioters either left the scene or were forced to leave by the remaining police. Unlike the Latino rioters, white rioters were not "chased" into their homes. The police seemed to consider Latino rioters more of a threat, pushing them from the scene first and violently pursuing them until they were all inside their (or someone's) homes, while many of the hundreds of white rioters were allowed to "drift" from the scene, as the *Boston Herald* described.[42] During the two nights of rioting, no one had been killed, and fewer than twenty people had been seriously injured.[43]

In the weeks and months after the riots, white rioting would often be minimized or forgotten, yet the equal participation of white rioters is echoed in the list of those arrested. The Lawrence police department had long faced accusations of bias against Latinos, but it seems that many more white rioters were arrested than Latinos on this second night (again using the inaccurate method of surnames). Overall, more than a dozen people had been arrested and several more were taken into "protective custody." Only a few of those brought in were Latino, arrested for crimes such as inciting a riot, breaking and entering, or looting. The rest, the overwhelming majority of those brought in, seem to have been white. A handful of white arrestees were the only ones charged with assault and battery of a police officer, although most of those arrested were charged with similar crimes, such as disorderly conduct or inciting a riot, or occasionally for possessing or throwing a Molotov cocktail. Most of those arrested were in their late teens or early twenties, and all were men.[44]

The bulk of those arrested were from the neighborhood, although some of the white rioters detained were from the surrounding suburbs of Methuen or Pelham, New Hampshire. The interest of white suburban residents in the riots was echoed by the *Eagle-Tribune*, which reprimanded out-of-towners: "Curiosity seekers must stay out. People have shown up from other parts of the city and surrounding communities to gawk and, at times, to add their two cents of prejudice or opinion to what is going on. . . . We urge them: STAY HOME."[45] Although suburban residents showed up to "gawk," city leaders truly feared a different kind of "outsider." Latino transurban connections with New York City remained strong, and there were fears that Latino rioters had sent for reinforcements from New York; "busloads of troublemakers" were rumored to be on their way.[46] This threat ultimately never materialized, however, as the rioting did not continue the next night.

FRIDAY, AUGUST 10, 1984

City Hall had done little during the first night of rioting, declining to issue a state of emergency or impose a curfew. Mayor John Buckley was the most steadfast in his attempts to minimize the significance of the riots. The day after the first disturbance, he had met with public safety alderman Raymond Johnson, and they decided to take a "low-key approach" to the possibility of another night of violence. While the second night of rioting brewed, Buckley attended a school committee meeting until nearly 10:00 P.M. and then drove through the riot area and decided not to take charge of any public safety measures. While many on the council pressed the mayor to declare a state of emergency, Buckley's boosterism and his desire to avoid drawing negative attention to Lawrence won out.[47]

The morning after the second night of rioting, however, the mayor called a special emergency meeting of the city council, much of which was spent behind closed doors in executive session. When the council emerged, Mayor Buckley addressed those in attendance, dismissing the riots as empty and irrational: "The past 48 hours has seen a situation develop which has been fueled by rumor and controversy. The events are both tragic and senseless and have led to a situation where too many people are reacting without reason or logic." After meeting with state and law enforcement officials, as well as with residents of the riot neighborhood, the council decided to declare a state of emergency in order to render the city eligible for more state and federal assistance. Under this state of emergency, the mayor declared a curfew in the riot neighborhood from 8:00 P.M. until 6:00 A.M. for the weekend.[48]

The curfew prohibited people from being out on the streets, sidewalks, or vacant lots of the area bordered by Broadway, Haverhill, Margin, and Essex Streets. In addition, "all places of amusement and entertainment within the area affected by the curfew" were to be closed, and the sale of gasoline in containers was banned in order to stem the production of Molotov cocktails.[49] The city attorney explained that anyone found violating the curfew would be subject to a fine of up to $300 and arrest and detention for up to twenty-four hours.[50] Afterward, public safety alderman Johnson downplayed the curfew to the press, explaining, "We're not going to stop people from living—if they have to go grocery shopping or go out or something. We just don't want people roaming the streets." But the city attorney was adamant: "All people—I repeat all people—who are out on the public ways will be subject to arrest. Going out to the store to buy cigarettes is not an emergency purpose."[51]

The Lawrence Police Department had three-quarters of its 100-member force on duty, but the council decided not to bring in extra police from out of town to help enforce the curfew. They did, however, keep them at the ready beyond Lawrence's borders.[52] The Lawrence police wanted to demonstrate that they had the situation under control. As Alderman Johnson explained, "We want people to realize the Lawrence Police can take care of this because when the tactical police and everybody else are gone we're still left here."[53] All media were banned from the curfew zone, and the *Boston Herald* reported that "police threatened to arrest reporters and photographers who refused to stay corralled behind police lines."[54] The city council established a rumor control hotline to dispel the hearsay they believed was at the root of the disturbance.[55] In preparation for the curfew, the police blocked off the entrances to the neighborhood with sawhorses, and "high-intensity street lights" lit up Oxford Street. At 8:00 P.M., the police began to move through the curfew area, ordering people off the streets. Those who tested the curfew were either arrested or told to go home, and the officers soon marched through deserted streets.[56]

Most residents of the area were not happy with the curfew. The *Boston Herald* reported, "Oxford street residents pleaded for an end to the violence in their riot-torn neighborhood yesterday, but insisted respect—not a curfew—was the solution."[57] Some Latinos clearly viewed the curfew not as protection but as further oppression from the city and from the police. Project residents posted signs that read, "Don't lock us in our cages—We are not animals."[58] Puerto Rican poet Martín Espada took a similarly critical view of "curfew signs" that "outlaw the conspiracy of foreign voices at night."[59] Jose Martinez argued, "The curfew won't work. Nobody can tell us what to do. This is supposed to be a free country. But what kind of freedom is that?"[60] Many white residents weren't happy either, although their complaints seem less explicitly protest-oriented; Ron Howard explained that he literally snuck out of his home to avoid the curfew. "Nobody is stopping me from going out to have a beer," he said. "This is stupid."[61]

Not everyone was displeased with the curfew, however. The Reverend James Keller of the Greater Lawrence Ecumenical Area Ministry, an organization that had long advocated for Latinos in Lawrence, said, "This is a time for prayer. Violence solves nothing and people should obey the authorities."[62] Nunzio DiMarca, an Italian American who spoke Spanish and spent decades involved in community service and organizing within the Latino community, addressed the residents of Merrimack Courts with Isabel Melendez. Using a loudspeaker attached to the roof of a car, DiMarca and Melendez urged project residents in Spanish to respect the curfew and end the violence. As they were speaking, police showed up to barricade off the curfew area, and project residents shouted to the police, "Go home, Go home."[63]

DiMarca and Melendez were both members of the Yellow Hat Brigade, a group of community leaders who worked with the police to keep the streets clear during the curfew. The name sprang from the special yellow caps they wore while patrolling the streets in order to identify themselves to the police,[64] but soon after the riots they named themselves the Alliance for Peace. Their cooperation with the police should not be taken as evidence of general collusion with the city in underplaying the riots. Members of the Alliance for Peace, including Isabel Melendez, were vocal advocates for deep changes in the city, but they were adamant that such change had to come through peaceful protest.[65]

WHAT MAKES A RACE RIOT?

By Saturday, a relative peace had returned to the streets of Lawrence, but people continued to struggle to explain and interpret the riots. As one Latina Lawrencian said, "The riots have no meaning. . . . What has meaning is what people are going to do about them."[66] In the conflicting interpretations of the riots, one can see the divergent interests and competing perspectives of three distinct groups within Lawrence: (1) City officials were generally desperate to downplay the riots in order to protect the city's reputation and attract new business, but they were also eager to garner state funds to ramp up the public safety services that had been undermined by Lawrence's economic decline. (2) White Lawrencians generally believed that the riots demonstrated a tragic decline in the city and that it was time for them to follow the tens of thousands of their former neighbors who had fled for the suburbs in the preceding decades. (3) Latino Lawrencians and their allies argued that the riots were a response to the pernicious exclusion and harassment of Latinos, as well as to the city's failed economy. They called for major changes in the city's housing, education services, and government, as well as for improved economic opportunities.

The conflict over what to call the events of August 1984 was symbolic of larger differences in perspective. Most residents, and the media that interviewed them, freely used the term "riot," with many further insisting that the riot was fueled by racial tension that had been developing for a long time—in other words, that it was specifically a race riot. The Spanish-language press in Boston used the term "*disturbios raciales*," which could translate to either "racial disturbances" or "race riots."[67] There seems to have been no attempt among local activists to label the events in Lawrence an "uprising" or "rebellion," but many Latino activists did explicitly refer to the riots as a "protest."

It was initially a challenge for the media to fit the Lawrence riots into existing conceptual categories. The TV news coverage couldn't even agree on how to define the two sides of the fighting: Hispanics versus Anglos, Latins versus whites, Hispanics versus French?[68] It was equally difficult to categorize the fighting: Was this a race riot if Latinos aren't precisely a race? And if most of the white people were actually French Canadian white ethnics? Was it an urban uprising similar to what African Americans did in Watts and other cities in the mid-1960s? If so, why were there so many white people involved?

Was it a nativist riot if it was mainly between white ethnics and Puerto Ricans, and as such neither group really had a stronger claim on an American identity than the other? The short answer is yes, it was all of those things (a race riot, an urban uprising, a nativist attack), in spite of the fact that the labels and identities did not fit as cleanly as the press might have liked. Those directly involved with the riot struggled less naming it; one Lawrence merchant stood in front of his store with a gun and told the press simply, "We've got a race riot here."[69]

The city's political leadership, however, strongly opposed the term "riots," and particularly the idea that the fighting constituted a "race riot." City officials were desperate to minimize the fighting, to make it simply a personal skirmish, a "domestic dispute" that got slightly out of control.[70] The initial claim of the city council was that the riots really didn't reflect any larger problems in Lawrence. Some in city government ultimately changed their opinion in the days and weeks after the riots, as the outcry forced them to look more closely at the living conditions in the neighborhood and to listen to the complaints of the residents. What did not change was the city government's virtually uniform insistence that the riots were unrelated to race or racial tension in the city. As Mayor Buckley summed up, "It was an isolated incident. It wasn't really racial."[71]

It is not exactly clear what city officials meant by this widespread assertion that the riot wasn't "racial." It most certainly was racial in the sense that each of the two groups who were rioting identified the other with racial slurs, and whites and Latinos allied themselves with people of the same group. What the city leaders likely meant was that racism was not the origin of the riot; people did not come out onto the street simply to express their bigotry and to hurt people who were different from them. That is partly true, as the riot was also about claiming public space, achieving a voice in local politics, and above all, protesting conditions in the crisis city. In this strict sense, however, no riot has ever really been racial. Racism is never simply about racial differences but about preserving or contesting privileges (economic, social, political) that are unequally divided along socially constructed racial lines. For white people in the United States, racial violence has historically been about preserving a "way of life" that they felt was under attack as a result of the growing number, growing power, or changing attitudes of people of color.[72] In this strictest sense of the term, then, the city leaders were correct that the riot was not about race, as it was not a simple and random expression of bigotry. For the white rioters, it was about a quality of life in Lawrence that they felt they were losing, a loss they attributed to the Latinos in their midst, a form of scapegoating in which a racial other was used to explain all the damage done by global restructuring and a sinking economy. For the Latino rioters, it was about a quality of life (dignity, safety, employment, and adequate housing) they perceived as being denied to them by discrimination and bigotry.

In this fuller sense, then, the riot was certainly and undeniably racial, as most of the rioters and almost all of the media onlookers agreed. City leaders, however, attempted to minimize the public perception of the racial stakes of the battle. Their interest in this seems to have been twofold. The first was a desire not to be seen as parochial, anachronistic, or out of touch with the presumably liberal values of the Northeast. The *Boston Phoenix* quoted a social service worker as saying, "There is a time warp. You come up I-93, and you are not talking 30 miles away from Boston, but light years away."[73] The former mayor of Lawrence, Kansas, for example, explained her surprise as she watched the TV coverage of the riots: "It doesn't usually happen in a city like Lawrence, Mass., it happens in a city like Montgomery, Alabama."[74]

By the 1980s, most U.S. Americans, especially northern liberals, understood that open expressions of prejudice had become taboo. The Civil Rights movement had successfully characterized bigots as ignorant throwbacks from an inglorious past, and the virulent racism expressed by white rioters was thus a shameful stain on the city. One observer explained that the bigoted comments made to reporters in Lawrence would not be heard in Boston, because "there's enough of a liberal veneer there so as not to say such things."[75] Of course, the "liberal veneer" that silenced *expressions* of prejudice didn't mean prejudiced *beliefs* had disappeared. In place of explicit bigotry, a coded language arose in the post–Civil Rights era that referred to people of color only indirectly, such as "inner-city youth" and "welfare queens." While prejudice had by no means disappeared, most of the nation, and particularly liberal Massachusetts, took pride in having moved beyond explicitly bigoted language by the 1980s, and shamelessly outspoken Lawrencians stood out against this. City leaders attempted to minimize the bigotry evident in the riots because they did not want Lawrence to get the reputation of a racist backwater, out of touch with contemporary New England.

Beyond the desire to avoid being seen as ignorant and parochial, city leaders had a second and more concrete reason to worry about the impact of the riots on Lawrence's reputation. Attracting private industry had long been Lawrence's main redevelopment strategy. Even after decades of failure, city leaders remained hopeful that they could revive the city's failing manufacturing economy by capitalizing on the historic charm and hardworking residents of Lawrence, thus providing both jobs and a necessary boost in tax revenue.

As discussed in Chapter 3, the official pursuit of an economic renaissance through attracting wealth to Lawrence, rather than building the assets of the people already in the city, was a long-standing vision of the city's leadership. Acquiring a national reputation as a bigoted little town with violent, rebellious residents had the potential to seriously undermine city leaders' vision for Lawrence.

The city had recently created an industrial park in an effort to recruit manufacturers, and Harold Brooks owned much of the land in the park. As a result, he was particularly invested in protecting the city's reputation. He argued that the rioters were working against their best interests. If they wanted jobs, he reasoned, they ought to protect the image of the city in order to attract investment. Brooks publicly dismissed the rioters and their right to the city, saying simply, "Whatever the trash is, get it out of here." In his view, the rioters were impeding Lawrence's economic recovery with their lack of concern for the city's reputation. Cleaning up Lawrence for its renaissance required ridding the city of its unruly poor—getting the "trash" out.[76]

The official denial of the racial tenor of the riots was shocking and outrageous to many residents, as well as to the nonlocal media. Reporters who came from out of town often had a slightly more critical perspective on Lawrence than the local paper, and they were much less likely to fall in line with official city perspectives. One reporter recalled, "I was amazed to hear the racist barrage of comments among the rioters and the total dismissal of racial overtones by city officials. . . . To the trained or untrained eye, the riots clearly expressed racial tensions and a cross-fire of racist hatred."[77] City officials' vocal dismissal of the idea that the violence was related to race struck many as discordant or even dishonest.

Most of the city council's meetings during the riots were held in executive session, so there is no direct record of what was said behind closed doors. State representative Kevin Blanchette, however, recounted events at a city council meeting during the riots that contrasted sharply with the neutral tone city officials took in public. Blanchette had stormed into the meeting with Congressman Jim Shannon to demand the council take action in the face of the growing disturbance. "We witnessed an incredible meeting of the city fathers [city council] that lasted only seven minutes. . . . We demanded they do something . . . call a state of emergency so the state police could be called in. . . . Several of the city [aldermen] yelled back: 'It's the state's damn fault for dumping all these minorities into Lawrence.' . . . 'It's your fault we have all this scum in the housing projects.' . . . 'Why don't you pass legislation to keep all these "spics" from moving here?' . . . Yes, said publically . . . from the same city council who, to this day, claims there were no racial overtones to the riots."[78] These quotes are secondhand, but the argument that Lawrence bore a disproportionate part of the state's burden of housing low-income residents is one that city officials had made before. These comments were attempting to draw attention to the metropolitan inequality that concentrated Latinos and the poor in cities, but it is difficult to recognize that kernel of truth through the heavy veil of bigotry in the comments.

As the city government denied the racial underpinnings of the riots, the police denied the charge that long-standing abuse from their officers had helped fuel the anger of the Latino rioters. Lawrence police chief Joseph Tylus denied that there was any special tension between his almost entirely white police force and the Latino residents of Lawrence. Only two of the ninety-six officers on the force were Latino, however, and the U.S. Department of Justice's Community Relations Service had been keeping an eye on interactions between police and the community in Lawrence for years. During the riot, several Latino Lawrencians had told the *New York Times* that the Lawrence police had conducted public strip searches of Latinos in the Essex Street projects. Tylus claimed he had "never heard" the accusations of public strip searches and called the idea "highly improbable" and "almost ludicrous." The chief went further and dismissed the idea that his officers might express bigotry at all. He claimed he knew of *no cases* in which police officers had used racial slurs toward Latinos, adding that in "99 percent" of such cases the person guilty of verbal abuse "turned out to be the civilian."[79] Tylus derisively denied Latino complaints of police misconduct, attempting to portray the police as the real victims of abuse.

Some city leaders, and even some Latino leaders, argued that the riots weren't about race, because it was only a certain type of Latino who had engaged in the rioting, specifically urban Latinos from New York City. The president of the city council, Anthony Silva, asserted that one reason for the city's ethnic tension and recent violence lay in the kinds of Latino immigrants who settled there: "They're coming to Lawrence very hardened, very tough, very street wise."[80] In Silva's mind, it was not simply that the rioters were Latino but that they were urban Latinos "hardened" by lives of poverty and struggle. His comments reflected the reality that many Latino Lawrencians had migrated from New York City to escape violence and overcrowding there. At least one Latino community leader, Cesar Caminero, apparently agreed with Silva, telling the city council that he had been in Lawrence for nineteen years and did not believe this violence was purely about animosity between whites and Latinos. He explained that "a lot of new people are living in the projects and some are different in cultur[e] and some probably from New York."[81] As Latino Lawrencians fought against stereotypes, Caminero's goal was likely to point out that Latinos in Lawrence were a diverse group, not all of whom had been or would choose to be involved in fighting against white residents. Yet such comments could easily be read as reinforcing a perception of Latinos as outsiders—if not as foreigners, then as thuggish New Yorkers—undermining Lawrence's quality of life.

If the riots were not racial, as city officials asserted, what can explain their destructive fury? City officials were quick to blame the media for fueling the riots. As Mayor Buckley argued, "If the media hadn't come in, we could have resolved this after the first night."[82] Silva added that the mindless pursuit of fame through violence was particularly enticing, given the rioters' economic background: "How often does a poor person get a chance to not just watch 'Fort Apache' on TV, but take part in it?"[83] "Fort Apache" refers to the 1981 movie *Fort Apache: The Bronx*, a crime drama about a police precinct set in a decaying Puerto Rican neighborhood in New York City (the movie included a neighborhood riot over police brutality). Once again, urban poverty, specifically the poverty of New York Latinos, was referenced to account for the rioters' behavior. Silva's argument was that fighting in the streets in front of TV cameras offered poor Lawrence residents a slice of the glamour created by a popular culture fascinated with urban decay and racial violence.

WE'VE BECOME A NASTY LITTLE CITY

While Latino organizers and their allies pressed for the riots to be read as a rational protest against systemic injustice, others in the city dismissed the riots as the irrational behavior of dangerous hooligans. One onlooker, Jose Santiago, explained, "This is just craziness for no reason."[84] For some observers, the violence against those trying to help seemed most irrational and most disappointing. Deputy fire chief Richard W. Fredette recounted that residents of the city's poorer neighborhoods had thrown rocks and garbage at firefighters all summer whenever firefighters had come into the neighborhood. Fredette was among the many white residents of the city for whom the riots symbolized Lawrence's precipitous decline. The attacks on firefighters signaled to some residents that many of their fellow Lawrencians had lost their moral compass. He explained, "I'm tired of euphemisms that gloss over the problems. We're not the friendliest little city in the United States. We've become a nasty little city with nasty, atrocious things going on."[85]

In a wide array of interviews he conducted after the riots as part of his master's thesis, Joseph Duran noticed this theme repeatedly: "The riots are seen as the acts of 'alienated,' 'disoriented,' 'crazy' citizens acting out their 'hysteria' because 'they didn't know what else to do.'"[86] Such perceptions could dangerously undermine the power of the riots as protest because the irrational acts of a few hooligans certainly do not require systemic changes to the city's political or economic system. After the first night of rioting, an *Eagle-Tribune* editorial argued, "A change of atmosphere is needed. The neighborhood—the housing project—needs something other than another hot night with nothing to do but hang out. A good rainstorm would help, or a community meeting with a goal of planning good things for the future, or, even, a street dance."[87] This is perhaps the most extreme expression of the dismissal of the riots' political element. According to the editorialists, what project residents needed was not improved living conditions or an end to discrimination, but a party!

Most Latinos, however, argued strongly that the riots were a protest or became an opportunity to protest once they were under way. One unemployed Latino resident said he had a friend from outside the neighborhood who tried to sneak past the blockades to participate in the riot. "Now's our chance," the friend told him, "our chance to band together and make people give us some attention." When asked if he participated, the interviewee responded, "Sure I joined in. . . . What the hell . . . I had a few things to get off my chest about the racist [leaders] who run this city."[88] Duran argued that many rioters joined in as a deliberate decision to send a message that Latinos in Lawrence were collectively "fed up with lack of access." Duran's informants discussed that they joined the riot as a "cry for help" or because the community's "needs [were] not being met" or out of "anger at the system," to name a few reasons. He also argued that the riots were clearly a deliberate protest, rather than irrational violence, because there was no sniper shooting at the police, "although many informants claim[ed] the number of citizen-owned handguns is quite high." According to Duran, the lack of sniper fire indicated the rioters' restraint, demonstrating that the disturbances were only a means to the end of making their voices heard.[89]

Many white Lawrencians, however, simply viewed the riots as another example of the lawlessness that had taken over their city and of the inability or unwillingness of the police to restore law and order. "The hoodlums own the street," said Jim John, a retired mechanic who lived next to the liquor store that was looted and burned.[90] Although he acknowledged the racial tension that had fueled the riots, he blamed alcohol and "lawless punks" for the bulk of the trouble.[91] Such beliefs that the rioters were "hoodlums" engaged in irrational violence had the potential to strip the riots of their power as political protest.

THIS USED TO BE A GOOD CITY . . .
BUT I THINK IT'S TIME TO MOVE

The white flight from Lawrence that had been under way for decades was reinforced by the accelerating urban crisis of the 1980s, and many white residents viewed the riots specifically as a catalyst to move. White residents of Lower Tower Hill reminisced sadly to reporters about Lawrence's imagined heyday. A thirty-five-year resident of the neighborhood, Carmen Ralph, reminisced, "It was really nice then. . . . We used to sit on the porch at night, and everyone knew each other so it was quite social. You could go out and not lock your door." She and other residents told the interviewer that the neighborhood had "changed complexion" in the last ten years, however, and in spite of their nostalgic love for the city, they had been persuaded that the Lawrence they cherished no longer existed.[92]

One resident called in to the local newspaper's "Sound Off" section to complain, "It was said Lawrence was the worst or nearly the worst city in which to reside in the United States. After the riots, Lawrence is the worst city to live in on the face of the earth."[93] Jim John, the retired mechanic quoted above, explained that he'd lived in Lawrence for forty years. The *Boston Herald* depicted him mourning the changes in Lawrence, shaking his head and saying, "This used to be a good city . . . but I think it's time to move."[94]

While white residents condemned the decline of the city and spoke of the necessity of moving out, Latinos expressed a firm commitment to remaining in the neighborhood and not being scared off. None of the Latino residents interviewed discussed a plan to leave the city. This did not mean Latinos lacked the desire to live somewhere free of Lawrence's troubles; rather, it was a result of constrained settlement choices. As a young Puerto Rican mother noted after the riots, "I have nowhere else to go. . . . I have to stay here."[95] The plans that whites made to leave the city reflected the reality that many had the option to move to the suburbs. They could leave Lawrence for a place without racial tension and largely without open violence, for a place without poverty or desperation or such political exclusion that rioting seemed the only way to be heard. For many Latino Lawrencians, however, moving to a place without open violence, poverty, or political marginalization was more difficult, whether because of explicit housing discrimination, the

The Riots of 1984

disproportionate concentration of public housing in struggling urban centers, the lack of multifamily rental housing in the suburbs, or the spiraling cost of suburban homeownership.

Furthermore, for Latinos, moving to Lawrence's lily-white suburbs would not bring an end to racial tension in their lives but would likely cause an exacerbation of it. As a Dominican teenager who had lived in Lawrence's most blue-collar suburb explained, "There was more prejudice in Methuen than there is in Lawrence. Our white neighbors used to call the police if we parked our car in front of their house."[96] In contrast to Lawrence's reputation for bigotry, breaking the racial homogeneity in the suburbs could be even more difficult than dealing with harassment in Lawrence, where at least there was strength in numbers for the city's Latinos.

The racialized political economy of suburban exclusion encouraged Latinos to focus their activism *within* the city, for access to city-level decision-making and street-level safety, but some white Lawrencians were also eager to point out the role of suburban exclusion in concentrating Latinos in the city. Eugene Declercq's opinion piece in the *Eagle-Tribune* was titled, "While Suburbs Duck, Lawrence Flounders: Riot Wasn't Just Urban Problem." Declercq challenged the accusations that the riots demonstrated a bigotry that was somehow unique to the small city and derided the "token liberalism" of the suburbs: "To say racism doesn't exist in Lawrence is stupid. To pretend it exists in any greater proportion in Lawrence than in ethnically homogenous suburbs is equally stupid."[97]

Declercq was one of very few commentators to take a metropolitan view of the riots, one that drew attention to the reality of the region's political economy. He challenged the suburban exemption from responsibility for the region's poor, an exemption premised on a politics of local control that enabled people living in the suburbs to exclude low-income residents as a way of protecting their property values and public services. "The cherished property values of the wealthy communities that surround Lawrence are secure because of a system that isolates its poor in cities like mine." Although he did not deny the bigotry within Lawrence, he focused blame instead on the political economy of suburbanization and Latino exclusion from suburban opportunities. Further, he questioned the naturalness of urban concentrations of poverty and communities of color: "Does anyone seriously think that Hispanics coming to the U.S. wouldn't rather live in Andover than in Lawrence? The success of suburban communities in seeing that low income housing is not built within their borders exacerbates the problem and forces cities like Lawrence into a vicious cycle of poverty."[98]

Declercq concluded his piece with what he ironically projected would be the future motto of the region if suburban political power held sway: "Give me your tired, your poor, your huddled masses yearning to breathe free—but make sure they live in Lawrence and not near us."[99] His critique of the racialized metropolitan political economy in Greater Lawrence made it clear that there was nothing natural about the designation of racial tension, poverty, and unemployment as "urban problems." There had been, rather, a long-standing effort to cordon off the city in many ways, to confine those social problems and the people associated with them to deteriorating urban centers. While white Lawrencians made plans to move away from the city in the wake of the riots, Latinos made it clear that they planned to stand their ground in Lawrence, however constrained that choice might be.

THIS IS WHAT YOU CALL AN ALL-OUT WAR

Media accounts often attempted to soften their depictions of the racial acrimony in Lawrence by discussing "racial tension" rather than racial inequality. Without any discussion of structural inequality, however, white and Latino rioters were implicitly portrayed as equally socially positioned and therefore equally culpable for the ostensibly mindless violence. The Boston Globe, for example, focused on "mutual hatred" and on the prejudices of "both sides," portraying racial hostility not as a means of maintaining or challenging the privileges of whiteness but as a result of unjustifiable mutual dislike.[100] This emphasis on mutual prejudices rather than on racial inequality reflected a specifically liberal view of race that came to dominate in the post–Civil Rights era, in which many whites imagined that society was now free of structural barriers to racial equality and thus ought to be beyond discussions of race. Old-fashioned prejudices would presumably evaporate if not voiced.[101] An even more watered-down version of this narrative focused not on "mutual hatred" but simply on cultural "misunderstandings." As a neighborhood priest explained, "People are afraid of the unknown. . . . They don't always understand cultures different from their own, and sometimes a lack of trust grows out of that misunderstanding."[102] These ideas reflected accurately the complicated racial status of Latinos but also served as a coded way to talk/not talk about race in the post–Civil Rights era.

Many observers attempted to bridge the cultural misunderstandings between the two groups by noting their shared history of immigration, including a shared experience of prejudice when they arrived. The Boston Herald argued, "The unique history of this factory town shows that each new group of immigrants that arrived faced similar problems. . . . [Textile mills] drew their first workforce from Irish immigrants fleeing famine. The succeeding waves of migrations put workers from Quebec, Italy, Poland and China into the crowded factories, earning Lawrence the nickname, 'The Immigrant City.' Harsher nicknames were given to the immigrant workers. City newspapers of the late 1800s are filled with references to 'noisy Irish rabble,' 'fighting Francais' and 'Pigtail Laundrymen.'"[103] This shared history of immigration and prejudice, the article implied, ought to unite white and Latino Lawrencians, not divide them. Yet this emphasis on Lawrence's history as the Immigrant City with a diverse population, all of whom had known but overcome prejudice, obscured the structural obstacles to Latino incorporation in Lawrence and their profoundly racialized position in the region. The narrative of a shared immigrant experience, like the narrative of cultural misunderstandings, reflected a liberal view that racial divisions were the result only of ignorance and could be overcome if different groups of people could be educated to recognize their essential commonalities.

Yet the relatively recent immigrant origins of many Lawrence whites did not necessarily lead to a sense of solidarity with Latinos. A seventy-five-year-old white resident of Lawrence, the daughter of Lithuanian immigrants, who had lived in Lawrence all her life, offered this illustration of "what happens" when Latino families move into the neighborhood: "First the storm door goes, then the window on the front door, then the bottom part of the fence when the kids kick them out." She asked rhetorically, "Who makes a slum?" and answered, "It's the people who live there." After blaming Latinos for the changes in her neighborhood, she concluded with a theme taken up by many of the children and grandchildren of immigrants who condemned the differences they perceived between their forebears and more recent migrants: "My parents came here with nothing and they made it."[104]

Her complaints touched on two of the key narratives in white opposition to Latino settlement in Lawrence. The first was that Latinos had been responsible for blight and neighborhood decline by failing to keep up the properties that they rented (obscuring both the legal responsibility of landlords, not tenants, to maintain properties and the disinvestment that preceded Latino settlement). The second was a familiar argument in this era from "white ethnics," the descendants of early twentieth-century European immigrants. Many argued that their immigrant forebears made it in America without help. Such a "boot-strap" argument, however, obscured the massive federal largesse that facilitated the social and economic mobility of early twentieth-century immigrants and their children and grandchildren. The New Deal, the GI Bill, and federally sponsored suburbanization had played a major role in separating the white ethnics of the 1980s from the squalor that many of their parents and/or grandparents had endured in the 1910s. Comparisons with early twentieth-century European immigrants also eclipsed the structural changes in the U.S. economy that had severely affected the urban job market and worker opportunities for upward mobility. Working-class immigrants in the earlier industrial era suffered a variety of hardships, but they certainly did not suffer the widespread urban unemployment that defined postindustrial Lawrence.[105] And of course, these comparisons to earlier European immigration also obscured that Latinos were mostly imperial migrants who arrived in Lawrence as a result of the long history of U.S. intervention in their home countries and thus had a different sense of the promise and perils of the United States.

Although many reporters tried to downplay the bigotry of white Lawrencians, a few white residents refused to adopt the liberal code of the post–Civil Rights era. They expressed the negative attitudes they held toward Latinos candidly to the press. Much to the chagrin of city leaders and more liberal white residents of the city, comments from bigoted white Lawrencians dramatically contributed to the city's reputation as a racist backwater. One white resident of Lower Tower Hill referred to "sandblasting" his Latino neighbors "just like graffiti."[106] A group of white youth in front of Cozy Café explained that the riot was "strictly racial" and told the press they hoped that the violence would continue.[107] Clearly, some white Lawrencians were not persuaded by the idea of cultural misunderstandings. "This is what you call an all-out war," one explained.[108]

Some white Lawrencians openly voiced their perception that Latinos received unfair privileges. One explained why white residents were leaving the city: "It's going downgrade. . . . There's too much one-sidedness [in favor of Hispanics]."[109] A white businessman in his sixties said of the violence, "It had to come. This used to be a good city but you get all these Spanish people in here and 90 percent of them don't work. I think they're pushy people." He claimed there were daily crowds of Latinos outside the welfare office on Lawrence Street and added, "You never see a white person there."[110] This claim—that Lawrence whites never received welfare—was, of course, untrue, yet it reflected the beliefs of many whites in the city that Latinos were actually being *over*served by the government, not marginalized as they claimed. This idea echoed the larger conservative movement in the 1980s aimed at dismantling the welfare state in the belief that it benefited the "undeserving" urban poor.[111] Many Lawrence whites embraced the idea that Latinos were simultaneously lazy and "pushy"—refusing to work yet milking the city government for underserved benefits. These narratives made it easy to blame the decline of the city on its newest residents. As one radio announcer explained, Latinos were the "whipping boys" of the city, the scapegoats for the city's decline.[112]

As much as the riots showcased the tension and conflict in Lawrence, some of the coverage displayed, intentionally or not, a remarkable degree of interracial cooperation and friendship also present in the city. Clips and photos of white and Latino neighbors and friends sitting together or talking were interspersed throughout the TV coverage. NBC focused on a large group of white and Latino young men who had gathered the day after the second night of rioting to discuss how they could prevent another night of violence. The main representative from each side agreed to talk to all their friends and try to calm everyone down, and the camera lingered on their hands as they shook on the agreement.[113] Many Lawrencians were anxious to point out the examples of racial harmony and cross-cultural friendships that existed within the city. A white resident who had lived on Oxford Street for eight years said, "We never had trouble. . . . The [Hispanic] families and us all live together. There's no racial problem."[114] In a press conference, Governor Michael Dukakis read a statement in English and Spanish that called on a presumed history of cooperation, or at least mutual tolerance, in Lawrence: "You have lived and worked and played together for years—in friendship and peace."[115] This racial harmony, however true and numerous the examples may have been, was not at the forefront of most residents' minds, particularly those Latino residents who viewed the riots as a rare opportunity to point out the racism and exclusion they faced in the city.

IT SEEMS THE AMERICANS HAVE A CHOICE ABOUT WHETHER THEY WILL RECOGNIZE US AS CITIZENS

Latino residents and community leaders were the most insistent that the riots were indeed racial. When asked about the riots, many Latinos emphasized the daily prejudice and harassment they encountered from whites. One resident of the riot neighborhood stated, "It's like a little drop of water that keeps hitting you in the back of your head. After a while it drives you crazy."[116] One Latina discussed the absurdity of white prejudice against Latinos, arguing that it was senseless to judge a person's worth based on skin color: "We [have] different colored skin and people don't want to understand that we're all the same. You know, they just think that just because we're a little darker . . . that we're just, what? Worse than them?"[117]

U.S. Representative Jim Shannon walked through Lower Tower Hill after the first night of rioting and met with Anna Ocasio, whose broken window had catalyzed the rioting. Her explanation put the incident into the larger context of the racist harassment Latinos endured in the city. "We don't mess around with nobody. . . . They hurt my kids. They said they was gonna burn this house. When we go to the store they call us names and everything."[118] Ocasio pointed out that Latinos were victims of pervasive threats and violence from neighborhood whites. Her comments make clear that the tension that erupted in the riots was a result of repeated incidents of harassment and intimidation. The confrontation stemmed, in this view, not from a desire for violence but from a desire for safety: for the right to walk to the store unmolested and live without the fear of glass raining down onto one's children.

Latinos argued that these prejudices led to frustration and dismay among immigrants to the city. One Latino explained, "We are disappointed that the opportunities that brought us here are affected by the attitudes of the townspeople . . . many of whom have told us to go back where we came from . . . just like what they yelled during the riots." The informant hypothesized that the perception of Latino Lawrencians as illegitimate residents of the city undergirded much of the white anger expressed during the rioting: "Actually that's what I think started the riots. . . . They assumed that we are all illegal aliens." This presumption of illegality was misguided (not that it would have justified the racist outrage of the riots even if it were true), as most Latino residents of the riot neighborhood were Puerto Rican. As the informant pointed out, "As Puerto Ricans we have no choice about U.S. citizenship . . . but it seems the Americans have a choice about whether they will recognize us as citizens."[119] The white rioters chanting of "U.S.A., U.S.A." and "Who's American? We are" must have been especially painful and absurd in this context.[120] Citizenship is assumed to entail full access to the privileges and responsibilities of the United States. The choice that white Lawrencians had, to either acknowledge or ignore the reality of Puerto Rican citizenship, reflected the enduring power of racism to create second-class citizens.

Many Latinos viewed the riots as a form of self-defense, as an expression of their commitment to fight against the prejudice and harassment they encountered. A young Latino resident of the neighborhood explained on NBC news that he and other young people had rioted because they had been continually denied basic respect: "We're tired of being put down. Please, we are tired of being put down."[121] One of Duran's informants summed up the hopes of Latinos for life in Lawrence and the obstacles they faced: "People tell us that to make it in America we have to work and study hard. . . . We would love to have a full chance to do those things . . . a good and decent job and opportunities for a good education. . . . But I do not see those opportunities here for everybody." In this context of frustration and disappointment, Latinos were compelled to struggle and protest for the most basic opportunities. "What it [may] come to is that we will have to fight for these things. . . . And believe me, if it comes to that, we will fight."[122]

One community leader called for "neighborly love" but added, "I am a realistic [woman], though, and I realize that even love must be fought for." She elaborated on her commitment to persevere in Lawrence, placing it in the context of U.S. revolutionary war: "I am not an educated [woman] but I have learned that this country itself was built by those willing to fight for their freedom. . . . As old as I am I will fight in whatever way is necessary to make sure my children and their children can have their rightful share of dignity and hope in Lawrence." By invoking her children's children, she affirmed the commitment of many Latinos to make Lawrence a permanent home. She continued by expressing her willingness to endure violence and unrest in the city to end the suffering of Lawrence Latinos: "If it takes riots then let it take riots. . . . We can no longer be ignored."[123] These statements reflected a clear commitment among many Latinos to embrace the riots as a protest, as a fight for the rights they were being denied, and as an insistence on their right to stay and build community in Lawrence.

Some Latinos emphasized that they were reluctant to protest, however. As one young Latino told ABC, "We all got families, you know? We don't need this." He argued that Latinos did not start the fighting but would not allow themselves to be pushed around and harassed.[124] Although Latinos were committed to fighting if necessary, their ultimate goal was not to struggle against the city but to contribute to it, to be fully at home in Lawrence. As one of Duran's informants said, "We want to be part of the total community . . . to contribute our culture . . . to raise our families. . . . But none of this is possible if we are kept in a position of earning such low wages . . . if we are kept at the bottom of the pile . . . if we are kept poor."[125] Another explained, "We [Hispanics] are not opposed to America. . . . We are here because we too believe in the freedom and the opportunity that is supposed to be what American democracy is all about. . . . Rather than ask whether Hispanics wanted to tear down the system, you should ask whether the system is keeping its part of the bargain . . . whether they are practicing democracy or just talking it."[126] The Spanish-language, Boston-based newspaper *La Semana* argued that Latinos needed to receive "*el apoyo necesario para acomodarse como un miembro armónico del cuerpo social de la ciudad, no como una minoría inconveniente que debe ser ignorada* [the support necessary to situate themselves as harmonious members of the social body of the city, not as an inconvenient minority that should be ignored]."[127] In these arguments, Latinos portrayed themselves as committed to an American Dream of opportunity, freedom, and democracy, as struggling simply for the right to contribute to the city.

WE ARE SLAVES TO THEIR INACTION

Many Latino Lawrencians blamed not only harassment from other city residents but also neglect specifically from the city government. One community leader noted that "many of the people who got involved wanted to turn the riots into a demonstration of how these city fathers . . . had better take care of their children." Dismissing the paternalism implicit in the common term "city fathers," the informant argued that "we pay more respect to our pets than they do to our people" and "they abuse and neglect their children." Foreshadowing the Latino political power that would transform the city in the following decades, the informant warned that "if they don't take better care of their 'children' then some of the children are going to have to take over as city fathers."[128] Another Latino resident said, "I do not understand the political system here . . . partly because I do not speak English and partly because when things are explained to me . . . about what the leaders say they are going to do . . . I look around and I see nothing. . . . Politicians here are masters of the words . . . and we are slaves to their inaction."[129] Many Latinos viewed neglect from city officials as one of the main causes of the riots.

Although city officials were careful with their language after the riots, many Latinos expressed the belief that city officials harbored hidden anti-Latino sentiments, such as those state representative Kevin Blanchette claimed city leaders revealed during closed council meetings. Echoing the rioters' taunts that Latinos should "go back where [they] came from," one Latino resident expressed his opinion that the city leaders felt the same way, and he suggested with outrage, "Maybe they should put us in an envelope and mail us home."[130] Another Latino resident said, "There is still an attitude at city hall that if they had their way they would kick all of us out of the city."[131] Many Latinos echoed this sense that they were not welcome in Lawrence, that city leaders considered the very presence of Latinos an obstacle to the city's success.

The words of a community leader best illustrate the mistrust that many Latinos felt toward the city officials: "We sense that the politicians mean only to intimidate us or dominate us. . . . They do [not] mean for us to join them in city hall, they only want us to put them there." Her comments focused on the injustice of Latinos' exclusion and depicted the riots as just one piece of a much larger struggle. "We asked them why they have ignored us and we are told to sit down, shut [up], or get out.... Always we are told to wait ... and we are made to feel that we have no place in city hall." Given the economic and living conditions that Latinos were forced to endure under an unresponsive city government, this organizer concluded, "To me this is more an act of war than the riots could ever be."[132] In this view, the exclusion of Latinos from city decision-making was itself a form of violence.

For other Latinos, particularly those who had participated in the riots, it was specifically the behavior of the police that was so infuriating. An unemployed nineteen-year-old Puerto Rican man recounted persistent police harassment: "The [police] call us bad names all the time." He added that the police were always slow to respond to calls for help "when it's from our area."[133] A young rioter argued that the protests resulted from frustration with years of police prejudice against Latinos: "We can't even ride a bike because they say it is stolen. We want even protection by the police."[134] A Latino restaurant worker in his mid-twenties (surrounded by a dozen people adding credence to his story) recounted that the Lawrence police had been conducting public strip searches in the projects, looking for drugs. In his view, the riots occurred because "we've been under pressure.... The police officers treat us like animals."[135] Some Latinos pointed out the unequal treatment of the police during the riots. A Latino teenager who admitted he was one of those fighting in the street explained that during the riots, "the police were in one corner protecting all the white people. They only came down to our corner to beat us up."[136]

WE ARE HUMANS AND WE ARE AMERICANS, TOO

Community leaders were very effective at casting the riots as a Latino protest against racism and political marginalization. Some Latino residents of Lower Tower Hill, however, saw the riots more clearly as an untamed explosion of their white neighbors' rage and bigotry. The insults shouted, the rocks thrown, and the fires started by white rioters, as well as the violence of the police, were simply further evidence of white Lawrencians' racist hatred. Latinos showed the press the wounds they received from violence during the riots. A five-month-old baby, Anna Ocasio's son, was the youngest victim. I quote the *Boston Herald* at length because the excerpt demonstrates the anti-Latino fury of the crowd and the hurt and anger of the victims:

"The baby was sleeping on the bed and the tear gas landed right outside the window. He was crying and crying and wouldn't stop. His lips turned purple."

The fumes quickly filled the woman's first-floor apartment.

"My eyes filled with tears and I felt like I was suffocating. I couldn't breathe and I felt helpless."

Ocasio said she ran out into the street and asked a police officer to call an ambulance. She said he told her to carry the baby out of the riot area and wait for the ambulance on the corner.

But that meant walking through an angry crowd of people who were screaming anti-Hispanic slurs.

The frightened mother handed the baby to her friend Jose Santana, 19, who ran through the crowd with little Daniel in his arms.

Santana said, "People were screaming and throwing stuff at me. If the police weren't around, they would've killed me."[137]

Ocasio and Santana voiced their anger at the anti-Latino harassment and violence they were forced to endure, including the riots as an example of that violence. Ocasio explained, "This has to stop. This is abuse." Ocasio wanted white Lawrencians to respect both the humanity and the citizenship rights of Puerto Ricans: "We are humans and we are Americans, too."[138]

Puerto Rican poet Martín Espada echoed Ocasio's perspective. In his poem *"Toque de queda,"* the riots were portrayed more as an act of violence against Latinos than as an act of protest by Latinos. For Espada, the mobs consisted of "white adolescents who chanted USA and flung stones at the scattering of astonished immigrants." Latinos were "astonished" and "scattering," not angry and demanding equality as many other accounts suggested.[139] Yet as Ocasio's account confirms, for some Latinos, the riots were exactly as Espada described. His poem and Ocasio's account illustrated that Latino residents of the riot neighborhood were a diverse group, and while some Latinos saw themselves as participants in an antiracist protest, others saw themselves as victims of a violent racist attack from their white neighbors. Ultimately the riots were multivocal: a Latino protest against racism and marginalization, a furious expression of white bigotry, a nativist protest against immigration, a working-class protest against urban economic decline and deindustrialization, and a popular protest against an out-of-touch city government.

Amazingly, no one was killed in the 1984 riots in Lawrence, and relatively few were injured.[140] Compared with other riots throughout the century, the violence was minimal. Yet the rioting and the conversations that followed it displayed the ongoing racialized competition over access to and control of the city's space and resources. White residents blamed Latinos for the city's decline and talked of moving out of the city, adding impetus to the suburban flight that had begun in the decades after World War II. Meanwhile, Latino residents talked of fighting for their rights and of their desire to be a part of the city. Latino activism centered on gaining access to decision-making power in Lawrence, and on the right to live safely and express themselves without fear of racist attacks. Ultimately, the meaning of the riots would be shaped as much by the activism that followed as by the violence itself.

FIVE

FORCING CHANGE

It's like somebody let the floodgate down in Boston and here
come all you folks with your notebooks and shit. . . . So now you
know about my anxiety and problems . . . now what are you going
to do? . . . Got a job for me, brother?

Latino Lawrencian quoted in Duran, "1984 Riots"

The *disturbios* in the streets of Lawrence in 1984 cracked the city open and
exposed its meanest divisions and hypocrisies. The rage of Lawrence's
disaffected was irrefutable, and the media loudly trumpeted the city's most
shameful failures. These circumstances generated tremendous political capital
for those who could harness it, and Latino organizers were quite successful in the postriot years at transforming the upheaval into political leverage
within the city and the state. Further, the riots helped to solidify a relationship between Latino activists and the federal government, in which the U.S.
Department of Justice served as a key ally in Latino efforts to gain access to
City Hall, culminating in a successful voting rights lawsuit in 1999. The growth
of Latino political strength in Lawrence after 1984 was simply undeniable, the
result of organizers building on the forceful protest of the riots to press their
claims for equal access to the city's resources and decision-making power.

Of course, the riots alone could not force white Lawrencians or city
officials to accept the growing presence of Latinos in the city. Indeed, in the
immediate aftermath of the disturbances, Latinos encountered a fierce backlash. For years after the riots, many Latinos complained that the prejudice they
faced in the city remained unchanged or had even worsened.[1] Yet this did not

preclude the riots from serving as an unprecedented platform for Latino organizing, as the media and state and federal officials shone a huge spotlight on Lawrence's "urban problems." The media (especially the *Boston Globe* and the *Boston Phoenix*) quickly focused on the recent mill closings and the deplorable living conditions in the city's public housing projects. State and federal officials focused on the absence of any meaningful Latino presence in city government and the discriminatory patronage system in place in City Hall. Latino Lawrencians used all of this attention to underscore their point that Lawrence was suffering from both pronounced economic decline and a form of systemic racism that condemned Latinos to suffer the brunt of urban crisis.

Over time, however, this twin emphasis on the city's economic *and* racial problems yielded to a more narrowly defined focus on ending discrimination and empowering Latinos politically within the city. This struggle against the political marginalization of Latinos within Lawrence was protracted but ultimately successful in many ways. Latino activism, augmented by the combined force of state and federal agencies (particularly the Massachusetts Commission against Discrimination [MCAD] and the U.S. Department of Justice), pushed city leaders to be accountable to Lawrence's Latinos. In the years after the riots, city leaders were ultimately compelled to respond to Latino demands for improved access to decision-making and to reorient the city's social services to meet the needs of Lawrence's most impoverished and fastest-growing demographic.

Yet increased Latino political power within the small city was not sufficient to transform the segregated and unequal metropolitan political economy in Greater Lawrence. Deindustrialization and suburbanization had devastated the city's job and tax base. Poverty, blight, and unemployment had been major causes of the riots, along with impoverished education, recreational, and public safety services in the city. These systemic problems were not necessarily forgotten in the years after the riots, but they were mitigated through increased state and federal aid rather than through larger structural changes. Money certainly flowed into Lawrence after the riots, but this did not reflect any broader improvements to the city's economic position. In effect, state aid came to be perceived as a form of charity given to the city by its wealthier neighbors, funds that could be given or taken away, directed or redirected, based on the vagaries of state politics. The economic crisis in Lawrence and the inequality between the city and its suburbs only became more pronounced in the years after the riots. Lawrence became increasingly reliant on funds doled out by a state government that too often reflected suburban interests.

Immediately after the riots, most media coverage considered the economic decline of the city to be absolutely central to understanding the riots. Observers seized quickly on Lawrence's economic situation, highlighting its deindustrialization, declining tax revenue, and increasing poverty. As an editorial in the Spanish-language Boston weekly *La Semana* argued, poverty had the power to spark violence. "*La violencia solo podrá desaparecer cuando se eliminen sus causas, y la pobreza es un peligroso detonante* [Violence will only disappear when its causes are eliminated, and poverty is a dangerous explosive]."[2] Many Latino community leaders were equally adamant that poverty, not simply bigotry, ignited the riot. The Reverend Daniel Rodriguez of the Hispanic Baptist Church argued, "This is a natural result of an economic situation. We cannot have so much poverty together."[3] It was not only shared poverty, however, but unequal poverty that inflamed these tensions. Although many Lawrencians were poor, observers noted that relative inequality still fueled Latino anger. Poverty mattered, but it did not create racial divisions; rather, it exacerbated these divisions. Poverty flowed along racial lines because Latinos had unequal access to jobs, housing, social services, and city government.

Inadequate and overpriced housing was particularly an issue for low-income Latinos. Patrick Smith, from the Immigrant City Community Housing Corporation, argued, "The tenements of Oxford Street have long served their purpose. . . . I wouldn't be surprised if the tenants there were paying 70 percent of their income in rents, and a lot of it to absentee landlords."[4] His estimate underscored the reality that Latinos were not finding "cheap rent" in the run-down neighborhoods in which they settled. Yet the worst conditions were reported in the housing projects, where the "absentee" landlord was the city government itself. As one project resident noted, "Why should we plant flowers when cockroaches crawl through our food, when the plumbing does not work, and heating does not work?"[5] Even Mayor John Buckley, the city official most eager to downplay the riots, later admitted that the conditions of the public housing projects reflected shameful neglect on the part of the city government. "The '84 riot involved no real racial problems. But I tell you kids, afterwards I went in to visit some Merrimack Project Apartments and my first thought was 'Shame on us—shame on every level of government responsible for this.' No bathtub, no shower, no play area. 250 families crowded in. No wonder they have problems."[6] Although Buckley maintained that the riots were not racial even after he left office, even he came to realize that the living conditions Latinos were forced to endure were simply shameful.

The *Boston Phoenix* suggested that the North Common controversy, discussed in Chapter 3, may also have inflamed feelings of animosity between Latinos and the city government. Community activists and city officials had long struggled over whether the city should focus on low-income or middle-income housing development. This struggle had played out in the city's efforts to exclude the development of low-income housing in the North Common urban renewal project, and it touched on a key difference between the visions of Latinos and white officials for the city: whether Lawrence should build adequate, affordable housing for its current residents or build higher-end housing to attract middle-income residents. Alex Rodriguez, chairperson of MCAD, argued that the city's efforts to exclude low-income housing from the North Common development had worsened relations between city officials and Latinos, as Latinos had been the majority of those cleared from the North Common area. Excluding affordable housing would mean that many of the displaced Latinos would be unable to return to the redeveloped neighborhood. Rodriguez argued that this sent a message to the city's poor along the lines of "Get out. You filled up the housing here when it was slummy, and now we, the city, are going to do something with that land, and we don't need you."[7]

Of course, the city's deindustrialization was emphasized in most media accounts as well. While the city's manufacturing sector had been declining in waves since the 1920s, the late 1970s and early 1980s had brought a new round of deindustrialization, as the city lost much of the remaining nondurable goods manufacturing that had enabled Latino settlement in the city. In August 1984, the *Boston Globe* noted that the small city had lost nearly 500 jobs since January, as three shoe manufacturers and a textile company had closed.[8] More important, perhaps, than the overall decline in manufacturing jobs was the fact that the remaining jobs in Lawrence did not afford the same opportunities to all workers; opportunities, once again, flowed along racial lines. The *Boston Phoenix* pointed out that most of the Lawrence workforce, whether white or Latino, was employed as "machine operators, assemblers, and inspectors in area factories." This common position relative to production obscured a stark difference in wages, however. In 1979, the last census available before the riots, the mean family income for whites was $18,137, while Latino families brought home just over half as much, $10,690. Poverty statistics made this divide even sharper, as the *Phoenix* noted that "roughly 50 percent of the 'Spanish-origin' population lives below the federally designated poverty level, compared to only 18 percent of the 'white' population."[9] Although factory work (and thus in some sense class status) was shared in

Lawrence, these statistics supported Latinos' claims that the economic system in the city favored white workers. With nearly half of Lawrence's Latinos living in poverty, it was obvious that the city's economic decline was having a disproportionate impact according to race.

This racial divide was evident in the unemployment figures as well. The overall unemployment rate in Lawrence was substantial. The *Globe* noted, "Unemployment in June, at 7.4 percent, was higher than any other city in the state, and even that rate was almost certainly an underestimate."[10] But Latino unemployment was both higher and growing faster than general unemployment. In 1980, unemployment among Latinos in Lawrence was 12 percent, much higher than the city's overall unemployment level of 7 percent. By 1990, Lawrence's general unemployment had risen to 15 percent, while Latino unemployment had grown to a mind-blowing 24.9 percent. At the time of the riots, unemployment was increasing, and Latinos were bearing the brunt of the joblessness. By 1990, while one-quarter of Latinos looking for a job could not find one, white unemployment in the city was only 9 percent. Although the media emphasized that unemployment and poverty contributed to the riots, the reality was that not only high but also *growing* and *unequal* poverty and joblessness were at work. Yes, the entire city was in a state of crisis, but that crisis did not play out evenly across racial lines. For imperial migrants, pushed toward Lawrence from Puerto Rico and the Dominican Republic in order to pursue opportunities foreclosed at home, the brutal joblessness wrought by deindustrialization generated extreme frustration. As one Latino resident summed it up, "The riots were about jobs . . . pure and simple. . . . Without decent employment the residents of this city have no investment here. . . . Why not riot?"[11]

As historian Andrew Diamond has noted, teenagers and young adults have often been the groups most willing to engage in urban riots, and Lawrence was no exception.[12] The circumstances for young people in Lawrence in 1984 were dire, and they highlighted the combined failures of the city's economy, its educational system, and its recreational services. The racial divide in unemployment evident among the city's adults was even more severe between white and Latino youth. White teenagers had only an 11 percent unemployment rate in 1985, compared with a shocking 35 percent unemployment rate for Latino teenagers. In addition, Lawrence's failing schools had contributed to a dropout rate of over 50 percent among Latinos. A Latino parent noted, "When you look at the mess the school is in . . . you begin to see why there were riots in Lawrence." The dropout rate combined with the high youth unemployment rate left the city with a remarkable abundance of young people who were neither in school nor employed.[13]

Forcing Change

Latino students made up more than half of the Lawrence public school population in 1984, and teachers and administrators struggled with how to teach students who were English-language learners and/or lived transnationally, frequently returning to the Dominican Republic or Puerto Rico. The *Boston Globe* noted, "Turnover rate in the classrooms is approaching 20 percent, with 1500 new students enrolling each year."[14] The superintendent complained of a student transiency rate of 55 percent and alleged that when there was racial conflict in the schools, they didn't know who the Latino student leaders were because Latino students came and went so frequently.[15] Although it was clearly unfair to blame the persistence of racial tension in the schools on the transiency of Latino students, the superintendent's comments capture the reality that the education system in Lawrence was neither designed nor equipped to build on students' bilingualism and transnational education and instead saw these things only as a hindrance to traditional schooling.

Lawrence public schools had difficulty adapting to the Latino student population in part because the school budget was in decline while student enrollment was increasing, as Latino immigration reversed the postwar flight of families from the city. A state law that capped local property taxes, Proposition 2½, went into full effect during fiscal year 1982. Before that, the *Boston Globe* noted, the Lawrence public schools had an $18 million budget to serve 7,800 students, 35 percent of whom were "minority" (almost exclusively Latino). The year before the riots, however, the school budget had declined to less than $16 million to serve 8,700 students, half of whom were "minority." This change meant a drop in per pupil spending from $2,307 to $1,839 in just a few years, and as a result, "classes met in book closets, gymnasiums and libraries."[16] In addition, the *Globe* noted that concentrated poverty in the city made Lawrence students, in many ways, disproportionately expensive to teach. "The schools reflect to an astonishing degree the sociological profile of a city with one of the highest poverty rates in the state. Three out of every four students qualify for free lunches, and two-thirds of the students require costly services in special education, bilingual and remedial programs."[17]

At the time of the riots, Lawrence Public Schools were in a state of crisis. Severely lacking in funds, the city had already been pressured by the state to dramatically improve its bilingual education program, and it was on the verge of implementing a desegregation plan, albeit one that critics claimed lacked Latino input and put too much of a busing burden on Latino students.[18] At least one Latino parent viewed the riots as protest against the city's failure to provide adequate educational services. "I don't condone violence, but I think those who rioted did the city a civic service . . . by bringing attention to the many problems for which the city is to blame. . . . If there are riots in the future, I wouldn't be surprised if parents, teachers, and students participated in them."[19] In this view, the riots were a "civic service" because they shone a spotlight on the city's failures and thus called city leaders to account.

While ending the city's marginalization of Latino students was essential, it would not be sufficient to address the larger funding problems contributing to the decline of the Lawrence public schools. One group of Latino parents offered this insight: "[The] typical response we have received when we have voiced our concerns to the school principals and teachers is that we need to understand the schools are bad for everyone and we should not be so upset because they are not discriminating." In other words, Latino parents were told that the city's public education services had declined to such an extreme that even white children were not receiving a quality education. While this must have been cold comfort for Latino families, it marks the degree to which an antidiscrimination strategy alone would ultimately be insufficient to transform the crisis city. The group of Latino parents didn't just want an end to discrimination; they wanted access to high-quality education: "[School officials] seem to think just because we are Hispanics that the only concern we have is discrimination. They do not take into account that we are no different than other parents when it comes to a quality education for our kids." Without schools that addressed the needs of all students, they argued, "none of our kids have prayer of a chance to survive or excel."[20] This group of parents wanted to transform the school system to make it work for everyone, not just to gain equal access to a failing system.

Not only did Lawrence have large numbers of young people who were neither in school nor working; the city also had very little to offer its youth in the way of recreational opportunities. As one of the Latino parents quoted above elaborated, "If the city does not provide good schools you certainly don't think they provide jobs or recreation for kids, do you?"[21] Public safety alderman Johnson argued that the riots were fueled by teenagers, mostly boys, who either were not old enough to work or could not find a job.[22] Normally, in the hot weather, restless teenagers could cool off in the public pool or at least open a fire hydrant; but the city had recently cracked down on the illegal opening of hydrants, and NBC noted that neighborhood hydrants had no water.[23] The public pool, meanwhile, had been closed for the past two years for lack of funds.[24]

Children playing on junked cars in the mid-1980s. After the 1984 riots, residents vehemently complained about the lack of recreational opportunities for youth in the city. Photo by Cheryl Senter, archived at the Lawrence History Center. Reprinted with permission from the *Eagle-Tribune*.

Education and recreation were not the only services that had been impacted by the city's decline. Public safety services were also clearly struggling, as was evident from the inability of the police to respond to the riots. Police and firefighters complained to the media about their lack of resources. The president of the police union explained that without the necessary "manpower," "the city could be burned down" before help arrived. He argued that city officials had "taken away 32 to 40 of our men" from a 132-person force in 1980. "We don't even have enough patrolmen to protect the cops on the street, let alone the public."[25] One firefighter told the *Eagle-Tribune*, "We only had 10 people for four pieces of apparatus.... Before we used to have 20."[26] Another explained, "We want to be proud of the city, do a good job, but how can we if we're scared?"[27] In the minds of many of the police and firefighters, the city's economic decline and fiscal crisis were directly responsible for its failure to provide adequate public safety services. Ending discrimination against Latinos was imperative, of course, but the riots also highlighted that the city's economic crisis had the power to undermine the hopes of all Lawrencians for a better life in the city.

Some observers argued that Massachusetts's Proposition 2½ could be blamed for a host of Lawrence's problems: not only lack of recreation but paltry school funding, insufficient numbers of police and firefighters, and the absence of a contract for teachers, firefighters, and police. Similar to California's "tax revolt" in 1978, Proposition 2½ had been passed by Massachusetts voters in 1980 in a conservative effort to limit the amount of property tax revenue a municipality could raise to 2.5 percent of the assessed value of taxable property. Mayor Buckley argued that it was Proposition 2½ that forced the city to shut down the public pool. Others argued, however, that the city actually had adequate money for public services; it was just not being apportioned fairly. The Reverend James Keller noted, "You can drive down the streets and see which (neighborhoods) get streets repaired, garbage picked up and snow removal."[28] Needless to say, predominantly poor or Latino neighborhoods were not among those served well by the struggling city. But the reality was that both sides were correct: Lawrence simply did not have enough money to offer its residents quality municipal services, and what little funds it did have were rarely channeled toward the city's Latino residents.

Still other observers pointed out that the city might be broke, but it wouldn't be if it were more diligent about collecting property taxes. A few months before the riots, a state revenue department report showed that Lawrence was short $2.4 million in uncollected fees and taxes dating back to 1980. While this missing revenue itself would not have solved the city's economic crisis, its absence drew attention to other structural problems in Lawrence beyond deindustrialization and competition with the suburbs. The city's failure to collect a portion of the tax revenue it was due reflected two situations: First, Lawrence had been a city of renters throughout its history and never had more than one-third of its housing units occupied by their owners. Absentee landlords had a prominent reputation as the scourge of the city, and it was presumably harder to collect money from property owners who did not live within city limits. Second, the city's failure highlighted Lawrence's long-standing struggle with political corruption. State representative Kevin Blanchette noted, "The system is rotten with patronage, it's like five little kingdoms." Many critics focused on Lawrence's alderman style of city governance. Unlike most cities, Lawrence had no professional administrators to head police, fire, street, or other departments. Instead, the city was run by the mayor and four aldermen, all elected at-large, and each was in charge of a major section of government, such as public safety. Each alderman was able to hire his or her own workers and set his or her own policy. No other city in Massachusetts maintained this form of government, and fewer than 3 percent of cities nationwide utilized it. Lawrence had developed legislation to transform its city government into the strong mayor and partially district-based city council form that was more common among late twentieth-century cities, but the new form of governance would not take effect until 1986, with the city's new charter.[29]

The *Boston Globe* noted that the alderman form of government was a city structure that "promote[d] an unusual amount of patronage and favoritism in the delivery of city services." As city services were provided by politicians, those services were delivered disproportionately to key election neighborhoods. Further, the at-large election of aldermen diluted Latino voting strength, because Latinos were concentrated in a few neighborhoods of the city. Alderman Kevin Sullivan, who would become mayor in 1985, acknowledged that, in Lawrence, the good jobs and lifetime appointments went to political supporters: "A good 90 percent of the people working for the City of Lawrence, except in police and fire, are politically motivated, are political appointments." Sullivan did not believe, however, that this overwhelming system of patronage made it difficult for poor Lawrencians to have their interests represented, asserting without irony, "I think the poor get treated very well."[30]

State representative Kevin Blanchette disagreed with the soon-to-be-mayor's assessment, however, arguing that "for years the City of Lawrence has been a closed shop. . . . People are fed up with the lack of access to decision-making in city government and policy-setting. . . . The riots broke out because they didn't know what else to do."[31] He argued that poor white Lawrencians also struggled to have their needs addressed by the city government under this system: "There is frustration with the city, both Anglos and Hispanics were feeling it . . . the lack of housing, city services and recreational opportunities."[32] Participants in the 1984 riots in Lawrence were evenly divided between whites and Latinos. They were fighting each other, but both sides were also clearly protesting the "closed shop" city government. White rioters had legitimate grievances; their city was in a profound state of economic decline, and they saw no clear path to change through the existing political system. While this certainly does not justify their violent scapegoating of Latinos, the corruption and unresponsiveness of the city government was part of what drove poor and working-class white rioters in Lawrence to take their complaints to the streets.

Observers who blamed the city's form of government for its neglect of Latinos anticipated that the situation might improve with the new charter, but most observers put the onus on Latinos to win political power and thereby force the city government to recognize them. Some believed that the ethnic/national diversity of Latinos in Lawrence caused their political powerlessness. Many equated Latino diversity with paralyzing divisions. As the *Boston Phoenix* argued, "They came not just from Puerto Rico, but from every Latin American nation. Their variety makes for colorful lifestyles, but it does not enhance political power."[33] Although the diversity of Latinos in Lawrence certainly precluded any easy consensus on a common agenda or strategy, it had not stopped decades of committed Latino activism in the city, both along and across ethnic lines. In retrospect, it seems obvious that Latinos in Lawrence were not suffering from a lack of leadership, a lack of commitment, or even a lack of cross-ethnic coordination; they were suffering from significant economic and political obstacles to their full incorporation into the city.

Nevertheless, some Latino community activists who had long been focused on ramping up voter registration agreed that if Latinos could overcome their ethnic divisions and apparent local political apathy, they could register enough voters to be an important political force in the city, as well as groom effective leaders for a united Latino movement. Virgil Perez, the city's director of equal opportunity and community relations, noted that of the 20,000 or so Latino residents of Lawrence, only about 5,000 were eligible to vote, and of those, only 1,500 were registered. He argued that Latinos could be a powerful voting bloc in local elections if all eligible voters voted.[34] Although this was most certainly true, alleged Latino apathy was not sufficient to account for the scale of neglect facing Latinos in Lawrence. A voting bloc should not be necessary to protect against police abuse or receive adequate maintenance in city-run housing. Further, Latino activists had already been working for decades to increase Latino voting, but they were faced with substantial obstacles created by the city until a successful U.S. Justice Department lawsuit in 1999, discussed below.

Even if the lack of Latino voting strength could explain the absence of elected Latinos in City Hall, it couldn't possibly explain the overwhelming exclusion of Latinos from city employment. Not only were there were no Latino elected officials in the city at the time of the riots; there were very few Latino staff in city government at all.[35] A 1977 executive order from Governor Michael Dukakis required cities to comply with equal employment standards or risk forfeiting state and federal funds. The goal was that 16 percent of Lawrence's workforce be Latino, equal to the Latino proportion of the population in the 1980 census. The city was under a voluntary agreement with MCAD to raise Latino hiring because it was quite far from the 16 percent goal. The most recent report before the riots, submitted by Virgil Perez, showed that of more than 800 employees in twenty-six municipal departments, only 18 were Latino, or 2 percent of the city's workforce. The *Boston Phoenix* noted that there were no Latinos among the "city's clerks, tax collectors, assessors, custodians, health-care workers, grave diggers, auto mechanics, water-department workers, librarians, assessors, purchasing agents, or engineers." There were two Latino police officers, one of whom was about to leave the force, and no more than 8 Latino firefighters out of nearly 200.[36]

A representative of MCAD explained that the lack of Latinos in city jobs sent a message to the community, and "nothing speaks louder than zero."[37] The reluctance of city officials to hire Latinos was blamed both for Latinos' sense of exclusion and for poor relations between Latinos and the police and fire departments. Rev. James Keller, from the Greater Lawrence Ecumenical Area Ministry, insisted to the *Boston Globe* that, at the very least, the city could teach firefighters and police officers some Spanish. This would not solve the problem of the lack of Latinos hired for city positions, but it would at least facilitate improved communication between the largely white police/firefighter forces and Latino communities.[38]

In the aftermath of the riots, the media, Latino activists, and state and federal antidiscrimination officials effectively drew attention to the legitimate complaints that had motivated the protests. They emphasized racialized poverty and joblessness, inadequate opportunities for youth, political corruption and patronage, and Latino exclusion from city governance and employment. This public attention gave leverage to Latino activists who were attempting to pressure the city to make changes, leverage that would be especially important given the white backlash Latinos faced in the city after the riots.

BACKLASH AND RECONCILIATION

Although the riots enabled a remarkable upswing in Latino political activism in the city, there was also a serious reentrenchment of white racism after the riots. This white backlash took two forms: renewed white flight and, in some cases, increased prejudice and discrimination. After Lawrence was broadly shamed in the media as a bigoted city during the riots, however, explicit prejudice generally yielded to coded scapegoating in the city's political discourse.

As discussed in Chapter 1, between 1940 and 1980, Lawrence had already lost 40 percent of its white population, even before Latinos made up a significant proportion of the city's population. This early white flight, encouraged by the pull of the suburbs, exploded in the 1980s as rejection of Lawrence's growing Latino presence fueled an unprecedented exodus of white residents. Although the total population of the city actually increased in the 1980s, from 63,000 to 70,000, the white population of the city decreased from 52,000 to 38,000, for a loss of 14,000 residents. In other words, a full quarter of the white people living in Lawrence in 1980 had left the city by 1990. This would be equivalent to a four-person family leaving the tiny city almost every day throughout the decade. Given the narrative examples in Chapter 4 of white residents whose decision to leave the city was spurred by the riots, it is very possible that the bulk of this exodus occurred in the latter half of the decade. Between 1990 and 2000, although slightly fewer than 14,000 white people left, this still amounted to 36 percent, or more than one-third, of the remaining white population leaving the city in these years.[39]

Within Lawrence, it seems that racial tension and quotidian expressions of anti-Latino sentiment actually grew after the riots. The surface calm in the Oxford Street neighborhood after the riots masked an underlying current of apprehension. As one Dominican resident recalled, "If you walked down the street, people looked at you funny. . . . It was calm, but you knew if somebody said something bad it would probably start all over again."[40] As Latina organizer Briseida Quiles explained it, the apparent calm in Lower Tower Hill a year after the riots was entirely attributable to the peace-oriented efforts of its residents, because little had changed structurally in the city: "The poverty is still here, and the aggressive police are still here."[41] As could be predicted from the plans expressed by white neighborhood residents to leave the city, the Lower Tower Hill neighborhood became predominantly Latino within a few years after the riots.[42] In the most basic sense, Latino rioters won the right to the neighborhood.

In addition to this tension and white flight, it seems that employment discrimination may have increased after the riots as well. One unemployed Latino reported, "I do not like to think it is discrimination but since the riots people seem afraid to hire us. . . . Others [employers] have told me plain to my face that I should go back where I came from."[43] Whether from increased discrimination or the ongoing processes of deindustrialization and suburbanization, Latino unemployment in the city had surged by 1990. It is very possible that the riots shifted the local image of Latinos among white employers from a docile labor force to urban insurgents. As discussed in Chapter 2, the recruitment of Latinos into industry in the late twentieth century was often premised on the idea that they were more tractable workers than African Americans (in the context of decades of Civil Rights and Black Power protest). The Lawrence riots and the persistent antiracist organizing that followed may have contributed to changing the perceptual frame through which Latinos in the city were viewed: from "hardworking immigrants" to "minorities" willing to fight for their rights. Gina Pérez observed a similar transformation in the discourse surrounding Puerto Ricans in Chicago after the Division Street uprising in 1966, from "model minority" to dangerous "underclass."[44] It is important to note, however, that negative stereotypes about Latinos circulated, and indeed dominated, in Lawrence long before the riots, as discussed in Chapter 3. However logically irreconcilable these two stereotypes may be (Latinos as hardworking immigrants versus Latinos as savvy welfare abusers), they could coexist discursively at the same historical moment, providing a flexible arsenal of anti-Latino rhetoric. Latino community organizer Felix Mejía summed up these malleable white beliefs about Latinos in the city: "If you work, you're taking the job away from someone else. If you don't work, you're on welfare." Mejía derided the unjustifiable white hostility against Latinos: "We work, we bring checks home, they treat us like pigs."[45]

The white backlash against Latino settlement in the city after the riots was perhaps most evident in the election of Alderman Kevin Sullivan to mayor in 1985. Latino activists argued that Sullivan ran on a coded anti-Latino campaign of "giving the city back to those who built it."[46] In a radio ad "paid for by the people that want their city back," Sullivan reportedly argued that "we've catered too much to groups that have no roots in the city."[47] Although he rejected the idea that he was referring to Latinos or immigrants as those who "have no roots" in Lawrence, his critics argued that this language was clearly a coded way to invoke anti-Latino sentiment without expressing explicit bigotry. Nunzio DiMarca summed up the common Latino criticism of Mayor Sullivan: "I still have many disagreements with Mayor Sullivan's views, who I believe got elected as mayor of Lawrence by being anti-Hispanic." Foremost among those disagreements was the mayor's discussion of welfare reform, which DiMarca and a number of organizers decried as "littered with racial innuendos."[48] In 1989, Guilmo Barrio, the Chilean-born director of the city's Human Rights Commission, resigned after submitting a letter to the *Eagle-Tribune*. The letter derided the mayor's anticrime rhetoric as racially coded. The mayor's "attacks on Hispanics and the poor are at best unsupported demagoguery," Barrio wrote. "At worst, they are vicious half truths designed to inflame racial and class hatred."[49] In Lawrence after the riots, explicitly bigoted commentary was no longer acceptable, particularly as Latino organizers marshaled the power of the state and federal government to protect their civil rights. Instead, a political language of racial innuendos and coded references to the city's Latinos evolved to take its place, as I discuss further in Chapter 6.

In spite of this backlash, the riots precipitated a host of positive changes. As Ramón Borges-Méndez has summarized, "In the aftermath of the riots, the city responded to the plight of Latinos with a number of policy measures that marked the beginning of a more open—although uneasy—sociopolitical relationship between Latinos and Anglos."[50] Religious leaders were some of the first to reach out to the city's Latino community in an effort to heal the breach in the wake of the riots. The day after the riots ended, Lawrence clergy appeared on local cable television "to call for peace and unity" and to announce that Archbishop Bernard F. Law would say a special mass at St. Mary's Church in Lawrence on Sunday.[51] Nearly 1,000 people showed up for the archbishop's mass, given in English, Spanish, and French. He told the congregation, "We are one," and asked members of different ethnic groups to stand up to rounds of applause. In a city whose public discourse had been filled for days with diversity as the source of Lawrence's tension, Law took the unusual step of celebrating that diversity: "What a blessing it is, what a strength it is. How much weaker this community would be if it would suddenly find itself bereft of any single group."[52] The archbishop's speech resonated with a sincere desire for unity and cooperation held by many white and Latino Lawrencians.

Another organization was moving quickly on a similar path. The so-called Yellow Hat Brigade, discussed in Chapter 4, lost no time mobilizing after the riots. They renamed themselves the Alliance for Peace and began a two-pronged approach to changing the city: They attempted to put pressure on the city council to be responsive to the community needs being articulated during and after the riots, while working to channel the anger of the riots into peaceful protest. The Alliance for Peace organized Latinos, especially those living in the housing projects, encouraging them to speak out and demand changes from the city government, but not through violence.[53]

In the months after the riots, the Alliance for Peace became the main bridge between the Latino community and the city. City leaders boasted of their relationship with the Alliance for Peace, using it as evidence of their willingness to engage with the community over issues such as housing conditions and Latino feelings of exclusion from city government. Community leaders in the Alliance for Peace, however, including Isabel Melendez, pressed the city for more than just improved communication, holding the city accountable for real changes. In the Lower Tower Hill neighborhood, for example, city officials yielded to community pressure to establish a recreation

Forcing Change

center in the Oxford Street area and opened a neighborhood housing services office. The city created a human rights commission to facilitate improved communication between city officials and the community and increased its efforts to hire Latinos in municipal jobs such as public administration and public safety.[54]

While city leaders committed themselves to improving communication between City Hall and the community, state officials increased oversight of city hiring to ensure antidiscrimination protocol was fully followed. After the riots, official exclusion of Lawrence's Latinos effectively became impossible. While these efforts did not eliminate racism in the city, the riots and the changes that they precipitated placed Latino needs and demands firmly on the city's agenda and served notice to white residents that prejudice and harassment would not go unanswered. The riots had made clear that Latino Lawrencians were willing to fight for their right to live, work, and raise their children in the city. Although the path to resolving the city's economic crisis remained unclear, it was now undeniable that there could be no future for Lawrence that did not include Latinos.

STATE AID AND SUBURBAN POLITICS

The initial response to the riots from the state government was ambivalent. Some politicians, like Governor Michael Dukakis, were adamant that the riots were a local problem that required local solutions and, indeed, that even city officials had little role to play beyond reestablishing "law and order." Dukakis argued that "the problems have got to be solved by the community itself. They can't be solved by the mayor or in the State House."[55] Yet many other state officials were adamant that the commonwealth must respond directly to the riots, particularly considering that the city needed the state to help foot the bill. Not only was the state legislature unlikely to grant funds to Lawrence without specific instructions on how they could be spent, but MCAD threatened to have the state freeze funds to the city entirely until Lawrence rectified its abysmal minority hiring record. Given the city's economic dependence, there was little chance it was going to be given the autonomy to solve its own problems.

In the wake of the riots, the state legislature passed two bills to aid Lawrence, aimed at both rebuilding the city and preventing future riots. Yet the process of acquiring state aid reflected the reluctance of suburban Massachusetts to foot the bill for "urban problems." The original proposed riot-aid package was for $5.5 million, including $3.5 million for social, educational, police, and other services in Lawrence. In December, Representative Kevin Blanchette asked for unanimous consent to introduce one of the bills before a proposed debate, a courtesy usually granted for local-interest bills. Representative Robert B. Ambler (a Democrat from Weymouth) objected, however, and the consideration of the bill was put off indefinitely, as the legislative session drew to a close. Blanchette told the *Boston Globe* that he asked Ambler, "What about the Lawrence bills?" and that Ambler allegedly replied with a "string of expletives." Ambler later denied cursing but said he opposed the bill because "my community and other communities would have to give up (local-aid) money." Ambler acknowledged that the legislature had approved emergency aid for communities such as Lynn and Peabody after fires, but he argued that the Lawrence aid went beyond the disturbance itself. Ambler added that he did not think Lawrence's social problems were more severe than those of other communities, claiming, "There's a lot of cities that have a lot of Hispanics, a lot of problems."[56]

Weymouth, the suburban town south of Boston that Ambler represented, had 55,000 residents in 1980, 319 of whom were Hispanic, or about one-half of 1 percent. The median household income was significantly higher than Lawrence's, and it had only a 7 percent poverty rate, compared with Lawrence's 19 percent.[57] Weymouth had successfully managed to keep "urban" problems out of its backyard, and Weymouth's representative refused to recognize them as shared state problems. Most importantly, he refused to sacrifice local aid to his thriving town in order to diffuse the burden of concentrated urban poverty. Although Weymouth was not one of Lawrence's immediate suburbs, Ambler's effort to block funds for Lawrence demonstrates the rise in the 1980s of what historians and political scientists have discussed as a distinctly suburban political agenda, an informal confluence of conservative political priorities that gained prominence across the nation in the 1970s, 1980s, and early 1990s. The suburban political agenda concentrated considerable political will on suburban concerns and rejected shared responsibility for what were considered urban problems.[58] Having benefited from decades of federal aid and soaring property values based on exclusions along race and class lines, suburban residents and politicians around the nation challenged the use of tax dollars to address problems in the inner cities.

The state legislature eventually approved riot aid to Lawrence (after a debate that Blanchette described as "acrimonious"), but with an amendment that nearly gutted the bill, stripping it of many of the key measures most Latino Lawrencians believed were necessary.[59] The original bill proposed by

Lawrence's state senator Patricia McGovern and Representative Blanchette (with others) allocated $400,000 for the city for operating costs from the riots and $200,000 to improve the city's management capacity and efficiency, both of which were allowed to stand, as well as allocations for public safety, which were cut but revived in another bill. The rest of the bill, however, was not so lucky. A $50,000 appropriation for the Division of Community Development "for contracts with organizations for the purpose of undertaking a program of services for Hispanic persons in the greater Lawrence area whose incomes are below the federal poverty line" was cut by the amendment. So too were a $100,000 appropriation for the Department of Social Services for adolescents in the city, including "counseling and outreach activities to reduce tension between youths of the various neighborhoods"; $200,000 for mental health community services; $75,000 for programs in the high school; $750,000 to provide in-service training to Lawrence schoolteachers, including "cultural and language familiarization instruction"; $500,000 for "updated textbooks and supplies"; and finally, a proposal to establish a housing court in the city. All were cut from the final bill. The second riot-aid bill successfully provided public safety departments in the city with a full million dollars to upgrade police and fire departments to prevent a future riot, as well as funds for the Lawrence Housing Authority. In the final version of the two riot-aid bills, the state legislature ultimately supported the city's need for riot gear but not for cultural sensitivity training, textbooks, or youth outreach to reduce interethnic tension.[60]

In spite of the continuous state rhetoric that emphasized helping Lawrence's Latinos, challenging their exclusion from politics, and correcting the underlying economic problems, the $2.6 million aid package that the state legislature eventually approved was slated largely for fixing the damage the city incurred during the riots and increasing the ability of the police to respond to future riots by modernizing their equipment. There was some money slated for repairs and recreation programs in the housing projects, but nothing that truly addressed the shambles of municipal social and educational services or the poverty of the city's Latino community. Latino residents were outraged. "We are talking about helping Hispanics here and the state is giving the police riot gear," complained one resident. "Is that a double message or what?" Riot gear requests from the police included shotguns and grenades, and many Latinos were sharply critical that state funds would support this militarization of the police. As one of Joseph Duran's informants pointed out, "It is a sign of a government afraid of its own people." Another said, "They want to shower down kids this summer with water to cool them off . . . and shoot their parents with shotguns to shut them up if they try to protest again." One resident explained simply, "I came to the United States to escape this kind of police state."[61] It seems the American Dream of political freedom that had spurred this Lawrencian's immigration had been derailed by urban crisis and the law-and-order response it had precipitated.

In the context of this "double message," residents questioned whether the city and state really had Latino interests at heart. "Are [we] supposed to feel like the city and the state cares for us just because we [are] going [to] get a few basketball courts? . . . While the police prepare for another riot? . . . And the fire department can use their new truck to put it out?" This Latino resident concluded that the emphasis on containing Latino violence was profoundly misdirected: "It is disgraceful that so much attention is placed on the fear that Hispanics will riot again. . . . Instead they should help us prepare for jobs . . . help improve our schools." Latino residents also called on the state to make the city more responsive to Latino needs: "The state should force the city to pay attention to us or else there will be more riots and this time people could get killed."[62] Yet the state legislature was unwilling to make that specific investment in solving "urban problems."

SOCIAL SERVICES

It became clear through the media and government attention to the riots that the social service system in Lawrence was inadequate to meet the needs of Latinos. As one Latino social worker explained to NBC, the riots would "make the political elites be aware that there is a need out there for more social programs such as education, welfare, housing, etc."[63] Social service systems comprise a complicated array of local, state, and federal programs and funding, but city officials held considerable sway over this system. As I will discuss in Chapter 6, many officials held the view that Latinos came to Lawrence specifically to avail themselves of welfare. In this view, the city had become a "welfare magnet," and adequate social service provisions would only bring more Latinos to the city. Many residents and observers thus believed that the inadequate and ill-fitting social service system in Lawrence reflected city leaders' prejudices, if not an explicit effort to deny public services to Latinos. As one social worker explained,

> Those in power in Lawrence today have a short historical memory. Their basic assertion, in opposition to Hispanics here, is that they made it in this society without welfare, bilingual education, job

Forcing Change

programs, and range of governmental benefits that we seek for immigrants today. They forget that it was the absence of many of those very programs that prevented many of their own from making it . . . and it was only through their incorporation into the political system that certain opportunities were opened up for them. . . . They forget, too, the riots, protest, strikes, demonstrations, that make up a part of their history. . . . Their history is one of a struggle for fair housing, education, jobs, decent treatment . . . the very things they actively seek to deny Hispanics today.[64]

In the bootstrap myth of immigrant incorporation, immigrants were not entitled to government support, because earlier generations of European immigrants had succeeded in the United States without such support and without audacious demands for more resources or government intervention. Of course, officials in this specific mill town should have known better, considering that immigrant textile workers had launched one of the most dramatic strikes in U.S. history in Lawrence in 1912, prompting congressional hearings on employment practices.[65] In addition, the array of New Deal programs begun during the Great Depression had been largely responsible for the upward mobility of European immigrants and their descendants in the postwar decades. Mortgages guaranteed by the Federal Housing Administration and the Veterans' Administration and college educations funded by the GI Bill were some of the largest government "welfare" benefits that the nation had ever seen. So the myth often invoked in Lawrence—that earlier European immigrants had not relied on welfare—was unfounded. Besides, Latinos in Lawrence were generally not "immigrants" in the way that Europeans had been in the early twentieth century; rather, the Latinos who settled in the city were imperial migrants pushed from one part of the U.S. empire to another, from its semicolonies to its crisis cities, and many were, of course, U.S. citizens. There was thus no justification for excluding or marginalizing Latinos within the city's social service system.

The riots, and the organizing and media attention that followed, drove home that the city's social services needed to be both better funded and better tailored to Lawrence's Latino population. Although the state legislature had cut much of the social service support in the riot-aid bill, the Executive Offices of Communities and Development and of Human Services put together a $1.4-million package for an overhaul to Lawrence's social service system, called the Lawrence Initiative. Most of it was designed to upgrade existing social services, but $33,000 was given to Inquilinos Boricuas en

Acción (a Boston-based Puerto Rican community development corporation with a history of successful grassroots advocacy in Boston's South End) to develop a new, multifaceted Latino social service agency in Lawrence, named Centro Panamericano.[66]

In perspective, $33,000 was not a major investment (even in 1984 dollars), and from its inception, Centro Panamericano was forced to grapple with fundraising, leaving the fledgling organization skeptical of its ability to engage in the kind of advocacy and policy work for which the community was hoping. It was, however, the first social service agency in the city explicitly tailored to and run by the Latino community, and it was a step in the right direction toward creating a social service network in Lawrence that could meet the needs of Latinos. Other social service agencies in the city, whether as a response to the needs so vocally expressed during and after the riots or to compete with Centro Panamericano for funds, began to ramp up their bilingual services and their outreach to Latinos.

Jorge Santiago, the first executive director for Centro Panamericano, who ran the organization for thirteen years, echoed the claims made after the riots that the human services system in Lawrence was profoundly ill-fitted to the needs of the city's Latinos. He described the social service landscape when he came to the city after the riots, arguing that traditional organizations in the city "had a lot of Latinos on the caseload [but] had very few Latinos in professional positions, staff positions. And if the state wanted more Latino staff, these agencies responded by saying, 'then give us additional resources.' They didn't want to shift the internal structure of the organization to accommodate this new client pool." Santiago argued that this refusal to tailor services to Latinos or to hire Latinos to help provide services had been long standing among many of the city's social service organizations. "Historically, Latinos have been used in this community to garner . . . funds and grant money. . . . Once they got the grants, they hardly ever gave any services to their Latino constituents at all." Not only were these organizations not tailoring their services to meet Latino needs; they were largely unwilling to hire or train Latino staff. Centro Panamericano was the first organization in Lawrence with both the goal and the means to systematically train local Latinos to be bilingual and bicultural service providers.[67]

Over the next few years, interagency competition for clients and funding then pressured other, more traditional, and overwhelmingly white-run organizations to prioritize hiring bilingual and bicultural staff. Within a few years, Centro Panamericano was no longer providing services that were distinct from other agencies in Lawrence, as bilingual and bicultural service provision had become the new norm in the city, thanks to the pressure exerted by the riots and the standards set by Centro Panamericano. As Santiago recalled, "I think we forced them [other service providers] to a large extent, especially initially, to change their practices. A lot of them wound up hiring my staff out from under me."[68] Although this loss of trained staff to other organizations proved frustrating for Centro Panamericano, the mainstream turn toward bilingual and bicultural service provision not only provided more inclusive services but also opened up significant opportunities for employment for Lawrence Latinos. By 2000, only about a quarter of Lawrencians were still employed in manufacturing, while over 40 percent were employed in service jobs, with half of those jobs in education, health, or other social services. The creation of a bilingual and bicultural service infrastructure was particularly significant in the employment of Latinas, who had been hit hard by deindustrialization. By 2000, over half of the city's employed Latinas worked in services, with the majority of them in education, health, or other social services.[69] In addition, the social service sector has been a key path to power for many Latino community and political leaders in Lawrence.[70]

For the purposes of this chapter, it is most essential to note the origins of the bilingual and bicultural service system in Centro Panamericano, a tangible result of the riots. Health and education services, in particular, were central to the "better life" migrants to Lawrence envisioned, and welfare and job training programs were key to surviving in the crisis city. The infusion of funds and the reorientation of the social service system in Lawrence was key to making the city livable for Latinos. The role of the riots in catalyzing the development of a Latino-oriented service sector demonstrates, however, that such a well-tailored service infrastructure was not an inevitable corollary of Latino population growth. Rather, it was the result of decades of activism, including the riots, geared toward making public and private services accountable to the Latino community. This bilingual and bicultural social service sector, however, was overwhelmingly dependent on state funds and grants, which would become painfully obvious when the state reformed its welfare system in the mid-1990s, radically undermining Massachusetts's commitment to providing a safety net for its poor, as discussed in Chapter 6.

The city also saw some increase in state (and federal) funds directed at housing after the riots. Duran reported that $18 million was allocated to housing improvements in the city in the year after the riots, including a million dollars provided as part of the state legislature's riot-aid package.[71] Although in 1985, many Lawrencians still complained of poor conditions, inadequate plumbing, and infestations, as well as absentee landlords and racism in the housing market, the Department of Justice's Community Relations Service (CRS) noted that residents were aware of and welcomed the growing investment of state and federal money in the city's public housing. "Minority residents expressed relief at 'seeing' ground-breaking, windows being installed, new kitchens being built, and new security and lighting systems being put into place.... In the largest [housing] project, basketball courts, handball courts, and a Youth Center have been opened and are being well attended." The CRS noted that it was "clear" that "better facilities" in the city's public housing had previously been reserved for white residents, but this was gradually changing. The Stadium Courts project, for example, had white residents in *all* of its 228 occupied units in 1980, but by 1985 it had Latino residents in 98 units.[72] The Merrimack Courts (Essex Street) projects that had been so central in the riots got a complete remodeling in the years afterward, including the construction of outdoor stairwells and the installation of plants and trees. In 1986, thirty-eight Lawrence Housing Authority employees even began a course in conversational Spanish that emphasized "cultural appreciation."[73]

Finally, the riots helped precipitate the Gateway Cities program in 1987, a landmark state initiative designed to increase services for immigrants and refugees. In the program's first year, the state approved $11 million, to be shared among thirty municipalities with large numbers of immigrants. With the support of Lawrence's Democratic state senator Patricia McGovern (conveniently, the chairperson of the Senate Ways and Means Committee), the Gateway Cities funds could be used flexibly, either by the city or by local community-based organizations. Gateway Cities temporarily brought a huge infusion of state funds to Lawrence organizations, including Semana Hispana, and enabled an impressive expansion of services to immigrants throughout the state, especially the provision of English as a Second Language classes. Yet, in 1988, the amount was cut to $3 million, and in 1989 Democratic governor Michael Dukakis vetoed the appropriation, ending funding for the project entirely. Although Gateway Cities provided crucial local services to meet local needs, it relied on state funding and thus was vulnerable to shifts in the priorities of state government.[74]

STATE AND FEDERAL CIVIL RIGHTS ALLIES

In the years after the riots, Latino activists welcomed the U.S. Department of Justice as a powerful ally in the struggle for the city. In the flurry of media attention during the riots, the Department of Justice's CRS announced that Lawrence had previously been placed on a "critical list" of cities in which

Forcing Change

race riots were most likely to occur. The CRS told the *Boston Globe* that "the appraisal was based on a number of 'warning signs,' including regular complaints of harassment and discrimination officials received from Hispanic residents."[75] One official told the *Boston Globe* that the CRS had tried years ago to address the tension and exclusion that had helped precipitate the riot by arranging talks between the city government and Latino community leaders, but that the talks had fallen apart because the Latino leadership "felt the city wasn't exhibiting good faith."[76]

After the riots, the CRS had increased leverage to pressure the city government to respect the civil rights of Lawrence's Latinos, and Latino activists had a powerful ally in prying open the closed doors of City Hall. The CRS had been involved in Lawrence since the late 1970s, fostering communication between city officials and the Latino community whenever Latinos alleged abuse or discrimination from city officials or the police. They repeatedly met with community leaders and city officials and ran training programs for the city on civil liability. After the riots, they met with the Alliance for Peace and other Latino organizations and helped amplify their calls for openness and accountability in City Hall. In addition, the CRS played a major role in establishing the city's Human Rights Commission and in training its members, as well as providing support for the city's affirmative action officer. Five years after the riots, thanks to this alliance between Latino organizers and the CRS, Latinos held nearly 11 percent of municipal jobs, up from just over 2 percent at the time of the riots; but this was still far short of their share of the population (approaching half), and there were still no Latino elected officials.[77]

Much of the CRS's work in Lawrence after the riots was devoted to planning a training program for the city's police department with the following among its goals: "to view the legal, historical and cultural imperatives of racism and culture"; "to share and discuss ideas and information pertaining to prejudice and its impact on our behavior"; "to examine myths and stereotypes around culture"; and "to explore Asian and Hispanic culture in American society." Although this training session was offered to some officers in August 1985, the police department successfully resisted it being required for all officers. In spite of this resistance and other challenges, the CRS concluded that its programs in Lawrence were still somewhat effective in mitigating the tension between city government and the Latino community, although not entirely. The CRS ultimately determined that the "major impediment to completely achieving all stated objectives was the lack of commitment of the City Government and the difficulties of overcoming historical racism and discrimination."[78]

Throughout the late 1980s, Latino activists frequently reached out to the CRS for leverage in their protests. In 1986, when a school official publicly made a disparaging joke about Puerto Ricans, the vice president of Lawrence's Bilingual Parents Advisory Council, Briseida Quiles, solicited the support of the CRS. The official, an assistant principal at a Lawrence junior high, had joked that there were no Puerto Ricans in the audience of a St. Patrick's Day event at the Ancient Order of the Hibernians because they were "all outside stealing our cars." He also joked that there had been an "accident" in the Arlington neighborhood in which "a bed broke and injured 14 Puerto Ricans."[79] These jokes invoked prominent stereotypes of Puerto Ricans as delinquents and poked fun at the overcrowded living conditions that many Latinos in Lawrence were forced to endure. Enraged, Latino activists demanded his resignation, asking, "What can the Hispanic parents and students [at the school] be expected to think about an Assistant Principal who apparently sees them all as prospective hoodlums?" When they received no remediation from the superintendent, they reached out to both MCAD and the CRS. As Quiles explained, "At this time we are requesting the U.S. Department of Justice come to Lawrence to investigate this matter. Too many times now we have seen how this sort of issue does not get resolved appropriately unless others outside of the Lawrence city administrative structure get involved." The CRS helped the city and Latino activists reach a settlement in which, although the assistant principal was not fired, he was not promoted to principal when that position opened. Instead, a Puerto Rican principal was hired, and the school official who had made the racist jokes was required to report to that Puerto Rican principal. In addition, the city brought in an outside organization, World of Difference, to conduct sensitivity training for school personnel.[80] Although far from a perfect solution, the increased leverage given to Latino activists by state and federal involvement in the city after the riots had a notable impact.

This relationship between Latino activists in Lawrence and the federal government would culminate in a successful voting rights lawsuit initiated in 1998. In this civil suit, the U.S. Department of Justice charged city officials with illegally restricting the practice and impact of Latino voting in the city. Although the city settled the case—so there was no official legal ruling as to whether or not the city was guilty of any wrongdoing—the settlement agreement required sweeping changes in city elections and dramatically increased Latino political power in Lawrence. Although the lawsuit was brought by the federal government, it had been *initiated* by citizen complaints. These complaints centered around issues evident in the 1998 elections and earlier, and the Justice Department specifically noted the investment in the case of thirteen Latino candidates in that election and a host of Latino community organizations, including People's Alliance for Rights and Equality, the Dominican American Voters' Council, Movimiento Puertorriqueño, the Bilingual Parents Advisory Council, the Greater Lawrence Community Action Council's Spanish Program, and even Semana Hispana. (The involvement of these last two organizations demonstrates again the blurred lines between activism, service provision, and cultural celebration among Latino organizations in the city).[81]

Latino politicians and community organizations leveraged the federal government to remediate disenfranchisement in the city of Lawrence through the Voting Rights Act of 1965, a key piece of Civil Rights legislation initially passed to end the disenfranchisement of African Americans in the South. Two sections of the Voting Rights Act were relevant in Lawrence: Section 2, which prohibits racially discriminatory voting practices, such as intentionally designing districts to dilute minority voter strength, and Section 203 (added in an amendment in 1975), which requires the provision of election materials in languages other than English whenever 5 percent or more of the population speaks a specific language and has depressed rates of literacy.[82]

The complaint centered on three main issues: inadequate provision of election materials in Spanish, failure to appoint and assign sufficient Latino pollworkers, and dilution of Latino voting strength through discriminatory districting. The Justice Department alleged that the city failed to fully translate all election-related materials into Spanish (including, but not limited to, official ballots for city elections, the annual register form used for voter lists, and certain absentee materials) and that pollworkers failed to provide effective, consistent oral language assistance. In addition, the suit claimed that the city failed to recruit, appoint, train, and maintain an adequate pool of bilingual poll officials on a consistent basis. The city already had an estimated Latino majority by the 1998 election; but only 53 of 250 pollworkers were Latino, and even this low number was attributable only to the Justice Department pressing the city to hire 40 additional pollworkers after Latino complaints regarding the 1997 election. As the Justice Department explained, "Because of the lack of Hispanic pollworkers, many Hispanic citizens, especially those with limited English proficiency, are intimidated by the process and discouraged from voting at polling places." This lack of Latino pollworkers contributed to a climate of exclusion and hostility for potential Latino voters. The suit elaborated, "A significant number of Hispanic citizens have not been comfortable voting at their assigned polling places because of the nature and location of the polling place. In some instances, pollworkers were instructed that they could not assist Hispanic voters."[83]

In addition to the complaints formally documented in the lawsuit, Latino activists alleged that among those counting the ballots when Puerto Rican José Santiago ran for state representative were members of his opponent's campaign. There were widespread stories of Latino voters being illegally asked to show identification at the polls as well as being denied help or information when they tried to vote.[84] Of course, official disenfranchisement was not the only force restraining Latino political participation, as quotidian acts of exclusion and intimidation still existed; one Dominican candidate recalled walking the streets in 1991 while running for office and encountering small, homemade "Spik go home" signs.[85]

The Justice Department had initiated the lawsuit after months of negotiating with the city but finding the city's progress to be inadequate.[86] Lawrence mayor Patricia Dowling derided the lawsuit as "Big Brother tactics." Rather than acknowledge the long-standing racial divisions Latino organizers and the Justice Department were aiming to redress, she argued that the suit itself was "divisive" in placing undue emphasis on race, asking rhetorically, "Aren't people elected based on qualifications?"[87] Indeed, ensuring that officials were fairly elected based on their qualifications was the point of the lawsuit; protecting the voting rights of all Lawrencians was essential to that process.

While the city formally denied all claims of unlawfully restricting Latino voting rights, it agreed to settle without trial, and the settlement agreement required major changes to the city's election procedures. While redistricting would wait until 2002 (after which five of Lawrence's six voting districts would have a Latino majority), issues of election materials and pollworkers were addressed immediately in the 1999 settlement agreement. The City of Lawrence was ordered to "provide to Spanish-language minority citizens full and complete information about all stages of the electoral process" and ensure that "the entire election process is equally accessible to Hispanic citizens." Compliance with this agreement explicitly required the city to coordinate with representatives of Latino community organizations (including those named above) and to engage in an outreach campaign via Spanish-language media. In addition, the city was required to appoint a fully bilingual coordinator as well as to encourage community organizations to appoint community election liaisons to review polling site selection. All registered voters were to receive election materials in both languages, and all precincts were to have a bilingual election officer present at all times throughout the day on election days. Finally, the city was called on to recruit and train Latino election officials and to ensure nondiscrimination in positions of responsibility, including warden.[88] As is obvious from these requirements, ensuring Latino voting rights was not simply something that city officials could do *for* Latinos; rather, it required actively engaging Latino Lawrencians in the civic process via the organizations and media outlets the community had already established.

The strategy of leveraging the power of state and federal governments to press for civil rights claims certainly did not begin with the riots, but the profound attention drawn by the riots to the discrimination Latinos faced in the city gave these efforts tremendous traction. Furthermore, as the city's economy continued to decline, the reliance of the city on external funding only amplified these calls. Immediately after the riots, many observers argued that state funds, in particular, ought to be withheld in order to force the city to end its discrimination against Latinos and to encourage their equal participation in city government. One opinion piece argued, "If the local [politicians] in the [Merrimack] valley can't or won't hit the streets and deal with the Latinos and broker with the white ethnics, then the state must do it for them. The state can withhold moneys from communities that don't address the needs of their poor and minorities."[89] In 1986, the Massachusetts Executive Office of Communities and Development informed the city that it had been conditionally awarded a $1 million community development and action grant to extend water and sewer lines. The award letter noted, however, that receipt of this grant was contingent upon the following conditions, set by MCAD: "that the City aggressively implement its affirmative action plans and submit its employment, housing, and contract compliance reports with improved performance on a quarterly basis" and "that the City develop an effective outreaching mechanism to increase its MBE [Minority Business Enterprise] participation in its contract awards, and submit complete reports on both MBE and contract compliance programs."[90] Receipt of these funds would be tied to the city's progress remediating its historic discrimination against and marginalization of Latinos.

While state and federal agencies strengthened Latino efforts to fight discrimination in the city, it is important to keep in mind that Lawrence was particularly susceptible to state and federal pressure, because its economic crisis left it so reliant on outside funds. Although antidiscrimination oversight from groups like MCAD or the Justice Department proved central to ensuring the growth of Latino political power in the state, addressing the deep social problems that precipitated the riots required an infusion of funding into the city.

Much of the initial media, activist, and official responses to the riots drew necessary attention to Lawrence's political economy: the crisis precipitated by deindustrialization and the inadequate services provided by the inefficient (or even corrupt) city government. These were issues that affected both white and Latino Lawrencians, and it was widely understood that the violent tension between the two groups could not be fully understood outside the context of the city's larger economic decline. In the months and years that followed, Latino organizers successfully used the attention garnered by the riots to press for crucial changes in the city. Thus 1984 marked the beginning of the end of decades of racial discrimination and marginalization from City Hall. In the context of the sustained Latino political organizing that followed the riots, it was quickly forgotten that white Lawrencians had been out in the streets as well, and that the riots reflected the frustration that both groups were feeling in the face of the city's decline. Instead, the media mainly adopted the narrative that the riots had been *Latino* riots. This erasure of white rioting was profound. A *Boston Phoenix* article compared the Lawrence riots to the disturbances "12 years ago when police clashed with Latinos in Boston's South End, and 17 years ago when blacks rioted in Roxbury and Dorchester," ignoring that white Bostonians had rioted against school desegregation just ten years earlier, in 1974.[91] Forgotten was the fact that whites in Lawrence rioted in numbers equal to those of Latinos. Five years after the riots, the *Boston Globe* described the city's residents, "many of them poor Hispanics whose anger had erupted in a flurry of firebombs, street fights and gunfire in the summer of 1984."[92] White rioting had been fully purged from this narrative. Clearly, white rioters violently targeting Latinos was unconscionable, but their disaffection was an important warning that, even without the added barriers of discrimination, Lawrence was failing to provide a good life for its residents. The structural changes and deteriorating quality of life in Lawrence—its failing economy, rising crime, inadequate schools and police force, and closed-shop political system—affected all residents of the city.

In the decade and a half after the riots, Latinos in Lawrence grew increasingly successful in challenging racial inequality within the city. Greater inclusion, however, meant less and less as white flight accelerated, and the line that separated the haves from the have-nots expanded to surround the city as a whole. This new bifurcation, distinguishing the decaying city from its prosperous suburbs, prevented remaining Lawrence residents of all races from receiving the economic opportunities they needed and the educational and public safety services they deserved. The riots were a protest against the city's crisis: against unemployment, poverty, inadequate housing, police harassment, failing schools, and apathetic "city fathers" who had no place for the current residents in their vision for Lawrence's future. It was undoubtedly essential to address the widespread discrimination against Latinos and their exclusion from the city's official life. Yet unless the serious structural inequality between Lawrence and its suburbs was also remedied, Latinos were doomed to incorporate into a failing city.

SIX

THE ARMPIT
OF THE NORTHEAST?

Bob and I couldn't help but smile when, at some of those same
Andover parties where we stopped the conversation with our
Lawrence address, we heard that so-and-so's daughter had gone to
Liberia to help the poor. Didn't she know that all she needed to do
was drive to Lawrence to find the Third World?

Jeanne Schinto, Huddle Fever

In 1992, the Immigrant City was in flames. The waves of arson peaked during
the summer months, when fires blazed nightly in Lawrence, lighting up the
small city's skyline of crumbling clock towers and abandoned brick mills.
The frequent fires sometimes drew gawkers from the surrounding suburbs (otherwise rare visitors to the troubled city), and firefighters cracked
jokes about how spectators should bring hot dogs. Frustrated Lawrencians
complained to one another about the slow response of the fire department.
Like the South Bronx in the 1970s, the burning city was a powerful symbol
of the continuing disinvestment and economic collapse in Lawrence.[1] In the
years after the riots, the city's crisis only deepened.

This chapter will examine the exacerbation of Lawrence's "urban
problems" in the late 1980s and 1990s. As the suburbs successfully blocked
a more equitable distribution of the burden of caring for the state's poor,
the city's economic decline accelerated, along with that of its educational
and other service infrastructure. Lawrence lacked the resources to address
its myriad economic and social problems, even during those rare instances
when there was agreement on what those problems were. Reliant on

state aid, Lawrence found itself at the center of larger struggles to reform Massachusetts's welfare and education systems, conflicts in which the divide between city and suburb was often starkly evident. Through decades of activism, Latinos came to have a strong political presence in the city by the end of the century, but at that point the city had little power, and even less money, to address the root of its urban problems. Economic and educational opportunities evaporated in the 1980s and 1990s, as did the tranquility that had brought so many Latinos to Lawrence.

Historians tend to focus on the urban crisis of the 1960s (rioting, white flight, and racialized poverty) and the 1970s (all of the above plus accelerated disinvestment and deindustrialization, often leading to fiscal crisis and a growing panic over urban crime). In many ways, however, the crisis in U.S. cities actually deepened in the 1980s and early 1990s. Racialized disinvestment and concentrated poverty worsened, leading to moralizing invocations of the specter of a permanent "underclass" of poor urban Blacks and Latinos. Professionals of color increasingly left urban ghettos for the formerly exclusive suburbs in this era, further concentrating the poor in the inner city, while crack cocaine set off a wave of addiction, crime, and violence in impoverished neighborhoods, the stakes of which were raised by the terrifying growth of militarized policing and mass incarceration during the "War on Drugs." Deindustrialization and disinvestment led to high rates of joblessness in many urban neighborhoods of color, as even poverty-wage jobs became difficult to obtain.[2] Finally, urban public schools were in a state of emergency. City school districts were often segregated from and unequal to their suburban counterparts, especially in the Northeast, and a Carnegie Foundation report in 1988 warned of an "imperiled generation," arguing that the "failure to educate" urban children had led many people to dismiss city schools as "little more than human storehouses."[3]

Yet the 1980s and 1990s also marked a new era of revitalization and gentrification in major metropolitan centers. While efforts to spur reinvestment in U.S. cities had persisted throughout the postwar era, particularly in the form of large urban renewal projects, this had not been sufficient to reverse larger decentralizing trends toward the suburbanization of offices, industry, and the middle class. In the 1980s and 1990s, however, the tide began to turn toward gentrification, as businesses and young professionals rediscovered the value of urban real estate and city living. In major metropolitan centers, a "tale of two cities" pattern emerged toward the end of the twentieth century, as gentrification existed alongside (and fed off) disinvestment.[4]

Cities like Lawrence had a very different experience. Unlike major metropolitan centers, small or second-tier postindustrial cities often experienced comprehensive urban economic decline; there was rarely a viable finance, insurance, and real estate sector to anchor the postindustrial economy; there were few medical centers or universities ("meds and eds") to maintain professional investment in neighborhoods; and there was virtually nothing to anchor or inspire reinvestment. Massachusetts had a number of these small, struggling postindustrial cities—Holyoke and Chelsea, for example—whose economies diverged sharply from that of Boston in this era, but similar cities existed throughout the Rust Belt, such as East St. Louis, Illinois, or Camden, New Jersey.[5] The persistent crisis *in* most U.S. cities in the 1980s and 1990s was a crisis *of* the city for many small postindustrial cities. Indeed, Jonathan Kozol, foremost chronicler of the crisis in urban education, reportedly referred to Lawrence at this time simply as "one big ghetto."[6] Experiencing disinvestment and fiscal crisis on a municipal scale meant that cities like Lawrence relied increasingly on state aid, a dependence that further stigmatized them and substantially compromised their autonomy.

URBAN/SUBURBAN DIVERGENCE

In the years after the 1984 riots, the economic situation of Latinos declined throughout the commonwealth. The "Massachusetts Miracle" of high-tech industrialization that brought about a massive boom in the state's economy in the 1980s largely bypassed Latinos. The recession that followed in the early 1990s, however, hit the state's Latino population particularly hard.[7] A 1993 Hispanic-American Advisory Commission report warned that, adjusted for inflation, the median household income for Latinos in Massachusetts declined a full 40 percent in the 1980s. Compared with that of white Massachusetts residents, this income decline was particularly stark: in 1979, Latino households earned 49 cents to every dollar earned by white households, but by 1987, the report estimated that Latinos earned only 25 cents per white dollar.[8]

The findings were equally grim when Latinos in Massachusetts were compared with Latinos across the nation. Massachusetts had the highest Latino poverty rate in the country: 37 percent in 1989, compared with a nationwide Latino average of 25 percent. Massachusetts also had the highest rate of Latino unemployment. This extreme poverty and unemployment compared with that of Latinos throughout the rest of the nation did not develop because Latinos in Massachusetts were "unskilled," as the report emphasized that their education levels were higher than that of the national average.[9]

Lawrence's history suggests that the overwhelmingly urban concentration of Massachusetts Latinos helps account for the extremes of Latino poverty in the state. Edwin Meléndez explained in 1993 that Latinos lived disproportionately in the state's cities, and urban residence was correlated to poverty regardless of race. Although Meléndez argued that the main cause of poverty among Latinos was their preponderance in the declining industry of nondurable goods manufacturing, he noted that the compounding effect of geographic concentration could not be dismissed.[10] The stunning rates of Latino poverty in Massachusetts's cities were not just about race, but also about space, about being *urban* Latinos in a radically segregated and unequal metropolitan political economy.

While many of Massachusetts's suburbs were thriving through the "miracle" of high-tech manufacturing in the 1980s, the state's small postindustrial cities experienced profound disinvestment. Kim Stevenson studied the evolution of the economy of Lawrence between 1980 and 1990 in relation to its surrounding region and described "the growing spatial polarization and isolation of poverty in Lawrence relative to the surrounding region." The origins of Lawrence's crisis stemmed from postwar shifts in the urban/suburban political economy, as discussed in Chapter 1, but the divergent paths of the city and its suburbs became most obvious in the 1980s and 1990s. Between 1980 and 1990, Lawrence's importance in the regional economy declined precipitously. Already by 1980, only about 30 percent of the region's jobs were located in Lawrence, but this declined even further to only 20 percent by 1990. Andover was the new employment powerhouse, with 21 percent of the region's jobs by 1990. Although Lawrence's decline has often been attributed to the flight of manufacturing to the South or overseas, it is significant that Andover gained nearly 3,000 jobs in the manufacturing sector during this decade. Continued successful suburban competition for industry played a major role in Lawrence's crisis.[11]

In the years after the riots, the growing gap between Lawrence and its suburbs was evident in housing as well. The Urban Studies Institute, a joint research venture between Phillips Academy in Andover and Lawrence High School, published a report on Lawrence's housing crisis in 1988, with a focus on the shocking inequality evident between Lawrence and its suburbs. In 1988, Essex County families needed a $62,400 yearly income ($125,019 in 2015 dollars) to buy and sustain an average-priced, single-family home in the area, an income far exceeding that of most Lawrence residents. But even this average obscured the urban/suburban housing gap. In 1984, the average cost of a home in the city was $57,250, already out of reach for most poor and working-class Lawrencians. In Andover, however, the average home in 1984 cost $152,320 and increased to $268,000 by 1989. For most residents of the city, the divergence in property values left suburban homeownership off the table, and of course, exclusionary zoning ensured that the availability of rental housing in the suburbs remained scarce.[12]

Reflecting on the low rate of homeownership in Lawrence, the faculty advisor for the Urban Studies Institute described her students' shock at the economic impact of suburban homeownership compared with urban tenancy in Greater Lawrence: "They saw that homeowners get farther ahead and the nonowners get farther behind."[13] Indeed, the role of homeownership in generating wealth in this era was remarkable. It was not simply that wealthy people moved to the suburbs, but that moving to the suburbs generally *made* people wealthier, both in terms of the increased job and education opportunities available to suburban families over time and because of the wealth generated by home appreciation in this era. By 1989, a full 80 percent of Methuen homeowners lived in houses they would not have been able to buy at their current incomes.[14]

The "housing bubble" of the late 1980s was partly responsible, but even over a longer time, the remarkable increase in suburban home values exceeded the (still notable) rise in suburban income. In 1980, the average home value in Andover, North Andover, and Methuen was only 2.6 times the median annual household income in these suburbs. By 2000, it had grown to 3.8 times the median suburban income.[15] Suburban incomes diverged from urban incomes in these years, but suburban home appreciation ensured that suburban *wealth* diverged even more, generating a distinctly suburban prosperity in Greater Lawrence for those privileged enough to have gained access to the suburbs earlier in the postwar decades.

THE CENTER OF DECAY FOR EVERYTHING

The increasing concentration of economic crisis within the city's boundaries provoked a social crisis in Lawrence by the late 1980s and early 1990s. Hundreds of arson fires ravaged the city: 100 in 1991, 150 in 1992, 102 in 1993, and at least 65 in 1994.[16] A state fire captain called Lawrence "the arson capital of the world" because of the many arsons that tore through the predominantly Latino Arlington District in 1992.[17] According to the *Boston Globe*, "In the earliest, darkest hours of the morning, throughout the poorest sections of the city, buildings are burning with mind-numbing regularity, the flames searing the psyche of a community where poverty is already a way of life.

The Armpit of the Northeast?

On Bromfield Street, in the predominantly Hispanic Arlington Mill district, there are three litter-strewn lots where, just a few months ago, three-decker homes once sat. Owners have abandoned buildings, while many of those who remain have abandoned hope, as they look down their street and see only scorched wood and boarded windows."[18] The paper noted that sections of the city "have begun to look like an urban war zone, with charred and vandalized vacant buildings on almost every street corner."[19] Arsons were not the only fires ravaging the city, as accidental fires were also common and particularly dangerous, given the city's density. In the fall of 1992, the *Boston Herald* noted that, in addition to the 140 arsons the city had experienced so far that year, 250 other fires had also set the city ablaze.[20]

The impact of these fires on the Latino residents in the Arlington District was brutal. As one Latina described it, "You never know when your home is going to be on fire. You get up at 2 or 3 in the morning and the street is filled with fire trucks. You never know if you are next."[21] The quiet, tranquil city that many Latinos hoped to find in Lawrence was going up in smoke, the remains either bulldozed or left to decay. A Latina resident on Oxford Street, where the 1984 riots had taken place, lived near a vacant house that had been set ablaze ten times over the past two years. She noted, "I'm in constant fear of the fires."[22] As the remaining whites left the neighborhood after the riots, the violent racial tension of the early 1980s evaporated; fear of racist harassment was replaced, however, by fear of the fires that resulted from extreme disinvestment.

The community organizing that had enabled Latinos to overcome earlier resistance to their settlement in the city was still at work, however, challenging the idea that Lawrence was an "urban war zone." In November 1992, 400 residents and community leaders marched on the Common in solidarity with fire victims, with signs declaring, "*No Más Apatía* [No More Apathy]" and "United in Hope." In spite of Lawrence's struggles, marchers asserted that the future of the city rested in unity, and this view held strong in the face of urban crisis. Speakers at the arson rally vowed that the city would live up to its reputation, not as the arson capital of the country but as "the city that would not die."[23]

The fires were clearly tied to the city's economic crisis, reflecting both disinvestment and the inadequate public safety services that could be marshaled by Lawrence's decimated tax base. Police Chief Allen Cole reflected on this relationship between arson and the city's economic decline in 1992. Lawrence contained hundreds of abandoned buildings, and he explained, "Owners are just walking away from them." Once the buildings were abandoned, they were often broken into, vandalized, and used as sites for drug use or sales. Chief Cole argued that this most basic form of disinvestment, property owners abandoning buildings in the city, played a major role in Lawrence's crisis: "It is almost like it is the center of decay for everything. It gives people the sense that no one cares." Once the buildings were abandoned, the understaffed Lawrence police and fire departments had little control over what happened in the buildings. The city had an operational budget of only $3.2 million the year before and had been unable to even send out property tax bills. Mayor Sullivan explained, "We are down about 43 positions in the Fire Department, and I just laid off about 10 policemen."[24] By the summer of 1993, the fire department had half the number of firefighters it had had in the early 1980s, although the city's population had grown considerably.[25]

Fire Chief Richard Shafer blamed the diminished investigative power of the fire department for the waves of arson. When city officials decided not to use scarce resources to investigate fires in vacant buildings in 1991, "a flicker erupted into flames." Chief Shafer argued, "When a vacant building burned up, obviously it was arson and the feeling was that it wasn't worth investigating. So when the fires started and no one was arrested, people got the feeling that they could light a fire and there was no chance of getting caught."[26] Even when the arsonist was known, diminished resources in the city to investigate the fires made arson difficult to prosecute, as the burden of proof was high. One state trooper commented, "There were no consequences so it was totally out of control. If you were going to a fire in Lawrence, you might as well take a hotdog." This joke about the burning of Lawrence being entertainment, a carnivalesque spectacle to be observed and enjoyed, was cruel but true, as during the arson peak in the summer of 1992, fire watchers, or "sparks," from outside the city crowded with residents in front of burning buildings on weekend nights.[27]

City officials claimed that arson for profit was rare, as very few of the owners of torched buildings actually maintained insurance policies.[28] Although this might seem plausible considering the city's remarkable financial distress, some buildings were undoubtedly burned by their owners or by people the owners hired. Even if an owner had no insurance, burning one's building could eliminate the need to find tenants, repair or maintain the building, or reduce taxes on the property. The *Boston Globe* reported that arsonists were paid for their work frequently enough for there to be a "going rate" for the task. One twenty-seven-year-old man who claimed to have set four fires compared the "work" of arson to the narrow range of other economic activities available to him in the crisis city. "You're out on the corner and you're stealing purses

The Armpit of the Northeast?

and selling baking powder and making $40 bucks a day, and someone comes up and offers you $400 to burn a place which'll take two minutes, and I say, 'What time should I be there?' . . . You offer me $10,000 and, boom, boom, I'll burn the . . . Police Department."[29] While some observers derided unruly Latinos for torching their own neighborhoods for thrills, the *Globe* article highlighted the role of property owners in the epidemic.[30]

North Lawrence, the portion of the city above the Merrimack River, was hit especially hard by the arson waves, and of course, few of the torched buildings were owner occupied. North Lawrence was already estimated to be approximately 75 percent Latino by 1993, and residents were rarely surprised by the decision of some absentee building owners to set their property ablaze rather than repair and rent it. After a house on Warren Street was burned, neighbors believed strongly that the owner was responsible. One Latino resident told the *Boston Globe* that the owner would return to burn the two buildings adjacent to the torched one, as they belonged to him as well: "Don't worry, he'll be back to burn the rest," he said. "He can't sell them so what else would he do with them?"[31]

Officials acknowledged that at least some of the arsons were landlord insurance schemes, but no building owners were indicted until October 1993, when two Derry, New Hampshire, men were accused of burning an apartment building one of them owned on Butler Street in Lawrence, by dousing it with paint thinner and setting it ablaze. It is significant that the Lawrence property owners/alleged arsonists lived not in Lawrence but in a nearby suburb (Derry is a short drive up Interstate 93 from Salem, New Hampshire), as many of the city's most egregious absentee landlords lived outside the city.[32] Whether arson-for-profit was frequent or rare, it demonstrates the impact that disinvestment in Lawrence had on the city and on the Latino residents who lived in fear of their homes going up in flames.

Not only were the fires rooted in the city's economic decline, but they contributed to its economic crisis as well, as banks and insurance companies hesitated to provide mortgages or policies for homes in Lawrence. Of course, for city elites, a main concern was that the fires would hamper the ability of the city to attract the "first-class" tenants it had been trying (mostly unsuccessfully) to recruit for decades. Mayor Sullivan explained, "The fire publicity starts going national, and the business people start getting wary. Those companies that are needed to expand the tax base become reluctant to locate here. The ability to deal with the problem becomes diminished. You depend on growth to fight the fires and tear down buildings."[33] This neoliberal argument reflected the reality of the metropolitan political economy: The city's ability to provide public services relied on its capacity to attract private capital, yet the crisis provoked by its inadequate public services discouraged private investment.

In addition to its image as arson center, Lawrence was named the nation's auto theft capital in 1990 by the National Insurance Crime Bureau after 3,356 cars were stolen in the city that year. That is an average of nearly 10 cars a night in a city that is less than seven square miles. A Lawrence police sergeant complained that "the majority of kids stealing cars are under the age of 16," so they were difficult to prosecute. The sergeant tied the rising car theft directly to the inadequacy of work, school, and recreational activities available for young Lawrencians: "You've got a high unemployment rate here. You've got a lot of kids with nothing to do, so a lot of them are spending their time going out stealing cars—sometimes selling the parts."[34] Unlike with arson, Lawrence's suburbs were not insulated from this "urban problem." Car theft in North Andover in 1990 was up 51 percent from the year before, a fact that the North Andover police chief attributed to the town's proximity to Lawrence. Meanwhile, Methuen instituted a decal program in which a resident could authorize police to stop his or her car without cause between the hours of 1:00 and 5:00 A.M., the prime time for auto theft, and check the driver's ID.[35]

The devastation of the city's tax base limited the public safety services Lawrence could provide. One could argue, however, that increased funding for the police might not have made the city's Latinos feel much safer, as the overwhelmingly white Lawrence Police Department had a reputation for harassing and even assaulting Latinos, particularly in the 1980s. The reality, however, is that inadequate funding for the police and police abuse against Latinos could coexist and actually reinforce each other. Inadequate training and oversight of the Lawrence police force (especially given the paucity of Latino officers) contributed to a hostile relationship between the police and the community, and this hostile relationship further hindered effective crime fighting. The Department of Justice's Community Relations Service noted in 1986 that Black and Latino residents of the city frequently complained of being addressed as "nigger" and "spic" by police officers and summed up Black and Latino opinions of the Lawrence officers as "abusive, cruel, liars, and racist." The Community Relations Service explained that "Hispanics do not call police when they need them because when police respond to calls from Hispanics, they tend to arrest the person who made the call instead of the criminal." Staff at the Lawrence Housing Authority argued that police refused to even respond to calls for help from project residents, and as a result of this neglect, the housing authority had to apply for a grant to form its own police force.[36]

Police abuse took place in the context of a department that was underresourced and in which officers were often overworked. Police officers alleged that a recalcitrant administration required existing officers to work six hours per week overtime rather than hire new offers in a manner consistent with affirmative action requirements; in other words, they made white officers work more to avoid hiring Latino officers. Inadequate resources limited the community relations training available to officers. The police department frequently concluded that training its officers in Spanish would improve community relations, but there were never sufficient funds available. The police department only accepted limited antiracism training when it was clear that it would not need to pay for such training out of the police budget. Finally, inadequate resources limited the oversight available to mitigate corruption and abuse within the department and may have led some officers to adopt an "if you can't beat 'em, join 'em" attitude, especially toward the drug trade. In 1985, the FBI was investigating the department for drug trafficking and protective gambling, while the department conducted an internal investigation around allegations that officers were protecting heroin dealers. A 1985 report by the Massachusetts Criminal Justice Training Council described "a police department in which 75 percent of officers surveyed felt no sense of pride and belonging, in which officers continue to perceive themselves as nonprofessionals, and in which Department personnel feel a growing sense of dissatisfaction with and alienation from the City's elected and appointed officials and the general public."[37] While increased resources might not have improved the department, it seems clear that the inadequacy of public safety funding contributed to its failures.

Concentrated racialized poverty, blight, arson, and crime gave the city a severe stigma in the surrounding region. A 1988 Urban Studies Institute report noted that Lawrence had the reputation of being "the armpit of the Northeast."[38] Former residents bemoaned the city's decline, and some refused to even drive through it. Jeanne Schinto noted in the early 1990s, "I often hear other people (non-Lawrencians) wonder aloud: Why don't they just bomb the place and start over from scratch?"[39] As a small local paper summed up the city's stigma, "During the 1980s and 1990s, Lawrence, Massachusetts was known throughout the nation as the arson capital of the country, the auto-fraud capital of the country, and a place where business went to die."[40] Many residents insisted that the positive aspects of the city were unfairly eclipsed by its bad reputation. As one Puerto Rican high school student wrote in a letter to Jeanne Schinto, "I came to Lawrence [in 1990] scared to death about the rumors I had heard about this beautiful city, but when I started school I loved it. . . . None of the garbage I heard was true. I was prejudiced of Lawrence just like many people are now. In fact, all *most* people see is drugs, violence, and all the negativity of the city. What most people fail to see is the talent hidden inside this beautiful city."[41] While the city was clearly facing momentous challenges, its stigmatization in the region as a site of urban danger and decay often loomed even larger than the reality.

The stark decline in Lawrence's municipal services resulted from the combined impact of two distinct forces: the decline of the city's tax base as a result of white flight, deindustrialization, and suburban competition, and a conscious political strategy among city officials to focus on recruiting "first-class" residents to the city rather than improving life for the city's current residents. City leaders were reluctant to invest scarce municipal funds in better serving Lawrence's poor and working-class Latinos, opting instead to pursue strategies (urban renewal, high-end redevelopment, keeping the tax rate as low as possible) that they believed would attract new industry, retail establishments, and middle-class residents to the city. In addition, many politicians even came to reject state and federal welfare funds, believing that such aid served to maintain the city's status as a "magnet" for the poor and foster a tradition of dependency in Lawrence.

WELFARE MAGNET?

As Lawrence's economy declined precipitously in the 1980s and early 1990s, its Latino residents often suffered from un- or underemployment, inadequate wages, and precarious living situations. Many Latinos thus relied on community-based, state, and federal support to ensure their and their families' survival in the crisis city. Cash payments through Aid to Families with Dependent Children (AFDC), food stamps, public housing, rental subsidies, job training programs, English as a Second Language classes, legal assistance (particularly with immigration paperwork), Medicaid, community health centers—all of these forms of "welfare" played an essential role in supporting Lawrencians in the face of the city's economic collapse. Yet this crucial safety net was under attack in the 1980s and 1990s, as the New Deal welfare state was in many ways being dismantled in the commonwealth and nationally.[42]

Lawrence relied on welfare. Not only did individuals and families rely on government funds and services, but welfare comprised a necessary infusion of capital into the postindustrial city. Landlords, grocers, and local retail establishments benefited directly from cash aid and housing/food voucher programs just as hospitals, doctors, nurses, and clinics benefited from

Medicaid and public health funds. In addition, provision of these services was a major source of employment for both city and suburban residents. Direct support for individuals and families was mirrored at the government level, as more than half of Lawrence's municipal budget by 1986 came from state aid.[43] Rather than reform the welfare industry to make it a better engine for economic growth, however, city leaders worked with suburban allies to remove Lawrencians from the welfare rolls, in the belief that such reform could stop the migration of poor and working-class Latinos into the city and reverse Lawrence's economic decline.

For better or worse, welfare was one of the few avenues through which capital flowed into the crisis city, and by the 1990s, social services had clearly become the backbone of Lawrence's postindustrial economy. Jeanne Schinto noted in the early 1990s that the regional field office of the state's welfare department was located on the first floor of the old Everett Mill: "Where rows of textile workers used to toil for hourly wages, there is now a honeycomb of little blue cubicles."[44] In many ways, welfare was just as crucial to the postindustrial city's survival as the textile industry had been to the city's industrial economy. In 1993, the *Eagle-Tribune* noted the scale of the city's welfare economy: "In Lawrence alone, the so-called 'misery industry' of non-profit social service agencies providing services to welfare recipients is worth close to $90 million a year. . . . The $4 billion a year Massachusetts welfare system is also a cash machine for local nursing homes, doctors, lawyers, landlords— even funeral homes and taxi drivers. . . . Landlords [in Lawrence], for example, earned $4.8 million in rental subsidies for welfare families last year."[45] Welfare was an obvious source of support for the doctors, lawyers, landlords, funeral homes, and taxis the paper listed. Nonprofit social service agencies were "economic engines" in the city, providing jobs as well as services, and the welfare system helped pay property taxes in the form of rental subsidies to landlords.[46] The paper noted that, all together, the Lawrence area welfare office spent over $300 million a year; this was $50 million more than the annual operating budgets of Lawrence and its suburbs combined![47]

The essential role that welfare played in the city was often perceived as a source of shame and outrage, however. In the minds of many Lawrence elites and white residents, the reliance of some Lawrence Latinos on welfare was not a *symptom* of the city's economic crisis but its *cause*. Welfare "abuse" (a powerful reference to addiction in the era of the War on Drugs) was supposedly rampant in Lawrence, and according to these observers, the abundance of services available in the city had made it a "welfare magnet" for Latin America's poor. In this view, Lawrence's economic crisis was the result of the sheer number of poor people who lived in the city, not the lack of economic opportunities available to them or the segregation that concentrated them within municipal boundaries.[48]

In response to these views, Mayor Kevin Sullivan initiated a local welfare reform campaign in the late 1980s. Although he was adamant that his reform did not have a racial motivation, he often explicitly discussed his belief that Lawrence had become a welfare magnet, arguing that "people are coming to Lawrence and Massachusetts in general from all over the world to get on public assistance."[49] In this sense, in spite of the mayor's protestations, welfare reform was explicitly geared toward discouraging immigrant settlement in the city. Rather than attribute the situation of impoverished families to structural factors that Latinos encountered *in* Lawrence (such as unemployment, low wages, discrimination in housing and employment, or a miserable education system), many city leaders and white residents declared that Latinos came *to* Lawrence because of the welfare the city and state provided. Indeed, rumors had long circulated of a sign in Puerto Rico that supposedly suggested, "Come to Lawrence for welfare."[50] Mayor Sullivan argued that Latinos came to the city to take unfair advantage of its social services and "use[d] poverty as a disguise to get hold of the system."[51] In response, Sullivan initiated a controversial plan in 1989 to revoke the benefit cards (including Medicaid and food stamps) of anyone even arrested for—not necessarily convicted of—selling drugs. The blatant illegality of denying people welfare without due process eventually brought a stop to the program, but it illustrated officials' perception that Latino use of welfare in the city was fraudulent.[52]

The drive for welfare reform in Lawrence found its fullest expression in the early 1990s under another mayor, Mary Claire Kennedy. In language reminiscent of the national discursive concern that a permanent "underclass" was taking shape in U.S. cities, Mayor Kennedy posited welfare reform as a solution to the city's economic crisis: "If our cities are ever going to turn themselves around, we need a welfare program that's temporary in nature, not a way of life. What we have are third generation families who have never worked." Rather than blame deindustrialization and suburban competition for Latino joblessness in Lawrence, Mayor Kennedy blamed welfare. Other Lawrence elites shared her view that welfare reform could solve Lawrence's economic problems; the president of the city's chamber of commerce optimistically predicted that welfare reform was "going to bring stability back to Lawrence."[53]

This enthusiasm for welfare reform as a solution to both urban crisis and unwanted immigration was echoed across the commonwealth, and Greater Lawrence politicians became major players in a successful campaign for state-level reform. This campaign culminated in 1995 when Massachusetts legislated a radical restructuring of welfare provision and eligibility designed to push poor families off the welfare rolls and into presumed self-sufficiency. The state's punitive reforms then served as a model in the national debate over welfare that led to the 1996 Personal Responsibility and Work Opportunity Reconciliation Act (PRWORA), designed to "end welfare as we know it."[54] Lawrence and its suburbs were absolutely central to the implementation of welfare reform in Massachusetts, and the Massachusetts law (in combination with other state-level reforms) subsequently became profoundly important in shaping the national legislation.[55] Indeed, a *USA Today* article in 1995 called Lawrence "the new ground zero" in the national battle for welfare reform.[56] Republican governor William Weld, a major force behind the state legislation, called Lawrence's Mayor Kennedy "my tutor on welfare reform."[57] The commissioner of the Massachusetts Department of Transitional Assistance claimed that "the whole idea of welfare reform really began in Lawrence."[58]

On the national stage, welfare reform invoked virulently racist narratives of African American "welfare queens" in the nation's cities. Politicians and the media demonized Black single mothers as either cunning abusers of the welfare system who preferred living off the generosity of taxpayers or as unwitting victims of a system that discouraged work through rewarding laziness and immorality (as having children out of wedlock was perceived). The truth was that white women were the largest group of single mothers who received welfare, but the dominant discourse did not reflect that reality.[59] Lawrence's history reminds us that this pathologizing rhetoric of welfare recipients as lazy, immoral, and fraudulent was not only directed at African Americans but also marshaled against urban Latinos, particularly Puerto Ricans, who shared the "culture of poverty" stigma with Black communities in this era. Welfare reform became an opportunity to address nativist concerns about rapid immigration in the 1990s, as fears of urban crisis intersected with racialized fears of broader demographic transformations.[60]

The narratives that connected welfare reform and Latino immigration in Lawrence had not dissolved by the time the debate reached the state level. On the contrary, one of the first welfare reform bills passed by the state senate in the early 1990s was designed to limit migrants' benefits to whatever they would have received in their home states, including Puerto Rico. Massachusetts did not offer the most generous benefits in the nation; but they were significantly higher than those offered on the island, and as a result, the bill would have sharply cut benefits for the state's Puerto Rican population. Although it did not in the end become law, the proposal illustrated legislators' efforts to eliminate the presumed welfare magnet; one of its sponsors defended the need for such a measure by arguing that "glossy brochures have been distributed in Puerto Rico outlining our benefits and urging people to come here."[61]

While the bilingual and bicultural social service infrastructure emerging in Lawrence certainly helped Latinos endure the city's economic devastation, the belief that Latinos came to Massachusetts specifically for welfare benefits was challenged by the numbers: In 1993, Massachusetts gave about the same amount to AFDC recipients as New York did ($579 and $577, respectively, for a single mother with two children), and both states gave far less than generous states such as Alaska and Vermont.[62] Given that most of the early migrants to Lawrence were secondary migrants, and that many kin networks would enable migration to New York as easily as to Lawrence, welfare does not seem to be the missing piece to explain why Latinos chose Lawrence. This similarity in benefits between Massachusetts and New York did not stop politicians from arguing that Massachusetts's generosity created a welfare magnet, however. This idea that welfare benefits were a magnet for poor migrants had been earlier directed at African Americans migrating from the U.S. South in the postwar decades. Indeed, the idea that welfare could draw poor people to a region had been used to justify welfare residency requirements until the Supreme Court rendered them illegal in 1969 in *Shapiro v. Thompson*. As Marisa Chappell has demonstrated, "discussions of migration and welfare receipt in the 1960s evoked images of black Southerners overrunning struggling industrial cities." These tropes that had been directed at Black migrants were easily recycled in later debates about Latino and/or immigrant poor.[63]

Although Lawrence elites had been pushing hard for local and state-level welfare reform for years, the "key architects" of the Massachusetts law were ultimately three suburban Democrats, two of whom hailed from Greater Lawrence: James P. Jajuga of Methuen and John D. O'Brien Jr. of Andover.[64] The important role of legislators from Lawrence's suburbs in welfare reform was not surprising in the context of the urban/suburban racial and economic polarization that had developed in Greater Lawrence over the preceding decades. Not only did Democratic legislators from Andover and Methuen shape the punitive Massachusetts welfare reform; they also subsequently pushed for a pioneering program to uncover welfare fraud by requiring all recipients to be fingerprinted, a program first tested in Lawrence and Springfield in 1996.[65] State senator O'Brien specifically referenced unequal urban development as the historical process responsible for Lawrence's economic decline. Like Mayor Kennedy, he proposed welfare reform as a solution to the city's crisis: "For people in the city of Lawrence, who aren't going to get megaplexes and who aren't going to get Central Arteries, this is the major issue: a small city that is overburdened with social programs that no longer work."[66] To this Andover legislator, it had already been determined that the factors responsible for suburban wealth—sites of mass consumption and highways—would not be available to Lawrence. The best that the state could offer Lawrence, in his view, was a deep cut to its welfare rolls, much of which were actually funded through state and federal money. He proposed cutting one of the few remaining infusions of capital into Lawrence, yet he described it as a way to save the city. Whether disingenuous or just inaccurate, the idea that Lawrence's social services were a "burden" to the small city, rather than a hard-fought and critical safety net, undergirded the suburban politician's push to erode the state's welfare program.

Welfare reform was a logical extension of the suburban push to disclaim responsibility for "urban problems" like poverty and unemployment. The liberal reputation of Massachusetts should not obscure the fact that it was at the vanguard of this erosion of collective support for cities and the urban poor. As USA Today described it, "Just as Massachusetts has been regarded as a liberal laboratory for social planning, it is now a leader in the backlash assailing decades of welfare policies." Massachusetts governor William Weld boasted that the Massachusetts law "scream[ed] for individual responsibility," and Massachusetts officials celebrated that the state's caseload dropped by 1,000 families before the law even went into effect.[67] As one North Andover resident asked in the Eagle-Tribune, in a letter to "all the welfare mothers who feel that their children deserve a decent life," "Would you please provide this without any assistance from my taxes?"[68] The suburban rejection of responsibility for urban problems found a natural expression in state welfare reform.

The 1995 Massachusetts welfare reform required able-bodied recipients with children six years of age and older to either work or provide twenty hours of community service each week. It also imposed a two-year limit for benefits within any five-year period, which could be suspended for up to a year in any county with extended unemployment of 10 percent or more. Particularly challenging for recipients who engaged in transnational child-rearing, benefits could be cut if children failed to attend school for a set number of days each year. The reforms also eliminated the $90-per-month increase for children added to the family while on welfare.[69]

After the passage of reform, the Massachusetts welfare commissioner reinvoked fears of the state's Latinization by discussing the role of reform in dissuading immigration. After the governor boasted of 1,000 families dropped from the welfare rolls, the commissioner added, "Just the talk of welfare reform has had a great impact on people deciding not to come to Massachusetts."[70] In a single sentence, the problems of Latino communities in Massachusetts were obscured, and Latino communities in Massachusetts *became* the problem. The issue was not that the people here were poor, but that the poor people were here; the goal was not to help them escape poverty, but to discourage them from coming to Massachusetts. Just a little more than a decade after the riots, when the clarion call had been to infuse state and federal money into Lawrence in order to solve the city's crisis, the goal had become to curtail the flow of state and federal money into cities like Lawrence. Welfare reform was seen as a silver bullet to end both urban crisis and Latino immigration.

These concerns over immigration and the "welfare magnet" persisted in the national debate over welfare reform and were reflected in federal legislation. The 104th Congress crafted both the PRWORA and the Illegal Immigration Reform and Immigrant Responsibility Act (IIRIRA), and the two bills were signed into law just weeks apart in 1996. Before the PRWORA, legal immigrants generally had the same access to benefits as citizens, but the national welfare reform legislation ended this equal treatment. Federal welfare reform restricted legal immigrants' access to means-tested benefits, such as cash payments (formerly AFDC, remade as Temporary Assistance for Needy Families), food stamps, and Medicaid, denying benefits to most legal immigrants for five years after entry. On the other hand, the IIRIRA required, for the first time, that the sponsors of legal immigrants have incomes higher than 125 percent of the federal poverty level, and it also required sponsors to support the immigrant until he or she naturalized or worked forty quarters. Sponsors became legally liable for reimbursing the government for any benefits the immigrant received in that time.[71] Christina Gerken has argued that these laws represented "a two-pronged attempt" to limit immigrants' access to welfare. She has highlighted the discursive link evident in welfare reform between fears of a permanent underclass in U.S. cities and fears of increased immigration, noting that "politicians implied that the current system not only discouraged American welfare recipients from finding work but also served as a magnet for paupers from all over the world."[72] Lawrence and other impoverished cities (or urban neighborhoods) that contained large Latino or immigrant populations represented the intersection of two major forces conservatives believed were eroding the nation: persistent poverty in America's ghettos and unrestricted immigration of the world's poor.

The Armpit of the Northeast?

Although it was signed into law by a Democrat, President Bill Clinton, the PRWORA was the creation of a resurgent Republican Party and had been a key part of the party's 1994 "Contract with America." As Kevin Kruse and Juliet Gainsborough have demonstrated, the early 1990s were the point at which a distinctly suburban political agenda was evident on the national level, and Republicans capitalized well on the suburban desire to reject responsibility for presumably urban problems.[73] The PRWORA marked the mainstream triumph of a conservative movement to restrict government benefits and lower taxes that had emerged in the 1960s in response to the urban crisis. The national War on Poverty expanded welfare-state programs for the poor at the precise historical moment when the poor were coming to be identified with rebellious communities of color in the nation's declining cities. The poverty in these communities and the anger expressed during this era through rioting and protest came to be seen by many white conservatives as ipso facto evidence that such communities were "undeserving" of taxpayer aid. This movement gained momentum through the tax revolts of the late 1970s and the Reagan era of the 1980s, and by the early 1990s much of the nation had been persuaded that welfare was an unfair transfer of funds from hardworking taxpayers (presumably white and suburban) to lazy, immoral people of color in the cities. Many who were not fully persuaded by this argument were convinced of its liberal corollary, that welfare damaged recipients by incentivizing unemployment and unwed childbirth and thus trapped recipients in a cycle of poverty and dependence.[74]

These stereotypes of welfare recipients were rampant in Massachusetts. One study on the state's welfare reform recounted the myths about poor women that were touted by politicians and the media—that they were "dependent," "lacking in motivation," and "welfare cheaters." The authors of the study, James Jennings and Jorge Santiago, emphasized that these negative stereotypes often focused on poor Latinas in Lawrence and other cities, and that these narratives were a major part of what enabled the state's punitive welfare reforms. Jennings and Santiago noted that when public assistance was perceived simply as a safety net for anyone experiencing temporary hardship, it was politically impossible to muster sufficient public opposition for reform. When politicians and the media, however, focused on the cost of (and problems within) the welfare system specifically in impoverished, heavily Latino cities like Lawrence, they successfully created a racialized image of rampant welfare abuse. "Once the movement of local and state economic and political leaders in the mid-1980s successfully localized welfare to communities of color, there developed the 'problem of welfare fraud,' and reform was able to garner widespread white support." The belief that welfare utilization was localized in cities like Lawrence and confined to women of color mitigated the public interest in ensuring that reform was enacted in such a way as to preserve the basic rights of welfare recipients, enabling the punitive aspects of reform.[75]

Lawrence's history illustrates that the impulse to restrict welfare was informed by highly mediated perceptions of urban crisis. The social disorder and cycles of poverty that were supposedly characteristic of specifically *urban* communities of color during an era of unprecedented economic hardship in U.S. cities inspired suburban residents to turn away from taxpayer-funded welfare programs that supposedly benefited only the "undeserving poor." In addition, while national welfare reform narratives focused on the supposedly pathological African American "welfare queen," on a local level the "undeserving" urban poor that welfare reformers were disparaging were often Latino and/or immigrant. Anti-Latino and anti-immigrant sentiment persisted in and enabled the state and national legislation. Welfare reform was an intentional strategy to discourage Latino migration into Massachusetts and part of a national strategy to discourage immigration more broadly.[76]

SAVAGE INEQUALITIES IN MASSACHUSETTS

By the 1990s, the explicit racialization of politics was taboo even in Lawrence, and the struggle over the city's resources often flowed along other lines, such as age. The flight of white families over the preceding decades and the immigration of Latino families had left the city with a large population of elderly whites and a comparatively young population of Latinos. This demographic shift ensured that even when political debates were ostensibly about something other than race, they were also about how white and Latino residents would share Lawrence's meager resources. In 1993, the city clerk estimated that about half of the registered voters in city were sixty-five or older, and Jeanne Schinto referred to the elderly as "Lawrence's most tyrannical voting block."[77] As the elderly were a powerful political force in the city, the city's priorities often reflected their concerns, and services for Lawrence's youth were not given preference.

The city's economic decline and its refusal to prioritize its young residents were reflected in the spectacular decline of its public schools. The most dramatic demographic change in Lawrence after the riots was the loss of white children from the city's public schools. White families continued to leave the city in unprecedented numbers, and many of those who remained

The Armpit of the Northeast?

sent their children to parochial schools.[78] In 1984, at the time of the riots, just over half of Lawrence public school students were Latino. By 1991, nearly three-quarters were.[79] It is impossible to tell if this proportional loss of white students from the public schools was a direct response to the riots, which many white Lawrencians described as the final provocation to leave the city, or just a result of the steadily increasing Latino population. It was perhaps encouraged by a school desegregation plan that was put into effect less than a month after the riots; but many critics described the plan as weak and placing most of the burden on Latinos, so it is unclear whether it would have pushed white families from the public school system.[80] With nearly three-quarters of the public school population Latino by 1991 and the district severely under-funded, no meaningful desegregation plan could possibly be put into effect within the city.

The shambles of the city's public school system were not unique to Lawrence. The late 1980s and the early 1990s were an era of national preoc-cupation with the crisis in urban public education. Prominent films of the era sensationalized the dysfunction of inner-city schools (*Stand and Deliver, Lean on Me, Dangerous Minds*), but journalists also provided ample evidence that inner-city students of color were receiving an education that was both separate from and profoundly unequal to that of their white suburban peers. One of the most riveting and influential accounts was Jonathan Kozol's *Savage Inequalities*. Published in 1991, this widely discussed book documented Kozol's national tour of U.S. schools. In vivid detail, it highlighted both the persistent racial segregation of the post–*Brown v. Board of Education* era and the extreme funding gaps between many urban and suburban districts. Kozol described city schools plagued by a range of issues, including overcrowded and deteriorating buildings, inadequate and out-of-date textbooks and equip-ment, and frustrated and/or prejudiced teachers and administrators.

Kozol attributed this state of crisis to the gap in resources between urban districts and their suburban neighbors and the realities of racial segregation between U.S. cities and suburbs. He emphasized the connection between race and class in this intrametropolitan inequality and the resistance of sub-urban politicians to increase funding for urban schools: "Many suburban legislators representing affluent school districts use terms such as 'sinkhole' when opposing funding for Chicago's children. 'We can't keep throwing money,' said Governor Thompson in 1988, 'into a black hole.' The *Chicago Tribune* notes that, when this phrase is used, people hasten to explain that it is not intended as a slur against the race of many of Chicago's children."[81] But of course, Kozol explained, this and other coded references to the race of urban students were barely veiled. *Savage Inequalities* concluded that a segregated and inferior "ghetto education" in inner cities seemed to be nationally accepted "as a permanent American reality."[82]

This crisis in urban public education was partly an outgrowth of the racialized metropolitan political economy of the postwar era, but it was also the result of specific legal decisions.[83] The U.S. Supreme Court had ruled in *Brown v. Board of Education* in 1954 that segregated education was inherently unequal, and over the next two decades, further Supreme Court decisions combined with executive and legislative action and grassroots Black activism compelled school districts to remedy past segregation through organized school desegregation plans. These efforts were quite effective in desegregating southern schools. In 1960, virtually all African American students in the Deep South attended schools that were 90 to 100 percent nonwhite. By the early 1970s, less than a quarter attended such highly segregated schools.[84] Yet the juridical regime put in place after *Brown* played no meaningful role in desegregating schools in the Northeast or Midwest, where segregation actually increased in the decades after *Brown*. In 1960, only 40 percent of students of color in the Northeast attended schools that were 90 to 100 percent nonwhite, but by the early 1970s more than half did. By 2000, the Northeast and Midwest were actually the most segregated regions in the country, with the majority of students of color in the Northeast (and a near-majority in the Midwest) attending schools that were between 90 and 100 percent nonwhite.[85]

School segregation in the Northeast and Midwest was partially the result of white flight and suburbanization. But its legal underpinning was the Supreme Court case *Milliken v. Bradley* (1974). In *Milliken*, the Supreme Court effectively exempted most suburbs from urban desegregation plans. A lower court had ruled that Detroit's suburbs must be included in any meaningful desegregation plan for the city, as the stark residential segregation between city and suburb meant that a city-only desegregation plan "would result in an all black school system immediately surrounded by practically all white suburban school systems."[86] The Supreme Court, however, rejected this argument and overturned the lower court's decision, ruling that desegregation did not need to occur across district lines unless there was evidence of intentional school segregation between city and suburb. *Milliken* ensured that suburban families would be protected from the "urban problem" of desegregating public schools in the Northeast and Midwest.[87]

Yet *Milliken* offered no protection from racial integration for *urban* white families, as courts began to insist on sweeping desegregation plans for northern cities. For many whites in the Northeast and Midwest, the threat of desegregation or "forced busing" in the cities combined with the promise of freedom from desegregation orders in the suburbs to further encourage white flight from urban public school systems. In 1974, the same year as the *Milliken* decision, Boston schools were desegregated in an incredibly controversial plan that its critics viewed as an unjust effort by the federal government to force white students to attend schools outside their neighborhood with students of color. White opponents to the desegregation plan protested violently.[88] As in Lawrence, white Bostonians argued that the burden of racial integration fell on poor and working-class urban residents; those with the resources to move to the suburbs were exempt from the pressures and friction of integration, and this was inextricably related to racially and economically segregated housing. Prominent antidesegregation activist Louise Day Hicks told her critics, "Take the Negro families into your suburbs and build housing for them and let them go to school with your children."[89] After desegregation was implemented in Boston, the number of white students attending public schools in the city declined precipitously. In 1974, 60 percent of Boston public school students were white; but by 1980, only approximately 40 percent were, and by the early twenty-first century, less than 15 percent of Boston public school students were white.[90]

If *Milliken* was a retreat from the principles of *Brown*, then *Milliken* combined with another Supreme Court case decided in 1973, *Rodriguez v. San Antonio*, marked a retreat even from the "separate but equal" principle expressed in *Plessy v. Ferguson* at the height of the Jim Crow era. In *Rodriguez*, the Supreme Court ruled that states did not have any legal obligation to equalize school funding between property-rich and property-poor districts. Ultimately it concluded that education was not a "fundamental right" provided for in the Constitution and that wealth (unlike race) was not a "suspect category" that required states to prove they were not acting discriminatorily.[91]

Mexican American families in San Antonio had initiated the *Rodriguez* case alleging that the Texas school finance system, which based school funding primarily on local property taxes, was a form of economic discrimination against students in property-poor districts, and thus a violation of students' Fourteenth Amendment rights to equal protection. This case had national importance, as every state in the United States except Hawaii used a similar school finance system that tied school funding to local property taxes. Had the Supreme Court confirmed the lower court's ruling, this decision might have provided for equalized school funding across districts within a state, regardless of a district's property wealth or tax base. Instead, the ruling calcified a growing inequality between districts.[92]

It was this juridical regime that governed the extreme divide between urban and suburban school districts described in Kozol's *Savage Inequalities* and evident in Lawrence classrooms. Even major metropolitan centers such as Boston and New York City were suffering from a crisis in urban education, not necessarily because they could not afford to spend as much as their suburban peers, but because metropolitan patterns of residential segregation had concentrated high-needs students within specific urban districts. Urban districts had vastly disproportionate numbers of poor students, English-language learners, and students whose parents had not completed high school. So even those large cities that maintained a sufficient tax base to spend on par with some of their suburban neighbors could rarely provide equal educational opportunities.

Yet the true impact of *Milliken* and *Rodriguez* and the separate and unequal educational system they helped to construct was clearest when viewed through the lens of small postindustrial cities, such as Lawrence, Holyoke, and Chelsea in Massachusetts. Indeed, the most evocative portrait in Kozol's *Savage Inequalities* was of East St. Louis, a small, impoverished, postindustrial city in Illinois whose population at the time of Kozol's visit was 98 percent African American.[93] These small or second-tier postindustrial cities often had the same (or higher) concentrations of high-needs students, but they were fundamentally unable to spend at a level comparable to that of their suburban neighbors because of the evisceration of their property tax bases. Small cities in Massachusetts were in such states of fiscal crisis that many of them were under control of a fiscal review board in the early 1990s (Holyoke, Lynn, Chelsea, Brockton, and Lawrence). A report from the Massachusetts Department of Education in 1991 noted what these small city districts had in common: "These districts contain some of the neediest students in the Commonwealth. If we look simply at economic indicators—the AFDC rate, the free and reduced price lunch rate, property wealth per student, net school tax rate, and per capita income—we find the three lowest ranking communities in the Commonwealth. Holyoke, one, Lawrence, two, Chelsea, three."[94] Boston certainly had poor neighborhoods, but Holyoke, Lawrence, and Chelsea were fundamentally poor cities.

While the nation fretted about "ghetto education" throughout U.S. cities, the reality was that major metropolitan centers had far more resources available to solve the crisis in urban education. In 1991, Boston actually spent much more per pupil than the state average and more on bilingual education than on monolingual education. This reflected the higher cost of educating urban students and English-language learners, and of course,

The Armpit of the Northeast?

Public School Spending per Pupil in Lawrence and Other Cities in 1991

	District total ($)	Bilingual K–12 ($)
Boston	6,345	6,723
State average	4,803	4,405
Holyoke	4,310	3,732
Lynn	4,149	3,882
Brockton	3,997	2,603
Springfield	3,995	2,641
Lawrence	3,668	2,876

Source: Massachusetts Department of Education, "Report on the Condition of the Public Schools in Holyoke, Lawrence, Brockton, and Chelsea," October 15, 1991

many suburban districts spent even more than Boston. The state's small postindustrial cities, however, spent far less than the state average per pupil and actually spent less on bilingual education than on monolingual education.[95] *Rodriguez* had not been about rich students versus poor students; it had been about property-rich districts versus property-poor districts, places where the tax base could support a quality education and places where it could not. Lawrence in the late 1980s and early 1990s was most certainly the latter.

Boston's television station WGBH visited Lawrence's schools in September 1989 to document the city's education crisis and explore its relationship to the declining tax base. The "Ten O'Clock News" broadcast began with a shot of about half a dozen teenagers at Lawrence High School shyly standing around the edge of a classroom while their classmates sat. These students were not out of their seats to be disruptive; rather, they were calmly standing through the class period because there were not enough seats to go around in many classrooms at Lawrence High. The news report noted that science students couldn't do labs because there were only three working lab benches for a class of thirty. In an algebra class, fifteen students were forced to sit on the floor for lack of desks, but the reporter pointed out that even if there was a desk for every student, there would still be forty students in the class.[96]

At the time of the report, Lawrence was one of the fastest-growing school districts in the state, with students from forty-five different countries, 70 percent of whom qualified for free lunch (i.e., were considered low income). Its marching band practiced on the sidewalk, and there were no playing fields for Lawrence High athletes. The dropout rate was estimated at a stunning 60 percent, and the majority of those who did manage to graduate did not go on to a four-year college.[97] The news report contrasted Lawrence with the wealthy Boston suburb of Wayland, noting that Wayland spent thousands of dollars more per pupil than Lawrence. The Lawrence public schools had a $7 million deficit in their budget that year, and although the state provided operating aid, it did not provide aid to update Lawrence's industrial-era school facilities. All of the teachers and administrators interviewed argued that the problems in Lawrence schools stemmed from inadequate funding, not from inadequacies in the students. The interim principal argued, "If you took our kids and put them in a Wayland setting, then you'd have exactly the same achievement level as Wayland, maybe more." Teachers acknowledged that money couldn't solve everything but that increased resources were needed to at least give students a chance.[98]

In 1990, WGBH returned to Lawrence, this time to explore an elementary school, the Rollins School. The report described the school building as "crumbling" and noted that the windows needed to be replaced and the slate roof leaked; kids wore their coats in school. The nearly 100-year-old school had seen its student population double in the last twenty years without expanding its physical plant. There was one set of bathrooms for 400 students. The auditorium had been sectioned into classrooms, and special education students were packed into overcrowded rooms in the building's basement. The mayor explained to reporters that the school's decline stemmed from the city's fiscal crisis and that its fiscal crisis was partly the result of Lawrence's distinct demographics: It was filled with the poor and the elderly. He explained that nearly a quarter of the city's residents were over sixty-five and that 80 percent of the students in Lawrence public schools come from families that received some form of public assistance. With its tiny tax base, the city relied hugely on the state, with 60 percent of the city's budget coming from the state.[99]

Without a doubt, Lawrence public schools were in shambles. In 1990, Lawrence's per-pupil expenditure was only $4,098, almost 20 percent less than the state average of $4,972. Further, more than 20 percent of the city's students had abandoned the public school system in favor of parochial schools. A 1991 report of Lawrence public schools noted that the inadequate school budget was taking a major toll: "In Lawrence, 17 percent of all elementary classes have more than 30 students, with many in the high 30's and one grade 8 class with 43. At the High School one Anatomy and Physiology class had 48 students, students must use two editions of the textbook, and because this is a lab class no hands on instruction will take place, the instructor will use demonstrations only." The report continued to discuss the conditions of the classrooms in Lawrence's school buildings: "Almost every school is old and in need of repair, and there are spaces used for classrooms which were never intended to be, including closets used for speech therapy and guidance counseling. Students sweep out classrooms every day. Almost every building reports problems with rats, mice, cockroaches and even bats, yet the city has no pest control contract." In addition to the structural decline, the public school curriculum had been gutted. Presumably extraneous courses had already been eliminated by 1991, including "Industrial Arts, art, music, foreign language, library, English as a Second Language support, physical education, nutrition, family and student health, [and] college prep courses especially those for bilingual populations." Not only did the school budget affect class size and course offerings, but there was a shameful lack of resources for students as well, including textbooks, the number of which had been reduced by nearly half. There was a "freeze" on supplies and materials after one week of school, and the report noted that "both Chelsea and Lawrence are soliciting ('begging' as one principal noted) used books from more wealthy school districts."[100]

The decline of the public schools partially reflected official city priorities in a political context dominated by elderly voters, and the 1991 report argued that Lawrence's tax burden was too low. But once again, a metropolitan frame is necessary to truly understand the education crisis in Lawrence in the early 1990s. Lawrence's situation was shared by cities across the nation whose tax bases had been undermined by decades of suburbanization and deindustrialization. The intrametropolitan inequality firmly established by the early 1990s left Lawrence in a position of relative powerlessness, "begging" resources from the surrounding suburbs.

The bilingual education program, which had been hard won by Latino organizing, was equally in shambles. In particular, the layoffs of teacher aides resulted in the city schools being in noncompliance with the law in both bilingual and special education class sizes and student/teacher ratios. A full 70 percent of the bilingual classes in Lawrence were in noncompliance.[101] Such extreme disregard of bilingual education guidelines demonstrates that the city was still reluctant to invest in its Latino students. In light of the city's economic crisis, it seems that the cost of bilingual education, in particular, caught the attention/resentment of cash-strapped white officials. In the mid-1980s, Mayor Sullivan allegedly complained to the city council that the city should not have to fund bilingual education because "minorities can't even speak their own language."[102] The 1991 Department of Education report confirmed that the cuts in aid to urban school budgets demonstrated a continued resistance to bilingual education on a school and community level in Lawrence. "One of the most disturbing results of the cuts," the report noted, "has been increased evidence of tensions and prejudice between regular education and special education and bilingual staff and within communities, because of the per-ception that burgeoning immigrant populations and the alleged high costs of bilingual and special education are responsible for the budget crisis."[103] It must have been especially galling to the state's oft-scapegoated Latinos that bilingual programs were simultaneously underfunded to the point of neglect and blamed for the overall lack of educational resources in the city.

Unsurprisingly, most suburban public schools were not suffering from such decline. Suburban students living just blocks from the Lawrence border were receiving a quality education relative to Lawrence students. The sepa-rate and unequal school system that the *Brown v. Board of Education* decision had been designed to abolish had in many ways been reestablished along urban/suburban lines. Thanks to *Milliken*, the suburbs were not compelled to participate in any meaningful metropolitan desegregation plan, and none of Lawrence's suburbs chose to participate voluntarily in such a plan with their nearest urban neighbor. An effort to create a voluntary "collab-orative school" in the late 1980s for students from Andover and Lawrence failed after it encountered intense opposition from Andover residents.[104] The project would have involved a jointly run (and largely state-funded) elementary school designed to admit students from both municipalities. The plan was unanimously approved by the Lawrence City Council, but the Andover School Committee voted to withdraw from the project in 1988 after voters overwhelmingly rejected the proposed school at a town meeting with near-record attendance. Although enrolling in the school would have been strictly voluntary and no Andover students would have been mandated to attend the collaborative school, many Andover residents opposed it on principle. As one resident explained, "Andover is Andover. . . . People move here in part because of the school system. We don't want an urban school in a suburban area."[105] In 1991, a Department of Education report noted that "school choice" programs had made no significant impact on improving the schools in Lawrence either, because schools in the surrounding suburbs had elected not to participate.[106]

Urban communities of color certainly did not abandon the effort to gain increased funding for their schools after the defeat in *Rodriguez,* but they did shift their approach. In the late 1980s and early 1990s, the new legal strategy adopted by parents and their allies in property-poor districts began to bear fruit, as a wave of court cases using the educational provision clause in many state constitutions successfully challenged school finance systems based on local property taxes. These court victories helped precipitate a swell of increased state and federal funding for urban education beginning in the

The Armpit of the Northeast?

early 1990s, although this reinvestment was often part of a wider "education reform" agenda that included an emphasis on high-stakes testing and privatization.[107] The benefits and pitfalls of this new legal strategy and the legislative changes it enabled were clearly evident in the commonwealth, making it a compelling case study of late twentieth-century education reform.

In Massachusetts, families from Lawrence and other cities and towns with low property wealth (not Boston) initiated a lawsuit against the state in *McDuffy v. Secretary of the Executive Office of Education*, arguing that Massachusetts's school finance system violated the obligation the state had under its constitution to "cherish" public education. The plaintiffs argued, "Just as parents who cherish their children would not allow them to remain undernourished and underclothed, so a government that cherishes its schools would not allow them to remain underfunded and inadequate."[108] The plaintiffs were very clear that they were not pushing for the state to *equalize* educational funding, because *Rodriguez* had effectively rejected the right to equal school funding. Rather, they wanted the state to provide *adequate* funding for districts with low property wealth.[109] This array of families from property-poor areas argued that they were suing for "equal access to an adequate education, not absolute equality."[110] Kozol submitted a full copy of *Savage Inequalities* as an amicus brief in this case, in support of the plaintiffs' charges that segregated, underfunded school districts did not provide an "adequate" education.[111]

As it became clear in the early 1990s that the *McDuffy* suit was going to be successful and that the court would compel the state to dramatically increase funding for property-poor districts, the Massachusetts legislature (after years of bitter struggle) managed to put together a major overhaul of its school finance system as part of the Massachusetts Education Reform Act of 1993 (MERA). MERA ensured each community a foundational budget sufficient to provide an "adequate" education for all the commonwealth's children. MERA was about much more than school finance reform, however; while it had been the dramatic inequality in school financing (exposed in *McDuffy*) that catalyzed the law, MERA was a political compromise. Almost everyone agreed that education needed reforming, but there was tremendous debate about what that reform should entail. Conservatives wanted increased accountability and privatization, but they did not want increased state funding, arguing that more money wasn't the answer to failing schools. Representative Mark Roosevelt (chair of the joint committee that had crafted MERA) responded, "Opponents say that finances have nothing to do with reform." He invited those opponents to "visit the students of Holyoke, or the students of Wales, of Lawrence, where we have had upwards of 73 children in a classroom in the fourth richest state in America as recently as last year." Roosevelt conceded that "maybe in the gentlemen's community finances have nothing to do with reform," but in small postindustrial cities, where the schools had "third-world conditions," finances and reform were inseparable.[112]

MERA's new school-funding formula resulted in an incredible reinvestment in urban education in Massachusetts's small cities. Over the course of the next decade, spending on education in the state more than tripled, from $3 billion to $10 billion a year.[113] State aid to Lawrence doubled immediately after its implementation, and just a few years later, the city was supplying only 1 percent of its own school budget.[114] This was a major win for families in property-poor districts, as they pushed the state to compensate for the pronounced spatial inequalities that had calcified in the postwar era.[115] Yet along with a new school-funding formula, MERA included provisions that emphasized administrative and teacher accountability, and the law also opened the door for charter schools in the state. A statewide common core was developed, enabling a standardized testing system to be implemented a few years later in order to assess student performance (and thus assess teacher and school performance as well, with a debatable degree of effectiveness).[116] Education analyst Susan Bowles explained the strings tied to the state's increased funding: "MERA mandates a foundation level of funding for all schools in the Commonwealth (the carrot) in exchange for a comprehensive accountability system based on student outcome measures (the stick)."[117]

In many ways, MERA marked the success of a grassroots movement to end "ghetto education" in Massachusetts, but the conservative impulses of education reform also clearly shaped the law. The drive toward privatization was evident in the charter provisions, and the loss of local autonomy was evident in the standardized curriculum, ultimately enforced through standardized tests. The state would not pour money into urban schools without some external measure to ensure the money was being well spent; state aid meant at least some measure of state control. Given the current controversy over high-stakes testing, however, it is significant that, in Massachusetts, the heightened importance of standardized testing emerged, at least partially, out of local efforts to end the neglect of property-poor districts and hold the state accountable for providing an adequate education for all students.[118]

When signing MERA, the governor explicitly referenced Kozol's work, arguing that the law would end the "savage inequalities" in the state's schools. It is important to note, however, that such was never MERA's intention, as the state constitution (as validated in *McDuffy*) required "adequate" funding, not

The Armpit of the Northeast?

"equal" funding, for property-poor districts.[119] In addition, there was nothing in *McDuffy* to blunt the continued interdistrict racial segregation permitted by *Milliken* or to soften the sharp economic inequality between cities like Lawrence and their prosperous suburbs. Finally, this reinvestment in urban education was reliant on a state legislature that was often reluctant to invest in solving "urban problems" when it was not pressed to do so by the courts.

QUESTIONING DEPENDENCE

As the 1990s drew to a close, Lawrence leaders were still trying to address urban/suburban inequality by spreading out the region's poor, asking the surrounding suburbs to assume their share of the responsibility to house low-income residents. As Lawrence Housing Authority president David DiFillipo said, "Low-income people are not unique to Lawrence. . . . The social problems of the poor are not exclusive to Lawrence. Our neighbor towns have some responsibilities here." The city, which was providing subsidized housing for one of every ten of its residents, announced a plan in 1999 to buy land and build more affordable housing. Instead of building this affordable housing within city limits, however, the city planned to build it in Andover, North Andover, and Methuen. The suburbs quickly put pressure on Lawrence to drop the idea, claiming that Lawrence had no right to force affordable housing development on them. What might seem like an excellent compromise—Lawrence would buy the land and pay for the development of affordable housing, while all the suburbs had to do was allow the housing within their borders—was clearly not perceived that way. Suburban officials agreed to discuss affordable housing issues and work together on a solution, but Andover town manager Buzz Stapczynski made it clear that such a solution did not involve "talking about building affordable housing in Andover or North Andover or Methuen."[120]

Lawrence's "urban problems" were tangled together in a way that defied simple solutions. Low wages, job insecurity, and high unemployment made Lawrence the poorest city in the state in the 1990s, and one of the poorest in the nation.[121] Low owner-occupancy rates in housing based on these low wages and this high unemployment enabled the proliferation of apartments owned by absentee landlords, some of whom severely neglected their properties. This neglect led to the high rates of arson in the 1990s and the public health nightmare of lead poisoning, as well as undercutting the city's property tax base. Terrible, underfunded schools, particularly in terms of bilingual programs, led to high dropout rates in the city, exacerbating the city's trouble with gangs and youth violence. Lawrence's poverty and its reputation for corruption, crime, and racial tension stalled its elite renewal efforts for decades, obstructing the recruitment of "first-class" business and residential tenants.[122]

Broad stigmatization of the city and persistent scapegoating of its Latino population discursively exempted the surrounding suburbs from responsibility for "urban problems," but the truth is that Lawrence was enmeshed in its region, economically, socially, and politically. Urban problems had metropolitan roots, but these were rarely discussed by the media. Lawrence was known as the car-theft capital of the country, yet the suburbanization of the region's jobs that required substantial numbers of employed Lawrencians to travel outside the city for work but that did not pay sufficient wages to enable the purchase and maintenance of a vehicle was not considered a contributing factor. In 1992, 150 buildings were burned by arson, yet the metropolitan political economy that kept Lawrence's owner-occupancy rate down near 30 percent for decades and that had refused to fund satisfactory oversight of absentee landlords was elided. Lawrence was also widely known as a drug hub, and its young Latinos were demonized as drug dealers, while the vast suburban New England marketplace where many of those drugs were consumed largely escaped criticism.[123]

Private market rhetoric obscured the path of capital *out* of the city and highlighted the infusion of capital *into* the city through state aid. The money that flowed out of Lawrence in the form of rent and consumption at suburban retail establishments and in the form of the productive labor that city residents performed in suburban industries was invisible in the discourse of Lawrence's dependence on outside aid. The reliance of the economy of the suburbs on the labor and consumption of Lawrence residents and the mutual interdependence of the metropolitan region was invisible. The "sweat equity" that Lawrencians contributed to suburban public services through their labor and consumption in suburban economies was not the subject of discourse and debate, but the welfare some Lawrencians received and the infusion of government aid into the city's public schools saturated the media. The image of Lawrence as a poor, pathetic, dangerous, and dependent city solidified, while the origins of its counterpart—the wealthy, safe, independent, and charitable suburb—were rarely questioned.

Poverty became an "urban problem" in the Northeast and Midwest largely because the postwar metropolitan political economy concentrated public and rental housing in cities from which economic and educational opportunities had fled. In small or second-tier postindustrial cities, urban

The Armpit of the Northeast?

crisis often occurred on a municipal scale and persisted through the 1980s and into the 1990s, in the same era that major metropolitan centers began to experience reinvestment. For Latinos in Lawrence, this meant that even as they fought to gain access to a fair division of resources within the city, they still needed to contend with the reality that the city itself did not possess an equal share of the state's and the region's resources. As in Puerto Rico and the Dominican Republic, economic dependence compromised Lawrence's autonomy while fiscal crisis undermined its public services and quality of life. Pushed to Lawrence to find a "better life," imperial migrants instead found a host of entrenched economic problems, a protracted crisis for which they themselves were often blamed.

SEVEN

CREATING THE LATINO CITY

Outsiders don't come in to see what it's all about. There's a lot of bad, but there's a lot of good, especially for the Hispanics. That's why there are so many Hispanics here. It's the best town in the world for me.

Dominican resident of Lawrence

The crowdsourced UrbanDictionary.com defines "Lawtown," a common slang term for Lawrence, as "the center of [the] Latin Universe in all of New England."[1] That's a big title for a small city, but it fits. In spite of its economic struggles, Lawrence remains a major Latino settlement site to this day, and it is home to the largest concentration of Dominicans outside New York City.[2] Lawrence became the first Latino-majority city in New England with the 2000 census, and its population today is nearly three-quarters Latino. It was not a simple demographic shift that made Lawrence a contender for "center of the Latin Universe," however; it was residents' activism and initiative that transformed the city.

Lawrence today is decidedly Latino. Much of the remaining white population is concentrated in South Lawrence or elderly, with many living in the senior housing projects constructed during urban renewal. There is a small Southeast Asian population and a small non-Hispanic Black population, each constituting about 2 percent of the city's residents.[3] Ultimately, though, public spaces throughout most of the city are unabashedly Latino. Spanish is the major language of commerce and conviviality in many parts of Lawrence, while official city business (signs and school notices, the staff at City Hall and

216

in the courts, etc.) is consistently bilingual. The sounds of merengue, bachata, and reggaeton, along with hip-hop, float out open windows in warm weather. The streets are packed with restaurants advertising *comida criolla*, nightclubs, stores featuring stylish but inexpensive clothing, barbershops with Dominican or Puerto Rican flags in their windows, and countless businesses of all kinds with *Borinquen* or *Quisqueya* in their names (believed to be the indigenous Taino names for Puerto Rico and Hispaniola, respectively). There is also an array of transnational service providers, such as travel agencies, money transfer sites, and shipping services. The Common, the main central park of the city, simply lights up when the weather gets warm. Adults sit at tables playing dominoes while children devour ice pops and teenagers chat in slang-filled English laced with Spanish.

This book has traced Lawrence's history along two distinct axes: the economic competition between the city and its suburbs, and the struggle between white and Latino Lawrencians within the city. Ultimately by 2000, the city had effectively lost the economic competition, resulting in a stark dependency on the state and an extreme divide between city and suburb. Yet this chapter will explore the other axis. In the most basic sense, Latinos won the struggle for the city. Latino activism and community development combined with white abandonment and disinvestment to transform the city demographically, socially, culturally, economically, and in a somewhat more limited fashion, politically. The decades-long struggle of Latinos to assert their right to make a home in the city and for equal access to its resources and public spaces was tremendously successful in a host of different ways by the end of the century.

Although Latinos were often scapegoated for the city's decline, the reality is that Latino migration into Lawrence reinvigorated a dying city. Latinos were responsible for reversing the city's population decline; for filling its abandoned homes and buildings; for bringing life to its streets, churches, restaurants, and parks; and for anchoring its tax base. There can be no doubt that Latino migration was good for the city of Lawrence. Yet what remains debatable is how good the city of Lawrence was for Latinos. Imperial migrants drawn to the American Dream found instead an urban nightmare of bigotry, segregation, unemployment, poverty wages, arson, crime, and failing schools. While the concentration of Latinos in Lawrence provided opportunities for some, many others expressed dismay and disappointment about life in the crisis city.

This chapter will attempt to do justice to this complicated reality, exploring the profound changes in the city without losing sight of how the larger racialized metropolitan political economy constrained many Latinos' spatial and social mobility and contributed to a sense of immense disappointment, frustration, and even betrayal. I will trace the continued Latino migration to Lawrence in the 1980s and 1990s, after the industrial job opportunities that had drawn the labor generation of migrants disappeared. This late twentieth-century immigration and the economic activity it generated reinvigorated the city, particularly its downtown and its streets and parks. Continued Latino political activism bore fruit in this era as well. Toward the end of the century, with the help of the U.S. Department of Justice, as discussed in Chapter 5, Latinos began to have political representation in the city commensurate with their numbers. Yet for all these positive developments, there is ample evidence that the struggling city did not provide the opportunities for which many Latinos had hoped.

Much of this chapter will focus on the experience of Dominicans, as they came to outnumber Puerto Ricans in this era and were overrepresented in the small business sector of Lawrence's economy.[4] Dominicans were often foregrounded in accounts of local and transnational political activity in this period as well. It is important to keep in mind, however, that Puerto Ricans remained a major force in the construction of the bilingual and bicultural service economy and in Latino activism in the city. Neither Dominicans nor Puerto Ricans monopolized a specific form of transnational or bilingual/bicultural activity, and all phases of Latino immigration to Lawrence (and all aspects of community formation within the city) have involved other Latin American nationalities as well. So this chapter will still refer broadly to "Latinos" in the city, at the risk of collapsing important differences in national origin.

THE BEST TOWN IN THE WORLD FOR ME:
LATINO OPPORTUNITIES IN THE 1980S AND 1990S

Latino settlement in Lawrence accelerated rapidly in the 1980s. Latinos were less than one-sixth of Lawrence's population in 1980, but over the course of that decade, their population nearly tripled from just over 10,000 to just under 30,000. This reversed the city's long-standing population decline in spite of continued white flight and made Latinos more than 40 percent of the city's population. Immigration to the city continued in the 1990s, although not at such an extreme pace. By 2000, there were more than 40,000 Latinos in Lawrence, constituting 60 percent of the city's population.[5]

Jobs in the city's declining manufacturing sector had attracted the earlier generation of Latino immigrants in the 1960s and 1970s. Yet it would be an oversimplification to conclude that employment opportunity explains Latino settlement in Lawrence. Many migrants expressed their frustration with the quality of the jobs available even in the earlier era. The reality of dangerous working conditions, poor treatment from employers, inconsistency of work, and low wages renders the term "employment opportunity" sadly ironic. By the 1980s, however, the era of peak Latino migration, the city was enduring yet another wave of deindustrialization, and even these jobs were disappearing. Latino immigration to the city occurred at the same time as a devastating economic contraction, and by 1990, Latinos in Lawrence had nearly a 25 percent unemployment rate, almost double the rate for Latinos in New York. Clearly by the 1980s, Latinos were not settling in the city because of the jobs available; they were settling in Lawrence *in spite of* the lack of jobs.[6]

This apparent contradiction can only be explained by looking beyond strictly labor motivations for migration. As much of the literature on immigration focuses on the "pull" of jobs in the United States, this seemingly irrational choice (from a strictly economic perspective) to move to a city in which work was widely unavailable encourages a more nuanced view. As discussed in Chapter 2, migrants struggled to improve their lives in a range of ways by coming to the United States, and a job was often just a means to that end. Further, settlement in Lawrence was the result of constraints, not just opportunities. Pushed from their home countries by economic or political crises often shaped by U.S. intervention, migrants from Latin America weighed their options and searched for improved circumstances. In the United States, however, their settlement choices were limited. Most poor and working-class Latinos did not have unrestricted options for housing and employment; instead racial and economic segregation often channeled their migration into areas, like Lawrence, suffering from disinvestment.

For Dominicans, increasing settlement in Lawrence during the crisis era can only be understood in the context of the strong "push" from the Dominican Republic caused by the economic catastrophe of the 1980s, especially the extreme dislocation faced by rural residents of the Cibao region. For many rural Dominicans, the rising cost of living and pervasive unemployment of the late twentieth century precipitated migration: Either they moved to the capital, the tourist zones, or the "free trade" manufacturing zones within the country, or they emigrated overseas. Although Latino unemployment was high in Lawrence in the early 1990s, Tenares, the rural town from which many (perhaps most) Lawrence Dominicans emigrated, had a 57 percent unemployment rate in 1993. While not every hardworking Dominican would be able to find a job in Lawrence, the odds were still better in a postindustrial U.S. city than in a postagricultural Dominican rural town.[7]

In addition to this extreme push factor, U.S. immigration law facilitated chain migration. As more Dominican immigrants became legal permanent residents or naturalized citizens, they were able to sponsor the immigration of greater numbers of kin, particularly those immediate family members who were exempt from the numerical limits on how many immigrant visas could be issued each year. In this context, Dominican immigration to the United States as a whole accelerated rapidly in the 1980s, and the burst of Latino immigration to Lawrence partly reflects that (trans)national development. As Isabel Melendez explained of the Greater Lawrence Community Action Council's work helping Dominicans sponsor the immigration of relatives, just a couple of families could, over decades, generate a hundred applications.[8] With kinship networks enabling migration, it is not surprising that Lawrence's Latino population grew, as divided families reconstituted themselves in the United States. Kinship alone cannot explain the concentration of Latinos within the city's boundaries, however. The factors that drew Latinos *toward* Lawrence were different from the factors that constrained them *within* the small city's borders. The segregated and unequal metropolitan political economy is the background to every story of immigrant settlement in the crisis city.

As Lawrence developed a sizable Latino population in the 1980s and 1990s, the presence of such a large community became its own draw. Latino activists and their allies had worked hard to make the city welcoming to and sustainable for Latinos. The growing Latino presence helped revive the city's economy, while Latino community organizations, small businesses, and social services made Lawrence a place where some migrants could indeed find a "better life," if not always a reliable livelihood. Although the challenges of the city were still considerable, the rewards of living in a densely networked Latino community often outweighed those challenges. In 1988, the *Boston Globe* reported that dozens of Latino families were arriving every week, drawn by friends and family who had already settled in the city. The reporter noted, "The city's huge Hispanic population—estimated at 20,000 to 30,000—seems to be the biggest attraction. Hispanics can find grocery stores, dry-cleaning shops and plumbing businesses run by other Hispanics." Jorge Santiago added, "The weather is different and the architecture is different but otherwise you could be walking around in your home town."[9] For Latinos displaced from their home countries and struggling to find economic opportunities in the United States, the presence of kin and a strong Latino community could be a crucial source of support, a key aspect of that "better life" for which migrants were searching.

Julia Silverio and her husband moved from Salem, Massachusetts, to Lawrence for the city's more substantial Latino population even earlier, in 1974. She recalled, "The Spanish-speaking population [in Salem] was not large and so [my husband] didn't have his friends and people that he could play—do sports with, so we ended up moving back to Lawrence."[10] The decision to move to Lawrence was precipitated by her husband's desire to live near friends and within a more sizable Latino community, but Julia Silverio herself subsequently built a prominent business selling insurance, arranging travel, and performing other assorted services for the Latino community in Lawrence. Her service-oriented entrepreneurship eventually helped launched her successful political career. In 1999, Silverio became the first Dominican woman elected to political office in New England when she became a city councilor in Lawrence.[11]

In 1992, the *Eagle-Tribune* profiled a young Latino couple, a machinist at Lawrence Pumps Inc. and a nursing aide, who had just married and bought a two-family house in the city (the husband's brother would live upstairs). The profile captured well the reasons why Latinos chose to settle in Lawrence in spite of the challenges created by the city's crisis: "They have read the stories about Lawrence that have made headlines nationwide this year, stories of stolen cars, fires, teen-aged pregnancy, insurance scams and welfare schemes. They know the city is home to all of those problems and more. But it is also home to their families and friends, their memories and their hopes." The husband was Dominican and had moved to Lawrence ten years ago with his parents and seven siblings, all of whom lived in the area. The wife was Puerto Rican, but she had been born in Lawrence and considered herself "more Lawrencian than Latina." The paper described the couple as "among many people in the city's Latino community who view Lawrence's problems as its shadow, not its substance." The profile argued that family ties were important but were not the city's only draw; Lawrence had elected its first Latino official, 200 Latino-owned businesses operated in the city, and community resources were abundant, including parents' groups that gathered in homes "sharing information about schools, city government, health and other neighborhood concerns." The article continued, "Latino churches are thriving, from storefront ministries to established parishes." The community organizations that Latinos had built in the city improved residents' quality of life, in spite of the economic challenges. Perhaps most shocking to city leaders who had been trying unsuccessfully to revitalize Essex Street, "Downtown

Lawrence has developed a decidedly Caribbean flavor. Clothes boutiques, restaurants and nightclubs catering to a Latin crowd are attracting people from Boston, Lowell, Worcester and New Hampshire." Latino migration and organizing had brought life to the city, and that vitality drew more Latinos.[12]

Longtime resident and community organizer Isabel Melendez echoed these conclusions in a 2010 interview in which she explained why so many Latinos were drawn to Lawrence in spite of the city's economic crisis. She began by explaining how the city used to be a "city of opportunity" for Latinos, with ample work and affordable housing:

> Había oportunidad, no te estoy diciendo ahora, en este momento. En este momento no tenemos trabajo, no hay viviendas. Pero Lawrence era una ciudad de oportunidad. Cuántas veces aquí llegaban, yo me acuerdo, en compañía, si tú me traes tres, te damos 50 dólares, te daban dinero a ti, para reclutar. Hoy no, hoy no existe eso pero aquí había trabajo. . . . Así fue que vinieron, porque era fácil, tú llegas hoy y mañana tú tienes un trabajo. Los apartamentos, las rentas eran bien baratas.

> There used to be opportunity, I'm not saying now, at this moment. At this moment, we don't have jobs, there isn't housing. But Lawrence was a city of opportunity. How many times people arrived here, I remember, at the company, if you bring me three [new employees], I'll give you fifty dollars, I'll give you money to recruit. Today no, today this doesn't exist, but there used to be jobs. The apartments used to be very cheap.[13]

Although those opportunities disappeared, they set Latino immigration to the city in motion in the 1960s and 1970s. Those Latinos who arrived began to develop the nearly abandoned city, creating both a strong community network and a Latino-oriented service and retail economy:

> Lawrence empezó a desarrollarse de inmediato . . . con el negocio latino. Aquí no hay otra ciudad que tenga de todo, no importa lo que tú busques. Tú buscas una guardería, tú la tienes, tú buscas una botánica, tú la tienes, tú buscas un restaurante, lo tienes. No importa lo que tú busques, aquí, aquí lo venden. Por eso es que te siguen atrayendo.

> Lawrence began to develop immediately . . . with Latino businesses. There is no other city around here that has everything, no matter

what you are looking for. You are looking for a daycare, you have it, you are looking for a *botánica*, you have it, you are looking for a restaurant, you have it. No matter what you are looking for, they sell it here. That is what keeps attracting people.[14]

As Melendez articulates, the services that Latinos organized to provide (whether profit-oriented or not) served to draw Latinos to the city, developing Lawrence into a relatively supportive community for Latino settlement. This was true *in spite of* the city's economic crisis and the difficulty of finding a job. Melendez explained that she tried to warn prospective migrants that the city's economy made life in Lawrence difficult, but migration persisted:

> IM: Ahora en este momento, aun así, que no hay trabajo, tú tienes personas nuevas, aquí me llegan personas. Y yo soy realista, cuando yo visito Puerto Rico y le digo cómo está la situación. . . . Y si yo estoy por allá en la Florida en algún lugar y yo digo la situación en Lawrence no está como estaba desde 25 años atrás, que tenías trabajo, que la renta era muy barata, ahora está todo muy alto, no hay trabajo, pero la gente sigue.
>
> Entrevistadora: ¿Sigue llegando porque es una ciudad latina?
>
> IM: Por eso, porque es latina, porque es latina.

> IM: Right now, even though there are no jobs, you have new people, new people arriving here. And I am a realist, when I visit Puerto Rico, I tell them the situation. . . . And if I am out there in Florida some place, I say the situation in Lawrence isn't what it was 25 years ago, when there were jobs, when the rent was cheap. Everything today is very expensive and there are no jobs, but the people keep coming.
>
> Interviewer: They keep coming because it's a Latino city?
>
> IM: That's why, because it's Latino, because it's Latino.[15]

Latinos looking for a better life, not simply labor migrants looking for work, transformed the city of Lawrence. Ultimately, decades of disinvestment in the city created space for Latino community and economic development, and the profoundly Latino city continued to draw new migrants. This was true even during the nadir of the city's economic crisis in the late 1980s and early 1990s. Lawrence Garcia, a Lawrence-born Dominican whose parents had named him after the city, drove a cab for Borinquen Taxi. Interviewed in 1992, he insisted that Lawrence was a prime settlement spot for Latinos, in spite of its struggles. "Outsiders don't come in to see what it's all about," he observed. "There's a lot of bad, but there's a lot of good, especially for the Hispanics. That's why there are so many Hispanics here. It's the best town in the world for me."[16]

HOMEOWNERSHIP

For some Latinos, particularly professionals, the city's allure was augmented by relatively low housing prices compared with those in the surrounding region, providing a unique opportunity for homeownership. The Urban Studies Institute began to see a rise in educated, professional Latinos settling in Lawrence during the late 1980s, migrants who "sought to put down roots in one of the few Eastern Massachusetts cities that seemed . . . to offer a chance for inexpensive home ownership."[17] Dalia Díaz is a great example of the draw Lawrence offered for some professional Latinos. Díaz had come to the United States from Havana as a teenager in 1963. After years in the United States improving her English skills, Díaz eventually got a job as a secretary at Prime Computer in Natick, with typing skills she had brought with her from Cuba. After her son was born, she moved from Chelsea to Natick for its school system. When her son finished school, she and her husband began looking to purchase a house north of Boston, as her husband was working in Malden. She recalled, "We started looking for properties along Route 93 and they were very expensive. When we looked around in Lawrence, it was a lot cheaper."[18]

She and her husband were no strangers to Lawrence, as it had already become a Latino hub in the region. "We were coming to Lawrence every weekend to the Hispanic restaurants and the factory outlets. Every single weekend we were coming here." They decided, "If this is the place where we come every weekend, why not live here?"[19] They settled in Mt. Vernon, in South Lawrence, a unique suburban-style neighborhood on the border with Andover. Díaz was deeply involved in Lawrence's Latino community as the founder of the bilingual newspaper *Rumbo*, and she and her husband had the means to buy one of the few single-family houses in the city, in a relatively tranquil section. For someone in her circumstances, Lawrence was not a "crisis" but an opportunity, especially considering that other houses in the region were prohibitively expensive.

The possibility of homeownership in Lawrence was a draw even for working-class Latinos. The Urban Studies Institute noted that Latino families worked together to buy and share triple-deckers in the Newbury Street area, "drawing on extended family members to help themselves into all the tax and equity advantages of homeownership."[20] Even workers with relatively low wages could eventually own their own home if there was more than one

Creating the Latino City

worker in a household. Jessica Andors cited a Dominican woman who grew up in Lawrence whose family was able to purchase a triple-decker house, even though they never made more than $8 or $9 an hour in their suburban manufacturing jobs.[21] The preponderance of triple-decker homes in a relatively depressed housing market presented an opportunity for Latino homeownership that single-family suburbs and towering big-city apartment buildings did not offer. Yet overall, the proportion of Latino families able to take advantage of this opportunity remained quite low, given the extreme rates of poverty and unemployment in the city. In 1990, only 12.7 percent of Latinos in Lawrence owned their own home.[22]

DISPLACEMENT FROM NEW YORK CITY

A good deal of Latino migration to Lawrence in the 1980s and 1990s was direct from Latin America, as a growing proportion of migrants chose to bypass the historic Dominican and Puerto Rican gateway of New York. By the late 1980s and early 1990s, New York City's urban crisis had accelerated in many ways, as disinvestment continued in low-income neighborhoods, unemployment remained high, and the drug trade, addiction, and the militarized War on Drugs ravaged inner-city communities. Like the earlier generation of migrants during the 1960s and 1970s, Latinos continued to move to Lawrence to escape or avoid urban crisis in New York. By the 1980s, however, Lawrence itself was in a deepening state of emergency. A young Dominican woman whose mother moved their family to Lawrence in 1989, for example, explained that her mother decided to leave New York "because there was a lot of drug dealing, a lot of stealing, gun shots. That wasn't a good area for us, to raise us. So she was concerned for our health, the way we [would] grow up, so she moved to Lawrence." Although the reasons behind this late 1980s move echoed the decisions of earlier migrants, once the family arrived in Lawrence, the young woman's mother was deeply disappointed to discover that their circumstances were similar to what they had left in New York. Within Lawrence, her family had to continue to move repeatedly in search of neighborhoods without drug dealing. By the late 1980s, Lawrence was no longer an escape from the crisis city.[23]

Not only racialized disinvestment and economic decline in New York City pushed Latinos toward Lawrence. By the late 1990s, economic revitalization in New York also came to play a major role in dispersing Latinos from the big city. While Lawrence's economy was declining in the early 1990s, Latino neighborhoods in New York City, including the Lower East Side and

East Harlem (*El Barrio*), were gentrifying. As Arlene Dávila and others have demonstrated, renewed investment in New York's Latino neighborhoods in the 1990s often made them unaffordable for poor and working-class residents. Most of the migration narratives used in this book were from Latinos who came to Lawrence by the early 1990s; as a result, the emphasis in these narratives is on the danger and crisis in New York, not gentrification. Yet the displacement of Latinos from New York City continued the process of Dominican and Puerto Rican dispersion evident in earlier eras, rendering alternative settlement sites like Lawrence increasingly important. Spatial mobility out of New York City did not necessarily mean upward socioeconomic mobility in the era of gentrification, however, and Dominicans and Puerto Ricans who settled in the Northeast's small postindustrial cities often experienced substantial hardship.[24]

Researchers at the Centro de Estudios Puertorriqueños at Hunter College studied Puerto Rican outmigration from New York City from 1995 to 2000 and reported that outmigrants from New York City varied significantly in their socioeconomic status and motivations for leaving. While some relatively successful Puerto Ricans left New York City for the surrounding suburbs or southern Florida or to retire in Puerto Rico, many of those who left New York to move to small cities in the Northeast fell into a category that the researchers termed "the displaced." They characterized "the displaced" as "individuals/families having difficulty in the New York City employment markets and housing markets," noting that such outmigration was "primarily responding to 'push' factors in New York City." The "displaced" outmigrants from New York generally had lower education and income levels, higher poverty levels, greater Spanish-language dominance, and a lower proportion of professional or managerial occupations than Latino outmigrants to other areas.[25]

This Centro study made clear that moving from a booming major metropolitan center to a small, segregated, and impoverished New England city rarely involved the improved economic circumstances typically associated with suburbanization. While middle-class, educated Puerto Ricans may have gained access to the tree-lined suburban ideal, the report noted that "for those at the other end of the socioeconomic spectrum—the displaced—leaving New York has not freed them from poverty conditions." Indeed, Puerto Ricans who went to small New England cities actually had higher rates of poverty than those who stayed behind in New York (42 versus 32 percent). The Centro researchers concluded that "for residents in smaller, de-industrializing Northeastern towns and cities, where they continue to face unemployment,

crime, and poor housing, relocation did not deliver substantial improvements in socioeconomic wellbeing." Changing census definitions have led to
the conflation of economically marginal small cities with suburbs (indeed,
the census no longer officially considers Lawrence a city), yet clearly, poor
and working-class Puerto Ricans who settled in the postindustrial Rust Belt
encountered distinct socioeconomic challenges.[26]

As gentrification forced the dispersal of poor and working-class
Latinos from New York, and as many suburbs in the Northeast remained
inaccessible, Lawrence and other small cities became increasingly important. Yet these struggling cities did not necessarily provide the better life
for which Latinos were searching. Using data from the 2000 census, José
Itzigsohn demonstrated that Dominicans in the smaller New England cities
of Providence and Lawrence fared much worse than those in New York
City in many respects. In all three cities, Dominican immigrants (the "first
generation") often had low median incomes and low educational attain-
ment and were largely concentrated in manufacturing jobs with low rates
of managerial and professional employment. U.S.-born Dominican Americans (the "second generation") generally had a higher proportion of individuals in professional and managerial positions and a higher proportion of
high school graduates compared with their parents' generation, indicating
some measure of upward socioeconomic mobility between the immigrant
and second generations. Yet there were troubling indicators that, taken as
a whole, Dominicans in Providence and Lawrence actually experienced
downward socioeconomic mobility across the generations. In New York
City, for example, second-generation Dominicans had a much higher
median income than Dominican immigrants (approximately $42,000 for
the second generation, compared with $33,000 for Dominican immigrants).
This increase in median income was true nationally for Dominicans as
well. In the smaller New England cities, however, not only were median
incomes substantially lower for Dominicans overall, but incomes were
actually lower for the second generation than for the immigrant generation. In Lawrence, the median income for Dominican immigrants was
approximately $32,000, but for the second generation it was only $29,000.
In Providence, the median income for Dominican immigrants was approximately $28,000, but for the second generation it was only $27,000. By 2000,
U.S.-born Dominican Americans were earning *less* than Dominican immigrants in both of these New England cities.[27]

Itzigsohn accounted for this intergenerational decline in median income
in Providence by noting the decrease in the number of relatively well-paid

manufacturing jobs and the growing concentration of second-generation Dominicans in the "services working class." Such service jobs, he pointed out, often meant that many Dominican Americans "live[d] their lives a paycheck away from poverty and, in some cases, as working poor." This movement of the second generation away from manufacturing and toward low-waged service jobs was true in Lawrence as well, but even poverty-wage jobs were often hard to find in the Massachusetts city. The unemployment rate for second-generation Dominicans in Lawrence was 10 percent, nearly twice the rate for Dominican immigrants. Rather than showing improved economic circumstances over the generations, these figures indicate that U.S.-born Dominicans in Lawrence often had a harder time finding work than their parents' generation did.[28]

Lawrence also diverged from New York City in terms of college completion rates. In New York (as in Providence), the second generation had a higher proportion of college graduates than the immigrant generation, but in Lawrence, the proportion of college graduates actually declined for the second generation. While 6.6 percent of Dominican immigrants in Lawrence had bachelor's degrees, only 2.2 percent of second-generation Dominicans did. This exceedingly low rate of four-year-college completion speaks to the relative lack of higher educational opportunities in and around Lawrence and likely also reflects the crisis in Lawrence public schools during the 1980s and 1990s, when many of these second-generation Dominicans were coming of age.[29] The urban economic decline that resulted from deindustrialization and suburbanization impacted the educational services that Lawrence could provide.

Itzigsohn emphasized the high degree of internal stratification among Dominicans to draw attention to the presence of some upwardly mobile, well-educated, middle-class Dominican entrepreneurs and professionals in all three cities, and indeed, Lawrence certainly has its share of success stories. Yet he argued (as the data illustrated) that for most Dominicans, opportunities for intergenerational social and economic mobility were limited by an array of factors, including their racialization and the low-wage service economy that came to dominate cities like Lawrence and Providence in the late twentieth century. In many cases, the dispersal of Dominicans and Puerto Ricans from New York to lower-tier cities in the Northeast *neither reflected nor provided* upward socioeconomic mobility. Latino settlement in Lawrence was beneficial for Lawrence, but this small postindustrial city seems to have provided poor and working-class Latinos with few educational or economic opportunities.

Immigration to the United States is typically imagined as a voluntary move-ment in pursuit of freedom and opportunity. Yet as Chapter 2 showed, economic dislocation (and sometimes political violence) often compelled migrants to leave behind their family, friends, communities, and countries, and many thus dreamed of being able to return home. The challenging circumstances that Latinos faced in Lawrence often exacerbated this longing to return, as migrants encountered unemployment, segregation, and inade-quate government services. Many imperial migrants who came to Lawrence continued to move, either returning to their home countries or living in different parts of the United States, in a peripatetic search for the elusive "better life." Some moved back and forth between Lawrence and New York City, while others tried out South Florida or cities in the Midwest.[30]

The dream of moving home was, for many, the most enticing, although it was often unrealized; many migrants simply did not have the means to return. As the *Eagle-Tribune* explained in 1984, "It has been an abiding flirta-tion, like the tide's with the shore. . . . In the last few decades, thousands of Spanish-speaking people have streamed into Lawrence—many to build new lives and dreams, others to turn and retreat, as their expectations dissolved like sand castles. Some have left and returned several times. But in the great pull and flow, most have found themselves with the same question asked by other immigrants before them: Where, exactly, is home?" The paper reported that "roughly half of the Hispanics interviewed for this story said they would like to return permanently to the country of their birth. Three out of four said they still have relatives there. But statistics show that most will never return, except for visits. They will, instead, live out their lives, . . . straddling two cul-tures, apart yet still a part."[31]

Many of those who intended to come to Lawrence temporarily wound up staying permanently. Some Latinos chose not to return home because they refused to give up access to the improved services and economic oppor-tunities available in the mainland United States. Specifically, many would not let go of their dreams that they, or more often their children, could have access to better health and educational services. Yet this did not mitigate the longing for home. A fifty-one-year-old Puerto Rican woman interviewed by the *Eagle-Tribune* illustrates this, as the interpreter reported, "She'd like to return to San Juan and have a little house of her own and die back in Puerto Rico." The paper argued that her longing to return was common among local

Latinos. She had come to the United States when she was thirty-six "not because she wanted to, but in order to help her sickly mother who wished to leave Puerto Rico." Initially, she wanted to return, but "thinking her children could get a better education here, she decided to stay for a time. That was 15 years ago." Although she had chosen to stay temporarily for the health and educational opportunities on the mainland, by the time of the interview, her economic situation had made her return impossible. She lived in the Beacon Street housing projects and could not afford her dream of having her own home in Puerto Rico. Yet she was unwilling to relinquish her hopes, maintaining a focus on returning even when it was not feasible. The interpreter explained, "She plays the lottery numbers and hopes that, through that, she can make her dream come true."[32]

For some Latinos, the racism they faced in Lawrence made them dream of returning home. As Peggy Levitt found with Dominicans in Boston, the experience of racism in the United States "reinforced migrants' transnational attachments . . . because they realized they would never be allowed to achieve full membership in the United States."[33] A young Dominican man in Lawrence was clear about his preference for his home country when he was interviewed in 1979. He argued that the prejudice he faced made the city simply unlivable: "They think we are all the same. . . . They think we are all from Puerto Rico. They call us spics."[34] In 1984, the paper interviewed a young Puerto Rican father who, in spite of his relative success in the United States, "still dream[ed] of raising his children in his homeland where they could not be singled out because of their race."[35] As was true for earlier generations, the economic difficulties of the crisis city merged with experiences of bigotry and discrimination to reinforce this desire to return to the home country. Jessica Andors reported, "One [Dominican] woman I talked with at the Department of Transitional Assistance, who had been in the States for 25 years (first in New York, then in Lawrence), informed me that she was leaving for the Dominican Republic the following week, despite the fact that most of her family was here, citing discrimination and the instability of temporary work as her main motivations for returning."[36] The longing for home was partially a response to the disappointments encountered in Lawrence—both the economic struggles and the bitter racism.

Although kinship was a crucial mechanism by which migrants settled in Lawrence, migration almost always entailed leaving loved ones behind as well. One woman who migrated from the Dominican Republic explained that she ended up in Lawrence because her sister-in-law invited her husband to move to the United States and, as a wife, she had to accompany him

Creating the Latino City

("*tuve que venir con él*"). When asked what she had to sacrifice to come to the United States, she replied, "*dejando todos mis hijos atrás* [leaving all my children behind]." As for many migrants, the move to Lawrence involved a painful family rupture, and she explained that it took a long time for her to adjust to her new home because she had to live in the United States without her children. Even when her children were eventually able to join her, she dreamed of returning, "*porque tengo mi madre atrás* [because I still have my mother there (in the Dominican Republic)]."[37] Puerto Ricans sometimes experienced the difficulties of divided families as well, but U.S. immigration law was not an obstacle to their reunification. For Dominicans, national borders could cause far more heartbreak. The displacements provoked by the U.S.-influenced political economy in the Dominican Republic pushed Dominicans to migrate for a better life; yet not only did urban disinvestment and segregation often render that better life inaccessible, but U.S. immigration policy made the process of family reunification on this side of the border protracted and sometimes impossible.

The longing to reunite one's family or to escape the crisis city and return home illustrates the hardships of transnationalism. For most migrants, the components of the "better life" they hoped for did not all exist in the same place. Tragically, the building blocks of their dream were often spread across national boundaries. As one Dominican explained, "*Yo te puedo asegurar que si hubiera un puente de aquí para allá, todos iríamos para allá ... vamos y venimos diario* [I can assure you that if there were a bridge from here to there, all of us would be going there ... going and coming daily]."[38] Without a bridge, this daily form of transnationalism was impossible, but many migrants visited frequently, communicated with kin even more often, and dreamed of returning home to stay. Such transnationalism was a way to mitigate the structural inequalities that made it impossible for migrants to have everything they needed within reach.

THIS WOULD BE A GHOST TOWN

With Lawrence devastated by decades of urban crisis, the growing numerical dominance of Latinos was not sufficient to address the city's economic ruin or the failure of its educational, public safety, and other city services. After half a century of suburbanization and deindustrialization, Lawrence had neither resources nor political leverage. Latinos had long argued that their marginalization prevented them from being able to fully contribute to the struggle of all Lawrencians to save their city. As the crisis deepened in the late 1980s and 1990s, it became obvious that simple inclusion in the city in its current incarnation would only mean a first-class seat on a sinking ship. Latinos instead worked for a transformation in the city: an economy based on transnational businesses and provision of bilingual, bicultural services in the public, private, and nonprofit spheres; a celebration of the city's Latino culture; an accountable city government; and community development strategies aimed at improving the neighborhoods for the people who were already in the city (rather than the long-awaited "first-class" residents who had yet to respond to the beckoning of city officials).

This transnational, bicultural approach reinvigorated the city, and it resituated Lawrence as a powerful player in international politics instead of a marginal charity case in state politics. Rather than accept their position at the bottom of the pile in Greater Lawrence and the state, Latinos sculpted for themselves a position vis-à-vis the Caribbean that was marked by relative wealth and definite political influence. In addition, by the late 1990s, when it became obvious that the city was clearly transitioning to a Latino majority, the argument that Latinos were the only hope for the long-awaited Lawrence renaissance began to gain purchase even with city leadership. The practice of excluding Lawrence's Latinos was supplanted by a practice of "bridge building" between the city's white and Latino communities.

White acceptance of the Latino community as a viable path to Lawrence's revitalization began with the growth of Latino-owned businesses in the 1990s. As the Latino population grew, small businesses emerged to serve it, and this became especially noticeable along the main downtown retail strip of Essex Street. Clothing stores, barbershops, restaurants, and auto repair shops oriented toward a Latino clientele proliferated alongside service businesses such as travel and insurance agencies, international shippers, van transportation to New York, and "multiservice" hubs that provided mailboxes, wire transfer services, notarization, and photocopies. The level of grassroots entrepreneurialism in Lawrence became truly remarkable.

These businesses, aimed at serving Latinos' local, interurban, and transnational needs, were partly a natural result of the demographic changes in the city. Yet they also reflected Latino agency, as they comprised a significant investment of capital and energy into the crisis city as well as a contested effort to shape its economy and landscape. As Latino community leader Eduardo Crespo argued, "The mere number [of Hispanics] has created an obvious marketplace. . . . We buy cars, we buy clothes, we rent, we own, we borrow. . . . Hispanics are bringing Lawrence back to life. . . . If we would, hypothetically, leave the city, this would be a ghost town."[39] With the flight

Creating the Latino City

of industry and retail to the suburbs, Crespo's assertion that Latinos brought life to the city and were, indeed, its major market was incontrovertible. Even Mayor Kevin Sullivan acknowledged in 1991 that almost three-fourths of the new businesses that opened in the last five years were Latino owned, citing car dealerships, insurance companies, groceries, and appliance stores. Crespo tied this growth of Latino-owned businesses explicitly to white flight and disinvestment, saying, "Hispanics are replacing traditional establishments that no longer believe in the city."[40]

Latino business ownership grew over the years, as did the faith of city leaders. In 1996, the *Eagle-Tribune* reported the results of a Census Bureau study of Latino business ownership. The study compared business ownership and revenue between 1987 and 1992, and the article—titled "Hispanic Businesses Boom"—noted with excitement that the number of Latino businesses in Lawrence had more than doubled during those five years. This dramatic growth rate significantly exceeded the national rate, which itself was considerable. By 1992, nearly one in seven businesses in the city was owned by Latinos, and officials enthused over the potential role of Latino-owned businesses in the city's imminent revitalization. When this study was released in 1996, Mayor Mary Claire Kennedy declared, "I along with others have been saying that the future of Lawrence, our economy and the downtown depends on the ability of the Hispanic population to be entrepreneurial, participate in the economy and climb in the economy. . . . If we're going to continue to grow and prosper, it's going to be because Hispanic-owned businesses continue to grow." This official proclamation that the fate of the city rested in the hands of Latino entrepreneurs was a pronounced turnaround from earlier policies designed to displace and exclude Latinos from the city.[41]

Unfortunately, Latino-owned businesses in 1992 were usually small and rarely generated major profits for their owners. Although they were 14 percent of the city's businesses, they generated only 1.6 percent of its business revenue, and that revenue had actually declined over the previous five years during the state's economic downturn. Not only did this forecast dim economic prospects for small business investment in Lawrence, but if the future of the city really rested on Latino-owned businesses, that future looked bleak.[42] Clearly, there were still obstacles in the early 1990s to Lawrence achieving its potential as a Latino economic enclave. At the same time, the proliferation of Latino-owned businesses in the context of severe economic decline throughout the rest of the city precipitated an important change: City elites began to realize that they needed to work with Latinos, rather than awaiting their eventual displacement, to bring about a renaissance in the city.[43]

By the late 1990s, there was more reason to be optimistic, as the city was in the midst of a significant expansion of Latino-owned businesses. Nelson I. Quintero, executive director of the Lawrence Minority Business Council, attributed this to the rising population of Latinos and the fact that the city was "getting an influx of immigrants who [were] well-educated and [had] a good foundation for running a business."[44] Between 1992 and 1997, the number of Latino-owned businesses in Lawrence more than doubled to 622, and after adjusting for inflation, the average per-business revenue increased almost 30 percent. Most importantly for the city, many of these businesses drew in customers from outside Lawrence, exactly what city elites had been trying unsuccessfully to do for decades. While Latino-owned businesses in the city were generally small (with three or fewer employees) and sometimes struggled to turn a profit, Latino entrepreneurialism was clearly playing an irreplaceable role in revitalizing the city.[45]

The growing importance of Latinos as consumers helped generate a bilingual and transnational service economy in the city. Latino entrepreneurs created an economic niche by providing transnational services and local services in Spanish, but other employers increased their hiring of Latinos as well. Business owners began to recognize the potential loss of profit if they refused to provide services in Spanish, and across the city, jobs for interpreters and bilingual employees multiplied. In doctors' offices and health centers; in schools, courts, and government offices; and in banks, restaurants, and stores, bilingualism was in high demand. This transition to a bilingual workforce was clearly evident by the 1990s. The *Eagle-Tribune* described how local business owners considered "bilingual workers, from secretaries to receptionists and administrative assistants, [to be] the cogs that keep the wheels of many Greater Lawrence businesses going" as the clientele became increasingly Latino. James V. Miragliotta, a lawyer on Common Street, confessed, "I don't know how a lawyer could function without a bilingual secretary. I think it's absolutely indispensable." His secretary, Carmen Falcon, said that "Do you speak Spanish?" was usually the first thing that people calling the office asked her.[46]

This demand for Spanish-speaking employees was one of the many ways in which the growth of the enclave in Lawrence was self-reinforcing. Although the manufacturing jobs that initially enabled migration to Lawrence declined severely at the same time that migration was increasing, the growing Latino population in the city created its own labor demand. Numbers alone did not create this change, however. There was a need for services in Spanish long before those services were provided, and this book offers sufficient examples

Creating the Latino City

of business owners acting against their own economic interest by refusing to serve Latinos, and of government agencies defying their public responsibility by refusing to provide services in Spanish. It was both the growth in numbers *and* the activism of the Latino community that created these jobs, the bridge services between the white institutional world and Lawrence's Latinos.

The transnational orientation of many Latino Lawrencians, including continued travel and communication with the islands, was significantly responsible for the persistence of bilingualism and biculturalism in the city. Although school administrators complained that they could not teach children who disappeared to Puerto Rico or the Dominican Republic for months each year, such frequent and prolonged trips gave students a different, but also important, education, allowing them to grow up both bilingual and fluent in the cultural modes of their parents' or grandparents' homeland. One interviewee explained that after she moved to Lawrence when she was seven years old, she alternated two years in Lawrence with two years in the Dominican Republic for the duration of her education before graduating from Lawrence High School. She credits this transnational education with her ability to speak, read, and write both languages fluently. When I asked her if she needed to be bilingual to work her current job, she replied that virtually all jobs in Lawrence required employees to be bilingual: "Oh yes, I'm thinking if you work in Lawrence you have to be."[47] The bicultural service sector became central to Lawrence's overall economy, and it is important to note that transnationalism was a major part of what enabled Lawrence-born youth to competently staff these services.

Transnationalism was nothing new, of course. Latinos in Lawrence had been writing and calling, sending money and gifts, and traveling and returning home for decades.[48] Although many white Greater Lawrence residents envisioned Latinos as welfare recipients, from a transnational perspective, the reality was the complete opposite: Latino Lawrencians were philanthropists, sending hard-earned money and other aid to their home countries, particularly in times of crisis. This aid contributed crucially to island economies. When asked whether Lawrence was important and well known in the Dominican Republic, Dominican consul Julio César Correa replied, "The city of Lawrence is widely recognized all throughout the island, but especially so in the region of El Cibao, from where most emigrate. Most important is the economic connection—most Dominicans here left family back in the island and constantly send money back to support them. This money is money that contributes to the economy of the island."[49]

It will come as no surprise to scholars of immigration that Latinos in Lawrence played a key role in the economies of their hometowns and home countries, as this has been amply documented among other Latino immigrants as well.[50] Yet given the pervasive stereotype of Lawrence Latinos as those who *received* aid, their transnational generosity is important to note. Perhaps more important for the city itself, however, was the fact that these transnational economic activities were key to the growth of many Latino-owned businesses in Lawrence. Many of these businesses were based on transnational activities, such as money transfers, travel agencies, and shipping companies. Thus transnationalism did not just involve sending money out of Lawrence; it also played a key role in reinvigorating the downtown business district.

Not only were Latino Lawrencians important to island economies; they were important in island politics as well, and this is especially true for the Dominican Republic. Ramón Borges-Méndez noted that his interaction with high-level Dominican politicians did not occur in the Dominican Republic or even in Boston; "as a matter of fact, I've met two of the former presidents of the Dominican Republic and the acting President of the Dominican Republic in *Lawrence*."[51] Julio César Correa had taught electrical engineering in a university in the Dominican Republic but had been forced to accept work as a machine operator at Malden Mills when he arrived in Lawrence, although he maintained his connection with the Partido de la Liberación Dominicana (PLD). When Leonel Fernández was elected president in the Dominican Republic in 1996, he named Correa as Dominican consul in Boston, and Correa left his job at Malden Mills to accept the post.[52] Correa is a clear example of how a person's marginal economic or political position in the United States was no indication of his or her potential importance in island politics. Another example was a Dominican barber from Essex Street, Carlos Jose Cepeda, who won a seat in the Dominican congress in 1995. He had joined the PLD in 1980 and had been a member of the Lawrence chapter since he arrived in the city nine years earlier. While working as a barber in downtown Lawrence, he was simultaneously building his political career in the Dominican Republic. Cepeda had been elected in the Salcedo Province (now called the Hermanas Mirabal Province), near Santiago, which contained the villages of Salcedo, Tenares, and Villa Tapia. His remarkable success in the Dominican election was directly attributable to transnationalism, as the *Eagle-Tribune* noted that 60 percent of Greater Lawrence Dominicans came from that province, particularly Tenares. Cepeda argued that local Lawrence support had been key to his success, and he planned to work on behalf of both his constituents on the island and his Lawrence supporters, explaining

Creating the Latino City

that Dominicans in Lawrence "now have a representative and even if they are here, they can come to me for any problems or needs in their towns back home which I can help solve there."[53]

This interest in homeland politics was not divorced from local concerns. As Correa explained, improving circumstances in the Dominican Republic and improving the country's image in the U.S. imagination were also key to improving the perception of Dominicans locally: "We have to start building up a new international image of our country, especially on the diplomatic end. And as a local resident, this affects our image in the city of Lawrence." As residents of a transnational city, Lawrence Latinos were invested in both local and homeland politics and were aware that the two were connected. Correa and his party, the PLD, encouraged both transnational and local political participation and cited the recent dual citizenship law that had been passed by the Dominican Republic as part of that process. As Correa explained, "The first step is for all Dominicans to become U.S. citizens so they can vote and share rights all citizens here have at their reach—this should be easier now more than ever with the new law passed recently which allows for dual U.S.-Dominican citizenship. Also, we encourage and sponsor English classes at our party headquarters so people understand the process better."[54] The transnational orientation of many Lawrence Latinos not only enabled them to contribute to the politics and economy of their home islands but encouraged a deeper engagement in Lawrence and the United States as well.

PUBLIC SPACE

The early 1990s marked the nadir of Lawrence's economic and social problems, yet it was also the period in which long-standing assertions by Latinos of their right to the city began to bear fruit. Most observers of Lawrence in this era emphasized the growth of Latino electoral power, but this involvement in official city politics built on community organizing and the quotidian contestations over public space discussed in earlier chapters.[55] The clearest manifestation of Latinos' growing public presence in the 1980s and 1990s was Semana Hispana. This annual celebration of Latino cultures continued to draw tens of thousands of attendees from near and far every summer to pack Lawrence's Common and fill its narrow streets. National origin groups had individual parades on different nights of the festival, followed by a pan-ethnic celebration on the weekend. Throughout the week of the festival, music filled the air as cars crawled through the streets proudly displaying Puerto Rican or

People dancing at a Semana Hispana event in 1986. Photo by Al Pereira, archived at the Lawrence History Center. Reprinted with permission from the *Eagle-Tribune*.

Dominican or other national flags and honking their horns, forming unofficial parades along with flag-waving pedestrians.

The festival celebrated the work of longtime community leaders by designating them grand marshals of the parade and profiling their contributions to the city in the annual program. In 1995, for example, the grand marshal was Orlando Ayala, known as "Cano." Born in Comerio, Puerto Rico, he came stateside in 1965. He started a grocery store on Water Street in Lawrence in 1969 and later opened the Club de Caguas, bringing to Lawrence, according to the program, "orchestras, bands and social activities so badly needed and that contributed to the development of employment opportunities in our society." He also established a major Puerto Rican social club in the city, Scorpio Hall, which he owned for ten years.[56] Ayala's contributions to the city illustrate the blurred lines between community formation, service provision, and small business entrepreneurialism in Lawrence. The advertisements in the annual programs also illustrated the wide array of Latino-oriented (and often Latino-owned) businesses in the city and their investment in the strength of this growing population. For example, the 1988 program included a full-page ad from Jesus Gonzalez, owner of the McDonald's on the corner of Essex Street and Broadway, which proclaimed that Gonzalez was "proud of being the first Latin owner of a McDonald's chain in New England."[57]

Creating the Latino City

Sponsoring Semana Hispana was a way of showcasing his pride not simply as an individual business owner but as a Latino business owner in Lawrence.

Performers included a mix of local and international artists and represented the diverse national origins and generational attachments of the city's Latinos. The 1988 schedule of events illustrates this well. With the support of Gateway Cities money from the state (a funding source that was at least indirectly related to the 1984 riots), this ten-year anniversary celebration was especially well funded and featured the renowned salsa percussionist Tito Puente. It is worth exploring the programming for this Semana Hispana in detail, as it reveals how widely this small city's festival ranged between local and international performers; between corporate, small business, government, and nonprofit sponsorship; between the national cultures of different Latin American countries and distinctly U.S. Latino/urban cultures; and between celebration, education, and politics.

The week began with a coronation ball on Saturday, June 11, at Central Catholic High School, sponsored by Uniglobe Travel, Park Street Auto Sales, Matosis Records, Díaz Boutique, and Graziano's Hair Design. National celebrations occurred throughout the following week, with an Ecuadorian night on Monday, a Puerto Rican night (at Scorpio Hall) on Tuesday, and a Cuban night on Wednesday, followed by an "Interfacing of Cultures" buffet dinner with a specialist in cross-cultural understanding addressing the diners. The major full-day celebrations began on Friday, June 17, starting with a video and panel discussion, "Youth against Aids," with many of the speakers from the local community college's Hispanic Cultural Club. Later in the evening came merengue artist El Zafiro, sponsored by Hispanic Week and Philip Morris USA, followed by a Guatemalan cultural presentation sponsored by the Gateway Cities program.

Saturday began with a softball tournament on the Common and a bicycle race, followed by a performance by Tito Caraballo and then the Lawrence High School Dance Group. At noon, the Essex Street McDonald's sponsored children's activities on the Common, while the rap group Jam Master Rockers performed nearby. In the afternoon, the Ramón de los Reyes Dance Group performed, sponsored by the Greater Lawrence Ecumenical Area Ministry, followed by a Colombian cultural presentation, also sponsored by the Gateway Cities program. Saturday evening, famed salsa/Latin jazz percussionist Tito Puente performed, sponsored by Miller Beer, followed by Grammy nominee Heriberto Colón y su Caribbean Express, sponsored by the Larry Carr Show. Sunday began with a parade headed by Senator John

Kerry followed by performances by Mariachi Guadalajara and Los Pleneros del 23 Abajo de Puerto Rico, sponsored by Pepsi-Cola. In the afternoon, the day's special attraction, Las Chicas del País—All Female Band performed, followed by a cultural presentation on Ecuador from Ecuatorianos Unidos, and then a performance by the Tenares Band. Finally, Caribe Orchestra, sponsored by New England Foundation for the Arts, performed last before the closing ceremonies.[58]

From a presentation on AIDS by the community college's Hispanic Cultural Club to a Tito Puente performance sponsored by Miller Beer, Semana Hispana blended and showcased the countless possible incarnations of *latinidad*. As in earlier years, the emphasis on Latino pride and community formation maintained a distinctly political element. As in the "national performances" by Puerto Ricans in Chicago described by Ana Y. Ramos-Zayas, home-country identities were marshaled and reconfigured in the context of U.S. racism and disinvestment in Lawrence. Tens of thousands of Latinos filling the streets and parks of the city and waving the flags of Latin American countries was a clear assertion of Latinos' right to be at home in Lawrence, to be neither forced out nor forced to assimilate. In addition, the festival continued to register hundreds of new voters each year.[59]

Yet the massive event was also designed to connect Latino Lawrencians with their white neighbors. Festival organizers wanted to showcase Latino cultures not only to generate pride and community among Latinos but also to build a bridge with white residents of the city.[60] It seems, however, that few white Lawrencians attended the exciting event in the heart of the city, a fact bemoaned by one organizer in 1997: "*Normalmente lo que hemos escuchado es que los anglos dicen que los latinos son muy bullosos y que si van al festival, sienten miedo de ser agredidos* [Generally what we have heard is that whites say Latinos are too rowdy and if they go to the festival, they're afraid they'll be victimized]."[61] Semana Hispana was a festive, family-oriented event clearly not considered dangerous by the tens of thousands of Latino attendees, but it seems that racialized associations between urban Latinos and crime may have kept many whites away.

This racialization of urban space and the perception that Latino-dominated spaces were inherently dangerous, unwelcoming, or inferior influenced white perceptions of the downtown retail district as well. While Latino-owned businesses grew along Essex Street, the Latino *presence* along Essex Street grew even faster, as Latino Lawrencians walked downtown to shop or stroll. The public presence of Latinos in the city's downtown played a major role in counteracting the feel of Lawrence as a "ghost town," yet it also

Creating the Latino City

seems to have contributed to white perceptions of Lawrence's decline. A 1991 report on Latino-owned businesses in the city surveyed business owners, shoppers, and strollers on Essex Street. While Latinos described the street generally as "nice," "clean," or "a good place to walk," white respondents generally derided Essex Street. They expressed their discomfort with or fear of "unsavory looking individuals," saying the "street is mostly filled with dubious looking characters," "groups of men hanging around," or "druggies in high powered sports cars."[62]

The survey asked people on Essex Street about whether they feared for their safety, and while only 18 percent of Latinos surveyed said they were frightened, nearly half of the "non-Hispanics" said they were. One white respondent explained, "I'm afraid of being attacked. It's depressing all the homeless and poor beggars looking in the trash. All there is are Spanish stores." This abrupt jump between the frightening and "depressing" aspects of downtown Lawrence and the ubiquity of Latino-run businesses was not uncommon. For some white Lawrencians, the mere presence of Latinos was clear evidence of the decline of the city.[63]

One respondent expressed quite frankly a distaste for the growing Latinization of downtown: "To be quite honest, I do not like feeling like a foreigner in my own country. On Essex Street you are surrounded by Spanish stores, signs, music, and people speaking Spanish." This respondent argued that many others shared this feeling, and as a result, downtown Lawrence had no hope of a renaissance; the respondent "[didn't] see how Essex Street could attract more customers." This racialized perception of the city's downtown demonstrates the associations many white Lawrencians made between Latinos and economic decline. It also demonstrates, however, a noteworthy transition in the public presence of Latinos. From an excluded minority in the 1970s, Latinos had become the main consumers downtown by the early 1990s, and the business district was increasingly shaped by their needs and preferences. Although in 1991, Latinos were still marginal in the city's political system, decades of quotidian assertions of their right to the city had incontrovertibly won Latinos a home in Lawrence's public spaces.[64]

As the example of Essex Street illustrates, many of the changes in Lawrence had a double-edged nature. Development of Latino-oriented businesses was tremendously important for the city's economy and for counteracting the "ghost town" trend of flight and disinvestment. In addition, the bilingual and bicultural social service industry that evolved out of decades of Latino activism was central to providing jobs in the city. Yet the economic situation for Latinos was still grim. Indeed, Lawrence was the poorest city in the state in 2000.[65] Persistent, devastating unemployment shouldn't lead us to overvalorize entrepreneurialism or the provision of jobs or to take for granted that working long hours for poverty wages or slim profit margins is significantly better than being out of work. On balance, by the late 1990s, the city had been transformed from one of unemployment, rage, and desperation to one of hard work with little reward for most of its residents. This may have improved the city in many respects—no rioting, less arson, less crime, more business—but this transformation did not necessarily provide a good life for the city's residents, as they worked long hours in the low-wage jobs that the restructured economy provided. Most importantly, as historians we should not fall victim to the false choice that urban crisis could be "solved" only in this double-edged neoliberal model, with private (albeit in this case, grass-roots) investment and the provision of poverty jobs.

Even the Latino social service organizations, conceived in struggle, that played such a major role in helping Latinos settle the city had a double edge. Their positive impact and their activist origins do not change the fact that they were most certainly not advocacy organizations. Structured to provide services, reliant on state contracts, constrained by Internal Revenue Service rules from engaging in certain forms of political activity, Latino social service organizations were channeled into addressing community needs in a narrow and specific way. This was certainly not unique to Lawrence; this was a transition that occurred nationally in the 1980s and 1990s that activists of an earlier era bemoaned. As José Duran, the executive director of the Hispanic Office of Planning and Evaluation, a Latino social service organization based in Boston that had a branch in Lawrence, observed in 1999, "We really have gone from community organizing to community organizations. And those community organizations are now extensions of the state. So many of us are so dependent on public funding that it has almost, by design or default, stopped our advocacy behavior."[66] As Lawrence revitalized, structural issues remained.

POLITICS

Decades of activism geared toward increasing Latino representation in city government finally began to produce results in the 1990s. As discussed in Chapter 5, Latino organizers in Lawrence made effective use of state and federal agencies, such as the Department of Justice's Community Relations Service, to pry open city government to Latinos, not only as voters but as appointed officials, contractors, and city workers. This process of Latino inclusion in city government accelerated in the 1990s as Latino electoral strength grew. Although a few Latinos had served in appointed positions in city government in the 1980s, such as the position of director of equal opportunity and community relations held by Virgil Perez at the time of the riots, appointed posts were most often held, as one scholar described it, by "Latinos from smaller, nonthreatening power bases (Chilean, Mexican American, and Venezuelan backgrounds)."[67] In 1991, however, Lawrence *elected* its first Latino officeholder, Ralph Carrero, the first Dominican politician elected in Massachusetts.[68] Carrero won a seat on the school committee, all members of which were elected at large. Two years later, José Santiago was elected to city council on a district seat. Santiago was later elected state representative in 1998, after redistricting created a legislative district where 70 percent of eligible voters were Latino. With this strong voter base and a growing local Latino media infrastructure, particularly Dalia Díaz's newspaper *Rumbo*, Santiago was not only able to win but to win by explicitly challenging the established power structure's neglect of problems facing the community.[69]

Santiago's victory was made possible through committed voter registration drives by Latino activists and their allies, who had increased the proportion of Latinos among the city's registered voters from 12 percent in 1991 to one-third by 1998. With the success of the Justice Department's voting rights lawsuit against the city in 1999, Latino politics got an enormous boost. The 1999 city election not only kept Carrero on the school committee; it also brought a number of new Latino officeholders into city government: Nilka Álvarez, Julia Silverio, and Marcos Devers were all elected to city council. The council now had a substantial number of Latino members, and Latino officeholders in the city included a mix of Puerto Ricans and Dominicans, men and women.[70] The redistricting required by the lawsuit in 2002 shifted city politics even further, leading to a Latino majority in five of the city's six voting districts.[71]

Although a dramatic assertion of the right to live and express themselves in the city was central to Latinos winning their right to Lawrence's public spaces, their growing electoral strength was premised on "bridge-building" with the city's white residents. The overwhelming emphasis of successful Latino candidates in Lawrence was on improving the city for everyone. This bridge-building strategy allowed many Latino candidates to win support from both the white and the Latino populations of the city. The first Latino elected to public office in the city, Dominican Ralph Carrero, pointed out that he could not have won without white support. Ramón Borges-Méndez noted that Carrero's "campaign and victory rested upon developing a wide political and social platform that demonstrated that all Latinos and Anglos could find common ground on certain issues."[72] As Carrero explained, "My candidacy and campaign were run very strategically in that this was going to be a campaign of bridging a community."[73] This emphasis on bridge-building was evident in Julia Silverio's vision for the city as well. She hoped "to make the city of Lawrence into a model city where all races and ethnicit[ies] can live together, learn to tolerate each other, respect each other, and learn from each other."[74] As Silverio's words demonstrated, Latino bridge-building politics were not premised on assimilation or an erasure of Latino identity; rather, Latino activists and their allies realized that if Latinos were given equal access to political participation, Lawrence could be a model of integrated politics, a "city on a hill" for the twenty-first century.

CONCLUSION

The Latinization of Lawrence was the result of decades of Latino struggles to claim the city as home. The political and cultural strength that Latinos had achieved in the city by the end of the century was hard won and reflects a triumph of individual perseverance and community organizing. Yet this strength was also inextricably tied to the city's relative decline in the metropolitan political economy. Although many cities in the Northeast and Midwest saw their power wane in the postwar era, nowhere was this process as thorough as in small or second-tier postindustrial cities like Lawrence. The lack of any real economic backbone in the city by 1990 was part of what enabled Latino-owned businesses and a bilingual and bicultural service economy to become so profoundly central to the city as a whole. At the same time, however, it left the city still struggling economically, as small businesses and social services (mostly dependent on state and federal funding) were not lucrative enough to enable Lawrence's self-sufficiency. The city's economic marginalization, Ramón Borges-Méndez has argued, was part of what allowed an ethnic enclave in Lawrence to flourish, as Latinos were not subject to the competition and displacement posed by gentrification. As he explained it, "The paucity of renewal allowed communities to prevail spatially, yet at the expense of other malaises like disinvestments and isolation."[75]

Although the drive for equal power in the city was by no means complete at the end of the twentieth century, Latinos were able to have a far greater impact on the social, political, cultural, and economic life of Lawrence than they could possibly have achieved in a city like New York. The fact that, even with such power in the city, major problems still remained simply highlights the relative powerlessness of the city itself. Even with an entirely Latino city government committed to addressing the needs of poor and working people, Lawrence could not have transformed its economy completely, as the city was a subordinate partner in a regional and global economy. Even if Lawrence had elected a progressive Latino mayor, she or he could not have undone the effects of deindustrialization or mandated that the suburbs share their immense wealth. Thus, even as Latinos brought about a renaissance in the city in countless ways, Lawrence remained a site of struggle and disappointment for many of its residents.

CONCLUSION

LATINO URBANISM
AND THE GEOGRAPHY
OF OPPORTUNITY

As any ten-year-old in East L.A., or Philly's El Norte knows,
borders tend to follow working-class Latinos wherever they live
and regardless of how long they have been in the United States.

Mike Davis, Magical Urbanism

As the twentieth century drew to a close, Lawrence barely resembled the city
it had been at the end of World War II. While its landscape was still dominated by brick mills and triple-decker homes, its economy and population had
been profoundly transformed by suburbanization, deindustrialization, and
Latino immigration. As scholars develop a distinct historiography of postwar
Latino urbanism, Lawrence may not prove to be typical—as no city could
possibly be—but its history nonetheless provides a set of essential questions
to address: What was the role of U.S. imperialism in the Latinization (and
globalization) of U.S. cities in the late twentieth century? How did race and
class segregation in the era of suburbanization and urban crisis impact Latino
settlement patterns and experiences? How did Latinos fight against disinvestment and discrimination and strive to claim their right to the city? Where
did Latinos fit in the larger stigmatization of the "inner city" and the broad
turn to conservatism that this discourse helped enable? From the periphery
of U.S. empire to the ghettos at its center, Latino migration in the crisis era
was a protracted struggle against containment and marginalization. Imperial
migrants fought to have in the United States what U.S. intervention had
denied them at home, pushing back against barriers of race and class in a
segregated metropolitan landscape.

In Lawrence, as in many U.S. cities, the growth of the suburbs in the decades after World War II drew families, industry, and retail businesses out of the city. Intentional zoning decisions largely limited the construction of multifamily and subsidized rental housing to the city, concentrating the poor within Lawrence, while the suburbs experienced an upward spiral of desirability, property values, tax revenue, and public services. Deindustrialization and suburban competition precipitated an economic crisis in Lawrence as the city's tax base and services declined. These were the circumstances into which Latinos migrated. Pushed from Puerto Rico and the Dominican Republic by political and economic conditions that the United States had helped to create, and pushed from New York by that city's own crisis, imperial migrants searched for a place to find a better life. Aided by recruitment into the city's dwindling manufacturing sector, Latinos reconstituted their families in Lawrence, overwhelmingly segregated within the small city's boundaries and largely excluded from its suburbs.

For many white residents in Lawrence, the growing Latino presence became a symbol of urban decline. As the city suffered economically, many white Lawrencians and officials attempted to halt or reverse Latino immigration into the city, in the hope that this could somehow halt or reverse the city's economic deterioration. This scapegoating was a fundamental misinterpretation of the roots of Lawrence's crisis and created a deeply hostile climate for Puerto Rican and Dominican settlement in the city. Through quotidian acts of resistance, community building, and political protest, Latinos fought to assert their right to the city. White bigotry and Latino activism found their most visible expression in the 1984 riots, as both sides vented their rage at the crisis facing the city. After the riots, Latino organizers and their allies used the protests as leverage to pry open city government to Latino political participation, but the larger economic issues that had fueled the *disturbios* remained.

Lawrence's crisis only deepened in the late 1980s and early 1990s. Major metropolitan centers began to experience reinvestment in this era, and in many big cities, brutal ghetto poverty and a pathologized urban "underclass" existed alongside gentrifying neighborhoods of wealth and influence. Lawrence, however, suffered from pervasive and persistent disinvestment, resulting in waves of arson and crime and a deeply troubled public school system. Dependent on infusions of state and federal aid, the city and its residents became broadly stigmatized as undeserving, and there was little political will to remedy the segregated and unequal political economy that characterized the region. Circumstances in the crisis city proved a tremendous obstacle to upward mobility for many Latinos and were a source of deep frustration. By the late 1990s, continued immigration and activism gained Latinos a prominent place in Lawrence's politics and public culture, and grassroots entrepreneurialism combined with a bilingual, bicultural service sector to revitalize the city's economy to some extent, lifting it from the nadir of its crisis. Yet overall, Lawrence remained impoverished and underresourced at the end of the twentieth century. As a result, while some Latinos found opportunities in the city, many others continued to find hardship and disappointment.

LAWRENCE IN THE TWENTY-FIRST CENTURY

In November 2009, Lawrence made history when it became the first city in Massachusetts to elect a Latino mayor. Latinos, by this point nearly three-quarters of the city's population, had fought for decades to gain political representation in the face of substantial white resistance.[1] In this context, the election of a Dominican, William Lantigua, was nothing short of a triumph. The *Boston Globe* reported, "Even before unofficial returns had been released, hundreds gathered at city hall to celebrate the apparent election of Lantigua. Chanting '*Si se pudo*,' or 'Yes, we did,' a crowd of hundreds—some dancing and crying—gathered in the city hall lobby." Lantigua sang "*Mi Gente*" (by the famous Puerto Rican salsero Héctor Lavoe) to the crowd and promised to represent all of the city's people.[2] This emotional moment was the culmination of decades of political activism and community organizing by Lawrence Latinos and their allies in the face of long-standing neglect and disenfranchisement by the city government. Without such activism, Latinos could have remained indefinitely *in* the city but not *of* the city, contributing to Lawrence but having no official power to help direct its future.

Lantigua had been a community leader and politician in Lawrence for over a decade before his election as mayor. Born in Santo Domingo, he had come to the United States as a teenager. He had lived in Lawrence and worked as a technician for an electric company for more than twenty years. Reflecting the broad Puerto Rican and Dominican political alliances that were central to Latino political strength in Lawrence, Lantigua had previously worked with two of the city's most important Puerto Rican politicians. He had served on José Santiago's successful campaign in 1998 (the first Latino to serve as Lawrence's state representative) and worked with Isabel Melendez on her campaign for mayor in 2001 (when she was the first Latina/o to win the Democratic mayoral primary). In addition, he had spent several terms as state representative himself after challenging Santiago in 2002.[3]

Yet it was not merely his local reputation and connections that helped land him in the mayor's office. The race had been close; Lantigua had won by only about 1,000 votes. Many speculated that the key to his victory had been the support he received from residents of the small town of Tenares in the Dominican Republic. Encouraged by local politicians and a morning talk-show host, many residents of Tenares had spent months calling and emailing friends and family in Lawrence, urging those eligible to go out and vote for Lantigua. This transnational support seems to have been crucial to Lantigua's election.[4]

The link between Tenares and Lawrence is strong despite the many miles and powerful national borders that divide the New England city and the Cibaeño town. Yet the role of Tenares residents in supporting Lantigua's election was just one very visible strand in a dense web of communication, support, travel, trade, and kinship that has long connected the two places. Of course, Lawrence's Latinos are diverse: native born, immigrant, citizen, legal resident, undocumented, and Puerto Rican, Dominican, Guatemalan, Cuban, and every other Latin American nationality. And many of these Latinos maintain various levels of connection to their (or their parents' or grandparents') home towns or home countries, even if for some that connection is largely symbolic. But there is a particularly sizable number of people from Tenares living in Lawrence; indeed, some estimate that between 50 and 70 percent of the city's Dominicans have roots there (the higher figure would mean that there are nearly as many Tenarenses in Lawrence as remain in the Dominican town). As a result, Tenares has been significantly impacted by its connections with Lawrence.[5]

Tenares is a town of just over 25,000 in the Hermanas Mirabal Province in the northern part of the Dominican Republic, in the Cibao region.[6] As discussed in Chapter 2, the Cibao's agricultural economy experienced dramatic decline in the second half of the twentieth century, at least partially due to pressures exerted by the United States on Dominican politics and economic policy. This rural economic decline spurred decades of emigration of Tenarenses to Lawrence and New York City. Migrants displaced by economic dislocation rarely sever ties to their home countries, however, often living transnationally as much as possible and dreaming of return. In the past couple of decades, many Lawrence residents from Tenares have invested in building houses back in their hometown in the hopes of eventually returning. Many of these houses stand empty or in states of half completion, as working-class Dominicans in Lawrence gradually accumulate (or fail to accumulate) the resources necessary to complete and furnish them. In the meantime, these construction projects generate considerable employment in the town, as do the remittances sent back to family members. In 2011, the mayor of Tenares estimated that as many as 80 percent of the town's inhabitants relied on money sent back from the United States, most of it from Lawrence. As one Tenares resident explained, "Whoever doesn't have someone in Lawrence sending them money won't survive here, won't be able to eat."[7] This reliance on remittances is not unique to Tenares, of course. Families and towns throughout the Dominican Republic depend on money sent from relatives working in the United States, as is true in many other Latin American countries, such as Mexico, where U.S.-shaped economic restructuring has made it a dreadful imperative that families straddle national borders.[8]

Given the Dominican town's dependence on Lawrence, it is no surprise that Tenarenses feel invested in ensuring Latino political empowerment and economic opportunity in the Massachusetts city. As the Tenares resident mentioned above explained, "They work in Lawrence so Tenares can survive."[9] This transnational investment in Lawrence's politics is a sharp corrective to the stereotype of U.S. Latinos too caught up in "homeland politics" to advocate for themselves locally or to engage in state or national politics in the United States; on the contrary, the stakes of U.S. elections are often well known in Latin America.[10] Yet the campaigning of Tenarenses for Lantigua also stands in contrast to the provocative image of wealthy foreign nationals attempting to corrupt U.S. democracy.[11] This transnational political involvement came most definitely "from below," as Dominicans attempted to exert some agency within the context of a serious structural dependency. Tenarenses' support for a Latino mayor in Lawrence could serve as a means to shore up a precarious system reliant on aid and investment from emigrant kin, kin who themselves were often struggling to make ends meet in the impoverished city.

As thrilling as the hard-won election of a Dominican mayor may have been, Lantigua's ascent also shows the limits of Latino political power in a small postindustrial city within an unequal metropolitan political economy. Although decades of activism brought Latinos political strength within the city, Lawrence's impoverishment put it at the mercy of a state government that was far less responsive to Latino hopes for self-determination and unlikely to address the intrametropolitan inequality at the root of the city's economic decline. Lantigua inherited a $24.5-million shortfall and a city suffering from decades of urban disinvestment from the previous administrations. State legislators passed a "bailout" for Lawrence in February 2010 designed to enable the city to borrow $35 million over two years from private sources, but the bailout also gave a state overseer authority over the city's spending. In addition, in November 2011, the Massachusetts Department of Education voted to place Lawrence public schools into receivership, the first time the state had ever taken direct control of a school district's finances and academics.[12] In effect, the small city was forced to surrender its autonomy in order to stay solvent.

There is a glaring parallel here, not only with other small postindustrial cities such as Flint, Michigan, whose fiscal crises left them undemocratically subject to outside control, but also with New York City in the wake of its fiscal crisis, with the Dominican Republic in the era of both "dollar diplomacy" and IMF-imposed "structural adjustment," and with Puerto Rico in its current debt crisis. Structural economic inequality was mitigated temporarily with loans, but that debt was then used as a mechanism for political and economic control by outside forces. Whether in Lawrence or on the islands, Latinos still found that crucial economic decisions were being made elsewhere; the political economic structure that determined the availability of jobs and services was shaped by factors over which local governments had little control. The impact of their activism was buffered by the larger, fundamentally undemocratic political economy that insulated economic decision-makers from popular pressure.

Overall, Lawrence has seen significant, albeit small-scale, reinvestment since at least the mid-1990s. Although this gradual and partial recovery pales beside the massive economic turnaround in major metropolitan centers like New York or Boston, Lawrence seems well past the nadir of its urban crisis era. As in cities and suburbs across the United States, immigrants have brought energy, education, and resources from their home countries to reinvigorate Lawrence. Grassroots activism has pushed to hold the city accountable to the needs of its poor and working-class residents. Lawrence has received a remarkable infusion of state funds (even if city residents do not always get to decide how they are spent). Crime has declined substantially since the early 1990s.[13] The city has developed a vibrant nonprofit sector able to attract government and foundation money and committed organizers, as well as developing home-grown community leaders. New businesses and residential developers are increasingly drawn to the Lawrence market, and Northern Essex Community College is expanding in the city.[14]

As in larger cities in the twenty-first century, there is evidence of growth and renaissance throughout Lawrence today; yet reinvestment has thus far not caused gentrification or displacement in this small city. As a result, unlike in major metropolitan centers, Lawrence's Latinos are not being pushed out of the slowly regenerating city. A particularly lovely example of Lawrence's renewal is the Spicket River Greenway, an interconnected series of parks, playgrounds, walkways, and community gardens along the river in the Arlington neighborhood. Turtles can be spotted along the river's banks, surrounded by the red brick of the city's industrial legacy (and fully bilingual signage, of course). The greenway was created out of vacant lots and brownfield sites or abandoned industrial spaces, many of which had become illegal dumping grounds and environmental hazards. The project was spearheaded by the local nonprofit Groundwork Lawrence and received massive state and federal funding. Grassroots action was key to the creation of the greenway, as thousands of city residents cleared the riverbanks of more than 115 tons of accumulated industrial and other debris.[15]

In spite of this obvious renaissance in Lawrence, fundamental structural issues remain. The metropolitan political economy still keeps Lawrence poor relative to its neighbors and dependent on external funds, and this economic dependence undermines the city's political autonomy. Lawrence reminds us that many postindustrial cities have simply not seen the economic turnaround of New York or Boston and that persistent spatialized inequality remains between municipalities. The Greater Lawrence area still shows few signs of racial or economic integration, and Lawrence continues to be profoundly stigmatized in the region. This is true in many urban Latino communities across the United States, as well as in areas where Latinos have moved into the suburbs: Racial and class segregation persists, even in the suburban landscape; local tax bases still determine school funding to a great extent; and Latino-dominant neighborhoods and municipalities are often stigmatized in a way that impacts their residents' economic opportunities. Finally, on the most basic level, the political and economic inequality that persists between the United States and much of Latin America continues to spur migration. It is clear that immigration does not necessarily mean opportunity, however, as many Latinos face long-standing structural constraints on social, spatial, and economic mobility in the United States.

Representations of Latinos in the media and popular discourse are oddly complicated in the current era; Latinos are alternately celebrated as hardworking, family-oriented immigrants or vilified as dangerous, degraded "illegals" who "take our jobs."[16] The reality of Latino diversity, of course, will never be captured in media stereotypes, but it is important to note that an earlier era's obsessive discursive concern with an urban Latino "underclass" of the perpetually jobless and welfare reliant seems to have been eclipsed in the past two decades by (both positive and negative) depictions of Latinos as *workers*. This is a welcome shift in rhetoric in many ways, but it hides as much as it reveals. Changes in U.S. policy since the 1990s have made immigration much harder for poor Latinos, have dramatically restricted immigrants' access to welfare, and have increasingly criminalized both authorized and unauthorized immigrants. Part of the aggressive policing of low-income communities of color in revanchist cities at the turn of the twenty-first century involved the widespread incarceration and deportation of even legal immigrants who failed to adjust to the straight-and-narrow neoliberal regime. Thus Latinos who do not fit the idealized immigrant narrative (law-abiding, hardworking, family-oriented) have no place in contemporary U.S. society; they are either locked up or pushed out of the country entirely, as the recent scholarship on Dominican and Salvadoran deportees illustrates.[17] Social acceptance for Latinos in the twenty-first century seems premised on their conforming to a higher standard of industriousness, docility, and gratitude than white U.S. citizens. Not only is this double standard unfair, but Lawrence's history illustrates that it is often simply impossible for many poor and working-class Latinos, particularly in areas suffering from disinvestment.[18]

Clearly, structural obstacles remain for Latinos, shaped by class and geography as much as by immigration status, language barriers, or the ever-shifting category of race. It is undeniable that Latino and other immigration has contributed immensely to the revitalization of cities and towns across the United States in the past few decades; but the benefits of this revitalization have been unevenly distributed, and access to its privileges has been restricted by an array of different types of borders. The boundaries may shift and move (no longer so tightly cutting city off from suburb, for example), and people may find innovative ways to cross them; but that does not mean the walls have fallen. A complex geography of opportunity and hardship persists in the twenty-first century, the nearly impregnable maze that stands between many Latinos and the American Dream.

NOTES

The following abbreviations are used throughout the notes.

AHS	Andover Historical Society, Andover, Mass.
BG	*Boston Globe*
BH	*Boston Herald*
DOJ-CRS	United States Department of Justice-Community Relations Service
ET	*Eagle-Tribune*
ICCHC	Immigrant City Community Housing Corporation, Lawrence, Mass.
LDIC	Lawrence Development and Industrial Commission
LHC	Lawrence History Center, Lawrence, Mass.
LPL	Lawrence Public Library, Lawrence, Mass.
MSA	Massachusetts State Archives, Boston
NARA-NE	National Archives and Records Administration Northeast Division, Waltham, Mass.
NYT	*New York Times*
SLM	State Library of Massachusetts, Boston
VTNA	Vanderbilt Television News Archives, Nashville, Tenn.

Introduction

1. For accounts of Lawrence's earlier history, see Cole, *Immigrant City*; Cameron, *Radicals of the Worst Sort*; Watson, *Bread and Roses*; Vecoli, "Anthony Capraro and the Lawrence Strike of 1919"; and Robbins, "Bread, Roses, and Other Possibilities." For classic accounts of earlier immigration more generally, see Handlin, *The Uprooted*, and Bodnar, *The Transplanted*. For broad and critical overviews of immigration history, see Reimers, *Other Immigrants*; Spickard, *Almost All Aliens*; and Waters, Ueda, and Marrow, *New Americans*.

2. Gonzales, *Reform without Justice*; Loyd, Mitchelson, and Burridge, *Beyond Walls and Cages*; Nguyen, *We Are All Suspects Now*.

3. For an overview of the debate over whether "Hispanic/Latino" should be considered a race, see Klor de Alva, Shorris, and West, "Our Next Race Question." See also the profoundly influential work of Flores, *Diaspora Strikes Back* and *From Bomba to Hip-Hop*.

For a classic study of how another group of immigrants (West Indians) negotiated their place in the U.S. racial hierarchy, see Waters, *Black Identities*.

4. For postwar urban and suburban histories, as well as accounts of racialized struggles over metropolitan space and resources, see Jackson, *Crabgrass Frontier*; Self, *American Babylon*; Sugrue, *Origins of the Urban Crisis*; Avila, *Popular Culture in the Age of White Flight* and *Folklore of the Freeway*; Cohen, *Consumers' Republic*; Seligman, *Block by Block*; Kruse, *White Flight*; Kruse and Sugrue, *New Suburban History*; Baxandall and Ewen, *Picture Windows*; Massey and Denton, *American Apartheid*; Freund, *Colored Property*; Lamb, *Housing Segregation in Suburban America since 1960*; Wiese, *Places of Their Own*; Gotham, *Race, Real Estate, and Uneven Development*; Gillette, *Camden after the Fall*; Williams, *Politics of Public Housing*; Biondi, *To Stand and Fight*; Thompson, *Whose Detroit?*; Singh, *Black Is a Country*; Theoharis and Woodard, *Freedom North*; Joseph, *Waiting until the Midnight Hour*; Young, *Soul Power*; Murch, *Living for the City*; Lemke-Santangelo, *Abiding Courage*; Kelley, *Yo' Mama's Disfunktional!*; Lassiter, *Silent Majority*; Schneider, *Vampires, Dragons, and Egyptian Kings*; and Satter, *Family Properties*.

5. For postwar Latino urban histories, see Acuña, *Community under Siege*; Avila, *Popular Culture in the Age of White Flight*; Fernández, "Young Lords and the Postwar City"; Hoffnung-Garskof, *Tale of Two Cities*; Whalen, *From Puerto Rico to Philadelphia*; Whalen and Vázquez-Hernández, *Puerto Rican Diaspora*; Thomas, *Puerto Rican Citizen*; Fernández, *Brown in the Windy City*; Lee, *Building a Latino Civil Rights Movement*; Snyder, *Crossing Broadway*; Muzio, "Struggle against 'Urban Renewal' in Manhattan's Upper West Side"; Otero, *La Calle*; Perales, *Smeltertown*; and García, *Havana USA*. For prewar and World War II–era Latino urban histories, see Sánchez Korrol, *From Colonia to Community*; Escobedo, *From Coveralls to Zoot Suits*; Molina, *Fit to Be Citizens?*; Innis-Jiménez, *Steel Barrio*; Alvarez, *Power of the Zoot*; Pagán, *Murder at the Sleepy Lagoon*; Romo, *East Los Angeles*; and Sánchez, *Becoming Mexican American*. For significant scholarship on urban Latinos in the contemporary era, see Pérez, *Near Northwest Side Story*; Dávila, *Barrio Dreams*; Stepick, Grenier, Castro, and Dunn, *This Land Is Our Land*; Levitt, *Transnational Villagers*; Itzigsohn, *Encountering American Faultlines*; Davis, *Magical Urbanism*; DeGenova and Ramos-Zayas, *Latino Crossings*; Flores, *From Bomba to Hip-Hop*; Haslip-Viera and Baver, *Latinos in New York*; Laó-Montes and Dávila, *Mambo Montage*; Smith, *Mexican New York*; Valle and Torres, *Latino Metropolis*; and Diaz and Torres, *Latino Urbanism*. For significant scholarship on other postwar and late twentieth-century urban immigrant communities, see Tang, *Unsettled*; Buff, *Immigration and the Political Economy of Home*; Abelmann and Lie, *Blue Dreams*; Bao and Daniels, *Holding Up More Than Half the Sky*; and Johnson, *New Bostonians*. Finally, for important studies of Latino communities outside traditionally urban spaces, see Fink, *Maya of Morganton*; Mahler, *American Dreaming*; Pitti, *Devil in Silicon Valley*; and Gordon, *Village of Immigrants*.

6. Guzmán, "Hispanic Population." For a clear articulation of the importance of Latino immigration to urban studies scholarship, see Sandoval-Strausz, "Latino Landscapes"; Diaz and Torres, *Latino Urbanism*; and Davis, *Magical Urbanism*.

7. In 1960, 69 percent of mainland Puerto Ricans lived in New York City alone, and 79 percent of Mexican Americans lived in cities; see Whalen and Vázquez-Hernández, *Puerto Rican Diaspora*, 3, and Waters, Ueda, and Marrow, *New Americans*, 513. In 1970,

of the 9.1 million persons of "Spanish origin," the census listed 7.9 million as "urban," including 3.9 of the 4.5 million Mexicans, but the data was not disaggregated for "central cities" versus other urbanized areas. The 1980 census listed 14.6 million persons of "Spanish origin," 7.35 million of whom lived in central cities (much fewer than those listed as "urban" or "inside urbanized areas"), but even with this narrow definition, half of Latinos were still in central cities. See *United States Census*, 1970, 1980, 1990.

8. For the economic contribution of immigrants to U.S. cities, see Millman, *Other Americans*; Foner, *One out of Three*; and García, *Havana USA*.

9. Tang, *Unsettled*, 5.

10. In their exploration of redevelopment in New York City and New Orleans, Kevin Fox Gotham and Miriam Greenberg have used the term "crisis cities" to refer to those cities impacted by event-induced disasters, like the 9/11 attacks or Hurricane Katrina. The crisis provoked by deindustrialization and suburbanization was a much more protracted process. A piece of graffiti in postindustrial Detroit pointed out the similarities in the devastation brought about by such disaster events and the decades of postwar urban decline; it read, "At least Katrina was quick." Photos of the graffiti are available on Flickr, Detroit Graffiti, https://www.flickr.com/groups/detroitgraffiti (accessed June 5, 2015); see also Gotham and Greenberg, *Crisis Cities*.

11. Sugrue, *Origins of the Urban Crisis*; Thompson, *Whose Detroit?*; Baugh, *Detroit School Busing Case*.

12. For the racialization of Puerto Ricans and Dominicans more broadly, see Candelario, *Black behind the Ears*; Itzigsohn, *Encountering American Faultlines*; Thomas, *Puerto Rican Citizen*; Jiménez Román and Flores, *Afro-Latin@ Reader*; Rubin and Melnick, *Immigration and American Popular Culture*; and Pérez, *Near Northwest Side Story*.

13. The fact that Lawrence never developed a sizable non-Hispanic Black population may have ensured that Latinos experienced the full brunt of systemic racism in Lawrence, unlike in other cities where Latino populations often occupied a place on the racial hierarchy between white and Black. For studies of Latinos occupying a position of relative privilege compared with African Americans but still facing racism from U.S. whites, see García, *Havana USA*, and Fernández, *Brown in the Windy City*.

14. Although the title of this book is *Latino City*, I make no claim that Lawrence's history captures the broad experience of all Latino groups in the United States. Readers will likely notice that people of Mexican descent, who make up nearly two-thirds of the 55 million Latinos in the United States today, are virtually absent from this story. Puerto Ricans and Dominicans are the second- and fifth-largest national origin groups among Latinos, constituting approximately 9 and 3 percent, respectively, of the mainland Latino population. As of the 2000 census, there were a few hundred each of Mexicans, Guatemalans, Cubans, Ecuadorians, and other Central and South Americans living in Lawrence, but there were more than 15,000 each of Dominicans and Puerto Ricans, as well as a remarkable 8,000 people in the category "Other Hispanic or Latino." This latter designation was assigned to anyone who did not record a national origin or who simply recorded "Spanish" (a common self-identifier for many Latinos in Lawrence) or "Hispanic" or who claimed more than one national origin. The fact that nearly 20 percent of Lawrence's Latinos identified this way suggests that the city's history has helped

forge a panethnic Latino identity, and Lawrence Latinos were more likely to identify as "Other Hispanic or Latino" (20 percent) than Latinos nationally (17 percent). See Stepler and Brown, "Statistical Portrait of Hispanics in the United States"; Motel and Patten, "10 Largest Hispanic Origin Groups" (note that the 3.7 million Puerto Ricans living on the island were not included in this count); Jones, "Latinos in Lawrence"; and Guzmán, "Hispanic Population."

15. Lefebvre, *Production of Space*. For a discussion of how to apply Lefebvre to the U.S. racial geography, see McCann, "Race, Protest, and Public Space." For Lefebvre and Latino suburban activism, see Carpio, Irazábal, and Pulido, "Right to the Suburb?"

16. For the idea of global or globalizing cities, see Sassen, *Globalization and Its Discontents* and *Global City*; Smith, *Transnational Urbanism*; Smith and Guarnizo, *Transnationalism from Below*; Chomsky, *Linked Labor Histories*; and Marcuse and Van Kempen, *Globalizing Cities*. For recent studies on second-tier global cities, see Chen and Kanna, *Rethinking Global Urbanism*. For studies on revitalization in small postindustrial cities, see Hoyt and Leroux, "Voices from Forgotten Cities," and Siegal and Waxman, "Third-Tier Cities."

17. Aviva Chomsky has noted the impact of transnational migration and global capital on Salem, Massachusetts, in "Salem as a Global City." For more studies on globalizing urbanism in New England, see Chen and Bacon, *Confronting Urban Legacy*.

18. Pho, Gerson, and Cowan, *Southeast Asian Refugees*; Nadeau, "Somalis of Lewiston"; Maggie Jones, "The New Yankees," *Mother Jones*, March/April 2004.

19. For studies of suburban diversity in the postwar through the contemporary era, see Lassiter and Niedt, "Suburban Diversity in Postwar America"; Katz, Creighton, Amsterdam, and Chowkwanyun, "Immigration and the New Metropolitan Geography"; Duncan and Duncan, "Can't Live with Them; Can't Landscape without Them"; Carpio, Irazábal, and Pulido, "Right to the Suburb?"; Baxandall and Ewen, *Picture Windows*; Wiese, *Places of Their Own*; Niedt, *Social Justice in Diverse Suburbs*, particularly Pastor, "Maywood, Not Mayberry" therein; Valle and Torres, *Latino Metropolis*; Singer, *Twenty-First Century Gateways*; Johnson, *New Bostonians*; Fong, *First Suburban Chinatown*; and Gordon, *Village of Immigrants*.

20. Two influential Brookings Institution reports were issued after the 2000 census, one of which noted that the majority of Latinos (both U.S. and foreign born) lived in the suburbs, and the other of which noted that the majority of immigrants (foreign born from all regions of the world) lived in suburbs. Brookings Institution researchers used their own guidelines to designate central cities and suburbs, and the report on immigrant suburbanization considered cities with fewer than 100,000 residents within a larger city's metropolitan area to be suburban. The report on Latino suburbanization notes that it did as well. See Audrey Singer, email correspondence with the author, November 2009; Suro and Singer, "Latino Growth in Metropolitan America"; and Singer, "Rise of New Immigrant Gateways."

21. Londoño, "Aesthetic Belonging"; Pastor, "Maywood, Not Mayberry." These small cities resemble Lawrence in some ways. In California, Maywood and Bell Gardens each had fewer than 100,000 residents in 2000. Both cities were dense (two or three times the population density of the city of Los Angeles itself), economically struggling areas, in which over 90 percent of the population was Latino, almost one-quarter living under

the poverty line, and approximately 70 percent living in rental housing. The New York metropolitan area had West New York and Union City, each with fewer than 100,000 residents, approximately 80 percent of whom were Latino, with almost twice the population density of New York City, one-fifth of their residents below the poverty line, and 80 percent of residents in rental housing. See *United States Census*, 2000, 2010.

22. The Boston Metropolitan Area Planning Council, established by the state legislature in 1963, does not include Lawrence or its suburbs as part of the Boston Metro area, although Lawrence is sometimes discussed as such. There is no official or universal definition for "suburb." The U.S. Census delineates metropolitan areas and cities, and municipalities that are inside a metropolitan area but outside a city are generally considered suburbs. Official methods of designating cities change over time. Until 1990, the census considered Lawrence to be the central city in its own metropolitan area, and it was not considered a part of Boston's metropolitan area. In 1990, the census considered Lawrence both a central city in the Boston-Lawrence-Salem CMSA (Consolidated Metropolitan Statistical Area) and the main central city in the Lawrence-Haverhill PMSA (Primary Metropolitan Statistical Area). In the 2000 census, Lawrence was only considered to be a central city in the Boston-Worcester-Lawrence CMSA. At the end of 2000, the Office of Management and Budget adopted new standards to define central cities (what they now termed "principal cities"), and Lawrence lost its city designation entirely. The new definitions of principal cities rely essentially on commuting patterns to determine the status of a municipality of Lawrence's size. Places with fewer than 250,000 residents that are not the largest city in their metropolitan area must provide either more than 100,000 jobs or more jobs than employed residents. Thus Lawrence's marginal position in its metropolitan economy (itself the *result* of it being a city, not a suburb in the postwar era) rendered it no longer a city for statistical purposes. See Boston Metropolitan Area Planning Council website, http://www.mapc.org/about-mapc; *United States Census*, Metropolitan and Micropolitan: Historical Statistical Area Delineations, http://www .census.gov/population/metro/data/pastmetro.html; and Office of Management and Budget, "Standards for Defining Metropolitan and Micropolitan Statistical Areas," *Federal Register*, December 27, 2000, 82236. For more on Boston and its metropolitan area, see Johnson, "Metropolitan Diaspora" and *New Bostonians*. Note that Johnson does not consider Lawrence as part of the Boston Metro area. See also O'Connell, *Hub's Metropolis*. O'Connell does include Lawrence but mentions the small city only a few times.

23. *United States Census* estimate, 2014; Mitch Smith, "Flint Wants Safe Water and Someone to Answer for Its Crisis," *NYT*, January 9, 2016.

24. Valle and Torres, *Latino Metropolis*, 15–43; Duncan and Duncan, "Can't Live with Them; Can't Landscape without Them"; Gordon, *Village of Immigrants*.

25. For a broader study of the political impact of the media's racialized attention to urban "dangers" in the 1980s and 1990s, see Macek, *Urban Nightmares*.

26. While the relationship between U.S. empire and immigration is foregrounded in much of the scholarship on Latino migration cited above, these ideas have been developed in other scholarship as well, particularly that related to Filipino migration. See Sánchez, "Race, Nation, and Culture in Recent Immigration Studies"; Bald, Chatterji, and Reddy, *Sun Never Sets*; Choy, *Empire of Care*; Fadiman, *Spirit Catches You and You Fall Down*; and Ngai, *Impossible Subjects*.

27. See migration narratives throughout this book. For bleak views of postwar U.S. cities in Latino literature, see Thomas, *Down These Mean Streets*; Pietri, *Puerto Rican Obituary*; Tobar, *Tattooed Soldier*; Viramontes, *Their Dogs Came with Them*; Quiñonez, *Chango's Fire*; and Díaz, *Drown*.

28. González, *Harvest of Empire*.

29. Pérez, "Hispanic Values, Military Values"; Dávila, *Latino Spin*.

30. Yohel Camayd-Freixas, MIT professor of urban studies, coordinator of the post-riot "Hispanics in Lawrence Symposium" series sponsored by the Department of Social Services, quoted in Duran, "1984 Riots," 43.

31. Carter, "Hispanic Rioting during the Civil Rights Era"; Valle and Torres, *Latino Metropolis*.

32. Duran, "1984 Riots," 31, 32, already translated from Spanish.

33. For more on neoliberalism, see Harvey, *Brief History of Neoliberalism*.

Chapter 1

1. For this and other depictions of class-inflected anti-Lawrence prejudice, see Schinto, *Huddle Fever*.

2. Jackson, *Crabgrass Frontier*, 283, 284.

3. As David Rusk has illustrated, many Sunbelt cities had (or were able to acquire) sufficient space for suburban-style development to occur *within* the city. Cities with open space for new growth after World War II were "elastic," able to "capture" suburban-style growth in a way that contributed to the urban tax base. Cities in the Northeast and Midwest were overwhelmingly "inelastic," already densely settled with little room for new growth and unable to expand their boundaries. The postwar suburban boom impoverished these cities, drawing residents and resources outside the municipal boundaries. See Rusk, *Cities without Suburbs*, 20.

4. Jackson, *Crabgrass Frontier*, 283, 284.

5. Rusk, *Cities without Suburbs*, 5.

6. Jackson, *Crabgrass Frontier*, 272.

7. *United States Census*, "Historical Census of Housing Tables," 2011.

8. Green and Wachter, "American Mortgage." The Federal Housing Finance Agency also offers a useful overview of this history on their website, http://fhfaoig.gov/LearnMore/History#Anchor36 (accessed July 12, 2013).

9. For studies of segregated suburbanization in the postwar era, see Jackson, *Crabgrass Frontier*; Self, *American Babylon*; Sugrue, *Origins of the Urban Crisis*; Avila, *Popular Culture in the Age of White Flight*; Cohen, *Consumers' Republic*; Seligman, *Block by Block*; Kruse, *White Flight*; Kruse and Sugrue, *New Suburban History*; Baxandall and Ewen, *Picture Windows*; Massey and Denton, *American Apartheid*; Freund, *Colored Property*; Lamb, *Housing Segregation in Suburban America since 1960*; Wiese, *Places of Their Own*; Gotham, *Race, Real Estate, and Uneven Development*; and Lassiter, *Silent Majority*.

10. Quoted in Vale, *From the Puritans to the Projects*, 169.

11. Vale, *From the Puritans to the Projects*. See also Hirsch, "Less Than *Plessy*."

12. Gotham, *Race, Real Estate, and Uneven Development*.

13. Baxandall and Ewen, *Picture Windows*.

14. Engler, "Subsidized Housing in the Suburbs." See also Geismer, *Don't Blame Us*.

15. Although there is also a Salem in Massachusetts, my use of Salem refers to New Hampshire unless otherwise noted.

16. Greater Lawrence here includes Andover, North Andover, Methuen, and Salem, N.H., as well as Windham, N.H. See Central Merrimack Valley Regional Planning District, "Population Report," September 1968, LPL.

17. Ibid. Not all of the growth in Lawrence's suburbs reflected flight from the city itself. No doubt some new suburbanites came from Boston or outside Massachusetts entirely. Indeed, the level of growth in the suburbs far exceeded the level of population decline in the city, which may be partly explained by the baby boom that occurred in the years after World War II. Yet a substantial portion of the suburbs' expanding populations was former Lawrencians, as white flight eviscerated the city. Suburban commentators frequently mentioned their Lawrence roots. The 1960 census indicated that nearly 40 percent of new Methuen residents had come from either Lawrence or Haverhill. Planning reports from this era made frequent reference to the flight from Lawrence to the suburbs, noting that many suburban residents had left Lawrence's aging housing stock in pursuit of "more modern housing in the suburbs" or that "the suburban towns of Andover, Methuen and North Andover have absorbed the greater part of the out-migration" from the city. See *United States Census*, 1960, and Lawrence City Planning Board, "Guide Plan for Lawrence, Massachusetts," 1957, LPL.

18. See Kruse, *White Flight*.

19. For a larger exploration of exclusionary zoning, see Danielson, *Politics of Exclusion*, and Lamb, *Housing Segregation in Suburban America since 1960*.

20. Median housing value and income data from *United States Census* and the U.S. Department of Housing and Urban Development, State of the Cities online database, http://socds.huduser.org/ (accessed throughout 2009 and 2010). Conversions were done using an online calculator from the Bureau of Labor Statistics, http://data.bls.gov/cgi-bin/cpicalc.pl.

21. Self, *American Babylon*, 269.

22. Chamber of Commerce of Greater Lawrence, "Greater Lawrence Economic Profile," 1980, Buckley Papers, LHC.

23. Legal Notices, *Andover Townsman*, April 10, 1936, AHS.

24. *Andover Town Report*, 1948 and 1955, SLM. For a discussion of how and when public housing became stigmatized, see Vale, *From the Puritans to the Projects*.

25. Harold Rafton quoted in Mofford, *AVIS*, 94. For the role of conservation efforts in shaping the suburbs, see Rome, *Bulldozer in the Countryside*.

26. Low income was generally defined as less than 80 percent of the area median income. For more on Massachusetts anti-snob zoning regulations, see Schuetz, "Guarding the Town Walls"; Engler, "Subsidized Housing in the Suburbs"; Merrimack Valley Planning Commission, "Chapter 774"; and Cowan, "Anti-Snob Land Use Laws."

27. Bernadine Coburn, "North Andover Opponents Fear Becoming 'Slurb,'" BG, February 19, 1973.

28. Archdiocese of Boston, Planning Office for Urban Affairs website, http://www.poua.org (accessed July 25, 2103).

29. Schuetz, "Guarding the Town Walls." In addition, Spencer Cowan concluded that, by 2000, the anti-snob zoning law had not substantially resulted in racial integration in

Massachusetts, noting "even after thirty years, the state's exclusionary suburbs are still disproportionately white" (Cowan, "Anti-Snob Land Use Laws," 308).

30. These figures are from before the construction of Wood Ridge Homes. See Merrimack Valley Planning Commission, "Chapter 774." Note that Chapter 705, 707, or Section 8 housing was not included in the definition of subsidized housing.

31. For an overview of urban renewal, see Avila and Rose, "Race, Culture, Politics, and Urban Renewal." See also Zipp, *Manhattan Projects*; Vale, *From the Puritans to the Projects*; and for a slightly different take, Rubin, *Insuring the City*.

32. Thomas, *Puerto Rican Citizen*, 193.

33. For a classic study of a working-class white ethnic neighborhood in Boston demolished by urban renewal in this era, see Gans, *Urban Villagers*.

34. For urban renewal's specific impact on Latino and Black communities, see Thomas, *Puerto Rican Citizen*; Avila, *Popular Culture in the Age of White Flight*; Diaz and Torres, *Latino Urbanism*; Otero, *La Calle*; and Self, *American Babylon*. See also the video documentaries *Chavez Ravine* and *The Case against Lincoln Center*.

35. Pernice, "Urban Redevelopment of Lawrence."

36. Ibid.

37. Ibid., 71, 72.

38. Ibid., 74.

39. Gans, *Urban Villagers*.

40. For an excellent discussion of the racialized use of the term "blight," see Avila, *Folklore of the Freeway*.

41. In the case of the Plains, the compensation amounts given to owners by the city were inadequate, even considering the depressed property values after years of rumors had allowed the neighborhood to deteriorate. See Pernice, "Urban Redevelopment of Lawrence," 112.

42. Pernice, "Urban Redevelopment of Lawrence."

43. Quoted in ibid., 30.

44. It is unclear if this redlining began before or after the neighborhood was included in the GNRA.

45. Pernice, "Urban Redevelopment of Lawrence."

46. Ibid., 35, 36.

47. "Mr. O'Connor," quoted in ibid., 108.

48. "Mr. DiFruscia," quoted in ibid., 109.

49. Quoted in ibid., 101.

50. Ibid., 64, 65.

51. Ibid., 2, 53.

52. For more on Lincoln Center, see Caro, *Power Broker*, and Thomas, *Puerto Rican Citizen*.

53. "History of the Lawrence Redevelopment Authority," LHC; John Farrell, "End of Decade: Urban Renewal—Still Going Forward," *ET*, December 31, 1969, clipping in Kiley Collection, LHC.

54. Chazy Dowaliby, "At Nick Maloof's They Meet the Dawn of Bygone Days," *Today in Greater Lawrence*, December 31, 1974, LPL.

55. For a national study of the grief and nostalgia precipitated by the shuttering of downtown businesses, see Isenberg, *Downtown America*.

56. For an excellent study of the impact of the suburban retail sector on urban economies, see Cohen, *Consumers' Republic.*

57. Liebke and Associates, "Analysis and Recommended Program for the Central Business District."

58. See, for example, Sugrue, *Origins of the Urban Crisis.*

59. Liebke and Associates, "Analysis and Recommended Program for the Central Business District."

60. Massachusetts Budget and Policy Center website, http://www.massbudget.org/documentsearch/findDocument?doc_id=621&dse_id=561 (accessed January 6, 2010).

61. Andrew Coburn, "Battle of the Buck: Methuen Mall Flexes Its Muscles and Downtown and Others Flinch," *Journal of Greater Lawrence*, November 29, 1973, LPL.

62. Ibid.

63. Walsh and Associates, "Action Plan Lawrence," 12–14.

64. Ibid., 36.

65. For more on this shift to electronics manufacturing, see Lampe, *Massachusetts Miracle*, and Tager, "Massachusetts Miracle."

66. Uncle Dudley, "City That Wouldn't Die," *BG*, December 11, 1960, reprint in LPL.

67. Mozingo, *Pastoral Capitalism*, 8, 17, 24. See also Sugrue, *Origins of the Urban Crisis.*

68. Tager, "Massachusetts Miracle."

69. Ibid.

70. Ibid., 112.

71. Vecoli, "Anthony Caparro and the Lawrence Strike of 1919."

72. Uncle Dudley, "City That Wouldn't Die," *BG*, December 11, 1960, reprint in LPL.

73. "Textile City Gets Along Despite Layoffs," *Business Week*, May 7, 1949, reprint in LPL.

74. Ibid.; "Lawrence, Mass.: Textile Town Stays Healthy," *Business Week*, December 19, 1953, reprint in LPL.

75. "American Woolen Co. May Leave N.E.," *BG*, January 18, 1952.

76. Ibid.

77. Robbins, "Bread, Roses, and Other Possibilities."

78. "Lawrence, Mass.: Textile Town Stays Healthy," *Business Week*, December 19, 1953, reprint in LPL.

79. Ibid.; Rear Admiral Thomas F. Halloran, "From Textiles to Electronics," as told to Jack McKallagat, reprint from *SIGNAL: Official Journal of the Armed Forces Communications and Electronics Association*, LPL.

80. For a detailed discussion of similar efforts to recruit and maintain urban manufacturing in Philadelphia, see McKee, *Problem of Jobs.*

81. For studies of deindustrialization, see Cowie and Heathcott, *Beyond the Ruins*, and McKee, *Problem of Jobs.*

82. "Comeback Incomplete, but It's There," *BG*, January 11, 1977.

83. Western Electric Company, Merrimack Valley Works documents, courtesy of AT&T Archives and History Center, Warren, N.J.

84. Ibid.

85. Andover Town Reports, 1955 and 1956, SLM.

86. Ibid., 1960–80.

87. "Industry Highlight Rezoning Special Meeting," *Andover News*, July 1968, AHS.

88. Raytheon Company website, http://www.raytheon.com/ourcompany/history/ (accessed January 7, 2014); "Industry Highlight Rezoning Special Meeting," *Andover News*, July 1968, AHS.

89. "Industry Highlight Rezoning Special Meeting," *Andover News*, July 1968, AHS.

90. Andover Town Reports, 1968, 1970, SLM.

91. Massachusetts Division of Employment Security, "Defense Spending and Massachusetts Employment."

92. Andover Town Reports, 1970, 1972, 1985, SLM.

93. Ibid., 1980.

94. Ibid., 1990.

95. Andover Finance Committee Report, 1989, SLM.

96. Manufacturers' News, Inc. website, http://www.manufacturersnews.com/info/massachusetts-manufacturers-register (accessed December 31, 2013).

97. LDIC, "Industrial Newsgram," November/December 1972, LPL.

98. Ibid., January/February, 1973.

99. The LDIC proposed a metropolitan approach to affordable housing, including the creation of a regional housing authority. A 1975 report by the Massachusetts Advisory Committee to the U.S. Commission on Civil Rights and the Massachusetts Commission against Discrimination had issued a similar recommendation for the Boston metropolitan area in a report on the impact of suburban development along Route 128. See ibid. and Massachusetts Advisory Committee, "Rt. 128: Boston's Road to Segregation."

100. Al White, editor of the *Eagle-Tribune*, personal correspondence, March 25, 2010. For simplicity's sake I generally refer to the paper by its current name, the *Eagle-Tribune*, throughout, including in the endnotes, although it should be noted that the paper was named the *Lawrence Eagle-Tribune* until 1987.

101. Tax data from the "Statistics" binder at LPL and from the Lawrence and Andover Town Reports at the SLM.

102. Lupo, "Lessons of the Street."

103. Tax data from the "Statistics" binder at LPL and from the Lawrence and Andover Town Reports at the SLM.

Chapter 2

1. *United States Census*, 1990.

2. Jose Zaiter quoted in Hilda Hartnett, "Lawrence's Latino History Diverse, Complex," *ET*, September 20, 1992. The term "blend in," however, was the journalist's paraphrasing of Zaiter's comments.

3. Ramón Borges-Méndez, quoted in a transcript of his presentation at the "Forgotten Cities" seminar series on October 27, 2004, hosted by the Department of Urban Studies and Planning at the Massachusetts Institute of Technology. Transcript archived with the Department of Urban Studies and Planning, and quote used with permission from the speaker.

4. Andors, "City and Island," 49. See also Garcia interview, Lamond interview, and Urena interview.

5. On the West Coast and in the Southwest, Latino agricultural labor and long-standing Mexican American communities complicated this postwar paradigm of racialized metropolitan development. For more on this see, Pitti, *Devil in Silicon Valley*.

6. Latino migration narratives include a handful of oral history interviews I conducted specifically for this project, more than twenty oral history interviews conducted by the Lawrence History Center over the past three decades, and interviews printed in newspapers and reports since the late 1950s. In total, this chapter makes use of several dozen accounts of migration to Lawrence, some very detailed and others representing no more than a single-line quote in a high school report. With no statistical claim to representing the full diversity of Lawrence's Latino community, and with such a paucity of detail among some of the accounts, I can only begin to sketch out some of the commonalities among migrants to Lawrence. For a full list of the complete oral history interviews used, please see the bibliography.

7. Borges-Méndez, "Urban and Regional Restructuring," 17.

8. González, *Harvest of Empire*.

9. Quoted in Urban Studies Institute, "Growing Up Hispanic," 8.

10. Quoted in Andors, "City and Island," 71, translated by Andors.

11. See Byrd, *Transit of Empire*; Goldstein, *Formations of United States Colonialism*; Williams, "United States Indian Policy and the Debate over Philippine Annexation"; and Drinnon, *Facing West*.

12. Jacobson, *Barbarian Virtues*.

13. Foraker quoted in Fernandez, *Disenchanted Island*, 2.

14. Quoted in ibid., 11.

15. Trías Monge, *Puerto Rico*, 86.

16. Dietz, *Economic History of Puerto Rico*, 159; Trías Monge, *Puerto Rico*, 77–87.

17. Representative Clarence Miller quoted in Fernandez, *Disenchanted Island*, 68.

18. Ayala and Bernabe, *Puerto Rico in the American Century*, 149. See also Dietz, *Economic History of Puerto Rico*, and Trías Monge, *Puerto Rico*.

19. The Partido Popular Democrático–controlled legislature in 1948 enacted Law 53, commonly referred to as the Gag Law, which made it illegal to advocate violent overthrow of the U.S. government. It was used broadly to silence nationalist opposition. See Ayala and Bernabe, *Puerto Rico in the American Century*, 160.

20. For more on Puerto Rico's complicated status, see Negrón-Muntaner, *None of the Above*; Grosfoguel, *Colonial Subjects*; and Duany, *Puerto Rican Nation on the Move*.

21. Quoted in Dietz, *Economic History of Puerto Rico*, 211.

22. Pérez, *Near Northwest Side Story*, 30–60.

23. This process of "fleeing the cane," is discussed in ibid. The phrase "industrialization by invitation," used to refer to Operation Bootstrap, quoted in Dietz, *Economic History of Puerto Rico*, 210.

24. Reducing the fertility of Puerto Rican women was also a part of solving the island's "overpopulation" problem, as documented by Briggs, *Reproducing Empire*, and Grosfoguel, *Colonial Subjects*, 108–10.

25. Whalen, "Colonialism, Citizenship, and the Making of the Puerto Rican Diaspora."

26. Chomsky, *Linked Labor Histories*, 108–12.

27. Brecher and Costello, *Global Village or Global Pillage*.

28. Grosfoguel, *Colonial Subjects*, 59, 95.

29. Whalen, "Colonialism, Citizenship, and the Making of the Puerto Rican Diaspora," 2. For studies of Puerto Rican migration and Puerto Ricans in diaspora,

see Whalen and Vázquez-Hernández, *Puerto Rican Diaspora*; Sánchez Korrol, *From Colonia to Community*; Pérez, *Near Northwest Side Story*; Whalen, *From Puerto Rico to Philadelphia*; Thomas, *Puerto Rican Citizen*; Fernández, *Brown in the Windy City*; Lee, *Building a Latino Civil Rights Movement*; Duany, *Puerto Rican Nation on the Move*; Flores, *Diaspora Strikes Back*; and Grosfoguel, *Colonial Subjects*.

30. Denis, *War against All Puerto Ricans*; Malavet, *America's Colony*; Ayala and Bernabe, *Puerto Rico in the American Century*; McCaffrey, *Military Power and Popular Protest*.

31. For a discussion of Dominican migration to Puerto Rico, including the prejudices faced by Dominicans, see Ricourt, "Reaching the Promised Land," and Duany, "Dominican Migration to Puerto Rico."

32. Quoted in Grosfoguel, *Colonial Subjects*, 68.

33. Dominicans celebrate their independence from Haiti in 1844 as their national founding, as the reannexation by Spain in the 1860s was short lived. For more on this complicated history, see Moya Pons, *Dominican Republic*, and Wucker, *Why the Cocks Fight*.

34. Moya Pons, *Dominican Republic*, 265–78. Moya Pons's comprehensive study is the classic English-language history of the Dominican Republic. See also Hernández, *Mobility of Labor under Advanced Capitalism*; Itzigsohn, *Developing Poverty*; Hoffnung-Garskof, *Tale of Two Cities*; Chester, *Rag-Tags, Scum, Riff-Raff, and Commies*; Black, *Dominican Republic*; Roorda, Derby, and González, *Dominican Republic Reader*; and Atkins and Wilson, *Dominican Republic and the United States*.

35. Moya Pons, *Dominican Republic*, 282.

36. Ibid., 287–95. The complete text of Roosevelt's annual message to Congress of 1904, in which the Roosevelt Corollary was articulated, is available online as part of NARA's 100 milestone documents series, http://ourdocuments.gov/doc.php?doc=56 (accessed June 1, 2015).

37. Moya Pons, *Dominican Republic*, 305–39.

38. Black, *Dominican Republic*, 23; Moya Pons, *Dominican Republic*, 300–325.

39. Black, *Dominican Republic*, 21–28; Moya Pons, *Dominican Republic*, 357–80. There is also an illustrative section on Trujillo in Roorda, Derby, and González, *Dominican Republic Reader*, 279–324.

40. Chester, *Rag-Tags, Scum, Riff-Raff, and Commies*; Wiarda, "United States and the Dominican Republic"; Roorda, Derby, and González, *Dominican Republic Reader*, 362.

41. Hoffnung-Garskof, *Tale of Two Cities*, 68–96.

42. Schrank, "Foreign Investors, 'Flying Geese'"; Hernández, *Mobility of Labor under Advanced Capitalism*, 51.

43. Hernández, *Mobility of Labor under Advanced Capitalism*, 58–61. See also Hoffnung-Garskof, *Tale of Two Cities*, 44–67. For a fascinating depiction of the cultural aspects of Dominican urbanization, see Pacini Hernandez, *Bachata*.

44. For more on this early immigration from El Cibao, see Hendricks, *Dominican Diaspora*.

45. Black, "Development and Dependency in the Dominican Republic."

46. Hernández, *Mobility of Labor under Advanced Capitalism*, 73.

47. Ibid., 81.

48. Smith, *Talons of the Eagle*, 213–40.

49. See Walton and Seddon, *Free Markets and Food Riots*, and Toussaint and Millet, *Debt, the IMF, and the World Bank*. For a video documentary of IMF and World Bank policies in Jamaica, see *Life and Debt*.

50. Walton and Seddon, *Free Markets and Food Riots*, 121; Hernández, *Mobility of Labor under Advanced Capitalism*, 78, 83.

51. Originally from Bernardo Vega, *En la Decada Perdida*, quoted in Hernández, *Mobility of Labor under Advanced Capitalism*, 79.

52. Black, "Development and Dependency in the Dominican Republic"; Raynolds, "Harnessing Women's Work."

53. For contemporary studies of the Dominican economy and the efforts of Dominicans to create lives and livelihoods for themselves within it, see Gregory, *Devil behind the Mirror*, and Brennan, *What's Love Got to Do with It?*

54. Migration Policy Institute, "Dominican Population in the United States"; Hernández and Rivera-Batiz, "Dominicans in the United States."

55. There are more than 4 million people currently on the waiting list for family-preference immigrant visas; nearly 200,000 of them are Dominicans; see U.S. Department of State, Bureau of Consular Affairs, "Annual Report of Immigrant Visa Applicants in the Family-Sponsored and Employment-Based Preferences Registered at the National Visa Center as of November 1, 2014." Average wait times for family-preference immigrant visas are published in the Department of State, Bureau of Consular Affairs's monthly "Visa Bulletin." For broader discussions of Dominican immigration, see Sagás and Molina, *Dominican Migration*; Grasmuck and Pessar, *Between Two Islands*; Pessar, *Visa for a Dream*; Georges, *Making of a Transnational Community*; Hernández, *Mobility of Labor under Advanced Capitalism*; Levitt, *Transnational Villagers*; Hoffnung-Garskof, *Tale of Two Cities*; Snyder, *Crossing Broadway*; and Itzigsohn, *Encountering American Faultlines*.

56. Information on the extensive application process for a nonimmigrant visa to the United States is available on the U.S. Embassy in the Dominican Republic's website, santodomingo.usembassy.gov (accessed June 1, 2015).

57. In 2000, the Immigration and Nationalization Service estimated that there were fewer than 100,000 undocumented Dominicans living in the United States, out of a total foreign-born Dominican population of nearly 700,000. See Hernández and Rivera-Batiz, "Dominicans in the United States," 15, 16.

58. For overviews of the history of U.S. intervention in Latin America, see Smith, *Talons of the Eagle*; Grandin, *Empire's Workshop*; and Nieto and Brandt, *Masters of War*. For broad studies of Latin American opposition to U.S. intervention, see McPherson, *Yankee No!* and *The Invaded*. For U.S. imperialism more generally, see the classic Kaplan and Pease, *Cultures of United States Imperialism*.

59. Ramón Borges-Méndez has argued that migrants in the 1960s often came straight from Puerto Rico. Jessica Andors has argued that, for Dominicans, the earliest migrants came from New York and direct migration from the island came later. There are many examples among the migration narratives of the move to Lawrence being a secondary migration for the Latinos who settled in Lawrence as early as the 1960s, for Dominicans particularly but also for some Puerto Ricans and Cubans. No quantitative study has been done, and it suffices to say that the earliest Latinos in Lawrence comprised a mix of direct

and secondary migrants. See Borges-Méndez, "Urban and Regional Restructuring," and Andors, "City and Island," 47.

60. Isabel Melendez quoted in Borges-Méndez, "Urban and Regional Restructuring," 135.

61. Lee, *Building a Latino Civil Rights Movement*, 44.

62. For portraits of New York City during the urban crisis era, see Snyder, *Crossing Broadway*; Mahler, *Ladies and Gentlemen, the Bronx Is Burning*; Schneider, *Smack*; Wallace and Wallace, *Plague on Your Houses*; Austin, *Taking the Train*; Chang, *Can't Stop, Won't Stop*; Reitano, *Restless City*; Thomas, *Puerto Rican Citizen*; Hoffnung-Garskof, *Tale of Two Cities*; Lee, *Building a Latino Civil Rights Movement*; Gonzalez, *The Bronx*; and Piri Thomas's classic memoir *Down These Mean Streets*.

63. Snyder, *Crossing Broadway*, 49; Baxandall and Ewen, *Picture Windows*.

64. Lee, *Building a Latino Civil Rights Movement*, 46–52; Thomas, *Down These Mean Streets*.

65. Snyder, *Crossing Broadway*, 116.

66. Lee, *Building a Latino Civil Rights Movement*, 215.

67. Schneider, *Smack*, 117–22.

68. Ibid., ix.

69. These agencies were the Municipal Assistance Corporation and the Emergency Financial Control Board. See Reitano, *Restless City*, 189–91.

70. Snyder, *Crossing Broadway*, 117.

71. Reitano, *Restless City*, 189–91; Snyder, *Crossing Broadway*, 117.

72. Wallace and Wallace, *Plague on Your Houses*, 47.

73. Quoted in Mahler, *Ladies and Gentlemen, the Bronx Is Burning*, 329; Gonzalez, *The Bronx*, 129.

74. Reitano, *Restless City*, 181.

75. Wallace and Wallace, *Plague on Your Houses*, 56.

76. For a comparative account of Mexican and Puerto Rican labor migration after World War II, see Fernández, "Of Immigrants and Migrants."

77. Quoted in Pessar, *Visa for a Dream*, xiii.

78. To give just a few examples, see Isabel Melendez, press conference transcript, December 14, 2003, http://www.notilatino.com/id9.htm (accessed October 27, 2009); Reyes Cardenas interview; Urena interview; Sara Saldana, quoted in Mary Fitzgerald, "An American Success Story," *ET*, March 18, 1994; and Urban Studies Institute, "Growing Up Hispanic."

79. Urban Studies Institute, "Growing Up Hispanic," 15–21.

80. Andors, "City and Island," 32, translated by Andors.

81. Ibid.

82. Charles Stein, "Lawrence Case Study: A Struggle of the Poor," *BG*, June 24, 1988.

83. "Dominican Student Unhappy with Education, Food, Weather," *ET*, April 30, 1979.

84. Urban Studies Institute, "Growing Up Hispanic," 10.

85. Snyder, *Crossing Broadway*, 162.

86. Time/CNN poll cited in Macek, *Urban Nightmares*, vii.

87. DeJesus interview.

88. Johnson interview.

89. Andrew Coburn, "The Puerto Ricans: Lawrence's Latest Wave of Immigrants," *ET*, July 21, 1967.

90. Piore, "Role of Immigration in Industrial Growth."

91. Chamber of Commerce of Greater Lawrence, "Greater Lawrence Economic Profile," 1980, Buckley Papers, LHC.

92. Julia Silverio, quoted in Hernández and Jacobs, "Beyond Homeland Politics," 288. See also Borges-Méndez, "Urban and Regional Restructuring."

93. Lamond interview.

94. Aparicio interview.

95. Ruth Weinstock, "New Immigrants in Old Sweatshops," *Today in Greater Lawrence*, June 26, 1974, LPL.

96. In 1975, the average hourly wage for manufacturing work in Puerto Rico was $2.59. See Dietz, *Economic History of Puerto Rico*, 248.

97. Ruth Weinstock, "New Immigrants in Old Sweatshops," *Today in Greater Lawrence*, June 26, 1974, LPL.

98. Díaz interview.

99. Ibid.

100. The remarkable rate of Latino unemployment in Lawrence, and indeed, the poverty, low wages, and unemployment of immigrants in general in the late twentieth century, was often attributed to the "unskilled" nature of those looking for work. As Evelyn Nakano Glenn has argued, however, this distinction between "skilled" and "unskilled" labor is often quite racialized and reflects access to formal education more than "skills" per se. See Glenn, "From Servitude to Service Work."

101. Rivera interview.

102. Interview with Dominican man in his forties, former professor, now factory worker, in Andors, "City and Island," 65, translated by Andors.

103. Ruth Weinstock, "New Immigrants in Old Sweatshops," *Today in Greater Lawrence*, June 26, 1974, LPL.

104. "Shoe Industry on Shaky Footing," *Mansfield News*, March 29, 1977.

105. Ward Morehouse III, "Help for New England Shoe Industry Getting Attention," *Lewiston Daily Sun*, February 5, 1977.

106. Morse Shoe, Inc., closed the Jo-Gal factory in Lawrence in January 1984. See "Morse Shoe, Inc. History" from Funding Universe website, http://www .fundinguniverse.com/company-histories/morse-shoe-inc-history (accessed January 7, 2014).

107. Massachusetts State Office of Affirmative Action, "Report of the Hispanic Task Force," 33.

108. For a discussion of the "underclass" debate, see Katz, *"Underclass" Debate*; Moore and Pinderhughes, *In the Barrios*; and Massey and Denton, *American Apartheid*. Also, see Chapter 6 in this volume.

109. *United States Census*. Although New York City Latinos may have had a higher cost of living, this does not seem to have been the case, as the Bureau of Labor Statistics indicated that the cost of living for the Boston metropolitan region was actually slightly higher than for the New York City metropolitan region, and rents in Lawrence tripled in the 1980s. Cost of living comparison from the Bureau of Labor Statistics website, http://data.bls.gov (accessed April 6, 2010). Lawrence rent information from Urban Studies Institute, "Family Housing Crisis."

110. By 1990, after the turbulent deindustrialization of the 1980s, only 46 percent of Lawrence Latinos worked in manufacturing, and less than one-third of employed Latinas worked as operatives. See *United States Census, 1990*.

111. Andors changed the names of her interviewees.

112. Andors, "City and Island," 48.

113. *United States Census, 1990*.

114. Andors, "City and Island," 33.

115. Loren McArthur, "Organizing Just-In-Time in the Merrimack Valley," *Social Policy*, Winter 2001/2002, 43–48.

116. This reality that rent in Lawrence was not "cheap" is clear in Urban Studies Institute, "Family Housing Crisis."

117. Oral history interviews often recount such discrimination against Puerto Ricans, particularly. See Jiménez de Wagenheim, "From Aguada to Dover," and Toro-Morn, "Boricuas en Chicago."

118. In addition, the report concluded that "discrimination against rental subsidy recipients posed an absolute barrier"; such testers were not offered any units. MCAD subsequently initiated formal complaints against all six real estate agencies and one property management company tested. See Rubin, "Housing Discrimination in the Rental Market."

119. For an excellent exploration of this idea, see Fernández, *Brown in the Windy City*. Regarding Philadelphia, see Katz, Creighton, Amsterdam, and Chowkwanyun, "Immigration and the New Metropolitan Geography." For a critical appraisal of the idea that Latinos might be "becoming white," see Vargas, "Latina/o Whitening?"

120. Massey and Denton, "Residential Segregation of Mexicans, Puerto Ricans, and Cubans." There are also many accounts of Puerto Ricans facing housing discrimination throughout Whalen and Vázquez-Hernández, *Puerto Rican Diaspora*.

121. Bluestone and Stevenson, *Boston Renaissance*, 170, 171.

Chapter 3

1. Kelley notes that he has adapted this approach from James C. Scott's idea of "infrapolitics"; see Kelley, *Race Rebels*. See also McCann, "Race, Protest, and Public Space."

2. Melendez interview by the author.

3. Quoted in Schinto, *Huddle Fever*, 268.

4. For more on "white ethnics," see Jacobson, *Roots Too*, and Sugrue and Skrentny, "White Ethnic Strategy."

5. For studies of "white fight" in other cities, see Diamond, *Mean Streets*; Seligman, *Block by Block*; and Kruse, *White Flight*.

6. Eugene Declercq, "While Suburbs Duck, Lawrence Flounders: Riot Wasn't Just Urban Problem," *ET*, August 12, 1984, clipping in Mayor Buckley scrapbooks, LHC.

7. Neff, "Facing Up to Our Prejudice."

8. Urban Studies Institute, "Growing Up Hispanic," 12. The Urban Studies Institute was run out of Phillips Academy, a prestigious private high school in Andover, and the report was a collaborative project by Phillips Academy and Lawrence High School students.

9. Neff, "Facing Up to Our Prejudice."

10. Urban Studies Institute, "Growing Up Hispanic," 15.

11. Neff, "Facing Up to Our Prejudice."

12. Rodríguez-Arroyo, "Never Ending Story of Language Policy in Puerto Rico"; Malavet, *America's Colony*, 113–16.

13. Urban Studies Institute, "Growing Up Hispanic," 13.

14. Ibid., 13, 14.

15. Thomasine Berg, "Lawrence: Can It Survive Its Ethnic Growing Pains? Two Leaders Voice Opinions," *ET*, November 22, 1981.

16. Ibid.

17. Urban Studies Institute, "Growing Up Hispanic," 13.

18. Neff, "Facing Up to Our Prejudice."

19. Kathie Neff, "Family Offers Window on Hispanic Life," *ET*, April 23, 1984.

20. Neff, "Facing Up to Our Prejudice."

21. Ibid.

22. Ibid.

23. Grosfoguel calls this the "African Americanization" of Puerto Ricans and then the "Puertoricanization" of Dominicans; see Grosfoguel, *Colonial Subjects*, 151. For the racialization of Puerto Ricans and Dominicans more broadly, see Candelario, *Black behind the Ears*; Itzigsohn, *Encountering American Faultlines*; Thomas, *Puerto Rican Citizen*; and Jiménez Román and Flores, *Afro-Latin@ Reader*. For how urban Chicanos often shared a similar stigma, see Brown, *Gang Nation*, and Suro, *Strangers among Us*. For more on the "culture of poverty" as the discourse was developed vis-à-vis Puerto Ricans, see Lewis, *La Vida*. For the broader stigmatization of urban communities of color during the crisis era, see Katz, *"Underclass" Debate*; Moore and Pinderhughes, *In the Barrios*; and Macek, *Urban Nightmares*.

24. Neff, "Facing Up to Our Prejudice."

25. Many of these condemnations were common early in the twentieth century as well, as European immigrants were blamed for the very slum conditions they were forced to endure. See Watson, *Bread and Roses*.

26. Garcia interview.

27. "Sound Off," *ET*, August 19, 1984.

28. Flores, *From Bomba to Hip-Hop*; Rivera, *New York Ricans from the Hip Hop Zone*.

29. Urban Studies Institute, "Growing Up Hispanic," 15.

30. Melendez interview by the author.

31. "Callahan: His Insensitive Behavior Insults the Whole City," *ET*, undated clipping, likely March 1980, LHC.

32. Thomasine Berg, "Lawrence: Can It Survive Its Ethnic Growing Pains? Two Leaders Voice Opinions," *ET*, November 22, 1981.

33. Marjory Sherman and Joe Sciacca, "Lawrence Gangs No 'Warriors,'" *ET*, April 22, 1979.

34. Photo by Rose Lewis, *ET*, April 22, 1979.

35. For excellent accounts of this desegregation process in the urban North, see Wolcott, *Race, Riots, and Roller Coasters*, and Biondi, *To Stand and Fight*.

36. Spindler interview.

37. *ET* photo and caption, August 3, 1971.

38. Bill Stetson, "I'll Sell the Shop—Green," *ET*, August 4, 1971. See also "Sign Cost Owner $200 and an Apology," *ET*, September 14, 1971.

39. Jack Wark, "Juanita's Family Worries: Maybe Leaving Puerto Rico Was Wrong," *ET*, December 7, 1970.

40. Ibid.

41. For studies of how movements, such as the Civil Rights movement, that often become associated with a single leader were truly the result of deeper grassroots efforts, see Payne, *I've Got the Light of Freedom*, and Ransby, *Ella Baker and the Black Freedom Movement*.

42. Melendez interview by the author.

43. Ibid.

44. *United States Census*, 1970.

45. Melendez interview by Margaret Hart.

46. Ibid.

47. Melendez interview by the author.

48. Ibid.

49. Ibid.; Melendez interview by Margaret Hart.

50. Lamond interview.

51. Mohl, "International Institute Movement."

52. The International Institute of Greater Lawrence has donated some of its records to the Lawrence History Center, but they are currently unprocessed.

53. For more on the War on Poverty, see Orleck, *Storming Caesars Palace*.

54. Melendez interview by the author; Melendez interview by Margaret Hart.

55. Melendez interview by the author.

56. Melendez interview by Margaret Hart.

57. Melendez interview and translation by the author, 2010.

58. Ibid.

59. Lamond interview; Jack Wark, "Accused's Testimony Translated for the Court by His Accuser," *ET*, August 4, 1970.

60. "Confrontation—Right to a Translator."

61. Jack Wark, "City and Spanish Rub Each Other," *ET*, December 10, 1970.

62. Melendez interview and translation by the author, 2010.

63. "Survey Questionnaires of Hispanics Living in the Downtown Areas Affected by Urban Renewal (Lawrence, Mass.) circa 1968," Urban Renewal and Redevelopment Collection, LHC.

64. Greater Lawrence Family Health Center website, http://glfhc.org/site/about-glfhc/glfhc-history and http://glfhc.org/site/about-glfhc (accessed January 9, 2014, and June 24, 2016).

65. Melendez interview and translation by the author, 2010.

66. Hospitals may provide telephone interpreters, but only in instances where they could not have reasonably foreseen a need to have an interpreter on call for a given language. See Massachusetts General Laws, Chapter 111, Section 25J. See also, Chen, Youdelman, and Brooks, "Legal Framework for Language Access."

67. Hernández and Jacobs, "Beyond Homeland Politics," 289.

68. For an excellent study of Latino claims on public space, see Ramos-Zayas, *National Performances*.

69. Melendez interview and translation by the author, 2010.

70. O'Neill interview.

71. Semana Hispana programs, LPL. Of course, not all Latinos speak Spanish, but it was nonetheless often invoked as a shared aspect of Latino identity.

72. Melendez interview and translation by the author, 2010.

73. Hernández and Jacobs, "Beyond Homeland Politics."

74. Joe Sciacca, "Redevelopment Target Is Lawrence's 'Last Frontier,'" ET, November 7, 1982, clipping, ICCHC.

75. Darlene Sordillo, "Questions over Development of 7 Acres Spark Tug-of-War among Lawrence Leaders," BG, undated clipping, ICCHC.

76. Mary Beth Donovan, "Low-Income Housing Limit to Be Asked," ET, November 8, 1983, clipping, ICCHC.

77. Darlene Sordillo, "Questions over Development of 7 Acres Spark Tug-of-War among Lawrence Leaders," BG, undated clipping, ICCHC.

78. Undated letter from "Clergy of Hispanic Churches" to "Mayor-elect John Buckley," ICCHC.

79. Letter from Nicholas Rizzo, on behalf of Lawrence Strategy, Inc. to Lawrence Redevelopment Authority, August 26, 1983, ICCHC.

80. Draft of proposed class-action lawsuit proposed by Immigrant City Community Housing Corporation, ICCHC.

81. Letter from Gaston Snow & Ely Bartlett, the law firm representing Immigrant City Community Housing Corporation, to David Dronsick of the Executive Office of Communities and Development, December 9, 1983, ICCHC.

82. Draft of proposed class-action lawsuit proposed by Immigrant City Community Housing Corporation, ICCHC.

83. Annemargaret Connolly, "Mayor, Council Score Victory as Low Income Homes Banned," ET, August 1, 1984, clipping, ICCHC.

84. Hyatt interview.

85. Melendez interview by the author.

86. Russell Contreras, "Melendez Won't Run for Mayor," BG, March 27, 2008.

Chapter 4

1. Sciacca, "Dusk-to-Dawn Curfew in Lawrence."

2. Kathie Neff, "Why Lawrence? Why This Neighborhood? Why Now?," ET, August 12, 1984.

3. Commission report quoted in Teaford, Metropolitan Revolution, 142–46; Woodard, "It's Nation Time in NewArk"; Isenberg, Downtown America; Abu-Lughod, Race, Space, and Riots; Mumford, Newark.

4. For an account of the Miami riot in 1980, see Portes and Stepick, City on the Edge, 46–50.

5. Sam Allis, "Racial Unrest: An Eye for an Eye," Time, September 9, 1991; Valle and Torres, Latino Metropolis, 45–66. Anna Deavere Smith's dramatizations of the multiple perspectives in both riots are evocative: Fires in the Mirror and Twilight.

6. Carter, "Hispanic Rioting during the Civil Rights Era." For an interesting discussion of this discourse on Latino political docility, see Lee, Building a Latino Civil Rights Movement, 211–48.

7. Yohel Camayd-Freixas, MIT professor of urban studies, coordinator of the post-riot "Hispanics in Lawrence Symposium" series sponsored by the Department of Social Services, quoted in Duran, "1984 Riots," 43.

8. Valle and Torres, *Latino Metropolis*, 45–66; Snyder, *Crossing Broadway*, 158–95.

9. For an analysis of the Draft Riots, see Jacobson, *Whiteness of a Different Color*, and the second episode of the documentary *New York*. For an account of the East St. Louis riot, see Lumpkins, *American Pogrom*.

10. White southern violence during the Civil Rights movement is amply documented; for a fascinating gendered analysis of it, see McGuire, *At the Dark End of the Street*. See also Tyson, *Radio Free Dixie* and *Blood Done Sign My Name*. For hate crimes against African Americans in New York City during the 1980s, such as the shooting of sixteen-year-old Yusef Hawkins in Bensonhurst, Brooklyn, in 1989, see Chang, *Can't Stop, Won't Stop*, and Pinkney, *Lest We Forget*.

11. Tager, *Boston Riots*, 197.

12. George Sánchez highlighted the nativist violence evident during the Los Angeles riots of 1992, and the FBI noted a pronounced acceleration in anti-Latino hate crimes in the 2000s. In addition, the Southern Poverty Law Center documented dozens of violent attacks against Latinos across the nation between 2004 and 2007. See Sánchez, "Face the Nation," and Mark Potok, "Anti-Latino Hate Crimes Rise for Fourth Year in a Row," October 29, 2008, Southern Poverty Law Center website, https://www.splcenter.org/hatewatch/2008/10/29/anti-latino-hate-crimes-rise-fourth-year-row (accessed June 22, 2016). Colorado assailant quoted in Pabón López, "Essay Examining the Murder of Luis Ramírez." See also *Deputized*; *Who Killed Vincent Chin?*; and Frank H. Wu, "Why Vincent Chin Matters?," *NYT*, June 22, 2012.

13. "Profile of a Changing Neighborhood," *ET*, August 9, 1984.

14. "Poverty, Bigotry—Terrible Legacy of 'Immigrant City,'" *BH*, August 11, 1984.

15. "Shannon Walks through His Troubled District: Communication Lines Need to Be Clear to Ease Tensions," *ET*, August 10, 1984. Much to the dismay of many Latino residents, no formal inquest into the riots was ever made. The sketch here is drawn from interviews, city council records, and TV coverage but relies heavily on newspaper reports, as the local and national newspapers did the most thorough investigations. Unfortunately, however, most papers interviewed far more white witnesses/participants than Latinos.

16. Cullen and Impemba, "New Riot Hits Lawrence."

17. Allan R. Andrews and Gregory Witcher, "Troopers Sent to Quell Violence in Lawrence; Firebombings, Shots Reported in Tower Hill Area," *BG*, August 10, 1984.

18. CBS news clip, August 9, 1984, VTNA.

19. Gwenn Friss, "Police Strategy Included Holding Back for 2 Hours," *ET*, August 9, 1984.

20. David Churbuck, "The Riot Began, Ended in One House: Feud Erupted over Windshield," *ET*, August 9, 1984.

21. Mary Beth Donovan, "Firefighters Felt Scared, Deserted," *ET*, August 9, 1984.

22. David Churbuck, "The Riot Began, Ended in One House: Feud Erupted over Windshield," *ET*, August 9, 1984.

23. Garcia interview.

24. "Those Caught in the Middle Called Everywhere for Help," *ET*, August 9, 1984.

25. Barney Gallagher, "The Riot Began with a Broken Windshield: When the Tactical Force Arrived, the Rioting Had Already Ended," *ET*, August 9, 1984; Gwenn Friss, "Police Strategy Included Holding Back for 2 Hours," *ET*, August 9, 1984.

26. "A Carnival Sideshow Turns Into an Ugly Riot," *ET*, August 10, 1984.

27. "Police Plan to Clear Streets."

28. ABC, CBS, and NBC news clips, August 9–12, 1984, VTNA; Elaine Cushman, with Yadira Betances contributing, "Does TV Coverage Add to Riot Tension?," *ET*, August 10, 1984.

29. "A Carnival Sideshow Turns Into an Ugly Riot," *ET*, August 10, 1984.

30. Elaine Cushman, with Yadira Betances contributing, "Does TV Coverage Add to Riot Tension?," *ET*, August 10, 1984.

31. Allan R. Andrews and Gregory Witcher, "Troopers Sent to Quell Violence in Lawrence; Firebombings, Shots Reported in Tower Hill Area," *BG*, August 10, 1984.

32. "Prayer Service Fails to Stop the Violence," *ET*, August 10, 1984.

33. Cullen and Impemba, "New Riot Hits Lawrence."

34. "A Carnival Sideshow Turns Into an Ugly Riot," *ET*, August 10, 1984.

35. "Massachusetts Town Rocked by Violence for a Second Night," *NYT*, August 10, 1984.

36. ABC, CBS, and NBC news clips, August 10, 1984, VTNA.

37. Garcia interview.

38. Cullen and Impemba, "New Riot Hits Lawrence."

39. "Police Saw Trouble Coming Weeks Ago," *ET*, August 10, 1984.

40. "Police Plan to Clear Streets."

41. Sciacca, "City of Anguish and Outrage."

42. Cullen and Impemba, "New Riot Hits Lawrence."

43. Hernandez, "Lawrence Police Enforce Curfew."

44. *ET*, August 10, 1984.

45. "Ending the Riots in Lawrence," *ET*, August 10, 1984, emphasis in the original.

46. Mary Beth Donovan, "Rumor Control Center Quashes Wild Tales," *ET*, August 11, 1984.

47. "City Wonders: Who's in Charge?," *ET*, August 10, 1984.

48. Lawrence City Council records, August 10, 1984.

49. Hernandez, "Curfew Lifted in Lawrence."

50. Lawrence City Council records, August 10, 1984.

51. "Police Plan to Clear Streets"; Hernandez, "Lawrence Police Enforce Curfew."

52. Lawrence City Council records, August 10, 1984.

53. Sciacca, "Dusk-to-Dawn Curfew in Lawrence." Although Alderman Sullivan pointed out that the state of emergency would allow the mayor to call in the National Guard, Johnson was clear that there were no plans to do so. See "Police Plan to Clear Streets."

54. Sciacca, "Dusk-to-Dawn Curfew in Lawrence."

55. Lawrence City Council records, August 10, 1984.

56. Robert Charest, "Curfew Holds: 27 Arrested but Riot-Torn Area Quieted: Rest of City Unaffected" *ET*, August 11, 1984.

57. Sciacca, "City of Anguish and Outrage."

58. Duran, "1984 Riots," 26.

59. Espada, "*Toque de queda*: Curfew in Lawrence," in *Trumpets from the Islands of Their Eviction*.

60. Sciacca, "City of Anguish and Outrage."

61. Sciacca, "Dusk-to-Dawn Curfew in Lawrence."

62. Ibid.

63. Sciacca, "City of Anguish and Outrage."

64. Sciacca, "Dusk-to-Dawn Curfew in Lawrence."

65. Duran, "1984 Riots," 67.

66. Ibid., 47.

67. Vicente Carbona, "17 Heridos y 50 Detenidos en Disturbios Raciales de Lawrence," *La Semana*, week 33, 1984.

68. Terms used by TV news outlets included "whites" and "Latins" on CBS, August 9, 1984; "white" and "Hispanic" on ABC, August 10, 1984; "Hispanic" and "Anglo" on NBC, August 11, 1984; and even "Hispanic" and "French" on CBS, August 12, 1984, VTNA.

69. John Impemba, "6 Shot as Street Riot Erupts in Lawrence," *BH*, August 9, 1984.

70. Hernandez, "Lawrence Police Enforce Curfew"; ABC news clip, August 10, 1984, VTNA. The paternalism in the view of the riots as a "domestic disturbance" is overwhelming, and it is compounded by the common reference to city officials as "city fathers."

71. Timothy Clifford, "Bishop Preaches Peace in Lawrence," *BH*, August 13, 1984.

72. See nn. 9 and 10 above for analyses of white racial violence, as well as Sugrue, *Origins of the Urban Crisis*, and Abu-Lughod, *Race, Space, and Riots*.

73. Lupo, "Lessons of the Street."

74. Marnie Argersinger, quoted in Marge Sherman, "From Miami to Chicago, the Talk Is of Lawrence," *ET*, August 12, 1984.

75. Lupo, "Lessons of the Street."

76. Marge Sherman, "Will the Rioting Hurt the City's Business Rebirth?," *ET*, August 12, 1984.

77. Duran, "1984 Riots," 68.

78. Ibid., 42.

79. Colin Campbell, "Hispanic Complaint Belittled in Riot-Struck Town," *NYT*, August 12, 1984.

80. Ibid.

81. Lawrence City Council records, August 10, 1984.

82. Robert Charest, "Curfew Holds: 27 Arrested but Riot-Torn Area Quieted: Rest of City Unaffected" *ET*, August 11, 1984.

83. Sciacca, "Dusk-to-Dawn Curfew in Lawrence."

84. Cullen and Impemba, "New Riot Hits Lawrence."

85. Lehman, "Struggle in Lawrence."

86. Duran, "1984 Riots," 64.

87. "Ending the Riots in Lawrence," *ET*, August 10, 1984.

88. Duran, "1984 Riots," 46.

89. Ibid., 64, 74.

90. Cullen and Impemba, "New Riot Hits Lawrence."

91. "A Tense City Explodes in Violence," *BH*, August 10, 1984. The phrase "lawless punks" is not a direct quote from Jim John; the quotation marks indicate the words the article's author used to paraphrase John.

92. "Profile of a Changing Neighborhood," *ET*, August 9, 1984. The phrase "changing complexion" is not a direct quote from Carmen Ralph; the quotation marks indicate the words the article's author used to paraphrase Ralph and other neighborhood residents.

93. "Sound Off Special," *ET*, August 10, 1984. These comments were anonymous, so there is no way to know whether the speaker was white (or even lived in Lawrence), but they strongly echo the narrative of many white Lawrencians after the riots.

94. "A Tense City Explodes in Violence," *BH*, August 10, 1984.

95. "Cries of Tiny Victim Haunt Tot's Mother," *BH*, August 11, 1984.

96. Urban Studies Institute, "Growing Up Hispanic," 13.

97. Eugene Declercq, "While Suburbs Duck, Lawrence Flounders: Riot Wasn't Just Urban Problem," *ET*, August 12, 1984, clipping in Mayor Buckley scrapbooks, LHC.

98. Ibid.

99. Ibid.

100. Kaufman, "Hostility Boils Over"; "Confrontation in Lawrence," *BG*, August 11, 1984.

101. For more on post–Civil Rights racial discourse, see Bonilla-Silva, *Racism without Racists*.

102. "Profile of a Changing Neighborhood," *ET*, August 9, 1984.

103. "Poverty, Bigotry—Terrible Legacy of 'Immigrant City,'" *BH*, August 11, 1984.

104. Kaufman, "Hostility Boils Over."

105. Roediger, *Working toward Whiteness*; Foner, *From Ellis Island to JFK*; Spickard, *Almost All Aliens*.

106. Lehman, "Struggle in Lawrence."

107. Campbell, "Two Nights of Rioting."

108. Cullen and Impemba, "New Riot Hits Lawrence."

109. Kaufman, "Hostility Boils Over."

110. Campbell, "Two Nights of Rioting."

111. Katz, *Undeserving Poor*. For a fuller discussion of welfare reform in Lawrence, see Chapter 6.

112. ABC news clip, August 10, 1984, VTNA.

113. NBC news clip, August 10, 1984, VTNA.

114. "A Tense City Explodes in Violence," *BH*, August 10, 1984.

115. Sciacca, "Dusk-to-Dawn Curfew in Lawrence."

116. Kaufman, "Hostility Boils Over."

117. CBS news clip, August 10, 1984, VTNA.

118. "Shannon Walks through His Troubled District: Communication Lines Need to Be Clear to Ease Tensions," *ET*, August 10, 1984.

119. Duran, "1984 Riots," 31, 32.

120. Gary Gerstle has offered a compelling history of French Canadians in Woonsocket, including their investment in their ethnic identity, and the strategic adoption of "Americanism" as a labor strategy in the 1930s. It is unfortunate that the riot coverage offers little insight into the French Canadian community in the neighborhood so that a more detailed exploration of the claim to Americanism by French Canadian rioters is not possible. See Gerstle, *Working-class Americanism*.

121. NBC news clip, August 11, 1984, VTNA.

122. Duran, "1984 Riots," 31, 32, already translated from Spanish in thesis.

123. Ibid., 90, 91.

124. ABC news clip, August 10, 1984, VTNA.

125. Duran, "1984 Riots," 31, 32.

126. Ibid., 74.

127. "Los Disturbios Raciales de Lawrence," *La Semana*, week 33, 1984.

128. Duran, "1984 Riots," 46.

129. Ibid., 91.

130. Sciacca, "Dusk-to-Dawn Curfew in Lawrence."

131. Duran, "1984 Riots," 24.

132. Ibid., 90, 91.

133. Campbell, "Two Nights of Rioting."

134. Sciacca, "City of Anguish and Outrage."

135. Campbell, "Two Nights of Rioting."

136. Sciacca, "City of Anguish and Outrage."

137. "Cries of Tiny Victim Haunt Tot's Mother," *BH*, August 11, 1984.

138. Ibid. Ocasio's story highlights a gendered element of the struggle to claim the right to live in Lawrence safely. The rioters seem to have been overwhelmingly male, while many of those claiming that the riots were a terrorizing force were female. For some of the city's female residents, particularly those with children, the riots were simply another example of the racist violence they faced in Lawrence. This gendered view of the riots as a terrorizing force, rather than as a chance to protest, should not preclude the possibility that some women participated in the Lawrence riots. Although all of those arrested were men, Marilynn Johnson has noted that arrest records generally substantially underestimate the participation of female rioters. Whether white or Latina women involved themselves in the actual fighting is unknown, but many were at least semi-involved as bystanders, adding strength to the crowds. In addition, in Ocasio's account of the initial conflict that precipitated the riots, she was *with* the group of young Latinos who went to confront John Ball and the others over the broken window; she was not passively being avenged. See Johnson, "Gender, Race, and Rumors."

139. Espada, "*Toque de queda*: Curfew in Lawrence," in *Trumpets from the Islands of Their Eviction*.

140. Reported injuries ranged from fifteen to "dozens." See Hernandez, "Curfew Lifted in Lawrence," and Cullen and Impemba, "New Riot Hits Lawrence."

Chapter 5

1. See repeated complaints throughout the records of the U.S. Department of Justice Community Relations Service, Significant Case Files, 1974–1994, NARA-NE.

2. "Los Disturbios Raciales de Lawrence," *La Semana*, week 33, 1984.

3. Quoted in "Prayer Service Fails to Stop the Violence," *ET*, August 10, 1984. See also Campbell, "Two Nights of Rioting"; "Confrontation in Lawrence," *BG*, August 11, 1984.

4. Quoted in Hernandez, "Curfew Lifted in Lawrence."

5. Duran, "1984 Riots," 26.

6. Urban Studies Institute, "Growing Up Hispanic," 28.

7. Lupo, "Lessons of the Street."

8. Lehman, "Struggle in Lawrence."

9. Michael Matza, "Down in the Valley: New Immigrants, Same Old Story," *Boston Phoenix*, August 21, 1984.

10. Lehman, "Struggle in Lawrence."

11. Duran, "1984 Riots," 27.

12. Diamond, *Mean Streets*.

13. Duran, "1984 Riots," 19–27.

14. Muriel Cohen, "Lawrence Schools Face a Series of Problems, Too," *BG*, August 20, 1984.

15. Lehman, "Struggle in Lawrence."

16. Ibid.

17. Muriel Cohen, "Lawrence Schools Face a Series of Problems, Too," *BG*, August 20, 1984.

18. Massachusetts Commission on Hispanic Affairs, "Hispanics in Massachusetts," 18.

19. Duran, "1984 Riots," 24.

20. Ibid., 22.

21. Ibid., 24.

22. "Police Plan to Clear Streets."

23. NBC news clip, August 9, 1984, VTNA.

24. Chinlund and Richard, "Lawrence's Charter for Trouble." As Victoria Wolcott has noted, many of the 1960s-era urban uprisings were also partially a protest against the lack of recreational opportunities available in communities of color as a result of urban disinvestment. See Wolcott, *Race, Riots, and Roller Coasters*.

25. Allan R. Andrews and Gregory Witcher, "Troopers Sent to Quell Violence in Lawrence; Firebombings, Shots Reported in Tower Hill Area," *BG*, August 10, 1984.

26. Mary Beth Donovan, "Firefighters Felt Scared, Deserted," *ET*, August 9, 1984.

27. Ibid.

28. Chinlund and Richard, "Lawrence's Charter for Trouble."

29. Ibid.

30. Ibid.

31. Duran, "1984 Riots," 42.

32. Chinlund and Richard, "Lawrence's Charter for Trouble."

33. Lupo, "Lessons of the Street."

34. Chinlund and Richard, "Lawrence's Charter for Trouble."

35. "Poverty, Bigotry—Terrible Legacy of 'Immigrant City,'" *BH*, August 11, 1984.

36. Michael Matza, "Down in the Valley: New Immigrants, Same Old Story," *Boston Phoenix*, August 21, 1984.

37. Representative of MCAD quoted in ibid.

38. Chinlund and Richard, "Lawrence's Charter for Trouble."

39. Of course, some of this decline in the white population would be due to death as well. See *United States Census*, 1980, 1990, 2000.

40. Garcia interview.

41. Andrew Torchia, "Lawrence: 1 Year Later," *BG*, August 9, 1985.

42. Garcia interview.

43. Duran, "1984 Riots," 28.

44. Pérez, *Near Northwest Side Story*, 71–79.

45. "Poverty, Bigotry—Terrible Legacy of 'Immigrant City,'" *BH*, August 11, 1984.

46. Quoted in Lindeke, "Latino Political Succession and Incorporation," 75. Lindeke notes that the mayor made these comments in "a widely circulated letter to the editor." I was not able to find the original letter, so it is possible the exact quote is inaccurate; but the coded anti-Latino spirit of the mayor's campaign is supported by the commentary that follows. See also Schinto, *Huddle Fever*, 277.

47. R. S. Kindleberger, "Mayoral Candidates Wage a Bitter Contest in Lawrence," *BG*, October 4, 1985.

48. Susan Forrest, "Hispanics Join Fraud Fight," *ET*, February 7, 1989.

49. Hohler, "5 Years after Riots."

50. Borges-Méndez, "Urban and Regional Restructuring."

51. Hernandez, "Lawrence Police Enforce Curfew."

52. Timothy Clifford, "Bishop Preaches Peace in Lawrence," *BH*, August 13, 1984.

53. Lawrence City Council records, August 10–14, 1984. Although the alliance was made up of both white and Latino residents of the city, it was profoundly geared toward supporting and representing the needs of the Latino community. Two of the main leaders of the group, Isabel Melendez and Nunzio DiMarca, were long-term organizers in the Latino community.

54. Borges-Méndez, "Urban and Regional Restructuring."

55. Sciacca, "Dusk-to-Dawn Curfew in Lawrence."

56. Kenneth J. Cooper, "Dispute Erupts over Lawrence Riot Aid; Legislator Charges Leadership Stonewalling," *BG*, December 12, 1984.

57. U.S. Census data from the State of the Cities Data System, http://socds.huduser.org (accessed throughout 2009 and 2010).

58. See Kruse and Sugrue, *New Suburban History*; Kruse, *White Flight*; and Gainsborough, *Fenced Off*.

59. Quoted in Duran, "1984 Riots," 50.

60. Duran, "1984 Riots," 49–53; *Massachusetts Session Laws*, Acts 1984, Chapter 429, "An Act Providing Funds for Emergency Remedial Measures to Prevent Civil Disorders in the City of Lawrence," and its accompanying legislative packet, and Chapter 435, "An Act Relative to the Alleviation of the Financial Burden Imposed on the City of Lawrence by the Civil Disturbances of Nineteen Hundred and Eighty Four," MSA.

61. Duran, "1984 Riots," 53–56; *Massachusetts Session Laws*, Acts 1984, Chapter 429, "An Act Providing Funds for Emergency Remedial Measures to Prevent Civil Disorders in the City of Lawrence," and its accompanying legislative packet, and Chapter 435, "An Act Relative to the Alleviation of the Financial Burden Imposed on the City of Lawrence by the Civil Disturbances of Nineteen Hundred and Eighty Four," MSA.

62. Duran, "1984 Riots," 55, 56.

63. NBC news clip, August 11, 1984, VTNA.

64. Duran, "1984 Riots," 36.

65. Watson, *Bread and Roses*; Cameron, *Radicals of the Worst Sort*.

66. Duran, "1984 Riots," 102–7. Inquilinos Boricuas en Acción was a Puerto Rican community organization that had been pivotal in protests in Boston's South End in 1969 and that had successfully campaigned for community-controlled public housing in the Villa Victoria project. See Moreno de Toro, "Oral History of the Puerto Rican Socialist Party in Boston," and Small, *Villa Victoria*.

67. Centro Panamericano was a direct recipient of a number of state contracts; see Santiago interview. It is very possible that the early success of the organization was due in part to the Gateway Cities program.

68. Santiago interview.

69. U.S. Census data from the State of the Cities Data System, http://socds.huduser .org (accessed throughout 2009 and 2010).

70. Lindeke, "Latino Political Succession and Incorporation."

71. Duran, "1984 Riots," 25.

72. DOJ-CRS, Significant Case Files, 1974–1994, boxes 2:9 and 2:24, NARA-NE.

73. Tour of the city's public housing and conversation with Don O'Neill, director of the Lawrence Housing Authority from the mid-1980s to the present, October 2013; DOJ-CRS, Significant Case Files, 1974–1994, box 2:24, NARA-NE.

74. Andrew Blake, "Immigrants Angered, Saddened by Cuts in Assistance Programs," *BG*, August 27, 1989; "Aid to Be Sought for Gateway Cities," *BG*, May 8, 1986.

75. Although CRS was clear that this was an internal document and that city leaders had not known of this designation, the agency also noted that it had already been working with some city officials and believed these warning signs should have been recognizable to city leaders. See Hernandez, "Curfew Lifted in Lawrence."

76. "US Official Says Town Had Clues to Unrest," *NYT*, August 13, 1984.

77. Hohler, "5 Years after Riots."

78. DOJ-CRS, Significant Case Files, 1974–1994, box 2:7, NARA-NE.

79. "Not Funny," clipping from the *ET* in DOJ-CRS, Significant Case Files, 1974–1994, box 2:29, NARA-NE.

80. DOJ-CRS, Significant Case Files, 1974–1994, box 2:30, NARA-NE.

81. Plaintiff proposal for case management order, *United States of America v. City of Lawrence, Massachusetts*, U.S. District Court, Massachusetts, Case No. 98 CV 12256 (1998).

82. The U.S. Department of Justice provides excellent overviews of the relevant parts of the Voting Rights Act online. See "Section 203 of the Voting Rights Act" and "Section 2 of the Voting Rights Act," http://www.justice.gov/crt/about/vot/ sec_203/203_brochure.php and http://www.justice.gov/crt/about/vot/sec_2/about_ sec2.php (accessed March 20, 2014).

83. Complaint, *United States of America v. City of Lawrence, Massachusetts*, U.S. District Court, Massachusetts, Case No. 98 CV 12256 (1998).

84. Lindeke, "Latino Political Succession and Incorporation," 90.

85. Marcos Devers, quoted in Hernández and Jacobs, "Beyond Homeland Politics," 291.

86. Zachary R. Dowdy, "Lawrence Hit with U.S. Suit on Voter Rights; Lack of Access for Hispanics Alleged," *BG*, November 6, 1998.

87. Quoted in Jordana Hart, "Lawrence Vote Process Defended; Mayor Says Suit Only about Race, while Latinos Cite Struggle to Change Status Quo," *BG*, November 7, 1998.

88. Settlement Agreement, *United States of America v. City of Lawrence, Massachusetts*, U.S. District Court, Massachusetts, Case No. 98 CV 12256 (1998).

89. Lupo, "Lessons of the Street."

90. DOJ-CRS, Significant Case Files, 1974–1994, box 3:1, NARA-NE.

91. Lupo, "Lessons of the Street."

92. Hohler, "5 Years after Riots."

Chapter 6

1. For a vivid depiction of arson in the Bronx and its impact on Puerto Ricans, see the documentary video *From Mambo to Hip Hop*. See also Mahler, *Ladies and Gentlemen, the Bronx Is Burning*. For an illustrative fictional account of arson in New York City, see Quiñonez, *Chango's Fire*.

2. Katherine Newman and Chauncy Lennon conducted a study in Central Harlem in 1993, for example, and found that even fast food restaurants generally had fourteen applicants for each available position; see Newman and Lennon, "Job Ghetto." For more on racialized disinvestment and concentrated poverty in U.S. cities in the 1980s and early 1990s, as well as analysis of the media and scholarly portrayals of the inner city, see Wilson, *When Work Disappears* and *Truly Disadvantaged*; Katz, *"Underclass" Debate*; Moore and Pinderhughes, *In the Barrios*; Massey and Denton, *American Apartheid*; and Macek, *Urban Nightmares*.

3. Carnegie Foundation, *Imperiled Generation*, xi. For an evocative depiction of the crisis in urban education, see Kozol, *Savage Inequalities*.

4. The term "tale of two cities" to describe the income inequality evident in contemporary cities is often associated with New York City mayor Bill de Blasio. See, for example, his "State of the City" address in 2015, available from *NYT*, February 3, 2015. For broader accounts of gentrification and reinvestment in U.S. cities, see Bluestone and Stevenson, *Boston Renaissance*; Zukin, *Naked City*; Smith, *New Urban Frontier*; Teaford, *Metropolitan Revolution*; Pérez, *Near Northwest Side Story*; Dávila, *Barrio Dreams*; and Martinez, *Power at the Roots*.

5. See Kozol, *Savage Inequalities*, for a depiction of urban crisis in East St. Louis, and for Camden, see Gillette, *Camden after the Fall*.

6. Quoted in Schinto, *Huddle Fever*, 36.

7. Meléndez, "Latino Poverty and Economic Development." For general information on the "Massachusetts Miracle," see Lampe, *Massachusetts Miracle*, and Tager, "Massachusetts Miracle." In 1990, more than half of Massachusetts's Latinos were Puerto Rican, and Dominicans were the next-largest group. See Jones, "Latinos in Massachusetts."

8. Massachusetts Hispanic-American Advisory Commission, "Final Report."

9. Ibid.

10. Meléndez, "Latino Poverty and Economic Development."

11. Stevenson's definition of the region is broader than mine, including the entire Lower Merrimack Valley. See Stevenson, "Spatial Analysis of Socioeconomic and Demographic Change."

12. Urban Studies Institute, "Family Housing Crisis." There were small parts of Methuen that were somewhat more accessible to Lawrence Latinos, as can be seen in the map of Latino settlement (map 2) in Chapter 2. Inflation adjustments from the Bureau of Labor Statistics inflation calculator, available online at http://data.bls.gov/cgi-bin/cpicalc.pl.

13. Andrew Dabilis, "Housing Study an Education in Itself," *BG*, July 10, 1989.

14. Urban Studies Institute, "Family Housing Crisis."

15. *United States Census*, 1980 and 2000.

16. Joe Heaney, "Gang-Related Arson Plagues City," *BH*, August 9, 1994.

17. Jill Harmacinski, "Lawrence Adopts New Law to Protect Neighborhoods from Blight," *ET*, March 6, 2008.

18. "In Lawrence, Hope Going up in Smoke."

19. "Lawrence Drug Gangs Add Arson to Arsenals," *BG*, April 20, 1992.

20. "Lawrence Residents Unite to Battle Arson," *BH*, November 2, 1992.

21. "In Lawrence, Hope Going up in Smoke."

22. "Lawrence Drug Gangs Add Arson to Arsenals," *BG*, April 20, 1992.

23. "Lawrence Residents Unite to Battle Arson," *BH*, November 2, 1992; Uncle Dudley, "City That Wouldn't Die," *BG*, December 11, 1960, reprint in LPL.

24. "In Lawrence, Hope Going up in Smoke."

25. Jacobs, "Fires in Lawrence Evoke Fear."

26. Ibid.

27. "Lawrence Declares State of Emergency and Seeks Help from National Guard," *BH*, September 25, 1992.

28. Ibid.

29. Jacobs, "Fires in Lawrence Evoke Fear."

30. The *Boston Globe* used the term "certain elements" to describe wayward Latino residents burning their own neighborhoods, and media and officials often suggested that gangs were mainly responsible for the arson. See ibid.

31. Ibid.

32. "N.H. Men Indicted on Arson Charges," *BG*, October 30, 1993. As Jeanne Schinto noted, "A typical list of 'nuisance properties' from the local paper, on the other hand, shows no owners in Lawrence. Instead, the roll call features a list of people with addresses in Windham, New Hampshire; Salem, New Hampshire; Chester, New Hampshire; Palm Beach, Florida; and Norristown, Pennsylvania" (Schinto, *Huddle Fever*, 220, 221).

33. "In Lawrence, Hope Going up in Smoke."

34. "Auto Insurance Fraud," *BH*, September 28, 1992.

35. "Car Theft a Growth Industry," *BG*, May 19, 1991.

36. DOJ-CRS, Significant Case Files, 1974–1994, box 2:24, NARA-NE.

37. Massachusetts Criminal Justice Training Council, "Management Survey of the Police Department"; DOJ-CRS, Significant Case Files, 1974–1994, box 2:9, NARA-NE.

38. Urban Studies Institute, "Family Housing Crisis."

39. Schinto, *Huddle Fever*, 69, 199, 200.

40. Paula Porten and Tom Duggan, "The Revival of Lawrence, Massachusetts," *Valley Patriot*, March 2006, http://www.tommyduggan.com/VP0308061awrence.html (accessed June 29, 2007).

41. Schinto, *Huddle Fever*, 298.

42. I am using the term "welfare" in a broad sense to include government provision of funds and services to ameliorate or mitigate poverty, regardless of whether the government provides these funds/services directly or through grants to a community-based organization. I am not including in this discussion the array of social insurance programs or government subsidies aimed at the middle class, not because they were unimportant, but because they were not under attack in the context of welfare reform.

43. City of Lawrence, "1985–1986 Budget," LPL.

44. Schinto, *Huddle Fever*, 215.

45. Gill, "'Misery Industry.'"

46. Massachusetts League of Community Health Centers, "Community Health Centers as Economic Engines."

47. Gill, "'Misery Industry.'"

48. Susan Forrest, "Welfare Benefits Can Act as Magnet, Studies Say," *ET*, February 25, 1990.

49. Charles Stein, "Lawrence Case Study: A Struggle of the Poor," *BG*, June 24, 1988.

50. Kathie Neff, "Lawrence and Hispanics: A Close-Up Look," *ET*, April 22, 1984.

51. *BG*, August 13, 1989.

52. NBC, August 14, 1989, VTNA.

53. Larrabee, "Community Braces for a Lifestyle Overhaul."

54. President Bill Clinton's promise in his State of the Union address, 1993.

55. Pamela Kathryn Wald has argued that state-level reforms were profoundly influential in shaping PRWORA. Although Massachusetts does not seem to have played as major a role as Wisconsin, Michigan, and New Jersey, the commonwealth's experiment with time limits for welfare was reflected in the national legislation. See Wald, "Bringing Welfare State Theories to the States," 186, 202.

56. Larrabee, "Community Braces for a Lifestyle Overhaul."

57. John Gill, "Welfare Reform to Make City Healthy," *ET*, February 12, 1995.

58. M. Brenda Smith, "Off Welfare and Making Money," *ET*, September 22, 1996.

59. Institute for Women's Policy Research, "Before and after Welfare Reform."

60. For overviews of welfare stereotypes, activism, and reform efforts from the 1960s through the 1990s, see Katz, *In the Shadow of the Poorhouse* and *Undeserving Poor*, and Chappell, *War on Welfare*. For an exploration of racialized welfare provision in an earlier era, see Fox, *Three Worlds of Relief*. For the broader stigmatization of urban communities of color during the crisis era, see Katz, *"Underclass" Debate*; Moore and Pinderhughes, *In the Barrios*; and Macek, *Urban Nightmares*.

61. Quote from David Locke, in John Gill, "Workfare, Boot Camp Plans OK'd," *ET*, June 14, 1991.

62. Gill, "'Misery Industry.'"

63. Susan Forrest, "Welfare Benefits Can Act as Magnet, Studies Say," *ET*, February 25, 1990; Chappell, *War on Welfare*, 70; Wald, "Bringing Welfare State Theories to the States," 89–130. See also Levenstein, "From Innocent Children to Unwanted Migrants and Unwed Moms," for the stigmatization of African Americans as welfare migrants. For a more general exploration of the idea of a "welfare magnet," see Peterson and Rom, *Welfare Magnets*.

64. The third state senator crafting Massachusetts's welfare reform was Therese Murray (D-Plymouth); see John Gill, "Clinton OKs Bay State's Welfare Plan," *ET*, September 4, 1995.

65. "Welfare Fingerprinting Begins," *ET*, April 13, 1996.

66. Gill, "'Misery Industry.'"

67. Larrabee, "Community Braces for a Lifestyle Overhaul."

68. Esther Bornstein, letter to editor, "Go to Work to Give Your Children All They Deserve," *ET*, May 7, 1995.

69. After negotiating with the federal government, the state compromised and allowed the two years to begin only after the recipient's youngest child had reached two years of age. See John Gill, "Clinton OKs Bay State's Welfare Plan," *ET*, September 4, 1995.

70. Larrabee, "Community Braces for a Lifestyle Overhaul."

71. Fix, Capps, and Kaushal, "Immigrants and Welfare"; Gerken, *Model Immigrants and Undesirable Aliens.*

72. Gerken, *Model Immigrants and Undesirable Aliens*, 48.

73. Kruse, *White Flight*; Gainsborough, *Fenced Off.* As both authors note, the 1992 election was the first time that suburban voters outnumbered both urban and rural voters combined. Given the demographic reshuffling of gentrification and suburban diversification, it does not seem that a distinct suburban political agenda has persisted on the national stage into the twenty-first century, although the broader turn toward conservatism evident in the 1970s clearly persists. See Schulman and Zelizer, *Rightward Bound*, and Frum, *How We Got Here.*

74. Evolving conservative and liberal views on welfare are well illustrated in Chappell, *War on Welfare.* For a broader account of the suburban origins of late twentieth-century conservatism, see McGirr, *Suburban Warriors.*

75. Jennings and Santiago, "Welfare Reform and 'Welfare to Work' as Non-Sequitur," 24.

76. For a larger study of the role of nativism and anti-immigrant sentiment in welfare reform, see Gerken, *Model Immigrants and Undesirable Aliens.* Also, for a powerful depiction of efforts to condemn another immigrant group for their welfare "abuse" (in this case Hmong refugees), see Fadiman, *Spirit Catches You and You Fall Down.*

77. Schinto, *Huddle Fever*, 259.

78. DOJ-CRS, Significant Case Files, 1974–1994, box 2:9, NARA-NE.

79. Edward Hardy, "Hispanic Enrollment Is Up This Year at Parochial Schools: Two Thirds Live in Lawrence," *ET*, December 3, 1984; "Parents Involved in Their Children's Schools," *ET*, September 22, 1992.

80. Massachusetts Commission on Hispanic Affairs, "Hispanics in Massachusetts."

81. Kozol, *Savage Inequalities*, 65.

82. Ibid., 5.

83. Jack Dougherty has demonstrated that the pursuit of superior schools has not just been a result of intrametropolitan inequality but indeed has helped to drive it. See Dougherty, "On the Line."

84. Clotfelter, *After Brown*, 56.

85. Ibid.

86. Judge Stephen Roth, quoted in Baugh, *Detroit School Busing Case*, 135.

87. Clotfelter, *After Brown.*

88. Theoharis, "'We Saved the City.'" See also Lukas, *Common Ground.*

89. Louise Day Hicks quoted in Teaford, *Metropolitan Revolution*, 152.

90. Katharine Q. Seelye, "4 Decades after Clashes, Boston Again Debates School Busing," *NYT*, October 4, 2012.

91. Sracic, San Antonio v. Rodriguez *and the Pursuit of Equal Education.*

92. Ibid.

93. Kozol, *Savage Inequalities*, 7.

94. Massachusetts Department of Education, "Report on the Condition of the Public Schools."

95. Ibid.

96. "Lawrence High School" clip from the "Ten O'Clock News," September 12, 1989, tape #6753, access code: 67486, WGBH archives, Boston.

97. Lindeke, "Latino Political Succession and Incorporation," 76.

98. "Lawrence High School" clip from the "Ten O'Clock News," September 12, 1989, tape #6753, access code: 67486, WGBH archives, Boston.

99. "Rollins School in Lawrence" clip from the "Ten O'Clock News," March 8, 1990, tape #7130, access code: 242305, WGBH archives, Boston.

100. Massachusetts Department of Education, "Report on the Condition of the Public Schools."

101. Ibid.

102. Unnamed administrator quoted in Duran, "1984 Riots," 21.

103. Massachusetts Department of Education, "Report on the Condition of the Public Schools."

104. Art Hagopian, "City-Town School Is in Doubt," *ET*, June 22, 1988.

105. "Andover Pulls Out of Joint School Plan," *Education Week*, August 3, 1988. For a discussion of METCO, the small-scale voluntary desegregation program that bussed Boston African American students to suburban schools, see Geismer, *Don't Blame Us*.

106. Massachusetts Department of Education, "Report on the Condition of the Public Schools."

107. For an overview of these school-finance lawsuits, see Bosworth, *Courts as Catalysts*. Another interesting, although highly critical, overview is Lindseth, "Legal Backdrop to Adequacy."

108. Plaintiff's reply brief in *McDuffy v. Secretary of the Executive Office of Education,* Massachusetts Supreme Judicial Court (1993).

109. States generally followed federal precedent in rejecting the principle of equal protection in school finance cases. An important exception to this is California's *Serrano v. Priest* (1971, 1977). See Bosworth, *Courts as Catalysts*.

110. Plaintiff's reply brief in *McDuffy v. Secretary of the Executive Office of Education,* Massachusetts Supreme Judicial Court (1993).

111. Amicus brief in *McDuffy v. Secretary of the Executive Office of Education,* Massachusetts Supreme Judicial Court (1993).

112. Video footage of House debates over the Massachusetts Education Reform Act, January 29, 1993, SLM.

113. Lindseth, "Legal Backdrop to Adequacy," 72.

114. Massachusetts State Auditor, "State Auditor's Report on Certain Activities of the Lawrence Public School System: July 1, 1993 through March 31, 1997," 1997, SLM.

115. It should be noted that some property-poor districts were back in court in the early 2000s, charging the state with still failing to provide adequate school funding, in *Hancock v. Commissioner of Education* (2005), although this suit was unsuccessful. See Stanczyk, "Public School Finance Litigation in New York and Massachusetts."

116. For a thorough overview of MERA and its implementation, see McDermott, "Incentives, Capacity, and Implementation"; University of Massachusetts Amherst School of Education, "Education Reform"; Anthony and Rossman, "Massachusetts Education Reform Act"; and video footage of House debates over the Massachusetts

Education Reform Act, January 26, 29, and June 8, 1993, SLM. The full text of MERA as well as the bill's legislative history is also archived at the SLM.

117. Susan Bowles, "School Accountability," in University of Massachusetts Amherst School of Education, "Education Reform," 24.

118. Like state-level welfare reform, state-level education reform also played a role in shaping federal legislation. The 2001 No Child Left Behind Act similarly tied federal education funding to standards-based reform. Massachusetts had been among the first states to adopt these now prevalent reforms. See McDermott, "Incentives, Capacity, and Implementation."

119. Governor's signing statement, MERA legislative packet, MSA.

120. Yvonne Abraham and Caroline Louise Cole, "Lawrence Heeds Neighbors on Housing," *BG*, March 7, 1999.

121. Lindeke, "Latino Political Succession and Incorporation," 76.

122. The reference to "first-class" tenants is from Walsh and Associates, "Action Plan Lawrence," 36.

123. See, for example, Hohler, "5 Years after Riots."

Chapter 7

1. Urban Dictionary website, http://www.urbandictionary.com/define.php?term=lawtown (accessed February 13, 2010).

2. Hernández and Rivera-Batiz, "Dominicans in the United States." Note that the authors of this report adjusted for the 2000 census undercounting of Dominicans.

3. *United States Census*, 2010. The census lists 1.8 percent of the population as Vietnamese or "other" Asian, and it is likely that Cambodians make up a substantial part of the latter. See Rambach and But, *Under the Sugar Palm Trees*.

4. Jorge Santiago and James Jennings found in 2000 that 83 percent of the Latino-owned businesses they surveyed were owned by Dominicans, and Andrea Ryan concluded in 2007 that 95 percent of Latino-owned businesses in Lawrence were Dominican owned. See Santiago and Jennings, "Latino Business Community," and Ryan, "Not My Brother's Keeper," 208.

5. *United States Census*, 1980, 1990, 2000.

6. Ibid., 1990.

7. Boburg, "U.S. Jobs Pay for American Dream." For a fuller discussion of Dominican economics and complete citations, see Chapter 2 of this volume.

8. Melendez interview by Margaret Hart.

9. Charles Stein, "Lawrence Case Study: A Struggle of the Poor," *BG*, June 24, 1988.

10. Silverio interview.

11. Yadira Betances, "Trailblazing Dominican Woman Receives Award," *ET*, October 8, 2005.

12. Hilda Hartnett, "For Latinos, a Dynamic Time," *ET*, September 20, 1992.

13. Melendez interview and translation by the author, 2010.

14. Ibid.

15. Ibid.

16. Lawrence Garcia, quoted in Hilda Hartnett, "Should It Be Called Latino or Hispanic?," *ET*, September 20, 1992.

17. Urban Studies Institute, "Family Housing Crisis."

18. Díaz interview.

19. Ibid.

20. Urban Studies Institute, "Family Housing Crisis."

21. Andors, "City and Island," 48.

22. Jones, "Latinos in Lawrence."

23. Maracayo interview.

24. For studies of gentrification in New York City and its impact on Latinos, see Dávila, *Barrio Dreams*, and Martinez, *Power at the Roots*. For Chicago, see Pérez, *Near Northwest Side Story*.

25. The study used IPUMS (Integrated Public Use Microdata Series) data to examine characteristics of Puerto Ricans who in 2000 said they had been living in New York City in 1995. See Marzán, Torres, and Luecke, "Puerto Rican Outmigration from New York City."

26. Ibid.

27. Itzigsohn, *Encountering American Faultlines*, 50–63.

28. Ibid.

29. Ibid.

30. For a fuller account of migration between Lawrence and other places in the United States, see Barber, "Latino Migration and the New Global Cities," 130–35. Oddly, I found very few accounts of movement between Lawrence and Boston. Peggy Levitt's superb exploration of Dominicans in Boston notes that most were from Miraflores on the south coast of the island, far from the Cibao region that was home to most Lawrence Dominicans. See Levitt, *Transnational Villagers*.

31. Kathie Neff, "Torn between Two Worlds," *ET*, April 24, 1984.

32. Ibid.

33. Levitt, *Transnational Villagers*, 111.

34. "Dominican Student Unhappy with Education, Food, Weather," *ET*, April 30, 1979.

35. Kathie Neff, "A Hispanic Middle Class Is Emerging," *ET*, April 25, 1984.

36. Andors, "City and Island," 77.

37. Pichardo interview.

38. Dominican woman in her forties, teacher, quoted in Andors, "City and Island," 75.

39. Eduardo Crespo quoted in Efrain Hernandez Jr. and Adrian Walker, "Hispanic Gains Don't Translate into Power," *BG*, March 24, 1991.

40. "In New England, Hispanics Have an Increasing Impact," *Philadelphia Inquirer*, April 21, 1991.

41. Ken Johnson, "Hispanic Businesses Boom," *ET*, July 10, 1996.

42. It is important to note, in the context of this low profit margin, that this type of grassroots immigrant entrepreneurship, particularly in the crisis city, was often brutally difficult work with very little remuneration. See Abelmann and Lie, *Blue Dreams*.

43. Ken Johnson, "Hispanic Businesses Boom," *ET*, July 10, 1996.

44. Ibid.

45. "Survey of Minority-Owned Business Enterprises," *U.S. Economic Census*, 1997; Santiago and Jennings, "Latino Business Community."

46. Al Lara, "Spanish-Speaking Secretaries Earn Special Recognition" *ET*, April 28, 1995.

47. Garcia interview.

48. For studies of Latino transnationalism, see Smith, *Mexican New York*; Grasmuck and Pessar, *Between Two Islands*; Georges, *Making of a Transnational Community*; and Pérez, *Near Northwest Side Story*.

49. Hernán Rozemberg, "Consul Knows Politics of 2 Lands," *ET*, November 18, 1996.

50. See Smith, *Mexican New York*, and Mahler, *American Dreaming*.

51. Ramón Borges-Méndez quoted in a transcript of his presentation at the "Forgotten Cities" seminar series on October 27, 2004, hosted by the Department of Urban Studies and Planning at the Massachusetts Institute of Technology. Transcript archived with the Department of Urban Studies and Planning, and quote used with permission from the speaker. Emphasis in the transcript.

52. Hernán Rozemberg, "Consul Knows Politics of 2 Lands," *ET*, November 18, 1996.

53. "Barber Helps Relatives Help Family Back Home," *ET*, March 11, 1995. The engagement of Dominicans in the United States in homeland politics was facilitated by two new laws in the 1990s. The first, in 1994, allowed dual citizenship, and the second, in 1997, allowed Dominicans abroad to vote in homeland elections.

54. Hernán Rozemberg, "Consul Knows Politics of 2 Lands," *ET*, November 18, 1996.

55. See Lindeke, "Latino Political Succession and Incorporation."

56. Semana Hispana program, 1995, LPL.

57. Semana Hispana program, 1988, LPL.

58. Ibid.

59. Ramos-Zayas, *National Performances*; Hernán Rozemberg, "Festival's Success Questioned," *ET*, July 28, 1996; "Dancing, Singing Chase Away Rain," *ET*, June 21, 1993; Yadira A. Betances, "18th Hispanic Week Kicks Off Tomorrow," *ET*, June 14, 1996.

60. For example, see Jaime Crespo, "Common Comes Alive with Sounds and Tastes of Cultures," *ET*, June 21, 1998.

61. Antonio López, quoted in Hernán Rozemberg, "Antonio López: Semana Hispana volverá a la cultura," *¡Fiesta!* by the *ET*, undated at LHC archives, most likely 1997, translated by the author.

62. Stevenson, "Hispanic and Minority Owned Businesses in Lawrence, Massachusetts."

63. Ibid.

64. Ibid.

65. Based on per capita income, not poverty rates. See *United States Census*, 2000.

66. Williams, "What's Going On?," 19. For other examples of this, see Võ, *Mobilizing an Asian American Community*, and for a criticism of this, see Incite! Women of Color against Violence, *Revolution Will Not Be Funded*.

67. Lindeke, "Latino Political Succession and Incorporation," 79.

68. Hernández and Jacobs, "Beyond Homeland Politics," 294.

69. Lindeke, "Latino Political Succession and Incorporation," 89.

70. Ibid., 91.

71. *United States of America v. City of Lawrence, Massachusetts*, U.S. District Court, Massachusetts, Case No. 98 CV 12256 (1998).

72. Borges-Méndez, "Urban and Regional Restructuring," 240.

73. Quoted in ibid.

74. Quoted in Hernández and Jacobs, "Beyond Homeland Politics," 290.

75. Borges-Méndez, "Migration, Settlement, and Incorporation," 37.

Conclusion

1. The *United States Census* in 2010 estimated that Latinos made up 73.8 percent of Lawrence's population.

2. Erica Noonan and Kathleen Conti, "Lawrence Elects State's First Latino Mayor," *BG*, November 3, 2009; "Alcalde oriundo RD enfrenta ola de críticas," *Hoy* digital, May 15, 2011, http://hoy.com.do/el-mundo/2011/5/15/375529/Alcalde-oriundo-RD-enfrenta-ola-de-criticas.

3. Lantigua was still serving as state representative when he was elected mayor and caused a firestorm of controversy by refusing to resign his seat in the state legislature to serve as mayor, hoping to continue to serve in both roles. See Maria Sacchetti, "Distant City Enjoyed Lantigua Largesse: Donated Vehicles and Political Connections Are Part of Ongoing Inquiry," *BG*, June 26, 2011.

4. Tenares residents were rewarded for their support with the donation of a garbage truck from Allied Waste (a major contractor with the city of Lawrence). Lantigua's chief of staff Leonard Degnan was later indicted for corruption for allegedly using his political position to pressure Allied Waste to donate the truck. See Michael Rezendes, Andrea Estes, and Sean P. Murphy, "2 with Ties to Mayor William Lantigua Indicted," *BG*, September 11, 2012.

5. Boburg, "U.S. Jobs Pay for American Dream."

6. The Salcedo Province was renamed Hermanas Mirabal Province in 2007. For statistical information on Tenares, see the Dominican government's statistical record, Oficina Nacional de Estadística, "Tu Municipio en Cifras: Tenares," http://one.gob.do/themes/one/dmdocuments/TMC/Hermanas%20Mirabal/Tenares.pdf (accessed March 19, 2014).

7. Maria Sacchetti, "Distant City Enjoyed Lantigua Largesse: Donated Vehicles and Political Connections Are Part of Ongoing Inquiry," *BG*, June 26, 2011; Fransisco Corniel, quoted in Boburg, "U.S. Jobs Pay for American Dream."

8. Mahler, *American Dreaming*; Hing, *Ethical Borders*; Smith, *Mexican New York*.

9. Fransisco Corniel, quoted in Boburg, "U.S. Jobs Pay for American Dream."

10. For another Lawrence-related critique of this stereotype, see Hernández and Jacobs, "Beyond Homeland Politics."

11. For an analysis of this idea, see Wang, "Beyond Identity and Racial Politics."

12. When Chelsea schools were put into receivership in the early 1990s, the state did not oversee them directly; rather, Boston University was put in charge of administering the schools. See James Vaznis, "State Sets Plan to Fix Schools in Lawrence; New Partnership with Charters a Key; Could Be a Model for Other Systems," *BG*, May 30, 2012.

13. John M. Guilfoil, "Lawrence Police, Fire Departments May Face 70 Layoffs," *BG*, May 11, 2010. The decline in crime from the early 1990s is true in New York City as well. See Zimring, *City That Became Safe*.

14. Robert Forrant, "City of Possibilities: Lawrence on the Merrimack," *MassBenchmarks* 15, no. 1 (2013): 13–19.

15. The project received a $2.6 million Commonwealth Gateway City Parks grant in addition to Community Development Block Grant and Federal Emergency Management Agency funds. See United States Environmental Protection Agency, "Community

Engagement Drives Progress in the Spicket River Revitalization Project," *Brownfields Success Stories*, April 2011, and Robert Forrant, "City of Possibilities: Lawrence on the Merrimack," *MassBenchmarks* 15, no. 1 (2013): 13–19.

16. Dávila, *Latino Spin*; Chomsky, *"They Take Our Jobs!"*

17. Gerken, *Model Immigrants and Undesirable Aliens*; Zilberg, "Fools Banished from the Kingdom"; Brotherton and Barrios, *Banished to the Homeland*. The term "revanchist city" is from Smith, *New Urban Frontier*.

18. For a brilliant exploration of the dangers in overvalorizing narratives of the hardworking, family-oriented immigrant, see Das Gupta, *Unruly Immigrants*.

BIBLIOGRAPHY

ARCHIVAL COLLECTIONS

Massachusetts
  Andover
    Andover Historical Society
  Boston
    Massachusetts State Archives
    Massachusetts Supreme Judicial Court Records, Clerk's Office and
      Social Law Library
    State Library of Massachusetts, Special Collections
    United States District Court Records, District of Massachusetts, Clerk's Office
    WGBH Educational Foundation, Media Library and Archives
  Lawrence
    Immigrant City Community Housing Corporation, Personal Collection of
      Armand Hyatt
    Lawrence History Center, Immigrant City Archives
    Lawrence Public Library, Special Collections
    Office of the City Clerk, Council Records
  Waltham
    National Archives and Records Administration Northeast Division
New Jersey
  Warren
    AT&T Archives and History Center
Tennessee
  Nashville
    Vanderbilt Television News Archives compilation DVD
      CBS, Thursday, August 9, 1984 (Massachusetts / Rioting 01:30)
      NBC, Thursday, August 9, 1984 (Massachusetts / Rioting 02:00)
      NBC, Friday, August 10, 1984 (Massachusetts / Rioting 02:00)
      CBS, Friday, August 10, 1984 (Massachusetts / Rioting 02:00)

ABC, Friday, August 10, 1984 (Massachusetts / Rioting 02:20)

CBS, Saturday, August 11, 1984 (Massachusetts / Rioting 02:10)

NBC, Saturday, August 11, 1984 (Massachusetts / Rioting 02:10)

CBS, Sunday, August 12, 1984 (Massachusetts / Rioting 02:10)

CBS, Friday, November 2, 1984 (Economy / Unemployment 01:50)

NBC, Monday, August 14, 1989 (Lawrence, Massachusetts / Drug War / Welfare 03:20)

NBC, Monday, May 25, 1992 (Lawrence, Massachusetts / Arson 01:50)

ABC, Tuesday, December 22, 1992 (Lawrence, Massachusetts / Crime Fight 01:50)

ABC, Sunday, February 12, 1995 (Welfare Reform / Massachusetts / Philadelphia, Pennsylvania, Program 05:20)

INTERVIEWS

Immigrant City Archives, Lawrence History Center, Lawrence, Massachusetts

Aparicio, Ester. Interviewed by Sandra DeVita, 1997.

DeJesus, Carolina. Interviewed by Joan Kelley, 1995.

Díaz, Dalia. Interviewed by Sandra DeVita, 1997.

Fernandez, Gloria. Interviewed by Margaret Hart, 1993.

Johnson, Mercedes. Interviewed by Yadira Betances, 1997.

Lamond, Father John J. Interviewed by Jeanne Schinto, 1992.

Lombardi, Morella. Interviewed by Yadira Betances, 1997.

Maracayo, Yamilis. Interviewed by Joan Kelley, 1995.

Mejía, Silvia. Interviewed by Rosemary Blessington, 2000.

Melendez, Isabel. Interviewed by Margaret Hart, 1988.

Montes Rentas, Marta. Interviewed by Rosiland Pestrana, 2007.

Muñoz, Lourdez. Interviewed by Marilenin Vásquez, 1998.

Narganes, Maria Teresa. Interviewed by Yadira Betances, 1997.

Nolberto, Fernando. Interviewed by Rodney Nolberto, 1998.

O'Neill, Daniel. Interviewed by Thomas Mofford, 1979.

Ortolaza Mane, Lucy. Interviewed by Joan Kelley, 2001.

Pichardo, Ana A. Interviewed by Euclida Pichardo, 1998.

Reyes, Rev. Jorge. Interviewed by Joan Kelley, 2008.

Reyes Cardenas, Ana. Interviewed by Joan Kelley, 2008.

Rivera, Daniel. Interviewed by Joan Kelley, 2003.

Ruiz, Maria. Interviewed by Sandra DeVita, 1997.

Silverio, Julia. Interviewed by Joan Kelley, 2002.

Urena, Francisco. Interviewed by Joan Kelley, 2007.

Interviews by the Author

Garcia, Ingrid. 2009.

Hyatt, Armand. 2009.

Melendez, Isabel. 2010.

Santiago, Jorge. 2009.

Spindler, Eric. 2006.

NEWSPAPERS AND PERIODICALS

Boston Globe
Boston Herald
Boston Phoenix
Business Week
El Diario/La Prensa
Eagle-Tribune (Lawrence Eagle-Tribune)
Journal of Greater Lawrence
Lewiston Daily Sun
El Mundo

New York Times
Rumbo
La Semana
Siglo21
Today in Greater Lawrence
USA Today
U.S. News and World Report
Valley Patriot

BOOKS, ESSAYS, AND ARTICLES

Abelmann, Nancy, and John Lie. *Blue Dreams: Korean Americans and the Los Angeles Riots.* Cambridge, Mass.: Harvard University Press, 1997.

Abu-Lughod, Janet L. *Race, Space, and Riots in Chicago, New York, and Los Angeles.* New York: Oxford University Press, 2007.

Acuña, Rodolfo F. *A Community under Siege: A Chronicle of Chicanos East of the Los Angeles River, 1945–1975.* Los Angeles: UCLA Chicano Studies Research Center, 1984.

Alvarez, Luis. *The Power of the Zoot: Youth Culture and Resistance during World War II.* Berkeley: University of California Press, 2008.

Asher, Robert, and Charles Stephenson, eds. *Labor Divided: Race and Ethnicity in United States Labor Struggles, 1835–1960.* Albany: State University of New York Press, 1990.

Atkins, G. Pope, and Larman C. Wilson. *The Dominican Republic and the United States: From Imperialism to Transnationalism.* Athens: University of Georgia Press, 1998.

Atkinson, Robert, and David Carey, eds. *Latino Voices in New England.* Albany: Excelsior Editions, 2009.

Austin, Joe. *Taking the Train: How Graffiti Art Became an Urban Crisis in New York City.* New York: Columbia University Press, 2001.

Avila, Eric. *Folklore of the Freeway: Race and Revolt in the Modernist City.* Minneapolis: University of Minnesota Press [Quadrant], 2014.

———. *Popular Culture in the Age of White Flight: Fear and Fantasy in Suburban Los Angeles.* Berkeley: University of California Press, 2006.

Avila, Eric, and Mark H. Rose. "Race, Culture, Politics, and Urban Renewal: An Introduction." *Journal of Urban History* 35, no. 3 (March 2009): 335–47.

Ayala, César J., and Rafael Bernabe. *Puerto Rico in the American Century: A History since 1898.* Chapel Hill: University of North Carolina Press, 2007.

Back, Adina. "'Parent Power': Evelina López Antonetty, the United Bronx Parents, and the War on Poverty." In *The War on Poverty: A New Grassroots History, 1964–1980,* edited by Annelise Orleck and Lisa Gayle Hazirjian, 184–208. Athens: University of Georgia Press, 2011.

Bald, Vivek, Miabi Chatterji, and Sujani Reddy. *The Sun Never Sets: South Asian Migrants in an Age of U.S. Power.* New York: New York University Press, 2013.

Baldwin, Davarian L. *Chicago's New Negroes: Modernity, the Great Migration, and Black Urban Life.* Chapel Hill: University of North Carolina Press, 2007.

Bao, Xiaolin, and Roger Daniels. *Holding Up More Than Half the Sky: Chinese Women Garment Workers in New York City, 1948–1992.* Urbana: University of Illinois Press, 2001.

Baugh, Joyce A. *The Detroit School Busing Case: Milliken v. Bradley and the Controversy over Desegregation.* Lawrence: University Press of Kansas, 2011.

Baxandall, Rosalyn Fraad, and Elizabeth Ewen. *Picture Windows: How the Suburbs Happened.* New York: Basic Books, 2000.

Biondi, Martha. *To Stand and Fight: The Struggle for Civil Rights in Postwar New York City.* Cambridge, Mass.: Harvard University Press, 2003.

Black, Jan Knippers. "Development and Dependency in the Dominican Republic." *Third World Quarterly* 8, no. 1 (January 1986): 236–57.

———. *The Dominican Republic: Politics and Development in an Unsovereign State.* Boston: Allen & Unwin, 1986.

Bluestone, Barry, and Mary Huff Stevenson. *The Boston Renaissance: Race, Space, and Economic Change in an American Metropolis.* New York: Russell Sage Foundation, 2000.

Boburg, Shawn. "U.S. Jobs Pay for American Dream in Dominican Town." *Eagle-Tribune,* December 16, 2005.

Bodnar, John. *The Transplanted: A History of Immigrants in Urban America.* Bloomington: Indiana University Press, 1985.

Bonilla-Silva, Eduardo. *Racism without Racists: Color-Blind Racism and the Persistence of Racial Inequality in the United States.* Lanham, Md.: Rowman & Littlefield, 2003.

Bosworth, Matthew H. *Courts as Catalysts: State Supreme Courts and Public School Finance Equity.* Albany: State University of New York Press, 2001.

Brecher, Jeremy, and Tim Costello. *Global Village or Global Pillage: Economic Reconstruction from the Bottom Up.* Boston: South End Press, 1994.

Brennan, Denise. *What's Love Got to Do with It?: Transnational Desires and Sex Tourism in the Dominican Republic.* Durham, N.C.: Duke University Press, 2004.

Briggs, Laura. *Reproducing Empire: Race, Sex, Science, and U.S. Imperialism in Puerto Rico.* Berkeley: University of California Press, 2003.

Brotherton, David C., and Luis Barrios. *Banished to the Homeland: Dominican Deportees and Their Stories of Exile.* New York: Columbia University Press, 2011.

Brown, Monica. *Gang Nation: Delinquent Citizens in Puerto Rican, Chicano, and Chicana Narratives.* Minneapolis: University of Minnesota Press, 2002.

Buff, Rachel. *Immigration and the Political Economy of Home: West Indian Brooklyn and American Indian Minneapolis, 1945–1992.* Berkeley: University of California Press, 2001.

Byrd, Jodi A. *The Transit of Empire: Indigenous Critiques of Colonialism.* Minneapolis: University of Minnesota Press, 2011.

Cameron, Ardis. *Radicals of the Worst Sort: Laboring Women in Lawrence, Massachusetts, 1860–1912.* Champaign: University of Illinois Press, 1995.

Campbell, Colin. "Two Nights of Rioting Bring a Curfew to Lawrence, Mass." *New York Times,* August 11, 1984.

Candelario, Ginetta E. B. *Black behind the Ears: Dominican Racial Identity from Museums to Beauty Shops.* Durham, N.C.: Duke University Press, 2007.

Carnegie Foundation for the Advancement of Teaching. *An Imperiled Generation: Saving Urban Schools*. Princeton, N.J.: Princeton University Press, 1988.

Caro, Robert A. *The Power Broker: Robert Moses and the Fall of New York*. New York: Knopf, 1974.

Carpio, Genevieve, Clara Irazábal, and Laura Pulido. "Right to the Suburb? Rethinking Lefebvre and Immigrant Activism." *Journal of Urban Affairs* 33, no. 2 (2011): 185–208.

Carter, Gregg Lee. "Hispanic Rioting during the Civil Rights Era." *Sociological Forum* 7, no. 2 (June 1992): 301–22.

Chang, Jeff. *Can't Stop, Won't Stop: A History of the Hip-Hop Generation*. New York: St. Martin's Press, 2005.

Chappell, Marisa. *The War on Welfare: Family, Poverty, and Politics in Modern America*. Philadelphia: University of Pennsylvania Press, 2010.

Chen, Alice Hm, Mara K. Youdelman, and Jamie Brooks. "The Legal Framework for Language Access in Healthcare Settings: Title VI and Beyond." *Journal of General Internal Medicine*, November 2007, 362–67.

Chen, Xiangming, and Nick Bacon, eds. *Confronting Urban Legacy: Rediscovering Hartford and New England's Forgotten Cities*. Lanham, Md.: Lexington Press, 2013.

Chen, Xiangming, and Ahmed Kanna. *Rethinking Global Urbanism: Comparative Insights from Secondary Cities*. New York: Routledge, 2012.

Chester, Eric Thomas. *Rag-Tags, Scum, Riff-Raff, and Commies: The U.S. Intervention in the Dominican Republic, 1965–1966*. New York: Monthly Review Press, 2001.

Chinlund, Chris, and Ray Richard. "Lawrence's Charter for Trouble; Critics Say Form of City Government Fosters the Inequalities That Led to Violence." *Boston Globe*, August 23, 1984.

Chomsky, Aviva. *Linked Labor Histories: New England, Colombia, and the Making of a Global Working Class*. Durham, N.C.: Duke University Press, 2008.

———. "Salem as a Global City, 1850–2004." In *Salem: Place, Myth and Memory*, edited by Dane Morrison and Nancy Lusignan Schultz, 219–47. Boston: Northeastern University Press, 2004.

———. *"They Take Our Jobs!" and 20 Other Myths about Immigration*. Boston: Beacon Press, 2007.

Choy, Catherine Ceniza. *Empire of Care: Nursing and Migration in Filipino American History*. Durham, N.C.: Duke University Press, 2003.

Clotfelter, Charles T. *After* Brown*: The Rise and Retreat of School Desegregation*. Princeton, N.J.: Princeton University Press, 2004.

Cohen, Lizabeth. *A Consumers' Republic: The Politics of Mass Consumption in Postwar America*. New York: Random House, 2003.

———. *Making a New Deal: Industrial Workers in Chicago, 1919–1939*. Cambridge: Cambridge University Press, 1990.

Cole, Donald B. *Immigrant City: Lawrence, Massachusetts, 1845–1921*. Chapel Hill: University of North Carolina Press, 1963.

"Confrontation—Right to a Translator (United States ex rel. Negron v. State of New York)." *St. John's Law Review* 46, no. 3 (1972), http://scholarship.law.stjohns.edu/lawreview/vol46/iss3/14. Accessed June 17, 2016.

Cowan, Spencer M. "Anti-Snob Land Use Laws, Suburban Exclusion, and Housing Opportunity." *Journal of Urban Affairs* 28, no. 3 (2006): 295–313.

Cowie, Jefferson. *Stayin' Alive: The 1970s and the Last Days of the Working Class.* New York: New Press, 2012.

Cowie, Jefferson, and Joseph Heathcott, eds. *Beyond the Ruins: The Meanings of Deindustrialization.* Ithaca, N.Y.: ILR Press, 2003.

Cullen, Kevin, and John Impemba. "New Riot Hits Lawrence: SWAT Team in Action against Wild Mob." *Boston Herald,* August 10, 1984.

Danielson, Michael N. *The Politics of Exclusion.* New York: Columbia University Press, 1976.

Das Gupta, Monisha. *Unruly Immigrants: Rights, Activism, and Transnational South Asian Politics in the United States.* Durham, N.C.: Duke University Press, 2006.

Dávila, Arlene. *Barrio Dreams: Puerto Ricans, Latinos, and the Neoliberal City.* Berkeley: University of California Press, 2004.

———. *Latino Spin: Public Image and the Whitewashing of Race.* New York: New York University Press, 2008.

Davis, Mike. *Magical Urbanism: Latinos Reinvent the U.S. City.* London: Verso, 2000.

DeGenova, Nicholas, and Ana Y. Ramos-Zayas. *Latino Crossings: Mexicans, Puerto Ricans, and the Politics of Race and Citizenship.* New York: Routledge, 2003.

Denis, Nelson A. *War against All Puerto Ricans: Revolution and Terror in America's Colony.* New York: Nation Books, 2015.

Diamond, Andrew J. *Mean Streets: Chicago Youths and the Everyday Struggle for Empowerment in the Multiracial City, 1908–1969.* Berkeley: University of California Press, 2009.

Diaz, David R., and Rodolfo D. Torres. *Latino Urbanism: The Politics of Planning, Policy, and Redevelopment.* New York: New York University Press, 2012.

Díaz, Junot. *Drown.* New York: Riverhead Books, 1996.

Dietz, James L. *Economic History of Puerto Rico: Institutional Change and Capitalist Development.* Princeton, N.J.: Princeton University Press, 1986.

Dougherty, Jack, "On the Line: How Schooling, Housing, and Civil Rights Shaped Hartford and Its Suburbs," http://ontheline.trincoll.edu/. Accessed February 11, 2014.

Drinnon, Richard. *Facing West: The Metaphysics of Indian-Hating and Empire-Building.* Minneapolis: University of Minnesota Press, 1980.

Duany, Jorge. "Dominican Migration to Puerto Rico: A Transnational Perspective." *Centro Journal* 17, no. 1 (Spring 2005): 242–69.

———. *The Puerto Rican Nation on the Move: Identities on the Island and in the United States.* Chapel Hill: University of North Carolina Press, 2002.

Duncan, James, and Nancy Duncan. "Can't Live with Them; Can't Landscape without Them: Racism and the Pastoral Aesthetic in Suburban New York." *Landscape Journal* 22, no. 1 (2003): 88–98.

Ehrenreich, Barbara, and Arlie Russell Hochschild. *Global Woman: Nannies, Maids, and Sex Workers in the New Economy.* New York: Metropolitan Books, 2003.

Escobedo, Elizabeth Rachel. *From Coveralls to Zoot Suits: The Lives of Mexican American Women on the World War II Home Front.* Chapel Hill: University of North Carolina Press, 2013.

Espada, Martín. *Trumpets from the Islands of Their Eviction*. Tempe, Ariz.: Bilingual Press/ Editorial Bilingüe, 1987.

Fadiman, Anne. *The Spirit Catches You and You Fall Down: A Hmong Child, Her American Doctors, and the Collision of Two Cultures*. New York: Farrar, Straus and Giroux, 1997.

Fernández, Johanna. "The Young Lords and the Postwar City: Notes on the Geographical and Structural Reconfigurations of Contemporary Urban Life." In *African American Urban History since World War II*, edited by Kenneth L. Kusmer and Joe W. Trotter, 60–82. Chicago: University of Chicago Press, 2009.

Fernández, Lilia. *Brown in the Windy City: Mexicans and Puerto Ricans in Postwar Chicago*. Chicago: University of Chicago Press, 2012.

———. "Of Immigrants and Migrants: Mexican and Puerto Rican Labor Migration in Comparative Perspective, 1942–1965." *Journal of American Ethnic History* 29, no. 3 (Spring 2010): 6–39.

Fernandez, Ronald. *The Disenchanted Island: Puerto Rico and the United States in the Twentieth Century*. New York: Praeger, 1992.

Findlay, Eileen. *Imposing Decency: The Politics of Sexuality and Race in Puerto Rico, 1870–1920*. Durham, N.C.: Duke University Press, 1999.

Fink, Leon. *The Maya of Morganton: Work and Community in the Nuevo New South*. Chapel Hill: University of North Carolina Press, 2003.

Fix, Michael E., ed. *Immigrants and Welfare: The Impact of Welfare Reform on America's Newcomers*. New York: Russell Sage Foundation, 2009.

Fix, Michael E., Randy Capps, and Neeraj Kaushal. "Immigrants and Welfare: An Overview." In *Immigrants and Welfare: The Impact of Welfare Reform on America's Newcomers*, edited by Michael E. Fix, 1–36. New York: Russell Sage Foundation, 2009.

Flores, Juan. *The Diaspora Strikes Back: Caribeño Tales of Learning and Turning*. New York: Routledge, 2009.

———. *From Bomba to Hip-Hop: Puerto Rican Culture and Latino Identity*. New York: Columbia University Press, 2000.

Foner, Nancy. *From Ellis Island to JFK: New York's Two Great Waves of Immigration*. New Haven, Conn.: Yale University Press; New York: Russell Sage Foundation, 2000.

———, ed. *One out of Three: Immigrant New York in the Twenty-First Century*. New York: Columbia University Press, 2013.

Fong, Timothy P. *The First Suburban Chinatown: The Remaking of Monterey Park, California*. Philadelphia: Temple University Press, 1994.

Fox, Cybelle. *Three Worlds of Relief: Race, Immigration, and the American Welfare State from the Progressive Era to the New Deal*. Princeton, N.J.: Princeton University Press, 2012.

Freund, David M. P. *Colored Property: State Policy and White Racial Politics in Suburban America*. Chicago: University of Chicago Press, 2007.

Frum, David. *How We Got Here: The 70's, the Decade That Brought You Modern Life (for Better or Worse)*. New York: Basic Books, 2000.

Gainsborough, Juliet F. *Fenced Off: The Suburbanization of American Politics*. Washington, D.C.: Georgetown University Press, 2001.

Gamm, Gerald. *Urban Exodus: Why the Jews Left Boston and the Catholics Stayed*. Cambridge, Mass.: Harvard University Press, 1999.

Gans, Herbert J. *The Urban Villagers: Group and Class in the Life of Italian-Americans.* New York: Free Press, 1982.

García, María Cristina. *Havana USA: Cuban Exiles and Cuban Americans in South Florida, 1959–1994.* Berkeley: University of California Press, 1996.

Geismer, Lily. *Don't Blame Us: Suburban Liberals and the Transformation of the Democratic Party.* Princeton, N.J.: Princeton University Press, 2015.

Georges, Eugenia. *The Making of a Transnational Community: Migration, Development, and Cultural Change in the Dominican Republic.* New York: Columbia University Press, 1990.

Gerken, Christina. *Model Immigrants and Undesirable Aliens: The Cost of Immigration Reform in the 1990s.* Minneapolis: University of Minnesota Press, 2013.

Gerstle, Gary. *Working-Class Americanism: The Politics of Labor in a Textile City, 1914–1960.* Cambridge: Cambridge University Press, 1989.

Gill, John. "The 'Misery Industry': Welfare Culture Blossoms as Rest of Lawrence Suffers." *Eagle-Tribune,* September 22, 1993.

Gillette, Howard, Jr. *Camden after the Fall: Decline and Renewal in a Post-Industrial City.* Philadelphia: University of Pennsylvania Press, 2005.

Glenn, Evelyn Nakano. "From Servitude to Service Work: Historical Continuities in the Racial Division of Paid Reproductive Labor." In *Unequal Sisters: A Multicultural Reader in U.S. Women's History,* 3rd ed., edited by Vicki Ruíz and Ellen Carol DuBois, 436–65. New York: Routledge, 2000.

Goldstein, Alyosha, ed. *Formations of United States Colonialism.* Durham, N.C.: Duke University Press, 2014.

Gonzales, Alfonso. *Reform without Justice: Latino Migrant Politics and the Homeland Security State.* Oxford: Oxford University Press, 2014.

Gonzalez, Evelyn. *The Bronx.* New York: Columbia University Press, 2004.

González, Juan. *Harvest of Empire: A History of Latinos in America.* New York: Penguin, 2011.

Gordon, Diana R. *Village of Immigrants: Latinos in an Emerging America.* New Brunswick, N.J.: Rutgers University Press, 2015.

Gotham, Kevin Fox. *Race, Real Estate, and Uneven Development: The Kansas City Experience, 1900–2000.* Albany: State University of New York Press, 2002.

Gotham, Kevin Fox, and Miriam Greenberg. *Crisis Cities: Disaster and Redevelopment in New York and New Orleans.* Oxford: Oxford University Press, 2014.

Grandin, Greg. *Empire's Workshop: Latin America, the United States, and the Rise of the New Imperialism.* New York: Metropolitan Books, 2006.

Grasmuck, Sherri, and Patricia R. Pessar. *Between Two Islands: Dominican International Migration.* Berkeley: University of California Press, 1991.

Green, Richard K., and Susan K. Wachter. "The American Mortgage in Historical and International Context." *Journal of Economic Perspectives* 19, no. 4 (Fall 2005): 93–114.

Gregory, Steven. *The Devil behind the Mirror: Globalization and Politics in the Dominican Republic.* Berkeley: University of California Press, 2007.

Grosfoguel, Ramón. *Colonial Subjects: Puerto Ricans in a Global Perspective.* Berkeley: University of California Press, 2003.

Halter, Marilyn, Marilynn Johnson, Katheryn P. Viens, and Conrad Eric Wright, eds. *What's New about the "New" Immigration? Traditions and Transformations in the United States since 1965*. New York: Palgrave Macmillan, 2014.

Handlin, Oscar, *The Uprooted: The Epic Story of the Great Migrations That Made the American People*. Boston: Little, Brown, 1951.

Hardy-Fanta, Carol. *Latina Politics, Latino Politics: Gender, Culture, and Political Participation in Boston*. Philadelphia: Temple University Press, 1993.

Hardy-Fanta, Carol, and Jeffrey Gerson, eds. *Latino Politics in Massachusetts: Struggles, Strategies, and Prospects*. New York: Routledge, 2002.

Harvey, David. *A Brief History of Neoliberalism*. Oxford: Oxford University Press, 2005.

Haslip-Viera, Gabriel, and Sherrie L. Baver, eds. *Latinos in New York: Communities in Transition*. Notre Dame, Ind.: University of Notre Dame Press, 1996.

Hayden, Dolores. *Building Suburbia: Green Fields and Urban Growth, 1820–2000*. New York: Pantheon Books, 2003.

Hendricks, Glenn. *The Dominican Diaspora: From the Dominican Republic to New York City—Villagers in Transition*. New York: Teachers College Press, 1974.

Hernandez, Peggy. "Curfew Lifted in Lawrence." *Boston Globe*, August 14, 1984.

———. "Lawrence Police Enforce Curfew in Riot-Torn Areas; No Resistance to Order Reported." *Boston Globe*, August 11, 1984.

Hernández, Ramona. *The Mobility of Labor under Advanced Capitalism: Dominican Migration to the United States*. New York: Columbia University Press, 2002.

Hernández, Ramona, and Glenn Jacobs. "Beyond Homeland Politics: Dominicans in Massachusetts." In *Latino Politics in Massachusetts: Struggles, Strategies, and Prospects*, edited by Carol Hardy-Fanta and Jeffrey Gerson, 277–96. New York: Routledge, 2002.

Hing, Bill Ong. *Ethical Borders: NAFTA, Globalization, and Mexican Migration*. Philadelphia: Temple University Press, 2010.

Hirsch, Arnold. "Less Than *Plessy*: The Inner City, Suburbs, and State-Sanctioned Residential Segregation in the Age of *Brown*." In *The New Suburban History*, edited by Kevin M. Kruse and Thomas J. Sugrue, 33–56. Chicago: University of Chicago Press, 2006.

———. *Making the Second Ghetto: Race and Housing in Chicago, 1940–1960*. Cambridge: Cambridge University Press, 1983.

Hochschild, Jennifer L., and Nathan B. Scovronick. *The American Dream and the Public Schools*. New York: Oxford University Press, 2003.

Hoffnung-Garskof, Jesse. *A Tale of Two Cities: Santo Domingo and New York after 1950*. Princeton, N.J.: Princeton University Press, 2008.

Hohler, Bob. "5 Years after Riots, Lawrence's Hispanics Feel Betrayed, Angry Community Activists Bemoan Budget Cuts, Crackdown by Mayor." *Boston Globe*, August 13, 1989.

Incite! Women of Color against Violence. *The Revolution Will Not Be Funded: Beyond the Non-Profit Industrial Complex*. Cambridge, Mass.: South End Press, 2007.

"In Lawrence, Hope Going up in Smoke: 70 Arson Cases Paralyze City Racked by Poverty." *Boston Globe*, May 29, 1992.

Innis-Jiménez, Michael. *Steel Barrio: The Great Mexican Migration to South Chicago, 1915–1940*. New York: New York University Press, 2013.

Isenberg, Alison. *Downtown America: A History of the Place and the People Who Made It.* Chicago: University of Chicago Press, 2004.

Itzigsohn, José. *Developing Poverty: The State, Labor Market Deregulation, and the Informal Economy in Costa Rica and the Dominican Republic.* University Park: Pennsylvania State University Press, 2000.

———. *Encountering American Faultlines: Race, Class, and the Dominican Experience in Providence.* New York: Russell Sage Foundation, 2009.

Jackson, Kenneth, *Crabgrass Frontier: The Suburbanization of the United States.* Oxford: Oxford University Press, 1987.

Jacobs, Sally. "Fires in Lawrence Evoke Fear of New Arson Outbreak." *Boston Globe,* June 25, 1993.

Jacobson, Matthew Frye. *Barbarian Virtues: The United States Encounters Foreign Peoples at Home and Abroad, 1876–1917.* New York: Hill and Wang, 2000.

———. *Roots Too: White Ethnic Revival in Post–Civil Rights America.* Cambridge, Mass.: Harvard University Press, 2006.

———. *Whiteness of a Different Color: European Immigrants and the Alchemy of Race.* Cambridge, Mass.: Harvard University Press, 1998.

Jennings, James, and Jorge Santiago, "Welfare Reform and 'Welfare to Work' as Non-Sequitur: A Case Study of the Experiences of Latina Women in Massachusetts." *Journal of Poverty* 8, no. 1 (2004): 23–42.

Jiménez de Wagenheim, Olga. "From Aguada to Dover: Puerto Ricans Rebuild Their World in Morris County, New Jersey, 1948 to 2000." In *The Puerto Rican Diaspora: Historical Perspectives,* edited by Carmen Teresa Whalen and Víctor Vázquez-Hernández, 106–27. Philadelphia: Temple University Press, 2005.

Jiménez Román, Miriam, and Juan Flores. *The Afro-Latin@ Reader: History and Culture in the United States.* Durham, N.C.: Duke University Press, 2010.

Johnson, Marilynn S. "Gender, Race, and Rumors: Re-examining the 1943 Race Riots." *Gender and History* 10, no. 2 (August 1998): 252–77.

———. "The Metropolitan Diaspora: New Immigrants in Greater Boston." In *What's New about the "New" Immigration? Traditions and Transformations in the United States since 1965,* edited by Marilyn Halter, Marilynn Johnson, Katheryn P. Viens, and Conrad Eric Wright, 23–50. New York: Palgrave Macmillan, 2014.

———. *The New Bostonians: How Immigrants Have Transformed the Metro Region since the 1960s.* Amherst: University of Massachusetts Press, 2015.

Joseph, Peniel E. *Waiting until the Midnight Hour: A Narrative History of Black Power in America.* New York: Henry Holt, 2006.

Kaplan, Amy, and Donald E. Pease. *Cultures of United States Imperialism.* Durham, N.C.: Duke University Press, 1993.

Katz, Michael B. *In the Shadow of the Poorhouse: A Social History of Welfare in America.* New York: Basic Books, 1986.

———. *The Undeserving Poor: From the War on Poverty to the War on Welfare.* New York: Pantheon Books, 1990.

———, ed. *The "Underclass" Debate: Views from History.* Princeton, N.J.: Princeton University Press, 1993.

Katz, Michael, Matthew J. Creighton, Daniel Amsterdam, and Merlin Chowkwanyun. "Immigration and the New Metropolitan Geography." *Journal of Urban Affairs* 32, no. 5 (2010): 523–47.

Kaufman, Jonathan. "Hostility Boils Over; Lawrence Residents Talk about Ethnic Tensions Simmering for a Long Time in Riot-Torn Tower Hill Neighborhood." *Boston Globe*, August 11, 1984.

Kelley, Robin D. G. *Freedom Dreams: The Black Radical Imagination.* Boston: Beacon Press, 2002.

———. *Race Rebels: Culture, Politics, and the Black Working Class.* New York: Free Press, 1994.

———. *Yo' Mama's Disfunktional! Fighting the Culture Wars in Urban America.* Boston: Beacon Press, 1997.

Klor de Alva, Jorge, Earl Shorris, and Cornel West. "Our Next Race Question: The Uneasiness between Blacks and Latinos." In *The Latino Studies Reader: Culture, Economy, and Society*, edited by Antonia Darder and Rodolfo D. Torres, 180–90. Malden, Mass.: Blackwell, 1998.

Kozol, Jonathan. *Savage Inequalities: Children in America's Schools.* New York: Crown, 1991.

Kruse, Kevin Michael. *White Flight: Atlanta and the Making of Modern Conservatism.* Princeton, N.J.: Princeton University Press, 2005.

Kruse, Kevin M., and Thomas J. Sugrue, eds. *The New Suburban History.* Chicago: University of Chicago Press, 2006.

Kusmer, Kenneth L., and Joe W. Trotter, eds. *African American Urban History since World War II.* Chicago: University of Chicago Press, 2009.

Lamb, Charles M. *Housing Segregation in Suburban America since 1960: Presidential and Judicial Politics.* Cambridge: Cambridge University Press, 2005.

Lampe, David R. *The Massachusetts Miracle: High Technology and Economic Revitalization.* Cambridge, Mass.: MIT Press, 1988.

Laó-Montes, Agustín, and Arlene Dávila, eds. *Mambo Montage: The Latinization of New York.* New York: Columbia University Press, 2001.

Larrabee, John. "Community Braces for a Lifestyle Overhaul." *USA Today*, March 13, 1995.

Lassiter, Matthew D. *The Silent Majority: Suburban Politics in the Sunbelt South.* Princeton, N.J.: Princeton University Press, 2006.

Lassiter, Matthew D., and Christopher Niedt. "Suburban Diversity in Postwar America." *Journal of Urban History* 39, no. 3 (March 2013): 3–14.

Lee, Sonia Song-Ha. *Building a Latino Civil Rights Movement: Puerto Ricans, African Americans, and the Pursuit of Racial Justice in New York City.* Chapel Hill: University of North Carolina Press, 2014.

Lefebvre, Henri. *The Production of Space.* Translated by Donald Nicholson-Smith. Cambridge, Mass.: Blackwell, 1991.

Lehman, Betsy A. "The Struggle in Lawrence: Poverty." *Boston Globe*, August 11, 1984.

Lemke-Santangelo, Gretchen. *Abiding Courage: African American Migrant Women and the East Bay Community.* Chapel Hill: University of North Carolina Press, 1996.

Levenstein, Lisa. "From Innocent Children to Unwanted Migrants and Unwed Moms: Two Chapters in the Public Discourse on Welfare in the United States, 1960–1961." *Journal of Women's History* 11, no. 4 (Winter 2000): 10–33.

Levitt, Peggy. *The Transnational Villagers*. Berkeley: University of California Press, 2001.

Lewis, Oscar. *La Vida: A Puerto Rican Family in the Culture of Poverty—San Juan and New York*. New York: Random House, 1966.

Lindeke, William A. "Latino Political Succession and Incorporation: Lawrence." In *Latino Politics in Massachusetts: Struggles, Strategies, and Prospects*, edited by Carol Hardy-Fanta and Jeffrey Gerson, 73–98. New York: Routledge, 2002.

Lindseth, Alfred A. "The Legal Backdrop to Adequacy." In *Courting Failure: How School Finance Lawsuits Exploit Judges' Good Intentions and Harm Our Children*, edited by Eric Hanushek, 33–78. Stanford, Calif.: Hoover Institution Press, 2006.

Londoño, Johana. "Aesthetic Belonging: The Latinization and Renewal of Union City, New Jersey." In *Latino Urbanism: The Politics of Planning, Policy, and Redevelopment*, edited by David R. Diaz and Rodolfo D. Torres, 47–64. New York: New York University Press, 2012.

Loyd, Jenna M., Matt Mitchelson, and Andrew Burridge, eds. *Beyond Walls and Cages: Prisons, Borders, and Global Crisis*. Athens: University of Georgia Press, 2012.

Lukas, J. Anthony. *Common Ground: A Turbulent Decade in the Lives of Three American Families*. New York: Knopf, 1985.

Lumpkins, Charles L. *American Pogrom: The East St. Louis Race Riot and Black Politics*. Athens: Ohio University Press, 2008.

Lupo, Alan. "Lessons of the Street: What Lawrence Never Learned." *Boston Phoenix*, August 21, 1984.

Macek, Steve. *Urban Nightmares: The Media, the Right, and the Moral Panic over the City*. Minneapolis: University of Minnesota Press, 2006.

Mahler, Jonathan. *Ladies and Gentlemen, the Bronx Is Burning: 1977, Baseball, Politics, and the Battle for the Soul of a City*. New York: Farrar, Straus and Giroux, 2005.

Mahler, Sarah J. *American Dreaming: Immigrant Life on the Margins*. Princeton, N.J.: Princeton University Press, 1995.

Malavet, Pedro A. *America's Colony: The Political and Cultural Conflict between the United States and Puerto Rico*. New York: New York University Press, 2007.

Marcuse, Peter, and Ronald Van Kempen, eds. *Globalizing Cities: A New Spatial Order*. Malden, Mass.: Blackwell, 2000.

Martinez, Miranda J. *Power at the Roots: Gentrification, Community Gardens, and the Puerto Ricans of the Lower East Side*. Lanham, Md.: Lexington Books, 2010.

Massey, Douglas S., and Nancy A. Denton. *American Apartheid: Segregation and the Making of the Underclass*. Cambridge, Mass.: Harvard University Press, 1993.

———. "Residential Segregation of Mexicans, Puerto Ricans, and Cubans in Selected U.S. Metropolitan Areas." *Sociology and Social Research* 73, no. 2 (1989): 73–83.

McCaffrey, Katherine T. *Military Power and Popular Protest: The U.S. Navy in Vieques, Puerto Rico*. New Brunswick, N.J.: Rutgers University Press, 2002.

McCann, Eugene J. "Race, Protest, and Public Space: Contextualizing Lefebvre in the U.S. City." *Antipode* 31, no. 2 (1999): 163–84.

McDermott, Kathryn A. "Incentives, Capacity, and Implementation: Evidence from Massachusetts Education Reform." *Journal of Public Administration Research and Theory: J-PART* 16, no. 1 (January 2006): 45–65.

McGirr, Lisa. *Suburban Warriors: The Origins of the New American Right*. Princeton, N.J.: Princeton University Press, 2001.

McGuire, Danielle L. *At the Dark End of the Street: Black Women, Rape, and Resistance— A New History of the Civil Rights Movement from Rosa Parks to the Rise of Black Power*. New York: Knopf, 2010.

McKee, Guian A. *The Problem of Jobs: Liberalism, Race, and Deindustrialization in Philadelphia*. Chicago: University of Chicago Press, 2008.

McPherson, Alan L. *The Invaded: How Latin Americans and Their Allies Fought and Ended U.S. Occupations*. New York: Oxford University Press, 2014.

———. *Yankee No! Anti-Americanism in U.S.–Latin American Relations*. Cambridge, Mass.: Harvard University Press, 2006.

Meléndez, Edwin. "Latino Poverty and Economic Development in Massachusetts." In *Latino Poverty and Economic Development in Massachusetts*, edited by Edwin Meléndez and Miren Uriarte, 15–37. Boston: Mauricio Gastón Institute for Latino Community Development and Public Policy, 1993.

Meléndez, Edwin, and Miren Uriarte, eds. *Latino Poverty and Economic Development in Massachusetts*. Boston: Mauricio Gastón Institute for Latino Community Development and Public Policy, 1993.

Millman, Joel. *The Other Americans: How Immigrants Renew Our Country, Our Economy, and Our Values*. New York: Viking, 1997.

Mofford, Juliet Haines. *AVIS—A History in Conservation*. Andover, Mass.: Andover Village Improvement Society, 1980.

Mohl, Raymond. "The International Institute Movement and Ethnic Pluralism." *Social Science* 56, no. 1 (Winter 1981). Immigration History Research Center, Reprint Series No. 5.

Molina, Natalia. *Fit to Be Citizens? Public Health and Race in Los Angeles, 1879–1939*. Berkeley: University of California Press, 2006.

Montero-Sieburth, Martha, and Edwin Meléndez. *Latinos in a Changing Society*. Westport, Conn.: Praeger, 2007.

Moore, Joan W., and Raquel Pinderhughes. *In the Barrios: Latinos and the Underclass Debate*. New York: Russell Sage Foundation, 1993.

Moreno de Toro, Angel A. Amy. "An Oral History of the Puerto Rican Socialist Party in Boston, 1972–1978." In *The Puerto Rican Movement: Voices from the Diaspora*, edited by Andrés Torres and José E. Velázquez, 246–59. Philadelphia: Temple University Press, 1998.

Moya Pons, Frank. *The Dominican Republic: A National History*. Princeton, N.J.: Markus Wiener, 2010.

Mozingo, Louise A. *Pastoral Capitalism: A History of Suburban Corporate Landscapes*. Cambridge, Mass.: MIT Press, 2011.

Mumford, Kevin. *Newark: A History of Race, Rights, and Riots in America*. New York: New York University Press, 2007.

Murch, Donna Jean. *Living for the City: Migration, Education, and the Rise of the Black Panther Party in Oakland, California*. Chapel Hill: University of North Carolina Press, 2010.

Muzio, Rose. "The Struggle against 'Urban Renewal' in Manhattan's Upper West Side and the Emergence of El Comité." *Centro Journal* 21, no. 2 (Fall 2009): 109–41.

Neff, Kathie. "Facing Up to Our Prejudice: First of a Series." *Eagle-Tribune*, April 22, 1984.

Negrón-Muntaner, Frances, ed. *None of the Above: Puerto Ricans in the Global Era.* New York: Palgrave MacMillan, 2007.

Newman, Katherine, and Chauncy Lennon. "The Job Ghetto." *American Prospect* 22 (Summer 1995): 66–67.

Ngai, Mae M. *Impossible Subjects: Illegal Aliens and the Making of Modern America.* Princeton, N.J.: Princeton University Press, 2004.

Nguyen, Tram. *We Are All Suspects Now: Untold Stories from Immigrant Communities after 9/11.* Boston: Beacon Press, 2005.

Niedt, Christopher, ed. *Social Justice in Diverse Suburbs: History, Politics, and Prospects.* Philadelphia: Temple University Press, 2013.

Nieto, Clara, and Chris Brandt. *Masters of War: Latin America and United States Aggression from the Cuban Revolution through the Clinton Years.* New York: Seven Stories Press, 2003.

O'Connell, James C. *The Hub's Metropolis: Greater Boston's Development from Railroad Suburbs to Smart Growth.* Cambridge, Mass.: MIT Press, 2013.

Ong, Aihwa. *Buddha Is Hiding: Refugees, Citizenship, the New America.* Berkeley: University of California Press, 2003.

Orleck, Annelise. *Storming Caesars Palace: How Black Mothers Fought Their Own War on Poverty.* Boston: Beacon Press, 2005.

Orleck, Annelise, and Lisa Gayle Hazirjian. eds. *The War on Poverty: A New Grassroots History, 1964–1980.* Athens: University of Georgia Press, 2011.

Otero, Lydia R. *La Calle: Spatial Conflicts and Urban Renewal in a Southwest City.* Tucson: University of Arizona Press, 2010.

Pabón López, María. "An Essay Examining the Murder of Luis Ramírez and the Emergence of Hate Crimes against Latino Immigrants in the United States." *Arizona State Law Journal*, Spring 2012, 155–73.

Pacini Hernandez, Deborah. *Bachata: A Social History of a Dominican Popular Music.* Philadelphia: Temple University Press, 1995.

Pagán, Eduardo Obregón. *Murder at the Sleepy Lagoon: Zoot Suits, Race, and Riot in Wartime L.A.* Chapel Hill: University of North Carolina Press, 2003.

Pastor, Manuel. "Maywood, Not Mayberry: Latinos and Suburbia in Los Angeles County." In *Social Justice in Diverse Suburbs: History, Politics, and Prospects*, edited by Christopher Niedt, 129–54. Philadelphia: Temple University Press, 2013.

Payne, Charles M. *I've Got the Light of Freedom: The Organizing Tradition and the Mississippi Freedom Struggle.* Berkeley: University of California Press, 1995.

Perales, Monica. *Smeltertown: Making and Remembering a Southwest Border Community.* Chapel Hill: University of North Carolina Press, 2010.

Pérez, Gina M. "Hispanic Values, Military Values: Gender, Culture, and the Militarization of Latina/o Youth." In *Beyond el Barrio: Everyday Life in Latina/o America*, edited by Gina M. Pérez, Frank A. Guridy, and Adrian Burgos Jr., 168–86. New York: New York University Press, 2010.

————. *The Near Northwest Side Story: Migration, Displacement, and Puerto Rican Families*. Berkeley: University of California Press, 2004.

Pérez, Gina M., Frank A. Guridy, and Adrian Burgos Jr., eds. *Beyond el Barrio: Everyday Life in Latina/o America*. New York: New York University Press, 2010.

Pessar, Patricia R. *A Visa for a Dream: Dominicans in the United States*. Boston: Allyn and Bacon, 1995.

Peterson, Paul E., and Mark C. Rom. *Welfare Magnets: A New Case for a National Standard*. Washington, D.C.: Brookings Institution, 1990.

Pho, Tuyet-Lan, Jeffrey N. Gerson, and Sylvia R. Cowan. *Southeast Asian Refugees and Immigrants in the Mill City: Changing Families, Communities, Institutions—Thirty Years Afterward*. Burlington: University of Vermont Press, 2007.

Pietri, Pedro. *Puerto Rican Obituary*. New York: Monthly Review Press, 1974.

Pinkney, Alphonso. *Lest We Forget: White Hate Crimes: Howard Beach and Other Racial Atrocities*. Chicago: Third World Press, 1994.

Pitti, Stephen J. *The Devil in Silicon Valley: Northern California, Race, and Mexican Americans*. Princeton, N.J.: Princeton University Press, 2003.

"Police Plan to Clear Streets after Second Night of Rioting: 8 PM Curfew in Force Tonight." *Eagle-Tribune*, August 10, 1984.

Portes, Alejandro. "NAFTA and Mexican Immigration." From the Social Science Research Council's website "Border Battles: The U.S. Immigration Debates," http://borderbattles.ssrc.org/. Accessed April 1, 2014.

Portes, Alejandro, and Alex Stepick. *City on the Edge: The Transformation of Miami*. Berkeley: University of California Press, 1994.

Pulido, Laura. *Black, Brown, Yellow, and Left: Radical Activism in Los Angeles*. Berkeley: University of California Press, 2006.

Quiñonez, Ernesto. *Chango's Fire: A Novel*. New York: Rayo, 2004.

Rambach, Peggy, and Nhek But. *Under the Sugar Palm Trees: Memoirs of Cambodian Refugees Living in Lawrence, Massachusetts*. Lawrence: Lawrence Cultural Council, Massachusetts Cultural Council, 2003.

Ramos-Zayas, Ana Y. *National Performances: The Politics of Class, Race, and Space in Puerto Rican Chicago*. Chicago: University of Chicago Press, 2003.

Ransby, Barbara. *Ella Baker and the Black Freedom Movement: A Radical Democratic Vision*. Chapel Hill: University of North Carolina Press, 2003.

Raynolds, Laura T. "Harnessing Women's Work: Restructuring Agricultural and Industrial Labor Forces in the Dominican Republic." *Economic Geography* 74, no. 2 (April 1998): 149–69.

Reimers, David M. *Other Immigrants: The Global Origins of the American People*. New York: New York University Press, 2005.

Reitano, Joanne R. *The Restless City: A Short History of New York from Colonial Times to the Present*. New York: Routledge, 2006.

Ricourt, Milagros. "Reaching the Promised Land: Undocumented Dominican Migration to Puerto Rico." *Centro Journal* 19, no. 2 (Fall 2007): 324–43.

Ricourt, Milagros, and Ruby Danta. *Hispanas de Queens: Latino Panethnicity in a New York City Neighborhood*. Ithaca, N.Y.: Cornell University Press, 2003.

Rivera, Raquel. *New York Ricans from the Hip Hop Zone*. New York: Palgrave Macmillan, 2003.

Robbins, Mark W. "Bread, Roses, and Other Possibilities: The 1912 Lawrence Textile Strike in Historical Memory." *Historical Journal of Massachusetts* 40 (Summer 2012): 94–121.

Rodríguez-Arroyo, Sandra. "The Never Ending Story of Language Policy in Puerto Rico." *Communicación, Cultura y Política* 4, no. 1 (2013): 79–98.

Roediger, David R. *Working toward Whiteness: How America's Immigrants Became White: The Strange Journey from Ellis Island to the Suburbs*. New York: Basic Books, 2005.

Rome, Adam Ward. *The Bulldozer in the Countryside: Suburban Sprawl and the Rise of American Environmentalism*. Cambridge: Cambridge University Press, 2001.

Romero, Mary, Pierrette Hondagneu-Sotelo, and Vilma Ortiz. *Challenging Fronteras: Structuring Latina and Latino Lives in the U.S.: An Anthology of Readings*. New York: Routledge, 1997.

Romo, Ricardo. *East Los Angeles: History of a Barrio*. Austin: University of Texas Press, 1983.

Roorda, Eric, Lauren Hutchinson Derby, and Raymundo González, eds. *The Dominican Republic Reader: History, Culture, Politics*. Durham, N.C.: Duke University Press, 2014.

Rubin, Elihu. *Insuring the City: The Prudential Center and the Postwar Urban Landscape*. New Haven, Conn.: Yale University Press, 2012.

Rubin, Rachel, and Jeffrey Paul Melnick. *Immigration and American Popular Culture: An Introduction*. New York: New York University Press, 2007.

Rusk, David. *Cities without Suburbs*. Washington, D.C.: Woodrow Wilson Center Press, 1993.

Sagás, Ernesto, and Sintia E. Molina, eds. *Dominican Migration: Transnational Perspectives*. Gainesville: University Press of Florida, 2004.

Sánchez, George J. *Becoming Mexican American: Ethnicity, Culture, and Identity in Chicano Los Angeles, 1900–1945*. New York: Oxford University Press, 1993.

———. "Face the Nation: Race, Immigration, and the Rise of Nativism in Late Twentieth Century America." *International Migration Review* 31, no. 4 (Winter 1997): 1009–30.

———. "Race, Nation, and Culture in Recent Immigration Studies." *Journal of American Ethnic History* 18, no. 4 (Summer 1999): 66–84.

Sánchez Korrol, Virginia E. *From Colonia to Community: The History of Puerto Ricans in New York City, 1917–1948*. Westport, Conn.: Greenwood Press, 1983.

Sandoval-Strausz, "Latino Landscapes: Postwar Cities and the Transnational Origins of a New Urban America." *Journal of American History* 101, no. 3 (December 2014): 804–31.

Sassen, Saskia, *The Global City: New York, London, Tokyo*. Princeton, N.J.: Princeton University Press, 2001.

———. *Globalization and Its Discontents: Essays on the New Mobility of People and Money*. New York: New Press, 1998.

Satter, Beryl. *Family Properties: Race, Real Estate, and the Exploitation of Black Urban America*. New York: Metropolitan Books, 2009.

Schinto, Jeanne. *Huddle Fever: Living in the Immigrant City*. New York: Knopf, 1995.

Schneider, Eric C. *Smack: Heroin and the American City*. Philadelphia: University of
Pennsylvania Press, 2008.

———. *Vampires, Dragons, and Egyptian Kings: Youth Gangs in Postwar New York*.
Princeton, N.J.: Princeton University Press, 1999.

Schrank, Andrew. "Foreign Investors, 'Flying Geese,' and the Limits to Export-Led
Industrialization in the Dominican Republic." *Theory and Society* 32, no. 4 (August
2003): 415–43.

Schuetz, Jenny. "Guarding the Town Walls: Mechanisms and Motives for Restricting
Multifamily Housing in Massachusetts." *Real Estate Economics* 36, no. 3 (2008): 555–86.

Schulman, Bruce J., and Julian E. Zelizer, eds. *Rightward Bound: Making America
Conservative in the 1970s*. Cambridge, Mass.: Harvard University Press, 2008.

Sciacca, Joe. "City of Anguish and Outrage: 'We All Just Want to Get Back to Living Our
Lives.'" *Boston Herald*, August 11, 1984.

———. "Dusk-to-Dawn Curfew in Lawrence: Top Pols in Plea for Calm." *Boston Herald*,
August 11, 1984.

Self, Robert O. *American Babylon: Race and the Struggle for Postwar Oakland*. Princeton,
N.J.: Princeton University Press, 2003.

Seligman, Amanda I. *Block by Block: Neighborhoods and Public Policy on Chicago's West
Side*. Chicago: University of Chicago Press, 2005.

Singer, Audrey. *Twenty-First Century Gateways: Immigrant Incorporation in Suburban
America*. Washington, D.C.: Brookings Institution Press, 2008.

Singh, Nikhil Pal. *Black Is a Country: Race and the Unfinished Struggle for Democracy*.
Cambridge, Mass: Harvard University Press, 2004.

Small, Mario Luis. *Villa Victoria: The Transformation of Social Capital in a Boston Barrio*.
Chicago: Chicago University Press, 2004.

Smith, Anna Deavere. *Fires in the Mirror: Crown Heights, Brooklyn, and Other Identities*.
New York: Anchor Books/Doubleday, 1993.

———. *Twilight—Los Angeles, 1992: On the Road: A Search for American Character*.
New York: Anchor Books, 1994.

Smith, Michael Peter. *Transnational Urbanism: Locating Globalization*. Malden, Mass.:
Blackwell, 2001.

Smith, Michael Peter, and Luis Eduardo Guarnizo, eds. *Transnationalism from Below*.
New Brunswick, N.J.: Transaction, 1998.

Smith, Neil. *The New Urban Frontier: Gentrification and the Revanchist City*. London:
Routledge, 1996.

Smith, Peter H. *Talons of the Eagle: Dynamics of U.S.–Latin American Relations*. New York:
Oxford University Press, 1996.

Smith, Robert C. *Mexican New York: Transnational Lives of New Immigrants*. Berkeley:
University of California Press, 2006.

Snyder, Robert W. *Crossing Broadway: Washington Heights and the Promise of New York
City*. Ithaca, N.Y.: Cornell University Press, 2015.

Spickard, Paul R. *Almost All Aliens: Immigration, Race, and Colonialism in American
History and Identity*. New York: Routledge, 2007.

Sracic, Paul A. *San Antonio v. Rodriguez and the Pursuit of Equal Education: The Debate
over Discrimination and School Funding*. Lawrence: University Press of Kansas, 2006.

Stanczyk, Michael T. "Public School Finance Litigation in New York and Massachusetts: The Bad Aftertaste of a Campaign for Fiscal Equity Win in New York." *Journal of Civil Rights and Economic Development* 21, no. 1 (Fall 2006): 353–70.

Stepick, Alex, Guillermo Grenier, Max Castro, and Marvin Dunn. *This Land Is Our Land: Immigrants and Power in Miami*. Berkeley: University of California Press, 2003.

Suárez-Orozco, Marcelo M., and Mariela Páez, eds. *Latinos: Remaking America*. Berkeley: University of California Press, 2002.

Sugrue, Thomas J. *The Origins of the Urban Crisis: Race and Inequality in Postwar Detroit*. Princeton, N.J.: Princeton University Press, 1996.

Sugrue, Thomas J., and Andrew P. Goodman. "Plainfield Burning: Black Rebellion in the Suburban North." *Journal of Urban History* 33, no. 4 (May 2007): 568–601.

Sugrue, Thomas J., and John D. Skrentny. "The White Ethnic Strategy." In *Rightward Bound: Making America Conservative in the 1970s*, edited by Bruce J. Schulman and Julian E. Zelizer, 171–92. Cambridge, Mass.: Harvard University Press, 2008.

Suro, Roberto. *Strangers among Us: Latino Lives in a Changing America*. New York: Vintage, 1999.

Tager, Jack. *Boston Riots: Three Centuries of Social Violence*. Boston: Northeastern University Press, 2001.

———. "The Massachusetts Miracle." *Historical Journal of Massachusetts* 19 (Summer 1991): 111–32.

Tang, Eric. *Unsettled: Cambodian Refugees in the NYC Hyperghetto*. Philadelphia: Temple University Press. 2015.

Teaford, Jon C. *The Metropolitan Revolution: The Rise of Post-Urban America*. New York: Columbia University Press, 2006.

Theoharis, Jeanne. "'We Saved the City': Black Struggles for Educational Equality in Boston, 1960–1976." *Radical History Review* 81 (Fall 2001): 61–93.

Theoharis, Jeanne, and Komozi Woodard, eds. *Freedom North: Black Freedom Struggles outside the South, 1940–1980*. New York: Palgrave-MacMillan, 2003.

Thomas, Lorrin. *Puerto Rican Citizen: History and Political Identity in Twentieth-Century New York City*. Chicago: University of Chicago Press, 2010.

Thomas, Piri. *Down These Mean Streets*. New York: Knopf, 1967.

Thompson, Heather Ann. *Whose Detroit? Politics, Labor, and Race in a Modern American City*. Ithaca, N.Y.: Cornell University Press, 2001.

Tobar, Héctor. *The Tattooed Soldier*. Harrison, N.Y.: Delphinium Books, 1998.

Toro-Morn, Maura I. "Boricuas en Chicago: Gender and Class in the Migration and Settlement of Puerto Ricans." In *The Puerto Rican Diaspora: Historical Perspectives*, edited by Carmen Teresa Whalen and Víctor Vázquez-Hernández, 128–50. Philadelphia: Temple University Press, 2005.

Torres, Andrés, ed. *Latinos in New England*. Philadelphia: Temple University Press, 2006.

Torres, Andrés, and José E. Velázquez, eds. *The Puerto Rican Movement: Voices from the Diaspora*. Philadelphia: Temple University Press, 1998.

Toussaint, Éric, and Damien Millet. *Debt, the IMF, and the World Bank: Sixty Questions, Sixty Answers*. New York: Monthly Review Press, 2010.

Trías Monge, José. *Puerto Rico: The Trials of the Oldest Colony in the World*. New Haven, Conn.: Yale University Press, 1997.

Tyson, Timothy B. *Blood Done Sign My Name: A True Story*. New York: Crown, 2004.

———. *Radio Free Dixie: Robert F. Williams and the Roots of Black Power*. Chapel Hill: University of North Carolina Press, 1999.

Vale, Lawrence J. *From the Puritans to the Projects: Public Housing and Public Neighbors*. Cambridge, Mass.: Harvard University Press, 2007.

Valle, Victor M., and Rodolfo D. Torres. *Latino Metropolis*. Minneapolis: University of Minnesota Press, 2000.

Vargas, Nicholas. "Latina/o Whitening? Which Latina/os Self-Classify as White and Report Being Perceived as White by Other Americans?" *Du Bois Review* 12, no. 1 (March 2015): 119–36.

Vecoli, Rudolph. "Anthony Capraro and the Lawrence Strike of 1919." In *Labor Divided: Race and Ethnicity in United States Labor Struggles, 1835–1960*, edited by Robert Asher and Charles Stephenson, 267–82. Albany: State University of New York Press, 1990.

Viramontes, Helena María. *Their Dogs Came with Them: A Novel*. New York: Atria, 2007.

Võ, Linda Trinh. *Mobilizing an Asian American Community*. Philadelphia: Temple University Press, 2004.

Wallace, Deborah, and Rodrick Wallace. *A Plague on Your Houses: How New York Was Burned Down and Public Health Crumbled*. London: Verso, 1998.

Walton, John, and David Seddon. *Free Markets and Food Riots: The Politics of Global Adjustment*. Oxford: Blackwell, 1994.

Wang, L. Ling-chi. "Beyond Identity and Racial Politics: Asian Americans and the Campaign Fund-Raising Controversy." *Asian American Law Journal* 5, no. 12 (January 1998): 329–40.

Waters, Mary. *Black Identities: West Indian Immigrant Dreams and American Realities*. New York: Russell Sage Foundation; Cambridge, Mass.: Harvard University Press, 1999.

Waters, Mary C., Reed Ueda, and Helen B. Marrow. *The New Americans: A Guide to Immigration since 1965*. Cambridge, Mass.: Harvard University Press, 2007.

Watson, Bruce. *Bread and Roses: Mills, Migrants, and the Struggle for the American Dream*. New York: Viking, 2005.

Whalen, Carmen Teresa. "Citizens and Workers: African Americans and Puerto Ricans in Philadelphia's Regional Economy since World War II." In *African American Urban History since World War II*, edited by Kenneth L. Kusmer and Joe W. Trotter, 98–122. Chicago: University of Chicago Press, 2009.

———. "Colonialism, Citizenship, and the Making of the Puerto Rican Diaspora: An Introduction." In *The Puerto Rican Diaspora: Historical Perspectives*, edited by Carmen Teresa Whalen and Víctor Vázquez-Hernández, 1–42. Philadelphia: Temple University Press, 2005.

———. *From Puerto Rico to Philadelphia: Puerto Rican Workers and Postwar Economies*. Philadelphia: Temple University Press, 2001.

Whalen, Carmen Teresa, and Víctor Vázquez-Hernández, eds. *The Puerto Rican Diaspora: Historical Perspectives*. Philadelphia: Temple University Press, 2005.

Wiarda, Howard J. "The United States and the Dominican Republic: Intervention, Dependency, and Tyrannicide." *Journal of Interamerican Studies and World Affairs* 22, no. 2 (May 1980): 247–60.

Wiese, Andrew. *Places of Their Own: African American Suburbanization in the Twentieth Century*. Chicago: University of Chicago Press, 2004.

Williams, Rhonda Y. *The Politics of Public Housing: Black Women's Struggles against Urban Inequality*. New York: Oxford University Press, 2004.

Williams, Walter L. "United States Indian Policy and the Debate over Philippine Annexation: Implications for the Origins of American Imperialism." *Journal of American History* 66, no. 4 (March 1980): 810–31.

Wilson, William J. *The Truly Disadvantaged: The Inner City, the Underclass, and Public Policy*. Chicago: University of Chicago Press, 1987.

———. *When Work Disappears: The World of the New Urban Poor*. New York: Knopf, 1996.

Wolcott, Victoria W. *Race, Riots, and Roller Coasters: The Struggle over Segregated Recreation in America*. Philadelphia: University of Pennsylvania Press, 2012.

Woodard, Komozi. "It's Nation Time in NewArk: Amiri Baraka and the Black Power Experiement in Newark, New Jersey." In *Freedom North: Black Freedom Struggles outside the South, 1940–1980*, edited by Jeanne Theoharis and Komozi Woodard, 287–311. New York: Palgrave-MacMillan, 2003.

Wucker, Michele. *Why the Cocks Fight: Dominicans, Haitians, and the Struggle for Hispaniola*. New York: Hill and Wang, 1999.

Young, Cynthia Ann. *Soul Power: Culture, Radicalism, and the Making of a U.S. Third World Left*. Durham, N.C.: Duke University Press, 2006.

Zilberg, Elana. "Fools Banished from the Kingdom: Remapping Geographies of Gang Violence between the Americas (Los Angeles and San Salvador)." *American Quarterly* 56, no. 3 (September 2004): 759–79.

Zimring, Franklin E. *The City That Became Safe: New York's Lessons for Urban Crime and Its Control*. New York: Oxford University Press, 2012.

Zipp, Samuel. *Manhattan Projects: The Rise and Fall of Urban Renewal in Cold War New York*. Oxford: Oxford University Press, 2010.

Zukin, Sharon. *Naked City: The Death and Life of Authentic Urban Places*. New York: Oxford University Press, 2011.

UNPUBLISHED THESES, DISSERTATIONS, AND PAPERS

Andors, Jessica. "City and Island: Dominicans in Lawrence: Transnational Community Formation in a Globalizing World." Master's thesis, Massachusetts Institute of Technology, 1999.

Barber, Llana. "Latino Migration and the New Global Cities: Transnationalism, Race, and Urban Crisis in Lawrence, Massachusetts, 1945–2000." Ph.D. diss., Boston College, 2010.

Borges-Méndez, Ramón. "Urban and Regional Restructuring and *Barrio* Formation in Massachusetts: The Cases of Lowell, Lawrence, and Holyoke." Ph.D. diss., Massachusetts Institute of Technology, 1994.

Duran, Joseph D. "The 1984 Riots: Lawrence, Massachusetts." Master's thesis, Massachusetts Institute of Technology, 1985.

Engler, Robert Edward. "Subsidized Housing in the Suburbs: Legislation or Litigation?" Master's thesis, Massachusetts Institute of Technology, 1971.

Morales, Julio, Jr. "Puerto Rican Poverty and the Migration to Elsewhere: Waltham Massachusetts: A Case Study." Ph.D. diss., Brandeis University, 1979.

Nadeau, Philip. "The Somalis of Lewiston: Community Impacts of Rapid Immigrant Movement into a Small Homogeneous Maine City." Conference paper, Brown University Center for the Study of Race and Ethnicity, August 14, 2003.

Pernice, Nicolas M. "Urban Redevelopment of Lawrence, MA: A Retrospective Case Study of the Plains Neighborhood." Master's thesis, University Of Massachusetts at Lowell, 2011.

Ryan, Andrea Dawn. "Not My Brother's Keeper: Ethnic Individualism, Civic Capitalism, and the Reinvention of Community in an Old Mill City." Ph.D. diss., Boston University, 2007.

Stevenson, Kim. "A Spatial Analysis of Socioeconomic and Demographic Change in the Lower Merrimack Valley and Lawrence, MA, 1980–1990." Master's thesis, Massachusetts Institute of Technology, 1992.

Wald, Pamela Kathryn. "Bringing Welfare State Theories to the States: How Ideas, Actors, and State Structures Affect Welfare Reform Trajectories in Minnesota and Wisconsin." Ph.D. diss., University of Minnesota, 2008.

REPORTS

Anthony, Patricia, and Gretchen Rossman. "The Massachusetts Education Reform Act: What Is It and Will It Work?" 1994. Reprint archived with the Education Resources Information Center.

Borges-Méndez, Ramón. "Migration, Settlement, and Incorporation of Latinos in Lawrence, Massachusetts." In "The Making of Community: Latinos in Lawrence, Massachusetts," edited by Jorge Santiago and James Jennings. 2005.

Fox, Radhika, and Miriam Axel-Lute. "To Be Strong Again: Renewing the Promise in Smaller Industrial Cities." PolicyLink, 2008.

Guzmán, Betsy. "The Hispanic Population." Census 2000 Brief, May 2001.

Hispanic-American Advisory Commission. "Final Report." Massachusetts, September 20, 1993.

Hernández, Ramona, and Francisco L. Rivera-Batiz. "Dominicans in the United States: A Socioeconomic Profile." CUNY Dominican Studies Institute, Dominican Research Monograph, October 2003.

Hoyt, Lorlene, and A. Leroux. "Voices from Forgotten Cities: Innovative Revitalization Coalitions in America's Older Small Cities." Department of Urban Studies and Planning at MIT, PolicyLink, and Citizens' Housing and Planning Association, 2007.

Institute for Women's Policy Research. "Before and after Welfare Reform: The Work and Well-Being of Low-Income Single Parent Families." 2003.

Jones, Charles. "Latinos in Lawrence, Massachusetts." Mauricio Gastón Institute for Latino Community Development and Public Policy, January 2003.

———. "Latinos in Massachusetts." Mauricio Gastón Institute for Latino Community Development and Public Policy, April 2002.

Liebke, James F., and Associates. "An Analysis and Recommended Program for the Central Business District: Lawrence, Massachusetts." 1957.

Marzán, Gilbert, Andrés Torres, and Andrew Luecke. "Puerto Rican Outmigration from New York City, 1995–2000." Policy Report from the Centro de Estudios Puertorriqueños at Hunter College (CUNY), 2008.

Massachusetts Advisory Committee to the U.S. Commission on Civil Rights and the Massachusetts Commission against Discrimination. "Rt. 128: Boston's Road To Segregation." 1975.

Massachusetts Commission against Discrimination. "Report on Civil Disorders: Could It Happen Here?" 1992.

Massachusetts Commission on Hispanic Affairs. "Hispanics in Massachusetts: A Demographic Analysis." August 1986.

———. "Hispanics in Massachusetts: A Progress Report." December 1985.

Massachusetts Criminal Justice Training Council. "Management Survey of the Police Department of the City of Lawrence, Massachusetts: Report to Massachusetts Criminal Justice Training Council." June 1985.

Massachusetts Department of Education. "Report on the Condition of the Public Schools in Holyoke, Lawrence, Brockton, and Chelsea." October 15, 1991.

Massachusetts Division of Employment Security. "Defense Spending and Massachusetts Employment, 1972–1980." 1982.

Massachusetts Hispanic-American Advisory Commission. "Final Report." September 1993.

Massachusetts League of Community Health Centers. "Community Health Centers as Economic Engines: An Overview of Their Impact on Massachusetts Communities and Families." October 2003.

Massachusetts State Office of Affirmative Action. "Report of the Hispanic Task Force." 1985.

Merrimack Valley Planning Commission, "Chapter 774 (the Anti-Snob Zoning Law): Its Impact on the MVPC Region." March 31, 1976.

Migration Policy Institute. "The Dominican Population in the United States: Growth and Distribution." September 2004.

Motel, Seth, and Eileen Patten. "The 10 Largest Hispanic Origin Groups: Characteristics, Rankings, Top Counties." Pew Research Center, June 27, 2012.

Piore, Michael Joseph, "The Role of Immigration in Industrial Growth: A Case Study of the Origins and Character of Puerto Rican Migration to Boston." May 1973.

Regional/Urban Design Assistance Team. "Lawrence R/UDAT." Boston Society of Architects, July 1990.

Rubin, Laurie F. "Housing Discrimination in the Rental Market: A Report on the Barriers Faced by Women with Rental Subsidies, Blacks, and Hispanics." Massachusetts Commission against Discrimination, 1988.

Rubin, Laurie, and Susan Forward. "Systemic Discrimination in the Private Rental Market." Massachusetts Commission against Discrimination, 1983.

Santiago, Jorge, and James Jennings. "The Latino Business Community of Lawrence, Massachusetts: A Profile and Analysis." 2000.

Santiago, Jorge, and James Jennings, eds. "The Making of Community: Latinos in
    Lawrence, Massachusetts." 2005.
Siegal, Beth, and Andy Waxman. "Third-Tier Cities: Adjusting to the New Economy."
    U.S. Economic Development Administration, 2001.
Singer, Audrey. "The Rise of New Immigrant Gateways." Brookings Institution, February
    2004.
Stepler, Renee, and Anna Brown. "Statistical Portrait of Hispanics in the United States."
    Pew Research Center, April 19, 2016.
Stevenson, Kim. "Hispanic and Minority Owned Businesses in Lawrence, Massachusetts:
    A Market Study of Essex Street and Downtown Lawrence." Prepared for the Lawrence
    Community Development Department, October 1991.
Suro, Robert, and Audrey Singer. "Latino Growth in Metropolitan America: Changing
    Patterns, New Locations." Brookings Institution, July 2002.
Urban Studies Institute, Lawrence High School/Phillips Academy. "The Family Housing
    Crisis in Greater Lawrence: A Backgrounder for Concerned Citizens." 1988.
————. "Growing Up Hispanic in Lawrence." 1986.
University of Massachusetts Amherst School of Education. "Education Reform: Ten
    Years after the Massachusetts Education Reform Act." 2003.
Walsh, E. Denis, and Associates. "Action Plan Lawrence Massachusetts: The Renovation
    and Reuse of Upper Story Space in a Block of Downtown Commercial Buildings."
    Prepared for the Commonwealth of Massachusetts, Department of Community
    Affairs, Building Reuse Project, 1978.
Williams, Loretta. "What's Going On? Welfare Reform, Race, and Communities in
    Massachusetts." Report on the proceedings from forum on "Welfare Reform and
    Communities of Color in Massachusetts." Trotter Institute, 1999.

TELEVISION AND VIDEO

The Case against Lincoln Center. New York: Third World Newsreel, 2007.
Chavez Ravine. Los Angeles: Tiny Projects, 2003.
Deputized: ¿Como pudo pasar? Brooklyn, N.Y.: Seedworks Films, 2013.
From Mambo to Hip Hop. Oaks, Pa.: MVD Visual, 2009.
Life and Debt. New York: New Yorker Films Artwork, 2003.
New York: A Documentary. Alexandria, Va.: PBS Video, 1999.
Who Killed Vincent Chin? New York: Filmakers Library, 1988.

INDEX

Abandonment, 3, 56, 71, 189–90, 216

Absentee landlords, 3, 15, 156, 162, 175, 191, 213

Affordable Housing Act (1969), 30

African Americans, 216; in central cities, 6, 7; in smaller cities, 13; suburban hostility to, 25; "culture of poverty" attributed to, 98

Aid to Families with Dependent Children (AFDC), 194, 198, 200, 206

Alameda County, Calif., 29

Alaska, 58, 198

Albizu Campos, Pedro, 59

Aldermanic system, 162–63

Alliance for Peace, 134–35, 168, 177

Alliance of Latins for Political Action and Progress, 96, 113

Alma (Dominican immigrant), 83

Álvarez, Nilka, 243

Ambler, Robert B., 170

American Built (shoe company), 80

American Woolen Company, 43, 61

Andors, Jessica, 54, 83–84, 225, 230, 267n59

Andover, Mass., 26–27, 92; taxes in, 21, 45–49, 51; housing prices in, 28, 188; housing stock in, 29; zoning in, 29–30, 45; Jewish residents in, 34; industry in, 41–42, 45–49, 50, 83, 187; income

levels in, 51, 52; failed collaboration with, 210; affordable housing proposed for, 213

Andover Village Improvement Society (AVIS), 20

Arlington District, 188–89

Armenians, 34

Arson, 6, 15, 20, 130, 188, 214, 217; revenue shortfalls linked to, 2–3, 190; in New York City, 53, 71, 72; racialized disinvestment linked to, 72, 189–90, 213, 247; spectators drawn to, 132, 184; for profit, 190–91; stigma of, 191, 193; declining rate of, 242. *See also* Disinvestment; Firefighting

AT&T, 45

Atkins, Thomas I., 50

Auto theft, 192, 214

Ayala, Orlando, 238

Ayer Mill, 43

Baby boom, 24

Balaguer, Joaquín, 16, 65–66

Ball, John, 126

Barrio, Guilmo, 167

Bilingual education, 104, 105, 111, 159, 172, 206–7, 209–10

Bilingual Parents Advisory Council, 111, 178, 179

Deindustrialization, 209; in Lawrence, 2, 4, 6, 9, 10, 14, 15, 23, 38, 42–44, 56, 82, 83, 155, 157, 158, 182, 194, 196, 219, 245; in Michigan, 8, 13; in New York City, 9, 55, 70–71; second wave of, 10, 82; in big vs. small cities, 51–52

Deportation, 5, 69, 76, 253

Desegregation, 101, 124, 159, 203–5, 210

Detroit, 8, 122

Devers, Marcos, 243

Devik, Rudolph, 129–30

Diamond, Andrew, 158

Díaz, Dalia, 79–80, 224, 243

DiFillipo, David, 213

Digital Equipment Corporation, 48

DiMarca, Nunzio, 115, 134, 167

Discrimination, 4, 6, 15; in employment, 8, 166, 196; in housing, 25–31, 34, 85, 91, 196

Disinvestment, 2, 3, 4, 8, 15, 18, 23, 75, 85, 93, 185, 189–90, 217, 223, 231, 247, 253; in New York City, 9, 55, 68, 70, 71, 72; in big vs. small cities, 13, 51–52; urban renewal and, 35, 37

Dominican American Voters' Council, 179

Dominican Republic, 15, 219, 236; U.S. interference in, 16, 57, 63–70, 88, 231, 247; foreign investment in, 61, 65–66, 68; sugar industry in, 63, 64, 65, 66–67; indebtedness of, 63, 66, 67, 71; chain migration from, 68–69; dual citizenship law in, 237; remittances to, 250

Dominicans, 2, 3, 5, 9, 10–11, 15, 19, 52, 53; racialization of, 8, 98; housing options for, 32; in New York City, 55, 65, 70, 72, 83, 123; emigration by, 62; segregation of, 86–88; immigration support to, 109–10; riots by, 123; Puerto Ricans outnumbered by, 218; unemployment among, 228; in Boston, 230; in elective office, 243–44, 248; deportation of, 253; businesses owned by, 287n4

Dowling, Patricia, 180

Draft Riots (1863), 124

Drinking water, 13

Drug abuse, 15, 53, 71, 74, 185, 193, 196, 214

Dukakis, Michael, 147, 164, 169, 176

Duran, José, 242

Duran, Joseph, 141, 148–49, 171, 175

Eagle-Tribune, 50, 97, 115, 195, 220; riot coverage by, 126–32, 141, 143–44

East St. Louis, Ill., 124, 186, 206

Ecuadorians, 257n14

Elderly population: housing for, 31, 35, 36, 216; growth of, 51, 202, 208; as political force, 202, 209

El Zafiro, 239

Eminent domain, 32, 33

Engler, Robert, 26

Entrepreneurship, 228, 232–34, 238, 248, 287n4

Espada, Martín, 121, 134, 152

Fair Housing Act (1968), 25

Federal Housing Act (1949), 32, 33

Federal Housing Administration (FHA), 24, 25, 173

Fernández, Leonel, 236

FIRE (financial, insurance, and real estate) sector, 52, 186

Firefighting: during riots, 1, 121, 126, 127–28, 140; funding of, 47, 72, 161–62, 171, 190; racial bias in, 100, 165. *See also* Arson

Flint, Mich., 13, 251

Florida, 11, 80, 223, 226, 229

Foley, Frank, 126

Food stamps, 61, 194, 196, 200

Foraker, Joseph, 58

Foraker Act (1900), 58

Foreclosures, 24

Framingham, Mass., 11, 13, 85

Fredette, Richard W., 140

Free Trade Zones, 67, 68, 219

French Canadians, 125, 135, 277n120

Gainsborough, Juliet, 201

Gangs, 15, 100–101, 214

Gans, Herbert, 33

Garcia, Lawrence, 223–24

Garment industry, 76

Gateway Cities program, 176, 239, 240

General Neighborhood Renewal Area (GNRA), 33

Gentrification, 13, 56, 75, 215, 244, 251; in New York City, 6, 225–26, 227; displacement caused by, 19, 227; in large cities, 52, 185, 247. *See also* Urban renewal

Gerken, Christina, 200

Gerstle, Gary, 277n120

Getaway Brothers (street gang), 100–101

GI Bill (1944), 24, 145–46, 173

Gill, Gary, 126, 128

Gillette Company, 48

Glenn, Evelyn Nakano, 269n100

Globalization, 55, 57, 69

Gonzalez, Jesus, 238

González, Juan, 17, 57

Gotham, Kevin Fox, 257n10

Great Depression, 24, 42, 173

Greater Lawrence Community Action Council (GLCAC), 92, 107, 109–10, 111, 179, 220

Greater Lawrence Family Health Canter, 111

Great Society, 4

Green, Joseph, 102

Greenberg, Miriam, 257n10

Grieco Brothers, 80

Grosfoguel, Ramon, 62, 271n23

Groundwork Lawrence, 252

Guam, 16

Guantánamo Bay, 58

Guatemalans, 257n14

Guzmán, Antonio, 110

Haiti, 62, 66

Haverhill, Mass., 80, 84

Health care, 110, 111–12

Heureaux, Ulises, 63

Hewlett Packard, 48, 49

Hicks, Louise Day, 205

Highways, 2, 24, 38, 41

Hispanic-American Advisory Commission, 186

Hispanic Office of Planning and Evaluation, 242

Holyoke, Mass., 11, 56, 186, 206

Homelessness, 15

Homeownership, 23–26, 28, 188, 224–25

Home Owners' Loan Corporation (HOLC), 24, 25

Housing: suburban prices of, 2, 9, 21, 23, 26, 28, 86, 88, 187–88; tenement, 2, 32, 34; discrimination in, 25–31, 34, 85, 91, 196; rental, 26, 29, 30, 31; suburban stock of, 29, 88; for elderly, 31, 35, 36, 216; affordable, 31, 118, 213; public, 32, 70. *See also* Absentee landlords

Howard, Ron, 134

Human Rights Commission, 167, 169, 177

Hyatt, Armand, 117

Illegal Immigration Reform and Immigrant Responsibility Act (IIRIRA) (1996), 200

Immigrant City Community Housing Corporation (ICCHC), 115, 116–18, 156

Imperialism, 5, 15–16, 56–70, 88

Incarceration, 5, 19, 185

Inflation, 67

Inquilinos Boricuas en Acción, 173–74

International Institute, 108–9

International Monetary Fund (IMF), 62–63, 67, 69, 71, 251

Irish, 34

Italians, 34

Itzigsohn, José, 227–28

Jackson, Kenneth, 23

Jajuga, James P., 198

Jennings, James, 201

Jewish residents, 34

Jo-Gal Shoes, 77

John, Jim, 141–42

Johnson, Lyndon, 65, 109

Johnson, Marilynn, 278n138

Johnson, Raymond, 132, 133, 160
Jones Act (1917), 16, 59
Juana Díaz, Puerto Rico, 74, 105, 106
Juanita (Puerto Rican migrant), 103–4

Keller, James, 134, 162, 165
Kelley, Robin, 91
Kennedy, Mary Claire, 196, 197, 198, 233
Kerner Commission (National Advisory
    Commission on Civil Disorders), 123
Kerry, John, 239–40
King, Martin Luther, Jr., 122
Kozol, Jonathan, 186, 203–4, 211
Kruse, Kevin, 201

Lamond, John J., 77, 108
Language differences, 94–95, 105, 110, 111,
    165, 193. See also Bilingual education
Lantigua, William, 248–49, 250
Law, Bernard F., 168
Lawrence Development and Industrial
    Commission (LDIC), 49–50
Lawrence Eagle-Tribune. See Eagle-Tribune
Lawrence Initiative, 173–74
Lawrence Maid (shoe company), 77–79,
    80, 81, 105
Lawrence Pumps, 221
Lawrence Redevelopment Authority
    (LRA), 33, 35, 115, 117
Lawrence Strategy, 116
Lead poisoning, 13, 213
Lebanese, 34–35
Lefebvre, Henri, 9
Levitt, Peggy, 230
Lewiston, Maine, 11
Lexington, Mass., 42
Lincoln Center (New York City), 36–37
Los Angeles, 7, 9, 18, 122, 123, 135
Los Trinitarios (social club), 106
Lot sizes, 26, 29, 30
Lowell, Mass., 11, 56
Lower Tower Hill, 142, 146; riots in, 99,
    117, 121, 124–25, 130, 148, 151; ethnic
    transformation of, 166; social services
    in, 168–69

Lucent Technologies, 45, 83
Lucero, Marcelo, 124
Lynn, Mass., 170, 206

Malden Mills, 236
Malls, 6, 9, 22, 26, 35, 37–39
Manufacturing: decline of, 2, 9, 10, 43,
    55–56, 76–77, 81, 82, 86, 103–4, 157,
    175, 187, 218, 227–28, 234, 247; in Rust
    Belt, 2, 13; high-technology, 21, 40, 45,
    48, 187; efforts to attract, 44, 137; in
    suburbs, 49, 83, 187, 225; of nondurable
    goods, 55, 68, 76, 81, 82, 83, 157, 187;
    in Puerto Rico, 60, 79; in Dominican
    Republic, 68, 219; in New York City,
    70–71, 82, 227. See also Computer
    industry; Defense industry; Garment
    industry; Shoe manufacturing; Textile
    industry
Martinez, Jose, 134
Massachusetts Commission against
    Discrimination (MCAD), 85, 155, 157,
    165, 169, 178, 181
Massachusetts Education Reform Act
    (MERA) (1993), 211–12
"Massachusetts Miracle," 42, 186
Maywood, Calif., 11
McDuffy v. Secretary of the Executive Office
    of Education (1993), 211, 212–13
McGovern, Patricia, 171, 176
Medicaid, 194, 195, 196, 200
Mejía, Felix, 167
Meléndez, Edwin, 187
Melendez, Isabel, 1, 70; as community
    advocate, 10, 90, 92, 104, 107–12,
    116–17, 168, 220, 222–23; stereotypes
    recalled by, 99–100; migration from
    Puerto Rico of, 105; as entrepreneur,
    106–7; Semana Hispana organized by,
    112–14; as mayoral candidate, 119, 120,
    248; nonviolence urged by, 134–35
Merrimack Courts projects, 131, 134, 176
Merrimack River, 2
Methuen, Mass., 26–27, 143; housing
    prices in, 28–29, 188; housing stock in,

110, 148, 231; housing options for, 32; in New York City, 36, 60, 71, 72, 225; perceived docility of, 76–77; in shoe industry, 78; segregation of, 85–88; stereotypes of, 95–100, 104, 167, 178, 197; social services established by, 110; in Lower Tower Hill, 125, 148

Puerto Rico, 16–17, 55, 57–62, 64, 66, 88, 95, 251

Quiles, Briseida, 166, 178

Rafton, Harold, 30
Ralph, Carmen, 142
Ramos-Zayas, Ana Y., 240
Raytheon Company, 21, 42, 45, 46–47, 49, 83
Reagan, Ronald, 67, 201
Recreational services, 155, 158, 60–61, 162, 163, 168–69, 171, 192
Redlining, 25, 34
Reitano, Joanne, 72
Rental housing, 26, 29, 30, 31
Restrictive covenants, 25
Retail, 6, 9, 22, 26, 35, 37–39
Riots
—in Lawrence (1984), 20, 93, 110, 121–53, 185; racial context of, 1, 2, 4, 10, 16, 91, 92, 125, 135–41, 146–53, 247; by whites, 1, 17, 124, 130, 131–32, 136–37, 148, 151, 152, 163, 182; firefighting during, 1, 121, 126, 127–28, 140; policing during, 1, 121, 126–28, 130–34, 138–41, 151, 161; economic context of, 2, 44, 81, 91, 125, 143, 155–56, 158, 182, 183; media coverage of, 10, 122, 126–32, 135–36, 137, 138, 141, 143–44, 156, 158, 165, 173; colonialist context of, 16, 17; tensions leading to, 99, 117, 120, 148; affordable housing and, 118; efforts to minimize, 132–33, 135, 136, 139, 156; changes brought about by, 154–69; school crisis and, 159–60, 202–3; backlash from, 165–66, 167–68, 201; state response to, 169–72, 239; social services spurred by,

172–76; civil rights claims spurred by, 176–81

—elsewhere: in Los Angeles, 7, 18, 122, 123, 135; in Detroit, 8, 122; in New York City, 18, 122, 123, 124; in Dominican Republic, 67; in Newark, N.J., 122; after King assassination, 122–23; in Miami, 123; in East St. Louis, Ill., 124; in Boston, 124, 182

Rivera, Daniel, 80
Rizzo, Nicholas, 116
Rodger, Kathy, 100
Rodriguez, Alex, 157
Rodriguez, Daniel, 129, 156
Rodriguez, Elsie, 131
Rodriguez, Oscar, 110–11
Rodriguez v. San Antonio (1973), 205, 206, 207, 210, 211
Roosevelt, Mark, 211–12
Roosevelt, Theodore, 63
Roosevelt Corollary, 63
Route 128, 11, 40–42
Ruiz, Carlos, 96
Rumbo (newspaper), 243
Rusk, David, 260n3
Rust Belt, 2, 7, 22

Salcedo, Dominican Republic, 236
Salem, N.H., 26–27, 35, 38, 50
Salvadorans, 9, 253
San Antonio, 7
San Domingo Improvement Company, 63
Santana, Jose, 152
Santiago, Eddie, 129
Santiago, Jorge, 174–75, 201, 220
Santiago, Jose, 140
Santiago, José, 180, 243, 248
Savage Inequalities (Kozol), 203–4, 206, 211, 212
Schinto, Jeanne, 184, 193, 195, 202
Schneider, Eric, 71
Schools, 10, 91, 247; funding of, 2–3, 15, 16, 47, 48, 77, 159–60, 162, 171, 203, 205–13, 252; suburban, 16, 21, 26, 27, 202–13; Latino enrollment in, 16, 110–11, 159,

203; private, 48, 93, 203, 208; in New York City, 72, 74; desegregation of, 118, 124, 182, 204–5; dropout rates in, 158, 207, 213–14; racist employees of, 178; charter, 212; transnational education in, 235; in state receivership, 251.

See also Bilingual education

Sears, Roebuck, 39

Segregation, 6, 7, 15, 19, 56, 187, 217, 219, 220, 226, 229, 231, 246, 247, 252; suburbanization and, 5, 13, 27, 28, 41, 55, 83–88, 196, 203; of African Americans, 8, 81, 98, 122; of Dominicans and Puerto Ricans, 85–88; fight against, 101, 118, 123, 124, 159, 182, 203–5, 210; of school districts, 185, 202–13. See also Suburbs

Self, Robert, 29

Semana Hispana, 112–15, 120, 176, 179, 237–40

Shafer, Richard, 190

Shannon, Jim, 138, 148

Shapiro v. Thompson (1969), 198

Shawsheen Mill, 46

Shoe manufacturing, 44, 76, 77–81, 157

Shopping centers, 2, 37

Silva, Anthony, 139, 140

Silverio, Julia, 76–77, 114, 221, 243, 244

Smith, Patrick, 156

Snyder, Robert, 71

Social clubs, 34, 104, 106, 119, 238

Somalis, 11

South Lawrence, 35, 44, 93, 216, 224

Spain, 16, 57, 58, 63

Spicket River Greenway, 252

Spindler, Eric, 101–2

Springfield, Mass., 84, 198

Stapczynski, Buzz, 213

Starr, Roger, 72

"Steering," 25

Stevenson, Kim, 187

Stevenson, Mary Huff, 86

Storefront churches, 104, 119, 221

Suburbs, 142, 162, 166, 196, 251, 253; housing prices in, 2, 9, 21, 23, 26, 28–29, 86, 88, 187–88; prosperity of, 3, 13, 22, 26–29, 52, 187–88, 245; transformation wrought by, 4, 22–23, 155, 194, 209, 228, 231, 246, 247; racial dimensions of, 5, 13, 24–26, 27–28, 32, 40, 41, 55, 70, 73, 83–88, 91–92, 93, 118, 143, 196, 203, 252; industry in, 5–6, 22, 40–42, 44–50, 76, 83, 185, 187, 214, 225, 232–33; policy bias toward, 6, 9, 23–25, 28, 41, 146, 170; of Detroit, 8; political agenda linked to, 10, 18, 29, 169–72, 201; geographic definitions and, 11, 13, 14, 227; diversity of, 11, 13, 185; schools in, 16, 21, 26, 27, 202–13; lot sizes in, 26, 29, 30; retail establishments in, 26, 37–39, 214, 232–33; elderly housing in, 31; urban renewal and, 32, 34–36; urban divergence from, 50–51, 186–88, 217; Latinos' choices constrained in, 55, 56, 73; in Greater New York, 70–71; health care and, 111; urban riots and, 122, 132, 135; crime in, 192; welfare reform and, 195, 197, 198, 199, 202; Puerto Ricans in, 226. See also Segregation; White flight; Zoning

Sugar industry, 17, 58, 59, 63, 64, 65, 66–67

Sugrue, Thomas, 8

Sullivan, Kevin, 163, 167, 190, 191, 196, 209, 233

Sullivan, Michael, 120

Sunbelt, 22

Syrians, 34

Tager, Jack, 42, 124

Tang, Eric, 7

Taxes: shrinking urban base of, 2–3, 6, 9, 22, 37, 45, 51, 71, 77, 83, 155, 156, 189, 191, 192, 194, 206–9, 213, 247; growing suburban base of, 21, 26, 40, 41, 44, 45–49, 51, 52, 84, 247; in Andover, 21, 45–49, 51; urban renewal and, 35, 36; on sales, 38; exemptions from, 41, 60, 61, 64, 68; in South vs. New England, 43; in Puerto Rico, 60; in Dominican Republic, 64, 67, 68; in New York City, 71; revolts over, 159, 162, 201, 202; failure to collect, 162,